Goa Handbook

Robert and Roma Bradnock

Footprint Handbooks

My village has shores and waving dunes,
hillocks and springs, shadows of palm trees,
chapels and devalayas, paddy fields and ponds
resting under red and white lotuses

My village is a plot of land stretched
along the mountain, and is fringed with surf.
My village is a corner of charm and restfulness.

Telo de Mascarenhas 'When the mango trees blossomed'

Footprint Handbooks
®

6 Riverside Court, Lower Bristol Road
Bath BA2 3DZ England
T 01225 469141 F 01225 469461
E mail handbooks@footprint.cix.co.uk

ISBN 1 900949 17 2 ISSN 1368-4272
CIP DATA: A catalogue record for this book is available from the British Library

In North America, published by

PASSPORT BOOKS
NTC/Contemporary Publishing Company

4255 West Touhy Avenue, Lincolnwood (Chicago), Illinois 60646-1975, USA
T 847 679 5500 F 847 679 24941
E mail NTCPUB2@AOL.COM

ISBN 0 8442 4807 X
Library of Congress Catalog Card Number: 97-68363
Passport Books and colophon are registered trademarks of NTC Publishing group

Every effort has been made to ensure that the facts in this Handbook are accurate. However travellers should still obtain advice from consulates, airlines etc about current travel and visa requirements and conditions before travelling. The editors and publishers cannot accept responsibilty for any loss, injury or inconvenience, however caused.

Maps - neither the coloured nor the black and white text maps are not intended to have any political significance.

Cover design by Newell and Sorrell; photography by Global Scenes; Tony Stone and James Davis Picture Library

Production: Design by Mytton Williams; Typesetting by Jo Morgan, Ann Griffiths and Alex Nott; Maps by Kevin Feeney and Aldous George; Illustrations by Shane Feeney; Proofread by Rod Gray.

Printed and bound in Great Britain by Clays Ltd., Bungay, Suffolk

Contents

4 Information for travellers

5
Rounding up

We try as hard as we can to make each Footprint Handbook as up-to-date and accurate as possible but, of course, things always change. Many people write to us with new information, amendments or simply comments. Please do get in touch. In return we will send you details of our special guidebook offer.

See page 259 for more information.

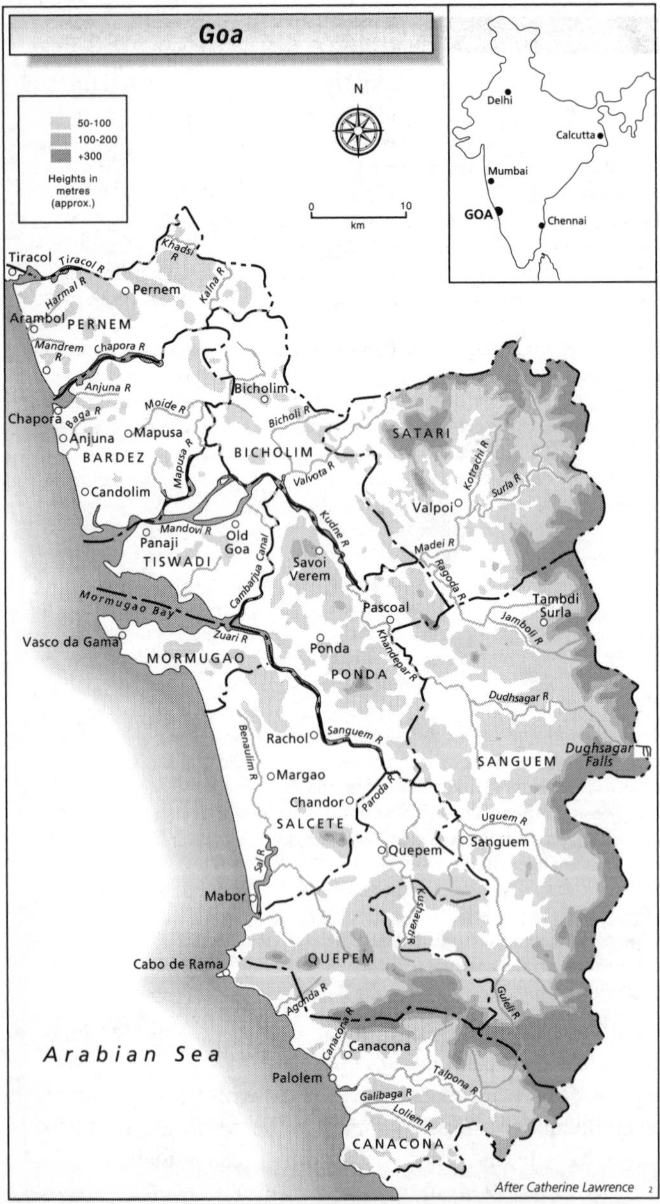
Goa
50-100
100-200
+300
Heights in metres (approx.)
N
0
10
km
Delhi
Calcutta
Mumbai
GOA
Chennai
Tiracol
Tiracol R
Khadsi R
Kalna R
Harmal R
Pernem
Arambol
PERNEM
Mandrem R
Chapora R
Anjuna R
Bicholim
Chapora
Baga R
Moide R
Bicholi R
Anjuna
Mapusa
SATARI
BARDEZ
Mapusa R
BICHOLIM
Kotrachi R
Valvota R
Surla R
Candolim
Valpoi
Kudne R
Mandovi R
Old Goa
Panaji
Madei R
TISWADI
Cambarjua Canal
Savoi Verem
Ragoda R
Tambdi Surla
Mormugao Bay
Pascoal
Jamboli R
Zuari R
Vasco da Gama
Ponda
Khandepar R
MORMUGAO
PONDA
Dudhsagar R
Benaulim R
Rachol
Sanguem R
Dughsagar Falls
SANGUEM
Margao
Paroda R
Chandor
Uguem R
SALCETE
Sanguem
Quepem
Sal R
Mabor
Kushavati R
Cabo de Rama
QUEPEM
Guleli R
Agonda R
Canacona R
Canacona
Arabian Sea
Talpona R
Palolem
Galibaga R
Loliem R
CANACONA
After Catherine Lawrence

WHERE TO GO?

Goa's superb beaches lie all along its magical coastline with sandy coves and estuaries to the north and long palm fringed quieter stretches to the south. You can choose a beach for its character – from crowded, lively, party-going **Anjuna** and **Chapora**, through the quieter and more sedate **Candolim** and **Mabor**, to the newly 'discovered' isolation and beauty of **Arambol** in the extreme north, or **Palolem** to the far south. Wherever you stay, on Wednesdays all roads (as far as foreign visitors are concerned) lead to **Anjuna** for the much publicised market, though many would find a lot more local colour in **Mapusa** on Fridays. Along the rocky headlands are remains of small Portuguese forts which can be fun to explore – tiny **Tiracol** in the northern most part of Goa, has been renovated to become a 'Heritage' hotel, while **Cabo de Rama**, to the south holds an aura of its historic past.

By venturing a short distance away from the idyllic coast you can explore the richness of Goa's cultural heritage. You need only make a couple of day trips and perhaps spend one night away from your resort hotel to see most of the suggested sights. Goa's Portuguese Catholic history is evident in the numerous attractive white painted churches along the central coastal section but is best captured in **Old Goa**, once described as the 'Rome of the Orient', with its numerous churches and convents and the renowned Basilica of Bom Jesus holding the relics of St Francis Xavier. Typical Portuguese village houses can be seen all across the Old Conquest territories but in addition a visit to **Chandor's** 'Menezes Braganza House' gives you an insight into the lifestyle once enjoyed by the elite. **Rachol Seminary** which has the Museum of Christian Art is another place to fit in to your itinerary.

Predominantly Hindu inland Goa has its best preserved ancient temple at **Tambdi Surla**. The vibrant, living temples dotted around **Ponda** give an insight into the strong religious tradition of the majority of its population. To get an idea of a 19th century Hindu house of substance, arrange to see the Deshprabhu Mansion in **Pernem**. You will also find a walk around the spice plantations near **Savoi Verem** or **Pascoal** near Tisk really rewarding. Although the wildlife reserves are rather disappointing as far as wildlife is concerned, they are in picturesque forest-rich areas and one has the famous **Dughsagar Falls**, spectacular in the wet months.

To see something of the astonishing diversity of India beyond, take a 2-3 day excursion and travel east to the ruins of the fabulous capital of the Vijaynagars at **Hampi** (Karnataka), or go through **Belgaum** with its Muslim past, or visit **Gokarna** on the coast to the south, alive and crowded with its present-day Hindu pilgrims. Cross near Tiracol in the north into Maharashtra to see a Maratha fort ruin at **Redi** which also has a beautiful deserted beach, and then climb the Ghats, up to the minor hill station of **Amboli**.

If **Mumbai** is your entry point, you will have the added opportunity to see a flourishing Indian regional capital and visit the superbly carved ancient cave temple on Elephanta Island, under an hour's boat ride away.

The authors

Robert Bradnock

Born in India, Robert Bradnock made his first visit to Goa in 1971. Since then he has been back five times, travelling throughout the state. Specialising in the Geography of South Asia at SOAS in the University of London, where he is now Head of the Geography Department, he has lived in India and travelled the length and breadth of the country over the last 30 years.

An international authority on India and its neighbours, Robert Bradnock broadcasts frequently on TV and radio about South Asian current affairs for the BBC and many other networks. With Roma he has also written the India Handbook and the Sri Lanka Handbook.

Roma Bradnock

A Bengali by birth, Roma was brought up in Calcutta, where after graduating she worked in the British Council Library. Travelling across the sub-continent had started in childhood but to widen her horizons she went to Europe and England subsequently became her home.

Her work with Footprint started with helping with the first edition of the South Asian Handbook 1992 while her two daughters were growing up. Working on the Handbooks allows her to return to her homeland each year to travel widely, often to seek out yet unexplored hidden corners. On her last visit in April/May this year, she concentrated on Goa in making final preparations for this new Handbook.

Acknowledgements

In addition to our own visits to Goa, we had assistance from several people we would like to thank very warmly.

Ian Large, covered most of Goa on a motorbike in the spring of this year and wrote exhaustive notes and invaluable comments. Ian particularly wants to thank Lisa Seeley from the UK for her help and Mr UD Kamat in Goa. Katharine Ainger sent back material while tracing her roots in the former Portuguese colony; Shelley Malgarin returned to India for 6 months' research and spent part of her time in Goa for the new Handbook.

Mr U D Kamat, the Director of Tourism in Goa, gave very freely of his time and his deep knowledge. We also wish to thank Mr Bharat from his office for accompanying us to some villages in central Goa and to young Nilesh at Savoi.

We wish to thank Mr BR Adwalpalkar of Bombay for sharing his deep knowledge of Goa and helping us to prepare the section on Konkani words and phrases. Jyotika Dandapani of SD Enterprises, Wembley, very kindly let us have the latest news on rail connections from Goa.

Roger Landau who has travelled in Goa for many years sent in very detailed reports of his most recent visit earlier this year. Many other users of our India Handbook have written recently with their suggestions and observations on the Goa section. Among them, James Hardy gave us the valuable perceptions of a first time traveller in India and Goa.

Goa

SINCE Afonso Albuquerque established the first Portuguese toehold on Goa, the lush coastal region of India has captured the western imagination. Yet while many today think of Goa almost as an extension of a Mediterranean culture grafted onto Indian stock, the image is misleading.

Certainly Goa has an often magical coastline, for three quarters of the year bathed in sunshine yet never suffering the gruelling heat of the Indian interior. From the sandy coves and estuaries of the north to the long palm fringed beaches of the south, sand and the warm waters of the Arabian Sea have been Goa's main attraction for foreign travellers ever since the 1960s.

But it isn't just the beaches that make Goa unique. The state has a relaxed and easy going feel, where the decaying buildings not of the British Raj but of the Portuguese have created a wholly distinctive atmosphere. It is still easy to get the impression that Goa is largely Christian. The coastal villages all have their beautifully white painted churches and piazza and wayside crosses, often creating a startling impression against the clear blue sky.

Yet inland Goa remains predominantly Hindu, and its position right on the border between north and south Indian influences has made its own mark on Goa's identity. Within the tiny state, barely 100 km from north to south and 60 from west to east, it is possible to see in microcosm something of the astonishing diversity of India beyond. Indeed, within two or three days you can easily visit the neighbouring Indian states, tracking back into some of India's great empires and kingdoms.

Goa is much more than just a place for a great beach holiday. It offers a wonderful chance to begin to sample something of India itself, of which today it is an integral if still highly distinctive part. And that indeed is part of its welcoming charm.

Robert and Roma Bradnock

Travel aids

Coloured maps

One of the fascinations of Goa is that it offers not only glorious beaches but also the chance to explore and see something of rural India. The coloured maps which appear in the centre of the book are organized by taluka - the administrative divisons of Goa. We have tried to help you find your way around the countryside by providing cross references to the maps in the text. Thus the entry for Anjuna appears as:

ANJUNA *M5C1*

This refers to coloured map 2. Anjuna will be found in square C1. We hope the maps help - good exploring.

Stars

❖ Stars have been placed in the text for places which we feel are particularly worth visiting. Within a town the stars highlight the most important sites.

Travel FAQs

OUR INTENTION here is to give the answers to Frequently Asked Questions about travel to Goa. The *Information for travellers* section, giving fuller details of the practicalities of both short stays and longer visits, is found on pages 231-253, *health matters* are carried on pages 260-264 and the directory of useful addresses, words and phrases and food glossary is under *Rounding up* on pages 255-288.

WHEN TO GO?

Goa is warm throughout the year, but its position on the coast means that it never suffers the unbearable heat of India's northern plains. However, from mid-April until the beginning of the monsoon in early June both the temperature and the humidity rise sharply, making the middle of the day steamy hot and the sand of the beaches almost untouchable. The monsoon itself makes June and July very wet months. On the coast, the heavy rain often comes as torrential storms accompanied by lashing winds, while up in the cooler Ghats, if it is not raining, the hill tops are often wrapped in swirling cloud and mist – it's a good time to see the waterfalls! Heavy showers can persist in August and September and humidity can remain unpleasantly high, but by October rainfall drops significantly. The beautiful warm clear and dry weather of Goa's tropical winter from October to March makes it justifiably the best time for foreign visitors.

HEALTH

Most travellers will return home having experienced no problems apart from travellers' diarrhoea. That said, Goa has clear health differences from Europe or the USA and sensible precautions should be taken *before* and *during* your stay which are outlined on pages 260-264. Health facilities are good in the main cities and details of chemists and hospitals are given town by town. Most hotels will call a local doctor in an emergency.

DOCUMENTS

All visitors require a visa which are at present valid for 6 months for tourists with multiple entry, and longer for other categories. Applications must be made on the prescribed form (the passport must be valid to cover the the period of the visit) and should be accompanied by 3 passport size photographs. Fees vary according to nationality and arrangements for application and collection vary from office to office (the list appears on page 231). A single visit may be sufficient for personal callers but allow 3-4 weeks for postal applications.

WHAT TO WEAR?

Light cotton clothes are useful in Goa at any time of year. Take some very lightweight long sleeve cotton shirts and trousers for evenings (light in colour), as they also give some protection against mosquitoes. Modest dress for women is very advisable. Dont forget comfortable shoes, sandals or trainers and cotton socks; also take a sunhat and sunglasses.

WHAT WILL IT COST?

Most food, accommodation and public transport, especially rail and bus, are exceptionally cheap. There is a widening range of inexpensive but clean places to stay and eat at. Budget travellers (sharing a room) can expect to spend about Rs 350-400 (about US$12-13 or £7-8) a day to cover cost of accommodation, food and travel. Those planning to stay in fairly comfortable hotels and use taxis for travelling to sights should budget for Rs 2,000 (US$65 or £40) a day.

MONEY

Indian currency is the Rupee (Rs). In November 1997 there were approximately Rs 60 to the £ (Rs 35=US$1). It is NOT possible to purchase these before you leave. If you want cash on arrival it is best to get it at the airport bank. Major credit cards are increasingly acceptable in the main centres although rarely in smaller cities and towns (beware it can sometimes be more expensive than payment by cash). Travellers cheques are accepted without difficulty but it can take 30 minutes or more to cash them in banks. Banks often give a substantially better rate of exchange than hotels. Large hotels change money 24 hours a day. **Visa** have a growing number of ATMs in major cities, and several Indian banks now have a wide network of ATMs for local account holders.

GETTING THERE

For international flights access to Goa is restricted to charter flights which arrive at the airport at Dabolim on certain days of the week. An increasing number of tour operators from UK as well as a few from Finland, Germany, Holland and Switzerland, offer good value package holidays between October and April. It is also possible to get to Goa easily by flying in to Mumbai (Bombay) which is served by airlines from countries around the world.

Discounts: package holiday prices are highest between mid-December and mid-January and again over Easter. There are good bargains early and late in the season. Airlines offer significant discounts on their scheduled flight fares to Mumbai, especially outside European holiday times, most notably from London.

TIME

GMT +5½ hours throughout the year (EST +10½ hours). Conception of time is different in India, being rather vague. Unpunctuality is common so patience is needed.

FIRST IMPRESSIONS

On arrival at Dabolim airport the exciting images of an ancient and richly diverse culture which draw many visitors to India can be overshadowed by the immediate sensations which first greet you. These can all be daunting and make early adjustment to Goa difficult. They are made even more so by the fact that nearly all planes arrive in the middle of the night. Even in a short visit you need to give yourself time and space to adjust! You need to be prepared for:

Heat and humidity

Even in December-January day time temperatures can be high and after a long flight it can be very trying.

Delays

Travel from the airport to beach hotels can be much slower than you expect. If you are going to the northern beaches be prepared for anything up to two hours or more, though if the Zuari bridge remains open the time should be much less.

Noise

Many people also find India incredibly noisy, as radios, videos and loudspeakers seem to blare in unlikely places at all times of day (some travellers find earplugs useful at night).

Smells

India has an almost baffling mixture of smells, from the richly pungent to the delicately subtle.

Begging

In Goa begging is rare. However, in Mumbai and other cities it is common and for some travellers, a disturbing experience as beggars are sometimes badly physically handicapped. It is best to give any donations to an organization rather than to individuals. A coin to one child or destitute woman on the street will make you the focus of demanding attention from a vast number before long. There are also networks of beggar rings that operate in various cities which are run on a business scale. Many Indians give alms to street beggars as a means of gaining spiritual merit or out of a sense of duty but the sum is very small – often a Rupee or less. Some find it appropriate to give food to beggars rather than money. Some travellers carry ball-point pens to India to give to children who have learnt to call out "school pen!" – these are most likely to be sold. It may also encourage some children to beg, who otherwise might not.

Pressure

If you arrive in Mumbai you may be overwhelmed by people clamouring to sell you things or give them something. Taxi and rickshaw drivers are always there when you don't want them, much less often when you do. There often seems to be no sense of personal privacy.

Public hygiene

Public hygiene – or lack of it. It is common in both town and country to see people defecating and urinating in the open.

SAFETY

In general the threats to personal security for travellers in India are remarkably small. Goa is still a very safe place compared to European and American holiday destinations. Over 99% of visitors enjoy a carefree and crimefree holiday in the sun. However, thefts and physical assaults have been increasing on certain beaches especially in dimly lit stretches within the tourist belt.

It is safer to walk in large groups, especially at night. It is essential to take good care of personal valuables both when you are carrying them, and when you have to leave them anywhere. It is best to keep your passport, TCs and valuables with you at all times. Money belts worn under clothing are safe although you should keep some cash easily accessible in a purse. You can't regard hotel rooms as automatically safe. Cheap accommodation without adequate security is particularly vulnerable; foreign currency, cameras and music systems being the usual draw so use a good padlock.

Keep a record of vital documents, (eg passport number, TC numbers). If you have anything stolen, report it to the police as soon as possible.

Drugs are widely available from local and foreign dealers at most resorts in Goa, especially at the northern beaches of Anjuna and Chapora. All night beach 'parties' are heavily involved with drugtaking. Some police have been suspected of planting drugs on likely looking travellers and then arresting them, hoping for substantial bribes for their release.

WARNING Anyone charged with the illegal posession of drugs risks facing a fine of Rs 100,000 and 10 years imprisonment.

WOMEN TRAVELLERS

Compared with many other countries it is relatively easy and safe for women to travel around India, even on their own, though most people find it an advantage to travel with at least one companion.

In Goa (and in major cities and tourist centres) some women have experienced harassment from local men. Cases of rape have been reported especially after beach parties. There are some problems to watch out for and some simple precautions to take which make it possible to avoid both personal harassment and giving offence.

WHERE TO STAY?

Goa has a wide range of accommodation in the popular beach resorts though the choice diminishes as you move to less popular beaches and inland towns. You will find luxurious 5-star resort hotels in superb beach locations in Goa (and in Mumbai city centre), or clean, comfortable and safe mid-price hotels and family guest houses which are excellent value, or very cheap simple rooms if you are travelling on a shoe string or aim to stay several weeks.

In the peak season (October to April) bookings can be extremely heavy so it is best to reserve hotel accommodation well in advance which you can do by fax either from abroad or in India itself. However, double check reconfirmation details, and always try to arrive as early as possible in the day, or your reservation may be cancelled.

FOOD AND DRINK

Most visitors are surprised – and often delighted – at the enormous variety of delicious food available in any Indian town. Restaurants and beach cafés in the main tourist centres offer freshly prepared seafood delicacies, traditional Goan dishes as well as a good range of specialities from other parts of India. To suit the unaccustomed palate, they also have some Western, Chinese and sometimes even Thai and Tibetan options. You will also have the chance to sample exotic sweets and many tropical fruits.

Drinking water used to be regarded as one of India's biggest hazards. It is still true that water from the taps or wells should never be regarded as safe to drink. Public water supplies are nearly always polluted and unsafe. Bottled mineral water is now widely available although not all bottled water is mineral water; some is simply purified water from an urban supply.

Tea and coffee are safe and widely available. There is also a huge variety of bottled soft drinks, including well known international brands, as well as fruit juice in small cartons, which are perfectly safe.

Goa has a reputation for charging the lowest prices in the country for its alcoholic drinks, be it the local *feni*, sweet wines or beer.

GETTING AROUND

Air

The national carrier Indian Airlines and a few private companies (eg Jet Airways, NEPC) connect Goa with Mumbai and some other major Indian cities. All the major airline offices are connected to the central reservation system. Book as early as possible, especially in the peak season. Sometimes this is possible from agencies outside India; Jet Airways has its own offices in UK, Dubai and Malaysia. In India, use a reputable travel agent only and remember foreigners must pay in foreign currency at the 'Dollar rate'.

Train

Trains offer a unique experience, and are often an excellent and cheap way of travelling long distances across India. The Konkan railway now allows you to reach Goa from either Mumbai or Mangalore in under 8 hours on a comfortable modern train. Equally, the new broad gauge service from Vasco and Margao to Londa allows easy connections to the Indian interior.

Since the fast trains on popular routes get heavily booked, it is best to reserve these in advance. An Indrail Pass allows foreign tourists special privileges and so are worthwhile for their convenience. You would, however, have to spend a high proportion of your time on the trains to make them pay. Foreigners may be able to make use of the special tourist quota when trains are otherwise 'full'.

Road

Roads offer the only way of reaching many sites of interest within Goa and the neighbouring states. State and private buses reach most places you are likely to want to visit off the rail network, and are very cheap. They can, however, be extremely crowded and uncomfortable, especially for long journeys.

Car hire with a driver can be an ideal option, and is reasonably affordable when shared by 3 or 4 people. However, roads are often in poor condition, progress very slow and for some the experience can be worrying since traffic rules are rarely obeyed.

Hitchhiking

This is fairly rare in India although within Goa, you may get a lift more readily, especially on a motorbike.

Local transport

For short distances, bicycles or motorcycles are fine and are widely available for hire. Motorcyclists in Goa can be picked on by the police so make sure you carry all documentation and an International Driving Licence.

City buses run in Mumbai and Goa's larger towns though 'three-wheelers' tend to be more convenient – the 'rickshaw' drivers often get commission from hotels and gift shops so avoid taking their advice. Mumbai has plenty of metred yellow-top taxis.

LANGUAGE

Konkani and Marathi are two languages most commonly spoken in Goa, while English is widely understood by many in the tourist belt. Portuguese is still spoken by some of the older generation. Hindi is India's official language and is quite widely understood. Public notices and road signs usually appear in English and Hindi.

TELEPHONE SERVICES

The international code for India is 00 91. STD codes for towns are printed after the town name in the main text. International Direct Dialling is now widely available in privately run call boxes. Current telephone directories themselves are often out of date.

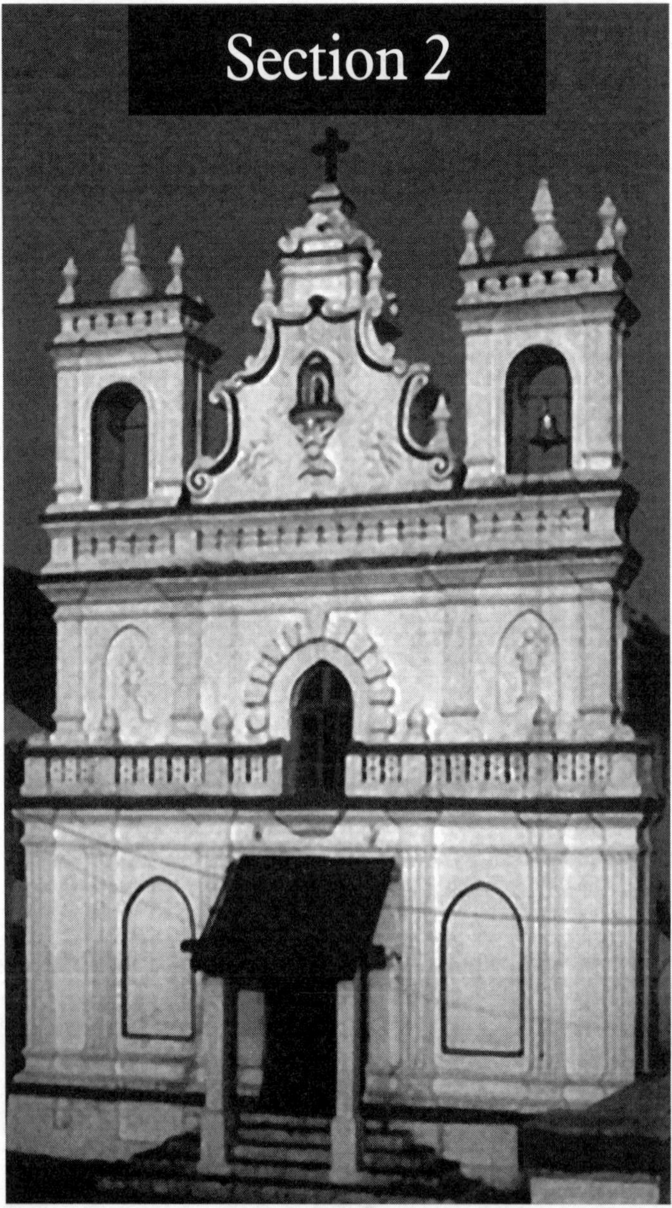
Section 2

Horizons

Official name
The Republic of India

National anthem
Jana Gana Mana

Constitution
Democratic republic

National flag
A horizontal tricolour with equal bands of saffron, white and green from top to bottom. At the centre is an Asoka wheel in navy blue.

Goa statistics
Area 3,800 sq km. *Population*: 1.170 million (Urban 41%, Scheduled Castes 2%, Scheduled Tribes 1%). *Birth rate*: Rural 15:1,000, Urban 16:1,000. *Death rate*: Rural 8:1,000, Urban 7:1,000. *Literacy*: M 74%, F 59%. *Religion*: Hindu 66%, Muslim 5%, Christian 29%, Jains 0.04%, Buddhists 0.03%.

India statistics:
Area: 3,287,000 sq km.Population: 940 million 1996. *Annual increase*: 18 million. *Birth rate*: Rural 34:1,000, Urban 27:1,000. *Death rate*: Rural 12:1,000, Urban 7:1,000. *Infant mortality rate*: Rural 105:1,000, Urban 62:1,000. *Literacy*: 52% (M 64%, F 39%). *Religion*: Hindu 765 million (Scheduled Castes: 139 million, Scheduled Tribes: 69 million), Muslim 105 million, Christian 25 million, Sikh 22 million, Buddhist 7 million, Jain 4 million.

The Land

BY INDIAN standards Goa is a tiny state. The coastline on which much of its fame depends is only 97 km long. The north and south of the state are separated by the two broad estuaries of the Zuari and Mandovi Rivers. Joined at high tide to create an island on which Panaji stands, these short rivers emerge from the high ranges of the Western Ghats less than 50 km from the coast and then glide almost imperceptibly to the sea. On either side of the rivers are extensive tidal marshes, and to north and south a series of minor streams run through flat bottomed valleys into the sea. From Tiracol in the north to Betul in the south these estuaries provided an important though far from wholly effective defence against intruders. Often overlooked by steep sided hillocks rising to the flat tops of the laterite plateaus which make up much of the area between the marshes, some of the estuaries contain the last remains of mangrove swamp and its associated ecosystem in western India.

The long sandy beaches which run for much of the length of both the north and the south coasts are backed by parallel sets of dunes. Apparently barren and economically useless the dunes have provided an important part of the wider ecosystem, providing shelter for housing and transport just inland. The beaches themselves are interrupted at various points by seaward extensions of the laterite plateaus which sometimes form impressive headlands. These provided ideal sites for coastal forts, as at Chapora, Fort Aguada or Cabo de Rama.

Inland from the coast Goa occupies a shallow indentation in the Sahyadri Ranges of the Western Ghats. Rising to around 1,000m along this section of their crest line, the Ghats were developed on the old fault which marked the separation of the Indian Peninsula from the ancient landmasses of Gondwanaland – which today have become

South Africa, South America and Antarctica. Separated from that great continental land mass less than 100 million years ago, the Indian Peninsula has been pushing northwards ever since. At its northern margins as it thrust under the Tibetan Plateau it was responsible for the creation of the massive mountain wall of the Himalaya. That has caused huge instability along the northern margins of the Peninsula, with earthquakes frequent in the foothills of the Himalaya themselves. In contrast, the land on which Goa stands is largely stable.

Despite its stability, geologically Goa represents a transition point in the Ghats. To the north the often precipitous ridge is formed by volcanic lavas which poured out over the Indian Peninsula over 60 million years ago, laying the foundation today for the rich black soils that cover so much of the Deccan to the northeast of Goa. In contrast, from Goa southwards the ridge of the Ghats is formed from the ancient and hard rocks of the Indian Peninsula, granites and gneisses. However, the ridge of the Ghats has been pushed back much further from the coast in Goa than anywhere else, because its short but powerful streams have eaten into the catchment areas of the great rivers of the Peninsula. This process has given Goa the 'breathing space' which marks it out from the rest of the much narrower strip of lowlands between the Ghats and the sea to both north and south.

The slightly greater extent of its coastal lowlands has not given Goa much easier access to the interior. The hill ranges rise sharply from the coastal plains, creating a wholly distinct, remote and rugged environment and pierced only by narrow gorges which lead up onto the plateau. Minor seasonal streams cascade down the mountain sides in the monsoon, while at the 600m high Dudhsagar ('sea of milk') falls the River Candepar plunges in a series of dramatic leaps throughout the year. The forested slopes of the Ghats are relatively sparsely populated, forming a natural barrier between the coastal lowlands and the much more open landscape immediately across the ridge of the hills in neighbouring Karnataka.

Where the laterite plateaus reach the coast, as at Chapora in the north, Dabolim in the centre or Cabo da Rama in the south, they produce rocky headlands jutting out into the sea, ideal sites for the string of coastal forts with which both the Portuguese and the Marathas defended their maritime and landward interests. The estuaries formed near such headlands – at Tiracol or Fort Aguada, Chapora or Betul – all suggest that in recent times sea level has risen slightly to flood the lower courses of the streams at high tide, pushing salt water several kilometres inland.

While the sandy beaches of the coast have provided the basis for Goa's rapidly expanding tourist industry the land of the interior of Goa has also become a vital resource. Rich in iron ore and manganese, huge open cast mines have provided enormously important exports. While the income derived from this has helped to boost Goa's foreign exchange, it often scars the landscape of the interior and has had a much criticized effect on neighbouring agriculture.

Climate

AT 15°N Goa lies well within the Tropics. Throughout the year therefore it is warm, but its position on the coast means that it never suffers the unbearable heat of India's northern plains. However, from mid-April until the beginning of the monsoon in mid-June both the temperature and the humidity rise sharply, making the middle of the day steamy hot and the sand of the beaches almost untouchable. But it is the monsoon itself which defines Goa's climate and its seasons, standing like a dividing wall between the heat of early summer and the beautiful warm clear and dry weather of its tropical winter, stretching from October to March.

Many myths surround the onset of the *monsoon*, derived from an Arabic word 'maunsam' which means simply 'season'. In fact its arrival is as variable as is the amount of rain which it brings. What makes the Indian monsoon quite exceptional is not its regularity but the depth of moist air which passes over the sub-continent. Over India, for example, the highly unstable moist airflow is over 6,000m thick compared with only 2,000m over Japan, giving rise to the bursts of torrential rain which mark out the wet season. Goa's location half way up India's west coast places it directly in line as the moisture laden winds sweep up from the southwest across the Arabian Sea. Forced to climb rapidly as it hits the Western Ghats the cooling air mass immediately releases its water, making June and July in Goa wet months. In an average year Panaji for example receives around 1,500 mm in just 6 weeks. On the coast itself this rain often comes as torrential storms accompanied by lashing winds, while up in the cooler air of the Ghats if it is not raining you can usually rely on the hill tops being in swirling cloud and mist. It's a good time of year for the waterfalls!

While heavy showers persist into August and September and the high humidity can continue to make life unpleasant the rainfall drops sharply away and in October most of the state receives less than 100 mm. Life returns to normal as the cooler dry air of the North East monsoon pushes southwards from the Tibetan plateau, bringing beautifully invigorating dry clear air to the rainwashed skies. It is the perfect season for visiting Goa, cool enough at night sometimes to need a pullover, but still hot in the open sun on the beach.

While the climate of Goa itself is

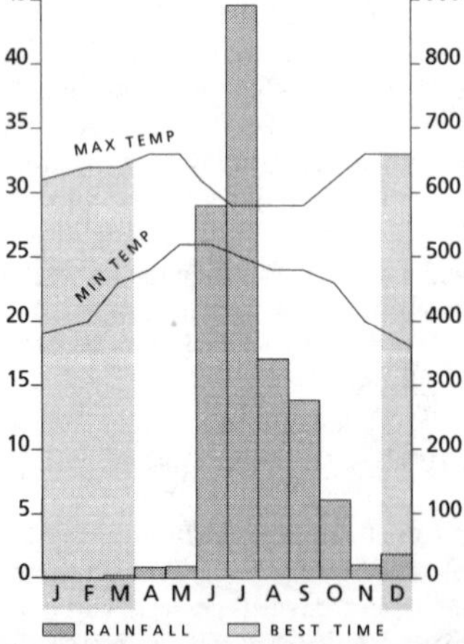

Climate: Panaji

74

dominated by its position to the west of the Ghats, the land immediately across the ridge of the hills experiences quite a different climate. Almost straight away on crossing the Ghats you notice the effects of far lower total rainfall. Although the entire region of neighbouring Karnataka and Maharashtra experiences exactly the same seasonal pattern of change in the wind system which brings Goa its wet monsoon, once the winds have climbed the Ghats and start their descent over the plains they dry out rapidly.

Wildlife

Goa has a fascinating range of birds and animals. According to one authority, Blanford, there are 48 genera of mammals, 275 genera of birds and 60 genera of reptiles, seven of which are endemic to the Western Ghats. The Wildlife Sanctuaries are worth visiting for their scenery, vegetation and birdlife but can be disappointing if you are expecting to see a variety of exotic animals.

MAMMALS

Deer There are several species, including the magnificent **sambar** (*Cervus unicolor*) which can be up to 150 cm at the shoulder. Sambar live on wooded hillsides in groups of up to 10 or so, though solitary animals are also quite common.

The much smaller **Chital** or spotted deer (*Axis axis*), only about 90 cm tall, are seen in herds of 20 or so, in grassy areas. The bright rufous coat spotted with white is unmistakable; the stags carry antlers with three tines.

Oxen By far the most visible member of the family is the domesticated **Water Buffalo** (*Bubalus bubalis*), widely seen in the coastal districts. The **Indian Bison** or **Gaur** (*Bos gaurus*) looks superficially like a large buffalo. The 'state animal' of Goa, this massive animal can be up to 200 cm tall at the shoulder, with a heavy muscular ridge across it. It usually lives in forested uplands. There are large herds in the Bhagwan Mahaveer Sanctuary and as far south

Flying fox

Sambar

Gaur

Hyena

Chital

Common Langur

Wild Boar

as Canacona.

The **Wild Boar** (*Sus scrofa*, known in Goa as *Ran Dukar*), although declining in numbers, is found in the foothills of the Ghats, and has the reputation of causing immense damage to paddy, banana and sugar cane crops.

One of the most important scavengers of the open countryside, the **Striped Hyena** (*Hyena hyena*) usually comes out at night. It is about 90 cm at the shoulder with a large head with a noticeable crest of hairs along its sloping back.

The **Sloth Bear** (*Melursus ursinus*), about 75 cm at the shoulder, lives in broken forest and has been seen in the Cotigao Sanctuary and Surla ghat. Unkempt and mangy looking, it has a distinctively long and pendulous lower lip.

The **Big cats** The Bhagwan Mahaveer Sanctuary, Goa's largest wildlife park, is reputed to have 18 panther. A few tigers are known to stray in occasionally from neighbouring Karnataka in the summer but are rarely seen. Despite their greater numbers panthers have the reputation of being even more elusive. The smaller species include the **Jungle cat** (*Felis chaus*) **Leopard cat** (*Felis bengaliensis*), **Small Indian Civet** (*Vivirrecula indica*)

The **Indian Elephant** (*Elephas maximus*) Although not normally found in Goa, a wild elephant is occasionally seen in the Bhagwan Mahaveer Sanctuary or the Bondla National Park when they wander in from neighbouring Karnataka during the summer months.

The **Common Giant Flying Squirrel** (*Petaurista petaurista*) which inhabits the Western Ghats, is found around Valpoi and the Bhagwan Mahaveer and Cotigao sanctuaries. The body can be as much as 45 cm long and the tail another 50 cm or so. They glide from tree to tree using a membrane stretching from front leg to back leg which acts like a parachute. **Indian Giant Flying Squirrel** (*Ratufa indica*) is noticeable by its strange call.

In addition to the animals that still live truly in the wild there are many species which have adapted to village and town life. India's various monkeys are rare on the coastal strip but inland they are far more common. The **Common Langur** (*Presbytis entellus*) is a long tailed monkey with a black face, hands and feet which lives largely in the forest. The **Bonnet Macaque** (*Macaca radiata*) is more solid looking with shorter limbs and a shorter tail, and has the distinctive whorl of longer hairs on the head. They are seen both in forests and near villages. All monkeys can be aggressively demanding and are carriers of rabies, so should be kept at a distance. Food, which invariably attracts them, should be kept concealed.

Palm squirrels are very common. The **Five-striped** palm squirrel (*Funambulus pennanti*) and the **Three-striped** palm squirrel (*Funambulus palmarum*), both about the same size (30 cm in length, about half of which is tail), look very similar. The five-striped squirrel is the one usually seen in towns.

The two bats most commonly seen in towns differ enormously in size. The larger is the so-called **Flying Fox** (*Pteropus giganteus*) which has a wing span of 120 cm. They roost in large noisy colonies, often in the middle of towns or villages, where they look like folded umbrellas hanging from the trees. In the evening they can be seen leaving the roost with *slow measured wing beats*. The much smaller **Indian Pipistrelle** (*Pipistrellus coromandra*),

Hoopoe
Paddy Bird
Pariah Kite in flight
Pariah Kite
Brahminy Kite
Common Myna
Little cormorant
Cattle Egret
Painted Stork
Openbill Stork

with a wing span of about 15 cm, is an insect eater. It comes into the house at dusk, roosting under eaves and has a *fast, erratic* flight.

The **Common Mongoose** (*Herpestes edwardsi*) lives in scrub and open jungle as well as in gardens and fields. It kills snakes, but will also take rats, mice, chickens and birds' eggs. Tawny coloured with a grey grizzled tinge, it is about 90 cm in length, of which half is pale-tipped tail.

Sea mammals An increasingly popular activity from several points on the Goa coastline is dolphin spotting. Both the **Long-beaked dolphin** (*Steno spa*) and the **porpoise** (*Phocaena phocaena*) are common right along the coast, and the **Dugong** or Sea Cow (*Dygong dugon*) is also found.

BIRDS

Like other parts of the Western Ghats and the west coast, Goa has a very rich birdlife. Many species have adapted to man and live in towns and villages.

Town and village birds Some perform a useful function scavenging and clearing refuse, one of the most widespread being the **Pariah Kite** (*Milvus migrans*, 65 cm), an all brown bird with a longish tail. The much more handsome **Brahminy Kite** (*Haliastur indus*, 48 cm) is also a familiar scavenger, but is largely confined to the waterside. Its chestnut and white plumage is unmistakable.

The common **White-backed Vulture** (*Gyps bengalensis*, 90 cm) is a heavy looking, ungainly, brown bird with a bare and scrawny head and neck. In flight the white rump and broad white band on the leading edge of the under surface of the wing identify it.

The **Feral Pigeon**, or **Blue Rock Dove** (*Columba livia*, 32 cm), is generally a slaty grey in colour and invariably has two dark bars on the wing and a white rump. The **Little Brown Dove** (*Streptopelia senegalensis*, 25 cm) is quite tame and shows little fear of man. It is bluey grey and brown above, with a pink head and underparts, and a speckled pattern on the neck. The **Collared Dove** (*Streptopelia decaocto*, 30 cm) is common especially in the drier parts of Goa, in gardens and open spaces. It has a distinct half collar on the back of its neck.

The **Red-vented Bulbul** (*Pycnonotus cafer*, 20 cm), a mainly brown bird, can be identified by the slight crest and a bright red patch under the tail. The **Common Myna** (*Acridotheres tristis*, 22 cm) feeds on lawns, especially after rain. Look for the white under the tail and the bare yellow skin around the eye, yellow bill and legs, and in flight the large white wing patch.

A less common, but more striking bird also seen feeding on lawns and in open country is the **Hoopoe** (*Upupa epops*, 30 cm), easily identified by its sandy plumage with black and white stripes, and long thin curved bill. The marvellous fan-shaped crest is sometimes raised. Finally there is a member of the cuckoo family which is heard more often than seen. The **Koel** (*Eudynamys scolopacea*, 42 cm) is commonly heard in gardens and wooded areas, particularly during the hot weather. The call is a kuoo-kuoo-kuoo, a double note which starts off low and flute-like, but rises in pitch and intensity, then suddenly stops, only to start all over again. The male is all black with a greenish bill and a red eye; the female streaked and barred.

Water and Waterside birds

Goa's marshes form an enormously rich bird habitat. Cormorants abound, the commonest, the **Little Cormorant** (*Phalacrocorax niger*, 50 cm) is an almost entirely black bird with just a little white on the throat. It has a long tail and hooked bill, and is seen both on the water and in colonies in waterside trees. The **Coot** (*Fulica atra*, 40 cm), another black bird, is found on open water, especially in winter. It sits much higher in the water than the cormorant and has a noticeable white shield on the forehead.

The **Openbill Stork** (*Anastomus oscitans*, 80 cm) and the **Painted Stork** (*Ibis leucocephalus*, 100 cm) are two of the commonest storks of India. The openbill stork is a white bird with black wing feathers, and a curiously shaped bill. The Painted stork is also mainly white, with a pinkish tinge on the back and greenish black marks on the wings and a broken black band on the lower chest. The bare yellow face and yellow down-curved bill are conspicuous.

By almost every swamp, ditch or rice paddy up to about 1,200m you will see the **Paddy Bird** (*Ardeola grayii*, 45 cm). An inconspicuous buff-coloured bird, it is easily overlooked as it stands hunched up by the waterside but as soon as it takes off, its white wings and rump make it very noticeable.

Goa is also home to wonderful kingfishers. The most widespread of the Indian kingfishers is the jewel-like **Common Kingfisher** (*Alcedo atthis*, 18 cm). With its brilliant blue upperparts and orange breast it is usually seen perched on a twig or a reed beside the water, or just a flash of eye-catching blue in flight. The much larger black and white **Pied Kingfisher** (*ceryle rudis*) is adept at fishing from the air and can sometimes be spotted hovering over water.

Birds of open grassland and cultivated land

The **Cattle Egret** (*Bubulcus ibis*, 50 cm), a small white heron, is usually seen in small flocks, frequently perched on the backs of cattle. Birds in breeding plumage have buff plumes on the head and shoulders, and a yellow bill.

The all black **Drongo** (*Dicrurus adsimilis*, 30 cm) is almost invariably seen perched on telegraph wires or bare branches. Its distinctively forked tail makes it easy to identify.

Weaver birds are a family of mainly yellow birds, all remarkable for the intricate nests they build. The most widespread is the **Baya Weaver** (*Ploceus philippinus*, 15cm). These birds nest in large colonies, often near villages. The male in the breeding season can be distinguished by the combination of black face and throat and contrasting yellow top of the head and the yellow breast band. In the non-breeding season the male and the female are both brownish sparrow-like birds.

REPTILES AND AMPHIBIANS

India is famous for its reptiles, especially its snakes which feature in many stories and legends, and despite its small size Goa has its share. The dense flora and heavy rainfall of the interior provide a pefect environment for many snakes. Although about 200 people a year report being bitten in Goa, snakes generally keep out of the way of people.

One of the most common in the well watered areas of the hills is the **Indian Rock Python** (*Python molurus*). Usually about 4m in length (and sometimes much longer). pythons are 'constrictors' which kill their prey by suffocation.

The *Dhaman* or *Sodne Nagin*, or **Indian Rat Snake** (*Pytas* mususus) is often seen in houses. The bright yellow snake grows to nearly 3m and has a strong and unpleasant smell. A common harmless snake in the forests of the foothills is the *Kalinagin* **Golden**

Tree Snake (*Chrysopelea ornata*), which despite its English name, can be almost black with greenish cross bars. Living on small mammals, geckos, birds and insects, the Golden Tree Snake can swing and 'jump' up to 6m from tree to tree.

There are several species of the poisonous cobra all of which have a hood, which is spread when the snake draws itself up to strike. The best known is probably the *Nag*, **Spectacled Cobra** (*Naja naja*), which has a mark like a pair of spectacles on the back of its hood. The largest venomous snake in the world is the *Raj Nag*, **King Cobra** (*Ophiophagus hannah*) which grows to 5m in length. It is usually brown, but can vary from cream to black. In their natural state, cobras generally inhabit forests.

Equally venomous, but much smaller in size, the *Kaner* or *Maniar*, the **Common Krait** (*Bungarus caeruleus*) grows to just over 1m. This is a slender shiny, blue-black snake with thin white bands across the body. The bands vary from very conspicuous,

to almost indiscernible. The slightly smaller and harmless *Pasko* (*Oligodon Taeniolatus*), common on farmland, is very similar as its brown spots resemble the krait's bands. It has green lines on the sides and lacks the hexagonal dorsal scales of the krait. Another common non-poisonous snake mistaken for a krait is the *Kaydya* or **Common Wolf snake** (*Lycodon aulicus*) which can be found near houses and in gardens. The grey-brown body has 12-19 darker cowrie-shaped markings which resemble the krait's cross bars.

Lizards In houses everywhere you cannot fail to see the **Gecko** (*Hemidactylus*) on the wall. There are several species of this small, totally harmless, primitive lizard which is active after dark getting rid of undesirable insects. One falling on your head is thought to bring luck! At the other end of the scale is the **Monitor** (*Varanus*), which can be up to 2m in length. There are several species in India and they vary from a colourful black and yellow to plain or speckled brown. Sadly, they are being threatened with extinction in Goa as people are killing them to eat.

The most widespread crocodile in India is the **Mugger** or **Marsh Crocodile** (*Crocodilus palustris*) which lives in fresh water and grows to 3-4m in length. The enormous **Estuarine** or **Saltwater Crocodile** (*Crocodilus porosus*), as much as 7m long, is a much sleeker looking species than the mugger. It is found in brackish waters and unlike the rather docile mugger, has an aggressive temperament. Both are found in the wild in Goa, notably in the Cumbarjua Canal which separates the island of Tiswadi from Ponda. Although **turtles** are commonly found in ponds, ditches and wells, the **sea turtles** including the **Olive Ridley** (*Lepidochelys olivacea*) which visit certain Goan beaches (Morjim, Calangute and Cabo de Rama among them) between October and December for laying their eggs, are being severely affected. Few baby turtles return to the sea since the eggs are taken to end up as a culinary delicacy despite attempts by the Forest Department to prevent the nests being plundered by villagers.

Vegetation

None of Goa's original vegetation remains untouched. The **mangrove** forests of the tidal marshes have been steadily eroded by the need to drain land for agriculture, while the estuarine waters have been increasingly polluted by mining activity. The most important mangroves are found today in the Mandovi-Zuari estuary, with minor forests remaining along the Chapora, Talpona, Galgibag and Tiracol estuaries.

Inland, the tropical rain forests which once covered both the Ghats and the lowland have been steadily reduced by clearance for farming and by cutting for timber. Two types of deciduous tree were once particularly common across peninsular India and even today they remain important. **Sal** (*Shorea robusta*), now found mainly in eastern India, and **teak** (*Tectona grandis*). Most teak today has been planted. Both are resistant to burning, which helped to protect them where man used fire as a means of clearing the forest, common along the Western Ghat ranges from north to south.

The most striking vegetation contrasts are provided by the regular succession of laterite plateaus and riverine valleys. The valley sides are still densely covered in cultivated trees – the tall and usually gently curving coconut palms and the equally tall but slender and arrow-straight areca palms, interspersed by a dense and rich cover of valuable nut and fruit trees. The most widespread – and economically the most important – is the shiny-leaved cashew, introduced originally from South America, with its distinctive almost pear-shaped fruit and highly valued nut. These drought-tolerant trees sprawl across the thin soils of the laterite pavements and down into the richer more fertile soils of the valleys, giving Goa one of its most important sources of income.

TREES

Goa's plantation economy depends heavily on two crops that every visitor will become aware of. One grows despite the little attention it receives, while the other is a part of daily life.

The **Cashew** tree (*Anacardium occidentale*) or *cazu* was introduced into India, but now grows wild as well as being cultivated. It is a medium sized tree with bright green, shiny, rounded leaves. The rather thick foliage casts a dense shadow. The nut grows on a fleshy bitter fruit called a cashew apple, although this looks more like a small squashed pear than an apple, and the nut hangs down below this. Both the fruit and nut are used in different ways and nothing is wasted (see box on 187). Despite its haphazard cultivation, it is Goa's most important economic crop and the nut is a good foreign exchange earner.

The **Coconut Palm** (*Cocos nucifera*) grows best along the coast and river banks of Goa and is a familiar sight along the country roads of coastal districts. It has a tall (10m-15m), slender, unbranched trunk, feathery leaves and large green or orange fruit (so different from the brown fibre-covered inner nut which makes its way to Europe).

The **Areca Palm** (*Areca catechu*), also known as betel nut, which grows abundantly in the Ponda taluka in particular,

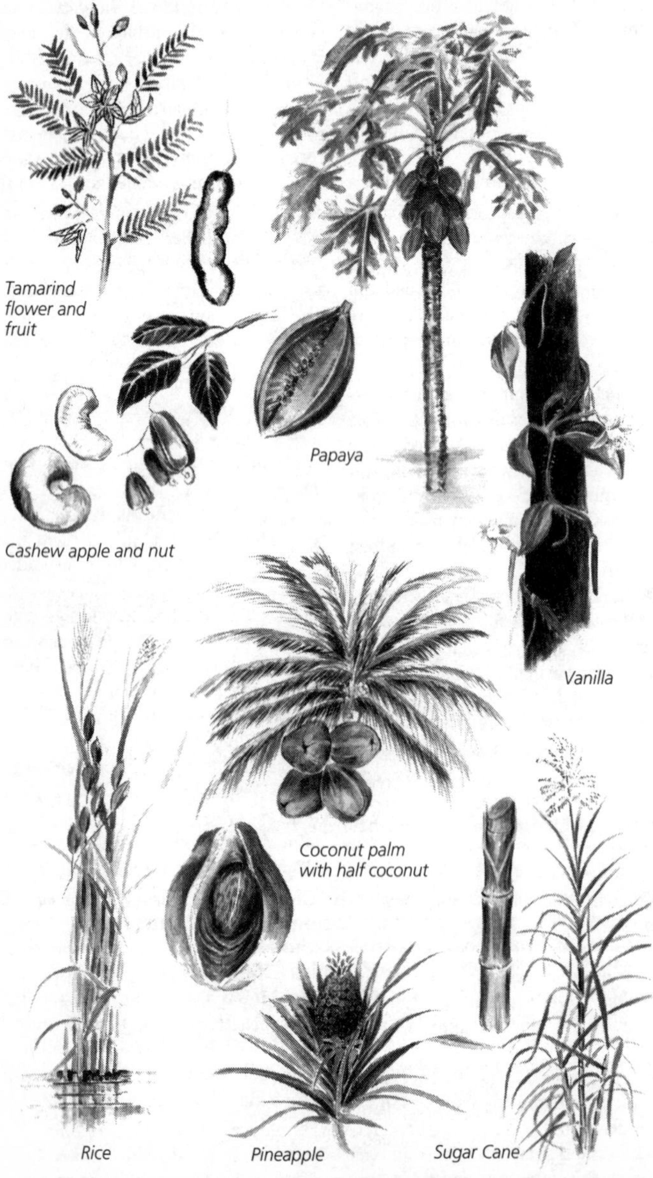
Tamarind flower and fruit
Papaya
Cashew apple and nut
Vanilla
Coconut palm with half coconut
Rice
Pineapple
Sugar Cane

is about the same height as the coconut palm, but prefers shade and needs more attention in the dry months. The leaves are similar, and fall cleanly off the trunk leaving decorative ring marks. Betel (areca) nuts, which grow in large hanging bunches, are smooth, round and only about 3 cm across.

The **Ashok** or **Mast** (*Polyalthia longifolia*) is a tall evergreen which can reach 15m or more in height. One variety, often seen in avenues, is trimmed and tapers towards the top. The leaves are long, slender and shiny and narrow to a long point.

Another plantation crop which is exported is the **Bamboo** (*Bambusa*) which is, strictly speaking, a grass. The larger varieties have stems strong and thick enough to be used for construction and as pipes in irrigation schemes in small holdings. Goa has a unique thornless type.

Of all Indian trees the **Banyan** (*Ficus benghalensis*) is probably the best known. Featured widely in Indian literature, it is planted by temples, in villages and along roads. In a wall, the growing roots will split the wall apart. If it grows in the bark of another tree, it sends down roots towards the ground. As it grows, more roots appear from the branches, until the original host tree is surrounded by a cage-like structure which eventually strangles it. The largest banyan in Goa is in a *math* (seminary) near the Cotigao Sanctuary.

Related to the banyan, and growing in similar situations, is the **Pipal** (*Ficus religiosa*), which also cracks open walls and strangles other trees with its roots. It has a smooth grey bark, and is commonly found near temples and shrines. It can easily be distinguished from the banyan by the absence of aerial roots,

The Indispensable Eco-friendly Coconut

The coconut palm, so much a part of the coastal strip and the interior waterside scene, is a great gift of nature. Grown as the second most important plantation crop, Goa is estimated to have over 2.5 million trees producing on average 30 fruit each per year.

The green fruit yields an excellent refreshing 'milk' which is on tap whenever the top is cut off. The 'shell' is split open to expose the soft white kernel which is edible. The outer fibrous coir, just under the skin, is soaked in tanks before being woven into mats or twisted into rope. The dry, older nut with a white layer of 'flesh' or kernel (*copra*), which is grated or pounded for cooking curries and preparing sweets, can be often seen being sold in market stalls. The Goans prize the sap which the toddy tapper collects every few weeks from the base of a fresh leaf. The fresh sap can be drunk as a sweetish juice before it begins to ferment in the warmth, or it can be processed to produce vinegar or jaggery sugar. Most Goans, however, prefer it as the lightly alcoholic fermented *urak* or the intoxicating *feni* which is produced through distillation, a method learnt centuries ago from the Portuguese. See also 'Sap Tappers' on page 134.

Palm oil and cattle feed in the shape of oil cakes are also products in demand. But, the trees' uses don't stop here since throughout the year the leaves are used for weaving baskets and providing thatch for shelter. Then, when the tree dies, its trunk comes in handy for cutting up for use in building.

It is not surprising that every Goan family living anywhere near water will tend a coconut or two.

and by the leaves which are large, rather leathery and heart shaped, the point of the leaf tapering into a pronounced 'tail'.

The **Casuarina** (*Casuarina*) is a slender, rather wispy looking tree which grows in poor sandy soil, widely seen on Goa's coast and village waste land. It has the typical leaves of a pine tree and the cones are small and prickly to walk on. Despite their normally modest size, they are said to attract lightning during a thunder storm.

The **Silk Cotton Tree** (*Bombax ceiba*), also known as the kapok, can grow to 25m in height. The bark is light coloured, often grey and often has conical spines. In big trees there are noticeable buttresses at the bottom of the trunk. Its wide, almost horizontal branches, though deciduous, keep their leaves for most of the year. The dramatic flowers, which appear when the tree is leafless, are cup-shaped, with fleshy red petals up to 12 cm long. It is the fruit which produces the fine silky cotton which gives it its name.

Fruit trees

The **Banana** plant (*Musa*) is actually a gigantic herb arising from an underground stem. The very large leaves grow directly off the trunk which is about 5m in height. The fruit grows in bunches of up to 100 fruit.

Bread Fruit trees are common, with large almost spiky leaves and fruit rather like giant knobbly acorns. The fruit (really a nut) is boiled and used in savoury dishes.

The **Jackfruit** (*Artocarpus heterophyllus*) is one of India's most remarkable fruit trees. A large evergreen with dark green leathery leaves, its huge fruit can be as much as 1m long and 40 cm thick. It grows from a short stem directly off the trunk and branches. The skin is thick and rough, almost prickly. The fruit of the main eating variety itself is almost sickly sweet. Each fruit has dozens of segments, each with a nut about the size of a Brazil nut at its centre.which are often roasted.

The **Kokum** (*bhirand*) is used in curries and is made into a syrup for making a refreshing cool drink in the summer. The peel is prepared into a magic cure (*sol coddi*) for hangovers!

The **Mango** (*Mangifera indica*) is widespread. It is a fairly large tree being 6-15m high, with spreading branches forming a rounded canopy. The distinctively shaped fruit is quite delicious and unlike any other in taste. A favourite variety is the Alphonso from Goa and Maharashtra.

The **Papaya** (*Carica papaya*) which often grows to only 4m has distinctive palm-like leaves. Only the female tree bears the shapely fruit, which hang down close to the trunk just below the leaves.

The economically valuable **Tamarind** (*Tamarindus indica*), which may have originated in Africa, is another handsome roadside tree with a straight trunk and a spreading crown. It is an evergreen with feathery leaves and small yellow and red flowers which grow in clusters. The valuable fruit pods are long and curved and swollen at intervals down their length.

CROPS

Goa's main crops are typical of India's whole coastal belt. The single most important crop is **Rice** (commonly *Orysa indica*). Soon after planting in the early monsoon the fields turn a beautiful light green as the young paddy shoots from the flooded fields. It takes between 3 and 5 months to mature, and some areas with irrigation manage to get two crops a year, so you can sometimes see rice ready for harvesting in November alongside newly planted seedlings. The tending of rice is very labour intensive, planting or harvesting often being done by hand.

Sugar cane (*Saccharum*), a commercially important crop in some areas, looks like a large grass which grows up to 3m. The sweet juice is sometimes extracted for selling along the roadside. It produces crude brown sugar which is sold as jaggery.

Pineapples (*Ananas comosus*) are often grown under trees, especially under coconut palms on the coast. The fruit grows out of the middle of a rosette of long, spiky leaves.

Of the many **spices** grown in India, the two climbers pepper and vanilla and the grass-like cardamom are the ones most often seen.

Vanilla (*Vanilla planifolium*), which belongs to the orchid family, also grows up trees for support and attaches itself to the bark by small roots. It is native to South America, but grows well in Goa as in other Indian regions which have high rainfall. It is a rather fleshy looking plant, with white flowers and the long slender pods can be seen hanging down.

The **Pepper** vine (*Piper Nigrum*) is indigenous to India. As it is a vine it needs support such as a trellis or a tree. It is frequently planted up against the betel nut palm, and appears as a leafy vine with almost heart-shaped leaves. The peppercorns cluster along hanging spikes and are red when ripe. Both black and white pepper is produced from the same plant, the difference being in the processing.

Culture

PEOPLE

Despite over four centuries of Portuguese dominance, earlier characteristics of Goa's population are still obvious. While during the Inquisition the Portuguese made systematic efforts to wipe out all social traces of the earlier Hindu and Muslim cultures, many of their features were simply modified to conform to external Catholic demands. Thus even in the Old Conquest areas the predominantly Catholic community is still divided along much earlier caste lines.

The four major varna groups of Hindus, the Brahmins or priestly caste, Kshatriyas (warriors), Vaishyas (merchants) and Sudras (agriculturalists) retained their designations in only slightly modified form. Thus according to the People of India project of India's Anthropological Survey, the different sub-castes of the Brahmin community in Goa merged into the single Catholic Saraswat group, the Vaishya sub-castes merged into one, the Charddo Catholic community, and the remainder became Catholic Sudras. There was a small community of Catholic Mestiços, most having left Goa for Portugal after Liberation. Today the two highest Catholic castes, the Brahmin and Charddo Catholics, have become a single group, inter-marrying and generally occupying high positions in society. Catholic Sudras, who include the Christian fishing communities, remain separate.

The Catholics are sub-divided into a number of occupational groups. In Salcete, Ponda and Quepem, for example the Carpenter group (Thovoi) is common, and many continue to depend on making small items of furniture or decorative images for Church buildings. Along the coast the Catholic Kharvi, or fishermen, claim to be Goa's original inhabitants. While their surnames – Rodrigues, Costa, Souza, Dias, Pereira – have all been adopted from the Portuguese they are direct descendants of the Hindu fishing communities of the coast.

Unlike the Christian communities the Hindu castes are still sub-divided along their original occupational lines. Thus the Brahmin community includes the Chitpavan Brahmins, present in all the talukas originally as priests. Most claim Marathi as their mother tongue although many also speak Konkani, and they are strictly vegetarian. The Daivadnya Brahmins in contrast are largely goldsmiths, taking the name Shett. Unlike the Chitpavan Brahmins they are not vegetarian, eating fish, mutton and chicken but abstaining from beef, pork and buffalo. They have strong cultural links with Maharashtra.

One of the most remarkable communities among the Hindus is that known today as the **Gomantak Maratha**

Samaj. The group belongs to the former *devdasis*, dancing women and prostitutes who had been dedicated to temples and the service of their deities. Ancient Hindu scriptures (the Puranas) had suggested that the most beautiful girls should be dedicated to temple service, and that they should be considered of high social status. In the social uplift movement of the 1940s and 1950s which sought to improve conditions for the devdasi community a number of different groups came together in the Gomantak Maratha Samaj. Among them were the *devlis*, who had been responsible for lighting the temple lamps or working as temple attendants, and the Chedvaan, Bandi and Farjand groups, who had been dependent on landlords. Before independence all large temples had a priest (*pujari*), lamplighters (*jyotkar*), musicians and people who recited religious songs (*kirtankars*), and groups of temple girl dancers (*bhavins*). It was the children of this last group who formed the distinct *devli* community, remaining under the control of the Mahajans (trustees) of the temple. Other members of this community include the *kalavants*, who claimed descent from the mythical *apsaras*. or divine dancers and singers, and *bandes* (meaning literally 'bound up') who were tied to landlords as maids and concubines.

There are also the tribal groups such as the Gavdes and Kunbis. **Gavdes** were originally nomadic hunters and fishermen who worshipped natural elements, while the **Kunbis** usually worked on the land and herded animals on the hillsides and lived in villages with mud and thatch huts. Some continue to wear traditional tribal dress. Kunbi women can be identified by row upon row of bead necklaces and copper bangles covering their arms from wrist to elbow and their long well-oiled hair coiled up into a distinctive shape.

LANGUAGE

Indian languages come in a seemingly baffling variety, many with their own scripts. Goa is located precisely on the dividing line which separates the Indo-European languages of North India from the Dravidian languages of the South.

The roots of nearly all the North Indian languages can be traced back to **Sanskrit** which originated with the Indo-Aryan pastoralists from Central Asia who moved into India from 2000 BC onwards. By the 6th century BC Sanskrit had become the dominant language of North India. The Muslims brought Persian into South Asia as the language of the rulers. Like Sanskrit before it, and English from the 18th century onwards, Persian became the language of the numerically tiny but politically powerful elite across the Sub-continent.

Out of the interaction between the Persian of the court and the native Sanskrit-based language developed Hindustani, separately identified as Hindi and Urdu. In the centuries which followed the major regional languages of North India developed, including **Marathi**, the language of Maharashtra, itself a sister language of **Konkani** spoken in Goa.

In sharp contrast, the dominant language of Karnataka, the state which borders Goa to the east and south, is **Kannada**, one of the four Dravidian languages (the others being Tamil in Tamil Nadu, Malayalam in Kerala and Telugu in Andhra Pradesh). Each has its own script.

All the Dravidian languages were influenced by the prevalence of Sanskrit as the language of the ruling and educated élite, although Tamil, which has a literature going back over 2,000 years, was least affected. Kannada was clearly established by AD 1000.

Portuguese was widely spoken until 1961 and even today many of the older generation can speak it, but local languages remained important. The two most significant were Marathi, the language of the politically dominant majority of the neighbouring state to the North, and **Konkani**, the spoken language of most Goans.

Konkani was introduced as the language of instruction in Church primary schools in 1991 and was added to the list of recognized languages in the Indian Constitution in August 1992. None the less, very few government primary schools teach in Konkani compared with over 800 that use Marathi, but the issue is still contentious. Hindi is increasingly spoken with the influx of non-Goan employees in hotel resorts. English and Hindi are widely used on road signs, bus destinations and tourism-related notices. In rural areas, however, Konkani predominates.

Scripts

It is impossible to spend even a short time in India without coming across several of the different scripts that are used. The earliest ancestor of scripts in use today was Brahmi, in which Asoka's famous inscriptions were written in the 3rd century BC. Written from left to right, a separate symbol represented each different sound. For about a thousand years the major script of northern India has been the Nagari or Devanagari, which means literally the script of 'the city of the gods'. Hindi and Marathi join Sanskrit in their use of Devanagari. In Goa, you are likely to come across widespread use of Hindi, and the Roman script for English. **Konkani** is written both in Roman and Devanagari scripts, though it is the latter which has now become the official script for the language.

Numerals

Many of the Indian alphabets have their own notation for numerals. This is not without irony, for what in the western world are called 'Arabic' numerals are in fact of Indian origin. In some parts of the sub-continent, local numerical symbols are still in use, but by and large you will find that the Arabic number symbols, familiar in Europe and the West, are common and in general use in Goa.

MUSIC AND DANCE

Goans are noted at home and abroad for their love of music. Although Indian classical music is performed and Goa has a rich heritage of folk music and dance, Goan popular music reflects modern western popular influences.

Indian music can trace its origins to the metrical hymns and chants of the Vedas, in which the production of sound according to strict rules was understood to be vital to the continuing order of the Universe. Over more than 3,000 years of development, through a range of regional schools, India's musical tradition has been handed on almost entirely by ear. The chants of the **Rig Veda** developed into songs in the **Sama Veda** and music found expression in every sphere of life, closely reflecting the cycle of seasons and the rhythm of work.

Over the centuries the original three notes, which were sung strictly in descending order, were extended to five and then seven and developed to allow freedom to move up and down the scale. The scale increased to 12 with the addition of flats and sharps and finally to 22 with the further subdivision of semitones. Books of musical rules go back at least as far as the 3rd century AD. Classical music was totally intertwined with dance and drama.

At some point after the Muslim influence made itself felt in the North, North and South Indian styles diverged, to become Carnatic (Karnatak) music in the South and Hindustani music in the North. However, they still share important common features: *svara* (pitch), *raga* (the melodic structure), and *tala* or *talam* (metre).

Hindustani music probably originated in the Delhi Sultanate during the 13th century, when the most widely known of North Indian musical instruments, the *sitar*, was believed to have been invented as well as the small drums, the *tabla*. The other important northern instruments are the stringed sarod, the reed instrument shahnai and the wooden flute. Most Hindustani compositions have devotional texts, though they encompass a great emotional and thematic range.

The essential structure of a melody is known as a raga which usually has 5 to 7 notes, and can have as many as 9 or even 12. The music is improvised by the performer within certain governing rules and theoretically thousands of ragas are possible though only about a hundred are performed. Ragas have become associated with particular moods and specific times of the day.

Veena

Carnatic (Karnatak) music Contemporary South Indian music is traced back to Tyagaraja, Svami Shastri and Dikshitar, three musicians who lived and worked in the 18-19th centuries. They placed more emphasis on extended compositions than Hindustani music. Perhaps the best known South Indian instrument is the stringed *veena*, the flute being commonly used for accompaniment along with the violin (played rather differently to the European original), an oboe-like instrument called the *nagasvaram* and the drums, *tavil*.

Dance

India is rich with folk dance traditions. The rules for classical dance were laid down in the Natya shastra in the 2nd century BC. It is still one of the bases for modern dance forms, although there are many regional variations. The most common sources for Indian dance are the epics, but there are three essential aspects of the dance itself, Nritta (pure dance), Nrittya (emotional expression) and Natya (drama). Like the music with which it is so closely intertwined, dance has expressed religious belief and deep emotion. Goa has its own folk dance traditions.

The religious influence in dance was exemplified by the tradition of temple dancers, *devadasis*, girls and women who were dedicated to the deity in major temples to perform before them. In South and East India there were thousands of *devadasis* associated with temple worship, though the practice fell into widespread disrepute, being associated with prostitution, and was banned in independent India. In Goa, in addition to girls and women who became *devadasis*, widows who escaped *sati* often sought refuge in temples and joined that group and subsequently became temple prostitutes. The practice of singing and dancing in the temples was expected in conjunction with serving influential and high caste members of the Hindu community sometimes as mistresses. The Portuguese codified the laws and customs relating to *devadasis* (both male and female) in the early 19th century.

SPORTS

Cricket and Soccer are very popular in Goa. Soccer is played from professional level to kickabout in any open space. Professional matches are played in Panaji and Margao in large stadia attracting vast crowds; the latter holds 40,000 spectators. The season is from October to March and details of matches are published in the local papers. The top class game tickets are Rs 25, but they are sold for much more on the black market. The crowds generate tremendous fervour for the big matches, and standards are improving. African players are now featuring more frequently with Indian teams and monthly salaries have risen to over Rs 40,000 per month, a very good wage by Indian standards.

Religion

THE VISITOR'S first impression of the religion of Goa's peoples is likely to be highly misleading. Most books about Goa give prominence to the Portuguese Christian legacy. To all appearances the drive from the airport to Panaji or south to any of the coastal resorts might appear to confirm that the state is predominantly Christian. Stunningly bright white painted churches dominate the centre of nearly every village, most with the heritage of the Portuguese influence stamped on every feature. Some however are modern, suggesting the continuing life of the overwhelmingly Roman Catholic Christian community.

Yet while in the area of the Old Conquests, including Bardez in the north, Mormugao and Tiswadi, and southwards into Salcete, tens of thousands of people were indeed converted to Christianity, the Zuari River represents a great divide between Christian and predominantly Hindu Goa. Today about 70% of the state's population is Hindu, and there is also a small but significant Muslim minority. Other minority groups are also found, notably Sikhs and Jains, though in far smaller numbers than elsewhere in India.

The misleading first impressions are easily reinforced by the lack of obviously recognizable Hindu buildings on the main tourist routes. Only when you get to Ponda or into the rural areas of the interior do you find significant Hindu temples, and these are mainly the product of the 18th and 19th centuries. Indeed, their curious blend of Muslim, Christian and Hindu features testifies to the distinctive influences on Hinduism in Goa over the last four centuries. For while nowhere in India is it possible to define a 'pure' Hinduism, either in terms of belief or practice, in Goa the interaction between the communities has blended features of each of the major religions. Thus it is no accident that the only Hindu temple with a design rooted in the traditions of the Peninsula is that of Tambdi Surla, deep in the forest and close to the border of Karnataka, and almost as far as it is possible to be from the Christianising influences of the West or the Muslim routes into

Goa of military and political control. It survived as it were by default.

But if there is only limited structural evidence of Hinduism's influence, the daily life of many Goan communities reflects the strong mutual respect for each other's traditions which is common. Village festivals are often shared, deities or saints are venerated by both communities, and mutual respect for each other's religious beliefs is shown at all levels of Goan society. This is not to say that there are no tensions between the communities, but many Goans will say that these have been created artificially by outsiders.

Yet if the people of Goa show hybrid versions of each of the major religions, the roots of each are none the less clearly discernible, and it is necessary therefore to appreciate the fundamental characteristics of each in its Goan context.

Hinduism

While some aspects of modern Hinduism can be traced back more than 2,000 years before the birth of Christ, other features are recent. As early as the 6th century BC the Buddhists and Jains had tried to reform the religion of Vedism (or Brahmanism) which had been dominant in some parts of South Asia for 500 years. Great philosophers such as Sankaracharya (7th and early 8th centuries AD) and Ramanuja (12th century AD) transformed major aspects of previous Hindu thought.

Key Ideas

A number of ideas run like a thread through intellectual and popular Hinduism. One recurring theme is 'vision', 'sight' or 'view' – **darshan**, used to describe the sight of the deity that worshippers hope to gain when they visit a temple or shrine hoping for the sight of a 'guru' (teacher). Equally it may apply to the religious insight gained through meditation or prayer.

The four human goals

Many Hindus also accept that there are four major human goals; material prosperity (*artha*), the satisfaction of desires (*kama*), and performing the duties laid down according to your position in life (*dharma*). Beyond those is the goal of achieving liberation from the endless cycle of rebirths into which everyone is locked (*moksha*). It is to the search for liberation that the major schools of

Indian philosophy have devoted most attention. Together with dharma, it is basic to Hindu thought.

Dharma

Dharma, an essentially secular concept, represents the order inherent in human life. The Mahabharata lists 10 embodiments of dharma, including truth, self-control, endurance, and continence. These are inseparable from five patterns of behaviour: non-violence, an attitude of equality, peace and tranquillity, lack of aggression and cruelty, and absence of envy.

Karma

The idea of *karma* – 'the effect of former actions' – is central to achieving liberation. As C Rajagopalachari put it: "Every act has its appointed effect, whether the act be thought, word or deed. The cause holds the effect, so to say, in its womb. If we reflect deeply and objectively, the entire world will be found to obey unalterable laws. That is the doctrine of karma".

Rebirth

The belief in the transmigration of souls (*samsara*) in a never-ending cycle of rebirth has been Hinduism's most distinctive and important contribution to Indian culture. The earliest reference to the belief is found in one of the Upanishads, around the 7th century BC, at about the same time as the doctrine of karma made its first appearance.

Ahimsa

Belief in transmigration probably encouraged a further distinctive doctrine, that of non-violence or non-injury – *ahimsa*. The belief in rebirth meant that all living things and creatures of the spirit – people, devils, gods, animals, even worms – possessed the same essential soul.

WORSHIP

The abstractions of philosophy do not mean much for the millions of Hindus living across South Asia today, nor have they in the past. The Hindu gods include many whose origins were associated with the forces of nature, and Hindus have revered many natural objects. Mountain tops, trees, rocks and above all rivers, are regarded as sites of special religious significance.

In Goa veneration of the *tulsi* (basil) plant is illustrated by the profusion of *tulsi* enclosures in front of houses and in temples. Stutley and Stutley recount how in one myth, when Krishna was chasing a nymph she changed herself into a *tulsi* plant, perhaps contributing to the widely held belief in its wide-ranging powers. Its religious virtues are summed up in the expression: "In its roots are contained all places of pilgrimage; its centre contains all the deities, and its upper branches all the Vedas." In addition to warding off mosquitoes and being an air purifier the *tulsi* is effective in warding off death, even being an antidote to snake venom. With all these desirable attributes it is not surprising that the herb should play such an important role in Hindu rituals from birth to death.

Puja

For most Hindus today worship (often referred to as 'performing puja') is an integral part of their faith. The great majority of Hindu homes will have a shrine to one of the deities. Individuals and families will often visit shrines or temples, and on special occasions will travel long distances to particularly holy places such as Varanasi. Goa's temples similarly are centres of periodic pilgrimage and of special festivals.

The popular devotion of simple pilgrims of all faiths in South Asia is remarkably similar when they visit shrines, whether Hindu, Buddhist or Jain temples, the tombs of Muslim saints or even churches such as Bom Jesus in Old Goa, where St Francis Xavier lies entombed. Perhaps Goa's most famous shrine at which both Christians and Hindus worship is the Church of St Jerome in Mapusa, better known as the Milagres Church, Our Lady of Miracles.

THE HINDU TRINITY

Brahma

Popularly Brahma is interpreted as the creator in a trinity alongside Vishnu as preserver and Siva as destroyer.

In the literal sense the name Brahma is the masculine and personalized form of the neuter word Brahman. In the early Vedas *Brahman* represented the universal and impersonal principle which governed the Universe. Gradually as Vedic philosophy moved towards a monotheistic interpretation of the universe and its origins this impersonal power was increasingly personalized. In the Upanishads Brahman was seen as a universal and elemental creative spirit. Brahma, described in early myths as having been born from a golden egg and then to have created the Earth, assumed the identity of the earlier Vedic deity Prajapati and became identified as the creator.

It is from Brahma that Hindu cosmology takes its structure. The basic cycle through which the whole cosmos passes is described as one day in the life of Brahma – the *kalpa*. It equals 4,320 million years, with an equally long night. One year of Brahma's life – a cosmic year – lasts 360 days and nights. The universe is expected to last for 100 years of Brahma's life, who is currently believed to be 51 years old.

By the 6th century AD Brahma worship had effectively ceased – before the great period of temple building, which accounts for the fact that there are remarkably few temples dedicated to Brahma, the most famous one being at Pushkar in Rajasthan. Goa is thus highly unusual in also having a Brahma temple at Carambolim. Nonetheless images of Brahma are found in most temples. Characteristically he is shown with four faces (each facing a cardinal direction).

Brahma's consort: Sarasvati

Sarasvati has survived into the modern Hindu world as a far more important figure than Brahma himself. In popular worship Sarasvati represents the goddess of education and learning, worshipped in schools and colleges with gifts of fruit, flowers and incense. She represents 'the word' itself, which began to be deified as part of the process of the writing of the Vedas, which ascribed magical power to words.

Normally white coloured, riding on a swan and carrying a book, Sarasvati is often shown playing a vina. She may have many arms and heads, representing her role as patron of all the sciences and arts.

Vishnu and his avatars

Vishnu is seen as the God with the human face, sometimes presented as the god of creation or preservation. From the 2nd century a new and passionate devotional worship of Vishnu's incarnation as Krishna developed in South India. By 1,000 AD Vaishnavism became closely associated with the devotional form of Hinduism preached by **Ramanuja**, whose followers spread the worship of Vishnu and his 10 successive incarnations ('avatars') in animal and human form. For Vaishnavites, God took these different forms in order to save the world from impending disaster.

Vishnu's ten incarnations		
Name	**Form**	**Story**
1. *Matsya*	Fish	Vishnu took the form of a fish to rescue Manu (the first man), his family and the Vedas from a flood.
2. *Kurma*	Tortoise	Vishnu became a tortoise to rescue all the treasures lost in the flood, including the divine nectar (Amrita) with which the gods preserved their youth. The gods put *Mount Kailasa* on the tortoise's back, and when he reached the bottom of the ocean they twisted the divine snake round the mountain. They then churned the ocean with the mountain by pulling the snake, raising the nectar, the other treasures, and the Goddess *Lakshmi*, Vishnu's consort.
3. *Varaha*	Boar	Vishnu appeared again to raise the earth from the ocean's floor where it had been thrown by a demon, Hiranyaksa. The story probably developed from a non-Aryan cult of a sacred pig.
4. *Narasimha*	Half-man, half lion	Having persuaded Brahma to promise that he could not be killed either by day or night, by god, man or beast, the demon Hiranyakasipu then terrorized everybody. When the gods pleaded for help, Vishnu burst out from a pillar in the demon's palace at sunset, when it was neither day nor night, in the form of a half man and half lion and killed Hiranyakasipu.
5. *Vamana*	A dwarf	Bali, a demon, achieved supernatural power by asceticism. To protect the world Vishnu appeared before him in the form of a dwarf and asked him a favour. Bali granted Vishnu as much land as he could cover in three strides. Vishnu then became a giant, covering the earth in three strides. He left only hell to the demon.
6. *Parasurama*	Rama with the axe	Vishnu (Parasurama) was incarnated as the son of a Brahmin, Jamadagni. Parasurama killed the wicked king for robbing his father. The king's sons then killed Jamadagni, and in revenge Parasurama destroyed all male kshatriyas, twenty one times in succession.
7. *Rama*	The Prince of Ayodhya	As told in the *Ramayana*, Vishnu came in the form of Rama to rescue the world from the dark demon, *Ravana*. His faithful wife Sita is the model of patient faithfulness while Hanuman, is the monkey-faced god and Rama's helper.
8. *Krishna*	Charioteer for Arjuna. Many forms	Krishna meets almost every human need.
9. *The Buddha*		Probably incorporated into the Hindu pantheon in order to discredit the Buddhists, dominant in some parts of India until the 6th century AD. An early Hindu interpretation suggests that Vishnu took incarnation as Buddha to show compassion for animals and to end sacrifice.
10. *Kalki*	Riding on a horse	Vishnu's arrival will accompany the final destruction of this present world, judging the wicked and rewarding the good.

AL Basham has summarized the 10 incarnations (see table).

Rama and Krishna By far the most influential incarnations of Vishnu are those in which he was believed to take human form, especially as Rama (twice) and Krishna.

In the earliest stories about Rama he was not regarded as divine. Although he is now seen as an earlier incarnation of Vishnu than Krishna, he was added to the pantheon very late, probably after the Muslim invasions of the 12th century AD.

Rama (or Ram – rhyme with *calm*) is a powerful figure in contemporary India, and for Goans Parasurama, Vishnu's sixth incarnation, is responsible for the creation of Goa itself. He had come to free the world by fighting the all-powerful king of the Kshatriyas. After his triumph he flung his axe from the top of the Sahyadri Range far out to sea and then commanded the sea to withdraw so that he could perform the most powerful of sacrifices, the Yajna. Thus Goa was created, pure, virgin land.

Vishnu's consort: Lakshmi Commonly represented as Vishnu's wife, Lakshmi is widely worshipped as the goddess of wealth. Earlier representations of Vishnu's consorts portrayed her as **Sridevi**, often shown in statues on Vishnu's right, while **Bhudevi**, also known as Prithvi, who represented the earth, was on his left. Lakshmi is popularly shown in her own right as standing on a lotus flower, although eight forms of Lakshmi are recognized.

Siva

Siva is interpreted as both creator and destroyer, the power through whom the universe evolves. He lives on Mount Kailasa with his wife **Parvati** and two sons, the elephant-headed **Ganesh** and the 6-headed **Karttikeya**.

Siva is also represented in Shaivite temples throughout India by the linga, literally meaning 'sign' or 'mark', but referring in this context to the phallus. The linga has become the most important symbol of the cult of Siva.

Siva's alternative names

Although Siva is not seen as having a series of rebirths, like Vishnu, he none the less appears in very many forms representing different aspects of his varied powers. In Goa his most common names are Nagesh, Mangesh or Saptakoteshwara. As Betall, who is shown naked with human skulls round his neck and covered in serpents, he is widely feared in Goan villages as having power over evil spirits. Other common names for Siva include: **Chandrasekhara**, **Mahadeva** and **Nataraja**, the Lord of the Cosmic Dance.

Siva is normally accompanied by his 'vehicle', the bull (*nandi* or *nandin*). Nandi is one of the most widespread of sacred symbols of the ancient world and may represent a link with **Rudra**, who was sometimes represented as a bull in pre-Hindu India. Strength and virility are key attributes, and pilgrims to Siva temples will often touch the Nandi's testicles on their way into the shrine.

OTHER HINDU DEITIES

Ganesh

Of thousands of Hindu deities, Ganesh is one of Hinduism's most popular gods. He is seen as the great clearer of obstacles. Shown at gateways and on door lintels with his elephant head and pot belly, his image is revered across India. Meetings, functions and special family gatherings will often start with prayers to Ganesh, and any new venture, from

Vishnu, preserver of the Universe

Siva as Nataraj, Lord of the Dance

Parvati, daughter of Parvata and wife of Siva

Ganesh, bringer of prosperity

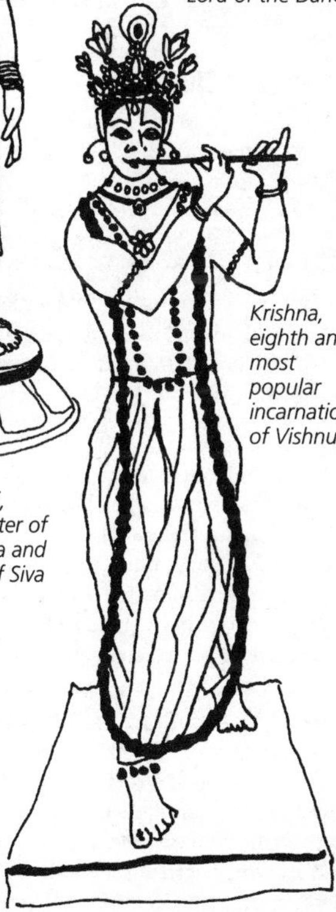

Krishna, eighth and most popular incarnation of Vishnu

the opening of a building to inaugurating a company will not be deemed complete without a Ganesh puja.

The Nagas and Naginis

The multiple hooded cobra head often seen in sculptures represents the fabulous snake gods, the Nagas, though they may often be shown in other forms, even human. Statues of divine Nagas are usually placed on uncultivated ground under trees in the hope and belief, as Masson-Oursel puts it, that "if the snakes have their own domain left to them they are more likely to spare human beings". The Nagas and their wives, the Naginis, are often the agents of death in mythical stories.

HINDU SOCIETY

Dharma is seen as the most important of the objectives of individual and social life. But what were the obligations imposed by Dharma? Hindu law givers, such as those who compiled the code of Manu (AD 100-300), laid down rules of family conduct and social obligations related to the institutions of caste and jati which were beginning to take shape at the same time.

Caste

Although the word caste was given by the Portuguese at the end of the 15th century AD, the main feature of the system emerged at the end of the Vedic period. Two terms – varna and jati – are used in India itself, and have come to be used interchangeably and confusingly with the word caste.

Varna, which literally means colour, had a fourfold division. By 600 BC this had become a standard means of classifying the population. The fair-skinned Aryans distinguished themselves from the darker skinned earlier inhabitants. The priestly varna, the Brahmins, were seen as coming from the mouth of Brahma; the Kshatriyas (or Rajputs as they are commonly called in NW India) were warriors, coming from Brahma's arms; the Vaishyas, a trading community, came from Brahma's thighs, and the Sudras, classified as agriculturalists, from his feet. Relegated beyond the pale of civilized Hindu society were the untouchables or outcastes, who were left with the jobs which were regarded as impure, usually associated with dealing with the dead (human or animal) or with excrement.

Jati The great majority of Indians do not put themselves into one of the four varna categories, but into a jati group. There are thousands of different jatis across the country. Many used to be identified with particular activities, and occupations used to be hereditary. Caste membership is decided simply by birth. Although you can be evicted from your caste by your fellow members, usually for disobedience to caste rules such as marriage, you cannot join another caste, and technically you become an outcaste.

The Dalits Gandhi spearheaded his campaign for independence from British colonial rule with a powerful campaign to abolish the disabilities imposed by the caste system. Coining the term *harijan* (meaning 'person of God'), which he gave to all former outcastes, Gandhi demanded that discrimination on the grounds of caste be outlawed. Lists – or 'schedules' – of backward castes were drawn up during the early part of this century in order to provide positive help to such groups. The term itself has now been widely rejected by many former outcastes as paternalistic and as implying an adherence to Hindu beliefs which some explicitly reject, and today many argue passionately for the use of the secular term 'dalits' – the 'oppressed'.

Affirmative action Since 1947 the Indian government has extended its positive discrimination (a form of affirmative action) to scheduled castes and scheduled tribes, particularly through reserving up to 50% of jobs in government-run institutions and in further education leading to professional qualifications for these groups, and members of the scheduled castes are now found in important positions throughout the economy.

The Hindu Calendar

While for its secular life Goa, in common with the rest of India, follows the Gregorian calendar, much of its Hindu and personal life follows the Hindu calendar. This is based on the lunar cycle of 29½ days, but the clever bit comes in the way it is synchronized with the solar calendar, by the addition of an extra month, known as the *adhik (extra) maas*, every 2 to 3 years.

Hindus follow two distinct eras. The *Vikrama Samvat* begins in 57 BC while the *Shalivahan Saka* dates from 78AD. Goa, in common with the rest of West India, follows the *Vikrama Samvat* whose New Year begins in the lunar month of *Kartik*, the seventh month of the lunar year. In most of South India except Tamil Nadu the New Year is celebrated in the first month, *Chaitra*, while in North India (and Tamil Nadu) it is celebrated in the second month of *Vaisakh*. Chaitra itself corresponds to the Gregorian month of March-April.

The year itself is divided into two, the first six solar months being when the sun 'moves' north, known in India as the *Makar Sankranti* and the second when it moves south, the *Karka Sankranti*. The first begins in January and the second in June, and Makar Sankranti in particular is celebrated by festivals in many parts of India.

Christianity

Although the Portuguese brought Roman Catholicism to Goa in the 16th Century, Christians probably arrived in India during the 1st century after the birth of Christ. There is evidence that one of Christ's Apostles, **Thomas**, reached Kerala on the west coast of India in 52 AD, only 20 years after Christ was crucified. He settled in Malabar and then expanded his missionary work to China. It is widely believed that he was martyred in Tamil Nadu on his return to India in 72 AD, and is buried in Mylapore, in the suburbs of modern Madras.

Roman Catholicism

Until the arrival of the Portuguese most Goans were either Hindu or Muslim. However, within 50 years of the Portuguese arrival Christian influence became a force to be reckoned with. The Jesuit, St Francis Xavier, landed in Goa in 1542, and in 1557 Goa was made an Archbishopric. Despite his brief stay, he left an indelible imprint on Goa's religious life.

The Jesuits set up the first printing press in India in 1566 and began to print books in Tamil and other Dravidian languages by the end of the 16th century. The Reformation which took place in Europe from the 16th century onwards resulted in the creation of the Protestant churches, which reasserted the authority of the Bible over that of the church. By virtue of the

Portuguese Catholic control Goa remained isolated from the developments through which Protestant missions subsequently worked extensively in other parts of India.

Although Goa remained almost entirely within the Catholic realm the influence of Catholicism varied sharply through time and in different parts of the Portuguese ruled territory. And, as Norma Alvares has written, "initially, despite their Christian skins, the Catholics remained furtive Hindus". The Inquisition was directed against this "unholy tendency" of these early converts to retain clandestinely their links with the Hindu faith. Certain phenomena, like caste, the Inquisition was unable to change. The Goan church eventually came to crystallize that institution in the form of the "*confrarias*".

The **Inquisition**, which lasted from 1560 to 1774, represented the most intensive, long term attempt to impose Catholic orthodoxy on the large non-Christian population. Because of the enormous lengths to which the courts of the Inquisition went to establish any opposition to Catholic belief its effective writ was geographically restricted to the area of closest Portuguese control – the Old Conquests – 'Ilhas' (comprising Tiswadi), Bardez and Salcete (including present day Mormugao). Every 2 or 3 years the Inquisition held great public trials with executions of the proven infidels. Here, not surprisingly, large scale conversions took place, and this area today retains by far the largest proportion of the Christian population.

CHRISTIAN BELIEFS

Christian theology had its roots in Judaism, with its belief in one God, the eternal Creator of the universe. Judaism saw the Jewish people as the vehicle for God's salvation, the 'chosen people of God', and pointed to a time when God would send his Saviour, or Messiah. Jesus, whom Christians believe was 'the Christ' or Messiah, was born in the village of Bethlehem, some 20 km south of Jerusalem. Very little is known of his early life except that he was brought up in a devout Jewish family. At the age of 29 or 30 he gathered a small group of followers and began to preach in the region between the Dead Sea and the Sea of Galilee. 2 years later he was crucified in Jerusalem by the authorities on the charge of blasphemy – that he claimed to be the son of God.

Christians believe that all people live in a state of sin, in the sense that they are separated from God and fail to do his will. They believe that God is personal, 'like a father'. As God's son, Jesus accepted the cost of that separation and sinfulness himself through his death on the cross. Christians believe that Jesus was raised from the dead on the third day after he was crucified, and that he appeared to his closest followers. They believe that his spirit continues to live today, and that he makes it possible for people to come back to God.

The New Testament of the Bible, which, alongside the Old Testament, is the text to which Christians refer as the ultimate scriptural authority, consists of four 'Gospels' (meaning 'good news'), and a series of letters by several early Christians referring to the nature of the Christian life. Roman Catholics also believe in the divine authority of the Pope as supreme head of the church and of the bishops and priests.

CHRISTIAN WORSHIP

Most forms of Christian worship centre on the gathering of the church congregation for praise, prayer and the preaching of God's word, which usually takes verses from the Bible as its starting point. Different denominations place varying emphases on the main elements of worship, but in most church services today the congregation will take part in singing hymns (songs of praise), prayers will be led by the priest or minister of the congregation, readings from the Bible will be given and a sermon preached. For many Christians the most important service is Mass (Catholic) or the act of Holy Communion (Protestant) which celebrates the death and resurrection of Jesus in sharing bread and wine, which are held to represent Christ's body and blood given to save people from their sin. Although Christian services may be held daily in some churches most Christian congregations in India meet for worship on Sunday, and services are held in Konkani and in English. They are open to all.

Islam

Islam reached Goa both by land and sea. Since before the birth of Christ. Goa, along with other ports along the west coast of India from Surat in the north to Cochin in the south, was on the Arab sea trading route to South East Asia and China. When the Arab world converted to Islam in the 7th century AD many of the traders based in these Indian settlements followed suit. However, Goa was never more than a relatively minor port on this route and the size of the Muslim community was much smaller than in Kerala to the south. Relations with neighbouring Hindus were generally good, Hindu rulers often giving grants of land to Muslim traders or help in building mosques. Indeed, Hutt records that when Goa was captured by the Muslim ruler of Honavar to the south the 10,000 Hindu inhabitants were moved out of the town centre but were allowed to remain in the suburbs.

Subsequently Islam has played a very different part in Goa's history. From the 13th century Turkish power brought Islam to India from the Northwest. Mahmud of Ghazni stormed into Punjab, defeating the Rajput rulers in 1192. Within the next 30 years Turkish Muslim power stretched from Bengal in the east to Madurai, in modern Tamil Nadu, in the south. On their way south the Muslims followed the path taken by generations of their predecessors who had migrated into the

The five pillars of Islam

In addition to the belief that there is one God and that Mohammed is his prophet, there are four further obligatory requirements imposed on Muslims. Daily prayers are prescribed at daybreak, noon, afternoon, sunset and nightfall. Muslims must give alms to the poor. They must observe a strict fast during the month of **Ramadan**. They must not eat or drink between sunrise and sunset. Lastly, they should attempt the pilgrimage to the Ka'aba in Mecca, known as the Hajj. Those who have done so are entitled to the prefix Hajji before their name.

Islamic rules differ from Hindu practice in several other aspects of daily life. Muslims are strictly forbidden to drink alcohol (though some suggest that this prohibition is restricted to the use of fermented grape juice, that is wine, it is commonly accepted to apply to all alcohol). Eating pork, or any meat from an animal not killed by draining its blood while alive, is also prohibited. Meat prepared in the appropriate way is called Halal. Finally, usury (charging interest on loans) and games of chance are forbidden.

'Deccan' (meaning simply "south"). A chain of Muslim kingdoms was established on the landward side of the Ghats who contested for power with each other and with the Hindu state of Vijayanagar. Some of the Muslim kingdoms retained important links with Persia and with the Arab world, and sea ports on the west coast became an important avenue for military supplies, especially horses, both for the Hindu Vijayanagar empire and the Muslim courts. Even in the 15th and 16th centuries business was business.

The early Muslim rulers looked to the Turkish ruling class and to the Arab caliphs for their legitimacy, and to the Turkish elite for their cultural authority. From the middle of the 13th century, when the Mongols crushed the Arab caliphate, the Delhi sultans were left on their own to exercise Islamic authority in India, a role which was taken over from the 16th to the 18th centuries by the Mughals who shaped the greatest of the Muslim led empires.

Muslim beliefs

The beliefs of Islam (which means 'submission to God') could apparently scarcely be more different from those of Hinduism. Islam, often described as having "five pillars" of faith (see box), has a fundamental creed; 'There is no God but God; and Mohammad is the Prophet of God' (*La Illaha illa 'llah Mohammad Rasulu 'llah*). One book, the Qur'an, is the supreme authority on Islamic teaching and faith. Islam preaches the belief in bodily resurrection after death, and in the reality of heaven and hell.

The idea of heaven as paradise is pre-Islamic. Alexander the Great is believed to have brought the word into Greek from Persia, where he used it to describe the walled Persian gardens that were found even three centuries before the birth of Christ. For Muslims, Paradise is believed to be filled with sensuous delights and pleasures, while hell is a place of eternal terror and torture, which is the certain fate of all who deny the unity of God.

Islam has no priesthood. The authority of Imams derives from social custom, and from their authority to interpret the scriptures, rather than from a defined status within the Islamic community. Islam also prohibits any distinction on the basis of race or colour, and there is a strong antipathy to the representation of the human figure. It is often thought, inaccurately, that this ban stems from the Qur'an itself. In fact it probably has its origins in the belief of Mohammad that images were likely to be turned into idols.

MUSLIM SECTS

During the first century of its existence Islam split in two sects which were divided on political and religious grounds, the Shi'is and Sunni's. Both sects venerate the Qur'an but have different traditional sayings of Mohammad *Hadis*. They also have different views as to Mohammad's successor.

The **Sunnis** – always the majority in South Asia – believe that Mohammad did not appoint a successor, and that Abu Bak'r, Omar and Othman were the first three caliphs (or vice-regents) after Mohammad's death. Ali, whom the Sunni's count as the fourth caliph, is regarded as the first legitimate caliph by the Shi'is, who consider Abu Bak'r and Omar to be usurpers. While the Sunni's believe in the principle of election of caliphs, Shi'is believe that although Mohammad is the last prophet there is a continuing need for intermediaries between God and man. Such intermediaries are termed Imams, and they base both their law and religious practice on the teaching of the Imams.

THE MUSLIM YEAR

The first day of the **Muslim calendar** is 16 July 622 AD. This was the date of the Prophet's migration from Mecca to Medina, the Hijra, from which the date's name is taken (AH = Anno Hijrae).

The Muslim year is divided into 12 lunar months, alternating between 29 and 30 days. The first month of the year is *Moharram*, followed by *Safar, Rabi-ul-Awwal, Rabi-ul-Sani, Jumada-ul-Awwal, Jumada-ul-Sani, Rajab, Shaban, Ramadan, Shawwal, Ziquad* and *Zilhaj*.

Significant dates

1st day of *Moharram* – New Year's Day; 9th and 10th of *Moharram* – Anniversary of the killing of the Prophet's grandson Hussain, commemorated by Shi'a Muslims; 12th of *Rabi-ul-Awwal* – Birthday of the Prophet (Milad-ul-Nabi); 1st of *Ramadan* – Start of the fasting month (around 2 January 1998); 21st of *Ramadan* – Night of prayer (Shab-e-Qadr); 1st of *Shawwal: Eid-ul-Fitr* – 3-day festival to mark the end of Ramadan (around 30 January 1998); 10th of *Zilhaj: Eid-ul-Ajha* – 2-day festival commemorating the sacrifice of Ismail; the main time of pilgrimage to Mecca (the Haj).

Buddhism

Despite its inaccessible location, for a time at least after 250 BC Goa was home to Buddhist communities in the foothills of the Western Ghats. Emperor Asoka is believed to have sent a missionary monk Dharmarak to the area and another monk Punna is thought to have preached Buddhism in Zambaulim in Sanguem. Today Buddhism is practised mainly on the margins of the sub-continent, from Ladakh, Nepal and Bhutan in the north to Sri Lanka in the south. Although there are approximately 5 million Buddhists in Maharashtra, most are very recent outcaste Hindu converts, the last adherents of the early schools of Buddhism having been killed or converted by the Muslim invaders of the 13th century.

Buddhists developed cave sites as monasteries or temples such as at Arvalem in Bicholim, Khandepar in Ponda and Rivona in Sanguem. However, they have none of the exceptional murals and rock carvings found at Ajanta and Ellora in Maharashtra, north of Goa, or in Sigirya in Sri Lanka, and are comparatively small and insignificant. The presence of Buddhist monks in the 11th century at the court of Jayakeshi I of the Kadamba Dynasty is recorded in Sanskrit texts a century later. However, the stronger influences of Shaivism and Vaishnavism during Kadamba rule in Goa virtually eradicated Buddhism (and Jainism) from the area. Today there are fewer than 400 Buddhists in the whole of Goa.

THE BUDDHA'S LIFE

Siddharta Gautama, who came to be given the title of the Buddha – the Enlightened One – was born a prince into the warrior caste in about 563 BC. He was married at the age of 16 and his wife had a son. When he reached the age of 29 he left home and wandered as a beggar and ascetic. After about 6 years he spent some time in Bodh Gaya. Sitting under the Bo tree, meditating, he was tempted by the demon Mara with all the desires of the world. Resisting these temptations he received enlightenment. These scenes are common motifs of Buddhist art.

The next landmark was the preaching of his first sermon on 'The Foundation of Righteousness' in the deer park near Varanasi. By the time he died the Buddha had established a small band of monks and nuns known as the *Sangha*, and had followers across North India. His body was cremated, and the ashes, regarded as precious relics, were divided up among the peoples to whom he had preached.

After the Buddha's death

From the Buddha's death – or parinirvana – to the destruction of Nalanda (the last Buddhist stronghold in India) in 1197 AD, Buddhism in India went through three phases. Not mutually exclusive, they were followed simultaneously in different regions.

Hinayana

'The Little Way' insists on a monastic way of life as the only path to achieving *nirvana*.

Mahayana

'The Great Way' believed in the possibility of salvation for all, practising a far more devotional form of meditation. The Bodhisattvas, saints who were predestined to reach the state of enlightenment through thousands of rebirths, gained prominence. The Buddha is believed to have passed through numerous existences in preparation for his final mission.

Vajrayana

'The Diamond Way' resembles magic and yoga in some of its beliefs. The ideal is to be 'so fully in harmony with the cosmos as to be able to manipulate the cosmic forces within and outside himself'. It had developed in the North of India by the 7th century AD, matching the parallel growth of Hindu Tantrism.

Buddhist beliefs

Buddhism is based on the Buddha's own preaching. He developed his beliefs in reaction to the Brahmanism of his time, rejecting several of the doctrines of Vedic religion: the Vedic gods, scriptures and priesthood, and all social distinctions based on caste. However, he did accept the belief in the cyclical nature of life, and that the nature of an individual's existence is determined by a natural process of reward and punishment for deeds in previous lives – the Hindu doctrine of karma (see page 41). In the Buddha's view, though, there is no eternal soul.

BUDDHISM'S DECLINE

The decline of Buddhism in India probably stemmed as much from the growing similarity in the practice of Hinduism and Buddhism as from direct attacks. However, the Muslim conquest dealt the final death blow, being accompanied by the large scale slaughter of monks and the destruction of monasteries. Without their institutional support Buddhism faded away.

Jainism

Like Buddhism, Jainism started as a reform movement of the Brahmanic religious beliefs of the 6th century BC. Its founder was a widely revered saint and ascetic, Vardhamma, who became known as Mahavir – 'great hero'. Mahavir was born in the same border region of India and Nepal as the Buddha, just 50 km to the N of modern Patna, probably in 599 BC. His family, also royal, were followers of an ascetic saint, Parsvanatha, who according to Jain tradition had lived 200 years previously.

Unlike Buddhism, Jainism never spread beyond India, but it has survived continuously into modern India, claiming 4 million adherents, though there are fewer than 500 in Goa itself.

JAIN BELIEFS

Jains (*Jina*, literally meaning 'descendants of conquerors') believe that there are two fundamental principles, the living (*jiva*) and the non-living (*ajiva*). The essence of Jain belief is that all life is sacred, and that every living entity, even the smallest insect, has within it an indestructible and immortal soul. Jains developed the view of ahimsa – often translated as 'non-violence', but better perhaps as 'non-harming'.

Unlike Buddhists, Jains accept the idea of God, but not as a creator of the universe. They see him in the lives of the 24 Tirthankaras (prophets, or literally 'makers of fords' – across the spiritual journey over the river of life), or leaders of Jainism, whose lives are recounted in the Kalpsutra – the 3rd century BC book of ritual. **Mahavir** is regarded as the last of these great spiritual leaders. Much Jain art details stories from these accounts, and the Tirthankaras play a similar role for Jains as the Bodhisattvas do for Mahayana Buddhists.

The five vows may be taken both by monks and by lay people: Not to harm any living beings (Jains must practise strict vegetarianism – and even some vegetables, such as potatoes and onions, are believed to have microscopic souls); To speak the truth; Not to steal; To give up sexual relations and practice complete chastity; To give up all possessions – for the *Digambara* sect that includes clothes.

JAIN SECTS

Jains have two main sects, whose origins can be traced back to the 4th century BC. The more numerous **Svetambaras** – the 'white clad' – concentrated more in eastern and western India, separated from the **Digambaras** – or 'sky-clad'– who often go naked and are now concentrated in South India.

Architecture

All Goan architecture is in some sense atypical. Domestic architecture in the Portuguese dominated areas reflects Portuguese influences, but is clearly adapted to local environmental conditions. Even church architecture is not a simple transplant from Europe, though the influence of the Baroque on many of Goa's most famous churches is obvious. In their turn, Hindu and Muslim architecture in Goa are strongly influenced by the mixture of cultural traditions from which they grew. Yet the distinctiveness of both Christian and Hindu traditions remains clear, and the fundamental features of their design can be traced back to their wholly different roots.

GOAN CHRISTIAN ARCHITECTURE

Almost nothing remains of the first great development of Portuguese church building during the reign of the Portuguese King Manuel I (r1495-1521). The doorway to the church of St Francis of Assisi in Old Goa, and the Church of Our Lady of the Rosary, the oldest church standing in Goa (1543) illustrate the incorporation of Indian features in its predominantly European model.

The dominant influence on Goan Christian architecture was that of the Italian late Renaissance and early Baroque, imported by the Jesuits. The Church of Il Gesu in Rome (completed in 1584, and where an arm of St Francis Xavier is still preserved and venerated) was a particularly important model. As Anthony Hutt points out it was designed by Vignola, the author of *The Five Orders of Architecture*, a work which has a profound influence on subsequent church building. Scrolls were used to link the high nave with the lower side aisles, as on a huge scale in the Se Cathedral. Towers flanking the west entrance were retained in Goan architecture, as in Portugal, long after they had been abandoned elsewhere.

Margao

Interestingly, the destruction of the northern tower of the Se Cathedral by lightning returned the cathedral closer to what may have been its original Islamic model from the Iberian peninsula, the tower being modelled on the Islamic minaret.

The most striking features of the religious building of the Baroque are in the decorated interiors, typifying the use of gilded wood to cover the whole of the reredos behind the altar. Such decoration, though usually on a much reduced scale, is typical of many of the Goan churches. Roman influence is clearly visible in one of the other great churches of Old Goa, the 17th century Convent Church of St Cajetan taking St Peter's Rome as its model. Despite the reduced scale recent restoration has highlighted the intrinsic quality of the building. Both its Michaelangelo-inspired façade and its interior, based on the form of a Greek cross with a central cupola, are strikingly effective. The evident importance of barrel vaulting, itself a reflection of the Roman arch dating back to the period of the Roman Empire, gives St Cajetan's a unique feel.

Many examples of Indian Baroque can be found outside Old Goa. Margao's Church of the Holy Spirit, the monasteries at Pilar or Rachol, or perhaps most spectacularly the Church of Santana (Saint Anna) at Talaulim are particularly good examples. In the second half of the 18th century Rococo features began to be expressed in a new bout of church building. Indian architects played a significant part in decoration, especially of the reredos and the pulpit. In *Golden Goa*, Dr José Periera lists 5 Goan churches as masterpieces of the Indian Baroque – the *Holy Spirit* (Old Goa) being the most sublime; *Holy Spirit* (Margao) the most magestic; the

Wayside cross

Santana (Talaulim) the most perfect; *St Stephens* (Santo Estevao, Jua Island) the most ornate, and the *Piedade* (Divar) as the most luminous.

DOMESTIC ARCHITECTURE

In the early 18th century Goa benefited directly from the huge wealth Portugal gained from Brazil, and while the court prospered as a result so individual noble families became wealthy through trading links with other Portuguese possessions in Africa and in Macau. Landed Goan families began to build houses to express their status and wealth, enough of which remain to give an insight into both the architecture and the life style of the time.

They borrowed some of the fundamental features from the coastal architecture of the Konkan, well adapted to the monsoon climate's demands for protection from torrential rainfall and powerful sun. The sloping roofs of red Mangalore tiles (augmented at times with disastrous aesthetic effects by modern corrugated iron) kept off the rain. Large reception rooms offered space and air for receiving guests, and the biggest houses had private chapels. Curved windows, sometimes filled not with glass but with translucent oyster shell (*nacre*) gave a "warm, filtered light" while also securing privacy. Central courtyards, another feature of Indian domestic architectural design, also gave families private space, although some of the new grand houses also had outward looking windows, in sharp contrast to the entirely inward looking courtyard houses of traditional Goan society. Verandas and balconies allowed families to enjoy cool shaded space. In many houses the entertaining rooms were all on the first floor, allowing any breezes to bring some freshness.

Unlike the great proliferation of highly ornate church building which in Portugal was funded largely by a flow of wealth from Brazil, Goa's élite (which was almost entirely Indian rather than Portuguese) prospered on locally created wealth, and built their new houses to reflect that increasing prosperity. They also took advantage of Portuguese trade with the east to provide Chinese ceramics for domestic use and eastern designs for wooden furniture, much of which was ultimately made in Goa by Indian craftsmen. Yet despite all the innovations Goan domestic architecture, even on the grandest scale, never entirely severed its links with earlier Hindu forms. One example was the universal practice of building private chapels, which as Hall points out can be seen as an extension of the Hindu tradition of every house having a shrine dedicated to the domestic deity. Village bungalows with distinctive porch roofs and *balcaos* often show columns borrowed from Hindu temple architecture. Outside the Old Conquests, domestic architecture retained even stronger links with Hindu traditional architecture of the coastal region and both to the north and south of Goa the housing in the border regions is almost indistinguishable from that of the neighbouring states of Maharashtra and Karnataka respectively.

HINDU TEMPLE BUILDING

The principles of religious building were laid down in the *Sastras*, sets of rules compiled by priests. Every aspect of Hindu, Jain and Buddhist religious building is identified with conceptions of the structure of the universe. This applies as much to the process of building – the timing of which must be undertaken at astrologically propitious times – as to the formal layout of the buildings. The cardinal directions of north, south, east and west are the basic fix on which buildings are planned. The east-west axis is nearly always a fundamental building axis. George Michell suggests that in addition to the cardinal directions, number is also critical to the design of the religious building. The key to the ultimate scale of the building is derived from the measurements of the sanctuary at its heart.

Indian temples were nearly always

Mandala

built to a clear and universal design, which had built into it philosophical understandings of the universe. This cosmology, of an infinite number of universes, isolated from each other in space, proceeds by imagining various possibilities as to its nature. Its centre is seen as dominated by **Mt Meru** which keeps earth and heaven apart. The concept of *separation* is crucial to Hindu thought and social practice. Continents, rivers and oceans occupy concentric rings around the mountain, while the stars encircle the mountain in another plane. Humans live on the continent of **Jambudvipa**, characterized by the rose apple tree (*jambu*).

Mandalas The Shastras show plans of this continent, organized in concentric rings and entered at the cardinal points. This type of diagram was known as a mandala.

Such a geometric scheme could be subdivided into almost limitless small compartments, each of which could be designated as having special properties or be devoted to a particular deity. The centre of the mandala would be the seat of the major god. Mandalas provided the ground rules for the building of stupas and temples across India, and gave the key to the symbolic meaning attached to every aspect of religious buildings.

Temple design

Hindu temples developed characteristic plans and elevations. The focal point of the temple lay in its sanctuary, the home of the presiding deity, known as the womb-chamber (*garbhagriha*). A series of doorways, in large temples leading through a succession of buildings, allowed the worshipper to move towards the final encounter with the deity himself and to obtain *darshan* – a sight of the god. Both Buddhist and Hindu worship encourage the worshipper to walk clockwise around the shrine, performing *pradakshina*. In contrast to the extraordinary profusion of colour and life on the outside, in most Hindu temples the interior is dark and cramped but here it is believed, lies the true centre of divine power.

Temple development in Goa

While some of the key principles underlying Hindu temple architecture remain the same in Goan temples the differences are striking, and the outward forms are wholly distinctive and unique. Both in design and in decoration many Goan temples, most of which are 18th century or later, have borrowed liberally from both Muslim and Christian architecture. The transformation was initiated by the Maratha leader Sivaji, who rebelled against the Muslim political dominance of Maharashtra and encouraged the development of a new temple style. The changes he introduced were subsequently developed into the Goan style. It took advantage of some features of Muslim architecture with which Sivaji was familiar in towns like Bijapur, including minarets, cusped arches and domes, or the beautifully curved *bangla* roofs loved by the Mughals. The Marathas also introduced long open pavilions in front of the temple, supported by columns, and what has become one of Goan temples' most distinctive features, the tall and often octagonal lamp towers or *deepmal* or *deepstambha*. Hutt writes that the "concept of the pillar with lamps on it as an offering to the deity is one of extreme antiquity, but seems to have been particularly developed at this period by the Marathas."

These large pagoda-like structures are peculiar to Goa and some suggest the influence of Western church ideas

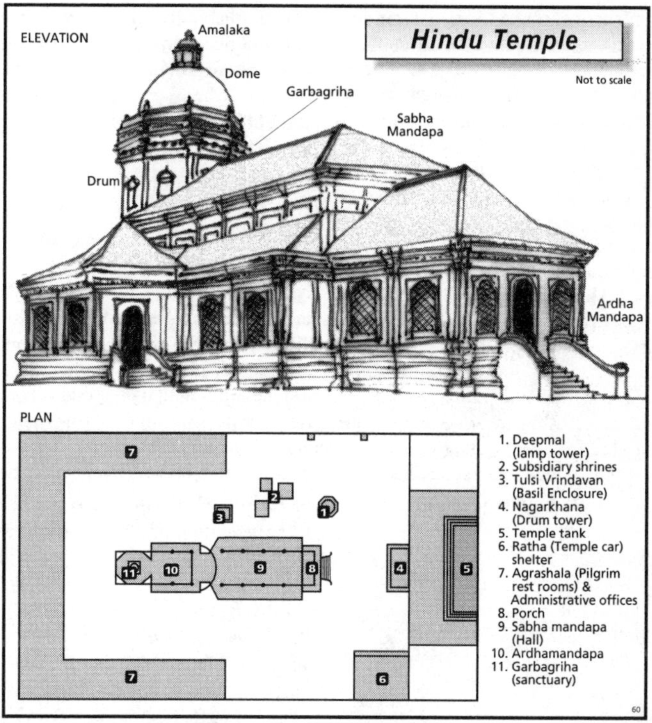

concerning the place of worship.

Goan architects also added a drum tower, a 'room' with a pyramidal tiled roof *nagarkhana* (or *naubatkhana*) where temple musicians would sit above the entrance gateway. Another distinctive feature was the prominent *tulsi vrindavana*(basil enclosure), which was similar in principle to the humbler container which is an integral part of Goan Hindu domestic architecture. The *tulsi*, which is believed to have many mystical properties, is widely associated with Krishna and Lakshmi. The 'enclosure' next to a temple would sometimes assume monumental proportions, and adopt features imitating the more commonly seen piazza crosses in front of churches.

In place of the pyramidal or curving towers that signal the *garbagriha* (main shrine) in most Hindu temples, Goan temples are uniquely surmounted by the kind of dome unknown in the pre-Muslim period. However, Gomes Pereira suggests that Goan architects went still further by introducing fundamentally European concepts into their temples. Classical styles, taking as their models churches in Old Goa like the Se Cathedral and Our Lady of Divine Providence gave both classical scales and the specific feature of the dome. The typical Goan temple comprised a regular series of features. The entrance porch would have an arch, sometimes surmounted by a dome. Inside, the pillared hall (*mandapa*), which could be regarded as similar to the nave of a church, was topped by a steep-pitched tiled roof, while the sanctuary itself was crowned by a dome which would sometimes sit over a European drum and be topped by a lantern.

Goan temples have other features that distinguished them from conventional Hindu temples. The interior is usually relatively open and light, even airy, in contrast to the dark stillness which pervades the sanctum of most temples in the rest of India. Decoration and embellishments in some of the temples are also of alien origin, imported glass chandeliers and tiles being particularly favoured.

The full distinctiveness of Goa's Hindu temples can only be appreciated in their context. Often set in the heart of lush valleys surround by dense greenery, instead of proclaiming themselves like the great hill top temples of peninsular India, Goa's temples are often completely hidden from view until the last moment. The temple tank provides not only the means of ritual cleansing but a beautifully cooling stretch of fresh water, usually close to the temple entrance. The pilgrim or worshipper is thus presented with an element of surprise up to the moment of entry, where at festivals the welcoming lamps flicker in the lamp tower and across the compound.

MUSLIM RELIGIOUS ARCHITECTURE

Although the Muslims adapted many Hindu features, they also brought totally new forms. Their most outstanding contribution, dominating the architecture of many north Indian cities, are the mosques and tomb complexes (*dargah*). The use of brickwork was widespread, and they brought with them from Persia the principle of constructing the true arch. Muslim architects succeeded in producing a variety of domed structures, often incorporating distinctively Hindu features such as the surmounting finial. By the end of the great period of Muslim building in North India in 1707, the Muslims had added magnificent forts and palaces to their religious structures. Both were testaments to imperial splendour, a statement of power as well as of aesthetic taste. Although Goa's Hindu temples reflected Muslim influence, true Islamic building can only be seen by travelling over the Ghats into Karnataka. Belgaum's fort and mosques are the nearest examples of the true Muslim peninsular styles.

History

EARLY GOA

Some identify Goa in the *Mahabharata* as Gomant, where Vishnu, reincarnated as **Parasurama**, shot an arrow from the Western Ghats into the Arabian Sea and with the help of the god of the sea reclaimed the beautiful land of Gomant. **Siva** is also supposed to have stayed in Goa on a visit to bless seven great sages who had performed penance for 7 million years. In the *Puranas* the small enclave of low-lying land enclosed by the Ghats is referred to as **Govapuri, Gove** and **Gomant**. The ancient Hindu city of Goa was built at the southernmost point of the island. The jungle has taken over and virtually nothing survives.

Myth and legend gradually intertwine with evidence as to the origins of settlement of the Konkan coast. On the interior plateaus just over the Ghats, India saw some of its earliest settlements, stone age cultures stretching back over 100,000 years being established on the upper reaches of great rivers like the Krishna and Tungabhadra, which rise just inland of Goa. It may be that some of the forest tribes are related to the aboriginal settlers who came in the first wave of *homo sapiens* settlement from Africa around 100,000 years ago. The modern population however is almost entirely descended from the **Indo-Aryans** who entered from the north west after 1500 BC. Between 1300 and 1000 BC the heartland of this new culture developed in the plains of North India, gradually stretching its influence southwards.

The great events of Indian history at this stage were taking place across the northern plains. Goa often found itself on the borders of developments taking place in both north and south. When Asoka (272 BC) extended his administration across the Deccan, the area of modern Goa was incorporated into the great **Maurya** empire of the 3rd to 2nd centuries BC, centred on Pataliputra (Patna in modern Bihar), while to the south the Cholas, Keralaputras and Pandiyas contested for power in the southern Peninsula.

The **Bhojas** followed the Mauryas and based their kingdom in **Chandrapur** (modern Chandor). From the 3rd to the 8th centuries AD the **Kadamba** dynasty established itself on the western borderlands, though it was normally seeking alliances with powers such as the Guptas or the later Rashtrakutas to the north or the Chalukyas to the south. Indeed some Goans actually claim the **Rashtrakutas** as their own dynasty. Some of the Rashtrakuta kings are revered for their patronage of the arts, Krishna I (r756-773), for example, commissioning the great Kailasanath temple at Ellora. From the 8th century AD until the arrival of the Muslims from the north in 1312 AD the Kadambas' power was reduced to a narrow coastal and hill belt, and they were almost entirely subservient to the dominant **Chalukyas** who controlled most of central peninsular India. One of the most remarkable of the Chalukyan kings, Someshvara III (r1126-1138) was passionately devoted to the arts and made an outstanding collection of folksongs, including Konkani songs.

In 1052, the Kadambas established their capital in the port town on the north bank of the Zuari (near Goa Velha) which had been developed by the Chalukyas as the flourishing port of **Gopakapattana** or **Govapuri** (Gove as it came to be known by traders).

Contact with the Muslim world

Since before the birth of Christ, the Arabs traded along the west coast of India and Arab geographers knew Goa as Sindabur. As the Arab world converted to Islam, the traders spread their new religion and many settled in Goa. However, while the Muslim-based coastal trade was largely peaceful, the penetration of Islam into the Deccan was anything but. In 1312, Muslim invaders from the Delhi Sultanate took power, destroying much of Govapuri and forcing the Kadambas to return to **Chandrapur**. In 1327 the Muslims under Mohammad Tughluq carried out further incursions into the interior going as far as Chandrapur. However, their power was challenged 20 years later by the Bahmanis.

In 1347 Muslims in the Deccan peninsula broke away from the Delhi Sultanate to the north and established the **Bahmani** dynasty (1347-1527). While the Bahmanis were in control of Goa from approximately 1348-1369 (and again for 26 years from 1470) they entered a renewed period of temple destruction and terrorising the Hindu population. From then until well after the arrival of the Portuguese, Goa's territory was the subject of repeated contests between the Hindu and Muslim powers of the interior and the maritime Portuguese.

The Bahmanis were, however, defeated by the Hindu **Vijayanagars** in 1378 and there followed nearly a hundred years of relative peace and prosperity. Goa had already become an important centre for the inward trade in Arab horses with the Vijayanagar Empire, who began to export the much prized spices and cotton cloth. The port of Govapuri had been silting up and power and attention was shifted to Ela on the south bank of the Mandovi which began to flourish and function as an alternative port.

It was control of maritime trade that attracted the peninsular powers into repeated conflict rather than ideological or religious competition. However, brutal attacks on the Muslim population of Bhatkal to the south of Goa by the Vijayanagar king encouraged the Bahmanis to return with renewed force in 1470. They destroyed what was left of the old capital Govapuri (which became known as Goa Velha) and moved the administration to the port of Ela on the Mandovi, taking the name 'Govapuri' (later Velha Goa). The Bahmanis themselves split into five different states, the largest of which, the **Adil Shahis of Bijapur** (1490-1686) played a key role in Goa's political fortunes. They took control from 1498-1510. When the Portuguese arrived, **Yusuf Adil Shah**, the Muslim Sultan of Bijapur, was the ruler. At this time Goa was an important starting point for Mecca bound pilgrims, as well as continuing to import Arab horses and, after

Cochin (Kochi), it was the major market on the west coast of India.

Under the Muslim Bahmanis, the new Govapuri (which was Ela and subsequently Velha Goa) developed into a significant town, prosperous as a result of the trade in horses and spices and of great geopolitical significance. Adil Shah, the Bijapuri Sultan himself had come from Iran, and links with the Middle East remained economically and politically important to the Deccan Sultanates. Ships from many lands laden with precious merchandise arrived in Velha Goa and traders came from Persia, Arabia, East Africa, Central Asia, Bengal, Deccan, the Malabar and China. The wide streets of the city were lined with shops and the Adil Shahs built mosques, mansions with gardens and an impressive palace facing the river.

THE PORTUGUESE

For the first Portuguese their encounter with Islam on the coast of India was simply an extension of the contest for power between Catholicism and Islam in the Iberian Peninsula. The Portuguese were intent on setting up a string of coastal stations to the Far East in order to control the lucrative spice trade.

Although Vasco da Gama landed in India in 1498, Goa was the first Portuguese possession in Asia and was only taken by **Afonso de Albuquerque** in 1510. For the intervening 12 years the Portuguese set up 'factories' along the Malabar coast (modern Kerala) and a fort in Cochin (Kochi). Originally intending to take his fleet up from Karwar, just south of Goa, to Egypt, to complete the previous year's destruction of the Egyptian fleet, Albuquerque changed his plans when he obtained vital information about Goa from his ally Timoja, an officer and spy of the Vijayanagar Empire. He discovered that the Muslims were building their ships in Goa, that the administration was fairly weak and that Bijapuri taxes were becoming increasingly unpopular among the local subjects.

Afonso de Albuquerque grasped the advantages of this island site, an excellent natural harbour, large enough to give a secure food-producing base but with a defensible moat, at the same time well placed with respect to the important northwest sector of the Arabian Sea. He found out details of the capital's defences and mounted an attack, successfully taking it on 1 March 1510. Yusuf Adil Shah died almost immediately after the defeat, but 2 months later his 13-year-old son and successor, **Ismail Adil Khan** (known to the Portuguese as the **'Idalcan'**), blockaded Goa with 60,000 men and recaptured

Afonso de Albuquerque

Historical table		
DATES	**EVENTS IN GOA**	**EVENTS IN INDIA AND THE WORLD**
Before 2000 BC	Earliest agriculture reaches the coast from the Peninsula	Indus Valley Civilization in North India
1200 BC		Earliest Vedas composed
600-500 BC		The Buddha born; Upanishads completed
250 BC	Mauryan Empire reaches Goa under Ashoka	
1st-3rd C AD	Trade with Arabia and Gulf begins	Discovery of monsoon winds
300-500		Gupta Empire in North India: the 'classical' period
6th-8th C	The Chalukyan kings dominate central peninsula and Goan coast	629 Death of Mohammad; 750 Rajputs become powerful in Northwest India
8th-11th C	Rashtrakutas dominate peninsula, followed by Kadamba control of Goan coast, Cholas control South India	
1050	Kadamban kings trade with Zanzibar and with Sri Lanka. Build Gopakapattana as capital.	
1192		Muslims defeat Rajputs nr Delhi. Angkor Wat built in Cambodia
14th C		Muslim Delhi Sultanate carries Islam south, 1290 Marco Polo reaches China
1351-88	Bahmani dynasty established, captures Goa	Incas centralise power in Peru
1367	Bahmanis defeated by Vijayanagar Empire	
1469	Bahmani Muhammad Shah II captures Goa	
1489	Yusuf Adil Shah establishes Bijapur Sultanate	
1498		Vasco da Gama lands in Calicut
1510	Afonso de Albuquerque captures Old Goa, looses it, recaptures it	Vijayanagar Empire contest with sultanates for control of peninsula.
1542	St Francis Xavier reaches Goa	Mughal Emperor Humayun re-conquers Delhi
1556		Akbar becomes Mughal Emperor
1560	The Inquisition starts	

Historical table		
DATES	**EVENTS IN GOA**	**EVENTS IN INDIA AND THE WORLD**
1565		Vijayanagar Empire defeated
1571	Portuguese granted rights over 'Old Conquests' by Bahmanis	
1603	Dutch blockade Goa	
1605		East India Company base at Surat
1667-83	Marathas extend control over Peninsula; attack Goa	
1690		Calcutta founded
1695	Viceroy moves residence out of Old Goa	
1737-39	Maratha wars, Portuguese victorious	Mughal Empire in decline
1774	Edict banning the Inquisition	1757 Clive wins battle of Plassey
1782-1791	'New Conquests' incorporated into Goa	
1787	The Pinto Revolt in Candolim	
1797-1813	British occupy Goa during Napoleonic wars in Europe	
1812	Inquisition finally ended	
1821	Goa representatives in Lisbon Parliament	
1843	Panaji declared capital	
1851		First railway in India – Bombay
1857		Indian Mutiny in North India
1881	First railway links Mormugao with peninsula	
1905	First iron ore and manganese mines	
1928	Founding of Goa Congress Party	
1947		Indian Independence
1946-58	Independence demands, leaders deported to Portugal	
19 Dec 1961	Indian Army enters Goa	
30 May 1987	Goa becomes full state of the Indian Union	

Vasco ship

it. Albuquerque and his men had to retreat to ships at sea. However, Adil Khan's victory was short-lived. Ismail found himself no match to defend the city against Albuquerque when he returned after the monsoon with reinforcements and recaptured the city on the 25 November (St Catherine's Day) in 1510, after a bloody struggle. He massacred all the Muslims and appointed a Hindu as Governor, thereby establishing his alliance with the Vijayanagar Empire which was more than happy to see the maritime power of its Muslim rivals curtailed.

The territory over which Albuquerque gained control was the roughly triangular shaped island with a rocky headland and two harbours which was given the name **Ilhas** ('island' in Portuguese), together with the islands of **Chudamani** (Chorao), **Dipavati** (Divar), **Vamsim** (the tiny island between the two) and **Jua**. In 1534 the adjoining lands of Bardez and Salcete which were dependencies of Govapuri came under Portuguese control. Although skirmishes continued with the Bijapuri Adil Shahs, the two territories were annexed by the Portuguese around 1543 to make up the territory known as **'The Old Conquests'**.

Once Albuquerque established his own control, the Portuguese started replacing the main Muslim buildings in Velha Goa with their own, took over the trading interests which had sustained the town, and started to develop it as a major Christian centre. To avoid conflict between missionaries in the Old Conquest territories, Bardez was offered to the Fransiscans (Grey Friars because of the colour of their habit), while Salcete was under the Jesuits and Ilhas was principally allotted to the Augustinians and Dominicans.

From 1510, until the establishment of British rule over the rest of India, the fortunes of Goa depended on quickly changing patterns of alliances and on the fortunes of the principal parties which were often determined by events outside Goa itself. For the first century of their occupation of the Old Conquests the Portuguese took advantage

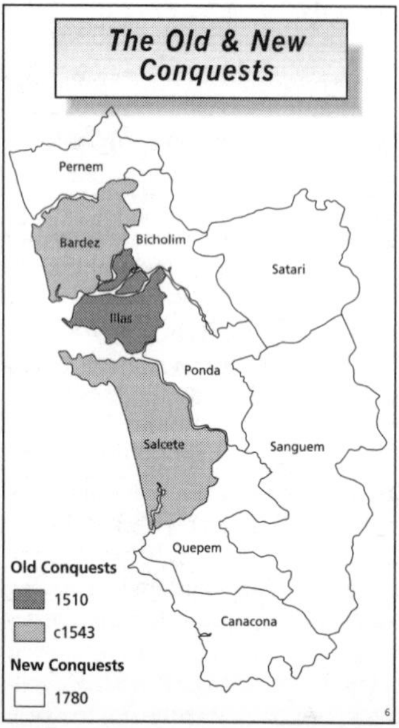

of the animosity between the powers on the Peninsula inland. Although some Hindu practices like *sati* (the burning of widows on the funeral pyre of their husbands), were stamped out by Albuquerque, in other respects he did little to interfere with local custom. By 1570 the colony had become so wealthy that it had acquired the sobriquet "Golden Goa". Goa became the capital of the Portuguese Empire in the East and was granted the same civic privileges as Lisbon.

During the 16th century, the Portuguese established themselves as a superior maritime power along the western peninsular coast, building forts in small enclaves (eg Daman, Diu) and close to Bombay (eg Bassein) and further south, along the coast of Goa. They terrorised Indian ships and those of the other colonizing countries to protect their monopoly in spices and the trade of cotton goods from the subcontinent to Southeast Asia.

Goa's reputation as a centre of culture and learning was enhanced by its association with **St Francis Xavier**, who visited Goa for the first time in 1542. His first mission was directed at ending the degeneracy of the *fidalgos* ('gentlemen'). He also contributed to the establishment of Goa's reputation as a centre of learning, setting up its first printing press. In the Ilhas and Salcete the Jesuits became dominant, while Franciscans worked throughout Bardez.

Throughout the 100 years after their arrival the Portuguese were intent on trying to build an empire in Asia. In that effort Goa played a pivotal role, acting as both a military and trading staging post between Portugal and its territories to the East. It was their misfortune that in 1565 the Vijayanagar Empire was suddenly – and unexpectedly – routed. Five years earlier the Portuguese had embarked on the Inquisition, attacking Hindus and Muslims alike within the Old Territories. In 1570 Muslim rulers from Bijapur to Sumatra attempted a concerted attack on Portuguese interests, and Goa was subjected to a 10 month siege. The harassment from the Bijapur Sultanate was only finally ended by the overpowering dominance of the much greater Muslim power of the Mughals.

When the Dutch began to control trade in the Indian Ocean Portuguese dominance of the sea declined. The fall of the Vijayanagar Empire in 1565 caused the lucrative trade between Goa and the Hindu state to dry up. None the less, by 1600 the population of the city may have been as much as 225,000, equal to London or Antwerp, then the largest cities in Europe. However, according to Della Valle who visited Goa in 1623 most of the population comprised slaves. Though this might have been an exaggeration, the Portuguese certainly had no objections to mixed marriages or inter-racial liaisons, so there was a large population of *mestizos*.

The Dutch blockaded Goa in 1603 and 1639. They weakened but did not succeed in taking it, but it was ravaged by an epidemic in 1635, and manpower was so severely depleted that the Portuguese brought criminals from Lisbon's prisons to maintain their numbers.

By the early part of the 18th century Portuguese fortunes had already experienced wide fluctuations and the territorial base was still restricted to the Ilhas, Salcete in the south and Bardez in the north. The greatest threat to security had come through the latter part of the 17th century from Sivaji (1627-80) and his Maratha confederacy (1674-1818). Sivaji and his son took the whole of the northern territories, only to be forced to withdraw in 1683 by the threat they faced from the Mughals on their own northern flank. Goa remained safe in its isolation, though it was threatened again briefly in 1739.

The risk of attack from both land and sea encouraged the Portuguese to establish a series of forts on the coast and inland. The forts are small compared with even the modest Indian forts, due to the small number of expatriate Portuguese who manned them. Even at the height of Portuguese domination Richards suggests that there were no more than 1000 Portuguese based in Goa, and over 700 of these were members of the religious orders. Through the 19th century the Portuguese developed Panaji as their capital, and it became a centre of education and civil administration.

Despite extraordinary cultural achievements, notably in the church building of Old Goa itself, Portugal's political base in Goa remained weak. In the mid-18th century a series of reforms were introduced under pressure from the Portuguese Government in Lisbon. These included the ending of the Inquisition and the confiscation of Jesuit property. These moves were matched by a determination to abolish racial discrimination, especially in the church.

In 1741 King Joao V of Portugal (r1706-50) had decided to extend Portuguese control to the provinces which were to become '**The New Conquests**'. The implementation of this plan had to wait four decades, when a succession of military victories led to the integration of the New Conquests into Portuguese territory. **Bicholim** and **Satari** were conquered in 1781 and 1782, victories which were celebrated by the first public display of the body of St Francis Xavier in 1782. **Pernem** was ceded to Portugal in 1788, while **Ponda, Sanguem, Quepem** and **Canacona** followed 3 years later, along with official acceptance by the Raja of Sunda of the capture in 1763 of the headland of Cabo de Rama. Portugal's hold on its Goan territory was complete.

While Portuguese Goa grew, Portugal's other Asian interests shrank. Struggles in continental Europe, notably between Britain and Napoleonic France, had an impact on alliances in India, and Goa itself was occupied by the British between 1799 and 1813.

It was during this period that Goa experienced its most important revolt against the Portuguese. In 1787 a group of priests met in the house of the Pinto family in Candolim and formed a plot to overthrow the government, a plot which became known as the **Pinto Revolt**. 15 of the 47 conspirators who were arrested and tortured were subsequently executed in Panaji. It was an event which left a deep feeling of unease, but may have speeded the process of reform and in particular the determination to end the racist policies by which Indians had been excluded from positions of authority both in the church and the state.

INDEPENDENCE

By the end of WW2 when the rest of India was on the point of achieving Independence there were less than 30 Portuguese officials based in Goa. The Portuguese came under increasing pressure in 1948 and 1949 to cede Goa, Daman and Diu to India, and in response despatched over 4000 troops to hold on to the territory. In 1955 *satyagrahis* (non-violent demonstrators) attempted to enter Goa. They were deported but later when larger numbers tried, the Portuguese used force to repel them and some were killed. At a demonstration in Margao, Portuguese police fired on the unarmed mob, killing 32 and injuring 225. The problem festered until 19 December 1961 when the Indian Army, supported by a naval blockade, marched in and brought to an end 450 years of Portuguese rule. Originally Goa became a Union Territory together with the old Portuguese enclaves of Daman and Diu, but on 30 May 1987 it became a full state of the Indian Union.

RECENT POLITICAL HISTORY

The Goa Legislative Assembly has 40 elected members while the state elects three members to the Lok Sabha. Although the Congress has been the largest single party, political life is strongly influenced by the regional issue of the relationship with neighbouring Maharashtra, and the debate over the role of Marathi led to the creation of the Maharashtrawada Gomantak Party which was in power in the Union Territory of Goa from 1963 until 1979. Regional issues remain important, but there is now also a strong environmental lobby, in which the Catholic Church plays a prominent part. In the Lok Sabha elections of 1996 the Congress lost both its seats, one to the Third Front and one to an Independent, and Goan politics remains sharply distinct from its neighbours.

Festivals

A few National holidays count as full public holidays throughout India: **26 January**: *Republic Day*; **15 August**: *Independence Day*; **2 October**: *Mahatma Gandhi's Birthday*; **25 December**: *Christmas Day*.

In addition to the widespread celebration of Hindu festivals, with Goa's significant Christian population and the small minority of Muslims, the corresponding religious festivals are also widely observed (see also above under Islam – Significant dates). Hindu and Muslim festivals fall on different dates each year, depending on the lunar calendar so check dates with the Tourist Office.

January

Feast of the Three Kings (6 January), celebrated in Cansaulim (Cuelim), Chandor and Reis Magos where a big fair is also held. See page 183.

Makarashankranti (14 January 1998) when Hindus distribute sweets among friends and relatives.

February

Mahasivaratri (12 February 1998) or *Sivaratri* marks the night when Siva danced his celestial dance of destruction (*Tandava*) celebrated with feasting and fairs at Siva temples, but preceded by a night of devotional readings and hymn singing. Special ceremonies are held at some temples eg Mangesh, Nagesh, Quela, Shiroda.

February/March: *The Carnival* (22-24 February 1998) is a non-religious festival celebrated all over Goa. On the first day (*Fat Saturday*), 'King Momo' leads a colourful procession of floats with competing 'teams' dressed in flamboyant costumes, as they wind through the towns' main streets. In Panaji, the procession starts near the Secretariat after mid-day. Dances are held in clubs and hotels through the 4 days and traffic comes to a halt on some streets from time to time.

March

Shigmotsav (12 March 1998) is a Hindu spring festival (Holi) held at full moon in the month of *Phalgun* and celebrated all over Goa but particularly in Panaji, Mapusa, Vasco da Gama and Margao on successive days starting at around 1600. The festivities are accompanied by percussive music of drums and cymbals.

Procession of all Saints (30 March 1998) In Goa Velha, on the Monday of Holy Week. See page 92.

April

Ramnavami (5 April 1998) Birthday of Lord Rama (the 7th incarnation of Vishnu), hero of the epic *Ramayana* is celebrated by Hindus.

Feast of Our Lady of Miracles, on the nearest Sunday 16 days after Easter (27 April 1998). See page 151.

May

(3rd) 30th *Goa Statehood Day*, an official

holiday when all Government offices and many shops are closed.

June

Feast of St Anthony (13th), songs in honour of the saint requesting the gift of rain.

Feast of St John the Baptist (Sao Joao) (24th) A thanksgiving for the arrival of the monsoon. See page 168.

Festival of St Peter (29th), Fort Aguada. A floating stage is erected on fishing boats tied together and a pageant is held as they float downstream.

July

Nagpanchami (28 July 1998) The *Naga* (Cobra/snake) is worshipped in the form of the thousand headed *Shesha* and *Ananta* (on which Vishnu reclined).

August

Raksha Bandhan (literally 'protection bond') (7 August 1998) commemorates the wars between *Indra* (the King of the Heavens) and the demons when his wife tied a silk amulet around his wrist to protect him from harm. The festival symbolizes the bond between brother and sister, and is celebrated at full-moon. A sister says special prayers and ties a *rakhi* (coloured threads) around her brother's wrist to remind him of the special bond. He in turn gives a gift and promises to protect and care for her. Sometimes *rakhis* are exchanged as a mark of friendship.

Janmashtami (Birth of Lord *Krishna*) (14 August 1998) mass bathing in the Mandovi River off Divar Island. Hymns are sung and night-long prayers are held.

Harvest Festival of Novidade (21st and 24th). The first sheaves of rice are offered to the priests on the 21st and to the Governor and Archbishop and placed in the Cathedral on the 24th. The festival includes a re-enactment of one of the battles between Albuquerque and the Adil Shah on the lawns of the Lieutenant Governor's Palace.

Ganesh Chaturthi: (26-27 August 1998) The elephant headed deity, the God of good omen is shown special reverence. The 5-day festival follows after harvest. On the last day, clay images of Ganesh (Ganpati) are taken in procession with dancers and musicians playing drums and cymbals (not always very tunefully) and are immersed in the sea, river or pond. The skies light up with fireworks displays and the air turns smoky from firecrackers.

October

Dasara (Dussera) (1 October 1998) is celebrated in honour of minor deities. The celebrations continue for 9 nights (*Navaratri*) when various episodes of the Ramayana story are enacted and recited, with particular reference to the battle between the forces of good and evil.

Narkasur (18 October 1998) On the eve of Diwali, Goan Hindus remember the victory of Lord Krishna over the demon Narkasur. In Panaji there are processions and competitions.

Diwali (Deepavali) (19 October 1998) The festival of lights; lighting of earthen lamps, candles. Fireworks have become an integral part of the celebration which are often set off days before Diwali.

December

Liberation Day (17 December) commemorates the end of Portuguese colonial rule and is a public holiday marked by military parades.

Christmas (25 December) is observed with Midnight Mass in churches across the state and usual family get-togethers and involves every community. Special Goan sweets made with ground rice and sugar and fried in oil are prepared.

Economy

GOA is one of India's most prosperous states. Its economy has been boosted both by remittances from Goans working abroad and by the inflow of foreign exchange from tourism.

Goans have scattered around the world, but although there are important communities of Goans in Europe and the United States, they have also taken up work in the Middle East and the Gulf States. They continue to play a crucial role in the economic development of the state and have contributed to the sharp rise in land prices through their interest in hotel and other tourism related development.

Industry and exports Goa's manufacturers produce fertilizers, sugar, textiles, chemicals, iron pellets and pharmaceuticals. Rice is the staple product with fruit, salt, coconuts, pulses and betel (areca nut) also produced. The principal exports are coconuts, cashew, fruit, spices, manganese and iron ores, bauxite, fish and salt.

Fishing For villages the length of India's west coast fishing has provided the basic source of livelihood for generations. It remains important today, but changing technology has brought mixed blessings. The rapid increase in deep sea trawler fishing has brought competition for inshore fishermen which is arousing increasing hostility. Locally caught fish continue to be sold in the markets, but many Goan fishermen are increasingly fearful that they will be unable to continue to survive largely by fishing and along the coastal tourist belt, an increasing number are using their boats for tourism during the season.

Tourism Tourism plays an important role in the economy and is growing fast. From 200,000 visitors in 1975 the figure reached over 1.1 million in 1997, of which about 15% were foreigners. Direct charter flights from Europe have given a boost (17 flights a week in the autumn of 1997); the demand will be better satisfied when a new civilian airport is built.

The private sector provides the bulk of tourist facilities and services and is responsible for most of the accommodation with even modest householders benefiting by taking in paying guests. Although tourism brings money into the Goan economy, there is considerable opposition to the expansion of facilities for tourists. Some Goans criticize the Government's expansion plans as bringing little benefit to the local economy, while threatening to damage traditional social and cultural values. The spread of hippy colonies in the late 1960s and 1970s was deeply resented by some, and more recently the rapid development of power, including plans to generate nuclear power on the coast south of Panaji, have raised protests. Tourism has also fuelled heavy immigration from other states, mainly from the rural poor from Karnataka, pushy salesmen from Kashmir and hotel staff from elsewhere in India.

The State Government is keen to stress that tourism to Goa should remain within limits so that the environment and ecology are not sacrificed. It has concentrated on improving road networks, increasing water supply and waste disposal to tourist areas. The number of well maintained 'Sulabh' pay toilets in heavily used tourist spots is being increased.

The vast majority of foreign visitors (95%, as compared to 77% of domestic tourists) stay on the coastal belt, the wonderful beaches being what draws them to this part of India. The authorities are keen to see that the rest of the state which has different architectural, cultural and scenic attractions, opens up to tourists. It has already taken steps to improve facilities at Old Goa, one of the premier places to visit away from the coast. It hopes to encourage watersports and has also earmarked three old forts (the Aguada plateau, Reis Magos and Cabo de Rama) for restoration and development by providers of quality accommodation and sports facilities

Transport Air transport through direct charter flights from Europe to the naval airport at Dabolim has brought great benefits. The State Government is now keen to have a civilian airport to cope with the growing demands of international tourists and is awaiting clearance on a site in North Goa, at Mopa in Pernem.

While Goa has become far easier to reach from Europe, communications internally and with the rest of India are also improving rapidly. New State Highways are planned to connect Mormugao to Chorlem and Pernem to Polem, though these have been long promised and as yet very slow to be built. Many estuaries have now been bridged, transforming travel by road along the coast. The Zuari bridge at Cortalim has however had major problems (possibly affected by salinity) with the superstructure cracking. Light vehicles continue cross the bridge in 1997 but heavy vehicles face a lengthy diversion via Ponda. Improved ferry ramps and new ferries will be in place before repair work begins. Work on the bridge across the Chapora estuary (Siolim-Chopdem) has begun but completion seems a distant dream.

A comfortable and fast Norwegian a/c **catamaran** service now operates in season between Mumbai and Panaji, taking about 8 hrs.

The progress of the **Konkan Railway** has been watched with great interest – and often huge controversy over its possible environmental impact – during the past few years. The southern section from Mangalore to Margao opened in August 1997 in addition to the northern section from Mumbai to Sawantwadi which had opened earlier in the year, and the whole line from Mumbai to Mangalore is expected to be operating by the end of 1997. Train services on the South Central Railway between Mormugao and Londa in Karnataka had been heavily disrupted during gauge conversion in 1996. However, work was completed in May 1997 and passenger trains were running in the summer. Dudhsagar Falls on the Karnataka border, a major tourist attraction, will again be accessible by rail.

Section 3

Panaji and Central Goa

CENTRAL GOA is the state's cultural heartland. The talukas of Tiswadi, Mormugao and Ponda contain in their compact space, elements of all the features which have given Goa such a distinctive identity. It was here that the Portuguese impact was first and most profoundly felt, but Old Goa, deserted and empty today, retains the atmosphere of a powerful political and religious city. Yet immediately to the east, across the Cumbarjua Canal, a muddy crocodile infested creek, lies Hindu Ponda with a wealth of temples and Goa's only significant remaining mosque. Alongside the traces of colonial history, in Panaji Central Goa also has the state's largest modern town with a full range of services. Few visitors stay in Central Goa, for it has limited beaches and relatively little accommodation, but it is the axis of the state's communication and it contains much of interest to see.

TISWADI TALUKA

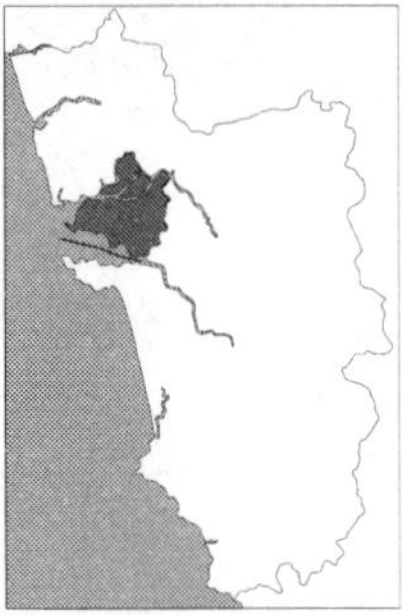

Stretching from the headland of Cabo de Raj Niwas in the southwest to the islands of Chorao and Divar in the Mandovi estuary to the north, Tiswadi is separated from what remained predominantly Hindu Ponda by the Cumbarjua Canal. The taluka is named after the 30 (*tis*) island areas (*wadi*, including 'Ilhas') that were brought under its administration.

At its centre is the thin-soiled laterite Teleigao plateau which reaches about 100m above sea level. Old Goa stands on the northern edge by the river while the modern University is on the southern edge of the plateau itself. In places the plateau drops steeply down to curving bays like Vanguinem or Bambolim, facing Mormugao across the Zuari estuary, while it juts out into the sea at its westernmost point of the Cape. The plateau also forms the high ground of the Altinho in Panaji.

Some of the great sights of Portuguese Goa are on this small territory. Old Goa, the Pilar Monastery and Santana Church, represent the central traditions of the Portuguese legacy, while the beaches and bays from Miramar to Bambolim give even the area closest to the capital access to fine sand and beautiful views. On the islands in the estuary, in contrast, are some of the remnants of the old estuarine marsh ecosystem.

Its central location means that all the important sites of Tiswadi can be seen relatively easily from either the northern or the southern beaches, as well as from Panaji itself. If the Zuari Bridge needs to be closed for repairs the capacity of the ferry may not meet the heavy demand and there could be very long delays. The alternative land route via Ponda is a long diversion but goes through a number of other places of interest in Ponda taluka.

Tiswadi (or the Ilhas) where Old Goa is situated, plus the neighbouring areas – Bardez (north of the Mandovi), Mormugao and Salcete – comprise the heart of the Portuguese territory and are known as the **Old Conquests**. They contain all the important Christian churches. In contrast the **New Conquests** came into Portuguese possession considerably later, either by conquest or by treaty.

The Mandovi-Zuari estuary The Mandovi and Zuari Rivers reach the sea after journeys of less than 70 km from their sources in the Western Ghats in a combined estuary which is one of the most important **mangrove** complexes in India, even though today mangroves cover less than 20 ha. Sea water penetrates a long way inland, especially in the dry season. However, there are approximately 20 species of mangroves, including some rare ones. The species *Kandelia candel* is still common despite being on the edge of extinction elsewhere. The estuary is a spawning ground for crustaceans and molluscs and many species of fish, and is host to huge numbers of migratory birds, especially ducks and shore birds. Jackals, water snakes, bats and marsh crocodiles are common.

Panaji (Panjim)

PANAJI has no great buildings or attractions which would make it a draw for a long stay, but it does retain enough character to make a pleasant visit. It is still the main point of arrival for people travelling by bus or catamaran from out of state, though as it is by-passed by the new Konkan Railway increasing numbers will use Margao and a visit to Panaji will become entirely optional. There are very pleasant walks over the Altinho and through the old district of Fontainhas.

Population 85,200; *STD Code* 0832

Panaji is the official spelling of the capital city replacing the older Portuguese spelling **Panjim** (see box). Occupying a narrow coastal plain between a low laterite hill – the 'Altinho' – and the mouth of the Mandovi, it still has the feel of quite a small town. It is laid out on a grid whose main roads run parallel with the sea front. It was its advantageous position guarding the estuary which first attracted the Muslim ruler **Yusuf Adil Shah** to build and then fortify a palace by the river in 1500, the Idalcao Palace, as the Portuguese called it. The palace remains today as the oldest and most impressive of the lower town's official buldings, but its service to the Sultan was very shortlived, for within 10 years **Albuquerque** had seized on the strategic value of Goa's *Ilhas* site. Although Albuquerque followed the Muslims' example and occupied the site of Old Goa as his main capital, he stationed a garrison at Panaji in 1510 and made it the customs clearing point for all traffic entering the Mandovi.

The town remained little more than a military outpost, and the first Portuguese buildings after the construction of a church on the site of the present Church of Our Lady of Immaculate Conception in 1541, were noblemen's houses built on the flat land bordering the sea. It remained no more than a staging post on the way to Old Goa, used by incoming and outgoing Viceroys, but with no real settlement, until the Portuguese Viceroy finally decided to move from Old Goa to Panaji in 1759. It was a further 84 years before it was officially declared the capital, by which time the population of Old Goa had followed the Viceroy to make it the largest town in the colony.

The *Altinho* (hill) to the south offered defensive advantages. Immediately above the Church of the

Travel tip

Motorcycle taxis with yellow mudguards are unique in Goa. A rider takes 1 passenger, often dangerously, down rough/muddy roads or narrow lanes and can be lethal (no helmets). **NB** Use (if you must) one with horizontal black/yellow pole fitted in front of rider. Min fare Rs 6, approx Rs 4/km thereafter, waiting charge Rs 6/hr. **Warning** Your insurance policy may not cover you if you are involved in an accident.

What's in a name?

The use of three languages in Goa is reflected in considerable confusion in naming of places and the spelling of many place names, with Portuguese, Marathi and Konkani variants all in use, making it very difficult to discover the original version of many names. Pronunciation adds to the confusion. The final "*im*" which appears in place names indicates a nasal ending, so that the "*m*" is never heard. *Betim*, *Siolim*, *Borlim*, *Cuncolim*, and formerly *Panjim* – Goa is full of place names ending in the nasalized but otherwise silent *m*.

So is it Pa-na-ji or Pan-jim? PP Shirodkar has reported that the first known reference to the site can be dated precisely to 7 February 1107, when it was named on a copper plate inscription as '*Pahajanikhali*', a name which refers to the starch used by fishermen to treat the threads of their fishing nets. Whatever its origins, the settlement has been known as Panjim for years, though another variant, Pangim, appears on old Portuguese maps. But in either spelling the final "*m*" was virtually silent, and not pronounced Pan-jim.

The modern official name, Panaji, recognised that. The central "*a*", appears as many Devanagari consonants have the sound "a" built into them. Thus in the Devanagari script "*n*" is normally pronounced "*na*", although the vowel sound is often so short as barely to be noticeable.

Either way you end up with a pronunciation that usually sounds to your authors' ears something like "Ponnjee" – with the "o" as in orange!

Immaculate Conception was Goa's first lighthouse, but most of the buildings on the Altinho today date from the 19th or 20th centuries. It is well worth walking up for the view over the estuary.

PLACES OF INTEREST

The riverside boulevard

The riverside boulevard (D Bandodkar Marg) runs from near the new Patto bridge, past the jetties, to the formerly open fields of the **Campal** to the southwest, offering picturesque views across the Mandovi towards the fort of Reis Magos. When Panaji depended on boats for communicating with the rest of Goa as well as with the world beyond, this road was the town's busiest highway. Along it are some of the town's main administrative buildings.

Idalcao Palace

Just behind the main Boat Terminal is the Idalcao Palace of the Adil Shahs, once their castle. The Portuguese expanded it after they captured it in 1510 and rebuilt it in 1615. Until 1759 it was the Viceregal Palace and then it became the Viceroy's official residence. In 1918 the Governor General (as the Viceroy had become) decided to move to the Cabo headland to the southwest, now Cabo Raj Niwas, and the old Palace was used for government offices. After Independence it became the Secretariat building for the Union Territory and it now houses the Passport Office.

The main entrance gate is a pilastered Romanesque arch in the south wall facing away from the river. The crest of the Viceroys which once adorned it has been replaced by the Ashokan 'Wheel of Law', the official symbol of India.

Next to it is an unusual and striking **statue of the Abbé Faria**, who became known in Paris as one of the discoverers of hypnotism. Abbé José Custodio de Faria was born on 30 May 1756 in Candolim, just inland of Calangute.

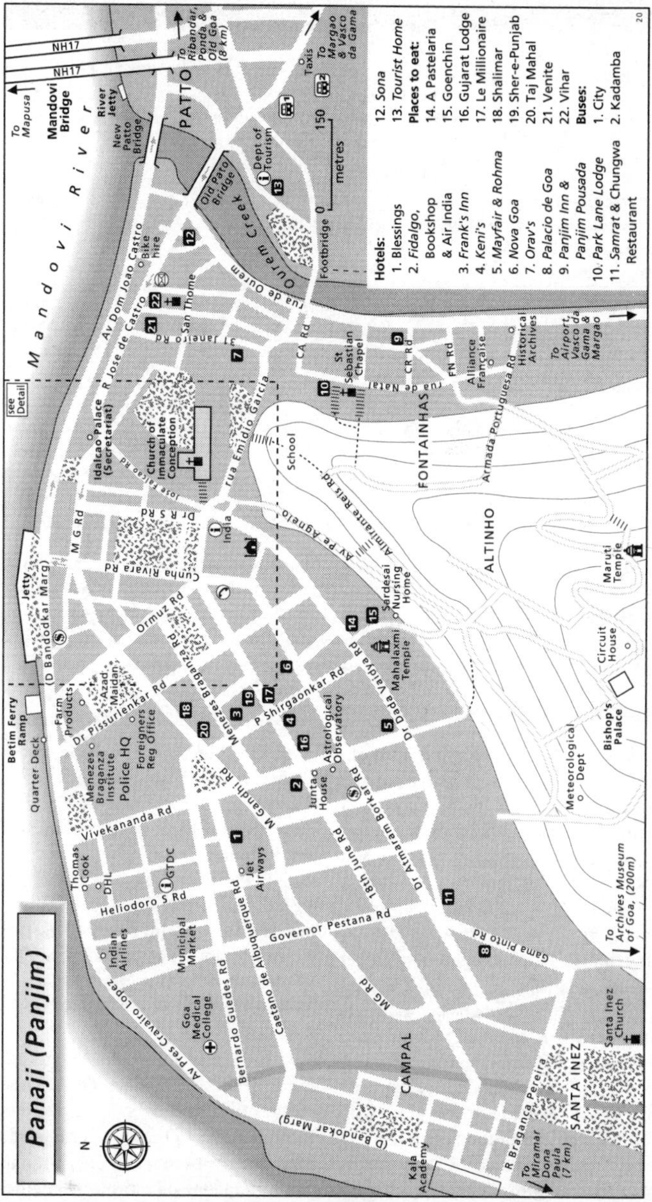
Panaji (Panjim)
N
Hotels:
1. Blessings
2. Fidalgo, Bookshop & Air India
3. Frank's Inn
4. Keni's
5. Mayfair & Rohma
6. Nova Goa
7. Orav's
8. Palacio de Goa
9. Panjim Inn & Panjim Pousada
10. Park Lane Lodge
11. Samrat & Chungwa Restaurant
12. Sona
13. Tourist Home
Places to eat:
14. A Pastelaria
15. Goenchin
16. Gujarat Lodge
17. Le Millionaire
18. Shalimar
19. Sher-e-Punjab
20. Taj Mahal
21. Venite
22. Vihar
Buses:
1. City
2. Kadamba
0
150
metres
Mandovi River
To Mapusa
Mandovi Bridge
NH17
NH17
River Jetty
New Patto Bridge
PATTO
To Ribandar, Ponda & Old Goa (8 km)
To Margao & Vasco da Gama
Taxis
Dept of Tourism
Old Pato Bridge
Ourem Creek
Footbridge
Rua de Ourem
Av Dom Joao Castro
Bike hire
R Jose de Castro
San Thome
31 Janeiro Rd
CA Rd
St Sebastian Chapel
CR Rd
FN Rd
Rua de Natal
Alliance Française
Historical Archives
To Airport, Vasco da Gama & Margao
see Detail
Idalcao Palace (Secretariat)
Church of Immaculate Conception
Jose Falcao Rd
rua Emidio Garcia
School
FONTAINHAS
Armada Portuguesa Rd
M G Rd
Dr R S Rd
India
Av Pe Agnelo
Almirante Reis Rd
ALTINHO
Maruti Temple
Jetty
(D Bandodkar Marg)
Cunha Rivara Rd
Ormuz Rd
Sardesai Nursing Home
Circuit House
Bishop's Palace
Betim Ferry Ramp
Quarter Deck
Farm Products
Azad Maidan
Dr Pissurlenkar Rd
Menezes Braganza Rd
P Shirgaonkar Rd
Mahalaxmi Temple
Dr Dada Vaidya Rd
Astrological Observatory
Menezes Braganza Institute
Police HQ
Foreigners Reg Office
Junta House
M Gandhi Rd
Meteorological Dept
Vivekananda Rd
Thomas Cook
DHL
GTDC
Jet Airways
Heliodoro S Rd
Bernardo Guedes Rd
Caetano de Albuquerque Rd
18th June Rd
Dr Atmaram Borkar Rd
Indian Airlines
Municipal Market
Governor Pestana Rd
Gama Pinto Rd
To Archives Museum of Goa, (200m)
Goa Medical College
Av Pres Cravairo Lopez
MG Rd
CAMPAL
Santa Inez Church
SANTA INEZ
R Bragança Pereira
(D Bandokar Marg)
Kala Academy
To Miramar Dona Paula (7 km)

Panaji and Goa tours

Goa Tourism tours can be booked at the Tourist Hotel, MG Rd, T 227103; GTDC, Trianora Apartments, Dr Alvares Costa Rd, T 226515; Directorate of Tourism, Tourist Home, Patto, T 225583; GTDC counters elsewhere including GTDC Tourist Hotels in other towns.

The tours which run regularly in season (1 October-16 June) leave from the Tourist Hotel, MG Rd, T 227103. Entrance fees are extra.

North Goa Tour includes Mapusa, Mayem Lake, beaches Vagator, Anjuna, Calangute, Fort Aguada; ***South Goa Tour*** includes Old Goa, Loutolim, Margao, Colva, Mormugao, Pilar, Dona Paula, Miramar (with optional river cruise at extra charge); both 0930-1800, Rs 70 (Rs 100, a/c). Similar tours are offered from Margao, Colva, Vasco, Mapusa and Calangute. The ***Village Tour*** includes a visit to Savoi Verem spice plantation and Hindu temples at Marcela. 2-day ***Dudhsagar Special*** (from Panaji and Margao): 1000-1800 (next day) via Old Goa, Bondla Sanctuary, Tambdi Surla. Overnight at Molem. 2nd Class return train to the Falls the following morning. Rs 350.

River Cruises by launch are organized on the Mandovi River, sometimes with live bands and sing-along entertainment (though no one seems to know the words yet most on board are keen to join in). Evening cruises "corny but pleasant at dusk" are recommended; "all-in-all it's good fun". It is not a "Luxury" launch – metal chairs are lined upfacing the band and dancers but you are free to wander around on deck. A bar also operates.

The GTDC, Santa Monica Jetty (east of New Patto Bridge): 1 hr *Sunset Cruise* (1800) Rs 55; *Sundown Cruise* (1915), Rs 55; *Full Moon Pleasure Cruise* (once a month!) 2 hrs (2030) Rs 100 (dinner available at extra cost); *The Mangrove experience* (1430) Rs 100, 2½ hrs. The private Emerald Waters Co also offers similar trips (tickets from various outlets in the city).

An ***Arab dhow cruise*** on the *St Anthonea* is available; book at Santa Monica jetty, Rs 600 (includes dinner). Cruises leave from the jetty between the New Patto and Mandovi bridges; tickets are also sold at the small booth near the jetty.

His family claimed descent from Brahmins from Colvale, but his parents separated after his birth, his mother becoming a nun and his father a priest.

José grew up with an adopted half sister under his father's care, but in February 1771 at the age of 15 his father took him to Lisbon - a journey that took over 9 months. His father found patronage in the court and he himself was given a scholarship to study in Rome where he was ordained a priest in 1780 and later completed his doctoral thesis. Abbé Faria then went on to Paris where he got involved with the French Revolution. He made a worldwide reputation as an authority on hypnotism through publishing his book 'On the causing of lucid sleep'. However, very little is known of his subsequent career, though he gave public lectures and demonstrations of 'magnetising power' (hypotnism) in Paris in the first two decades of the 19th century. He died at the age of 64 in 1819 in Paris, never having revisited the Goa which he had left 48 years before.

The character in Dumas' *Count of Monte Christo* may have been based on him.

The Braganza Institute and the Azad Maidan

Further west, almost opposite the wharf are the **library** and public rooms of the **Braganza Institute**. The blue tiled frieze in the entrance, made in 1935, is a "mythical" representation of the Portuguese colonization of Goa. The tiled panels, *azulezos*, about 3m high, are set against a pale yellow background. They should be read clockwise from the entrance on the left wall. Each picture is set over a verse from the epic poem by the great Portuguese poet **Luis Vaz de Camoes**, whose statue stood in front of the Se Cathedral until it was removed to the museum in Old Goa by the post-colonial Goa government. Camoes had served in North Africa before travelling to Goa in 1553, staying in India and the far East for 17 years. He was a fierce critic of the Portuguese colonial enterprise, evidenced in his epic poem *Os Lusiadas*.

The Institute is also home to the **Menezes Braganza Institute** (formerly the Instituto Vasco da Gama), which was established on 22 November 1871, the anniversary of the date on which Vasco da Gama sailed round the Cape of Good Hope. It was founded to stimulate an interest in culture, science and the arts and has 24 Fellows who must all be residents of Goa. Luis Menezes de Braganza (1878-1938) whose home at Chandor is open to the public, gives a fascinating insight into the lives of the elite Portuguese-speaking Goan families. He was an outstanding social and political figure in early 20th century Goa. It is open Monday-Friday 0930-1300, 1400-1745. Exhibits include paintings, mainly by European artists of the late 19th and early 20th centuries and Goan artists of the 20th century. There are also sculptures, coins and furniture, the last including a remarkable seven legged rectangular table used for interrogation during the Inquisition. Three legs on one side are carved to represent two lions flanking a central eagle, while the four other legs are carved into the form of human heads.

Azad Maidan ("Freedom Square")

This is immediately to the south of the Braganza Institute has a pillared memorial in the gardens which originally housed a statue of Albuquerque but now has a black stone memorial to Dr Tristao de Braganza Cunha, one of Goa's

Panaji houses

most venerated Freedom Fighters. Antonio Sebastiao Pedro dos Remedios Francisco Tome Tristao de Braganza Cunha was born on 2 April 1891 in Chandor village. After an education in Pondicherry and then an electrical engineering degree in Paris he returned to Goa in 1926. From that point. until his death in 1958, he became a leading opponent of colonialism and an advocate of full independence within India. Despite his background of conservative Catholicism rooted among the landed gentry, "TB" became a radical rationalist. In 1946 he was arrested by the Portuguese as a leading subversive and imprisoned, first at Fort Aguada jail and then in Vasco da Gama, in transit to jail in Portugal. Released in 1950 but under compulsion to stay in Lisbon, he escaped to Paris and then back to India in September 1953. However, India's freedom had left Goa isolated, and until his death on 26 September 1958, he struggled against widespread apathy through newspaper articles to press the case for Goan independence. Disowned by the Catholic church he was buried in a Church of Scotland cemetery in Bombay

Largo da Igreja

The main (Church) square is south of the Secretariat. This was marsh until in the mid-19th century when the marshes were reclaimed to create the Praca de Flores (Square of the Flowers). It is dominated by a white-washed church.

The **Church of Immaculate Conception** (1541) stands at the top of a flight of steps. It was built to serve the needs of arriving sailors rather than for the town population. Through the 16th and 17th centuries Panjim remained no more than a marshy fishing village. Once affiliated to the Teleigao parish when Panaji was of little importance it became the parish church of the capital in 1600. The low hill offered a landmark for boats coming into the Mandovi estuary and the Portuguese established their Customs Post just below the hill, making it the first landing point for sailors from Europe.

The church was completely rebuilt in 1619 to its present design, modelled on the church in Reis Magos across the estuary. Before the hill was cut and the imposing stairway built in the 1780s, access was by a narrow staircase on the west side. In 1871 the central supporting arch had to be modified and strengthened to support the great bell, the second largest in Goa after the bell in the Se Cathedral (originally from the tower of the Church of St Augustine in Old Goa, this had been placed above Fort Aguada 30 years earlier). A few years later it fell and fatally wounded a member of the congregation.

Inside the church the main altar reredos and the altars on either side to Jesus the Crucified and to Our Lady of the Rosary, are typically ornate gilded Baroque, in turn flanked by marble statues of St Peter and St Paul. The panels in the Chapel of St Francis, in the south transept, came from the chapel in the Idalcao Palace in 1918. The *Feast Day* is on 8 December.

In 1945, the statue of Our Lady of Fatima was installed and a crown of gold and diamonds was gifted by parishioners 5 years later. This statue is carried in a candle light procession each year on 13 October.

The domeless **Jama Masjid** (mid-18th century) can be seen to the left looking from the steps in front of the church.

The Hindu **Mahalaxmi Temple** (originally 1818, but rebuilt and enlarged in 1983) is now hidden behind a new building, but is by the *Boca de*

Vaca ('Cow's Mouth') spring, further up Dr Dada Vaidya Rd, on which all these places of worship are situated. The Mahalaxmi Temple was the first Hindu place of worship to be allowed in the Old Conquests after the ending of the Inquisition. Even then permission was slow to be granted and raised fierce opposition from Archbishop Galdino. The deity, which had been removed to Bicholim in the 16th century, was restored only after a temporary resting place was found in the house of Mahamay Kamat, near the Secretariat. However, the Archbishop did not give up his opposition to the project and in 1827 "ordered that the priests should announce that it would be a very grave sin of idolatry for anyone to engage himself in the works of Hindu temples even when ordered to do so by the Government."

St Thome and Fontainhas

On the eastern promontory, sandwiched between the Altinho, the Mandovi River and the Ourem Creek, is San Thome, with Fontainhas to its south. Drained in the 18th and early 19th century the area still has its original narrow lanes and houses. Under Portuguese rule the only buildings allowed to be painted all white were the churches, while various shades of ochre predominated for secular buildings. Features such as window or door frames were picked out in other colours or white, and the sloping tiled roofs and wrought iron fronted balconies, often covered in climbing plants, created a very picturesque urban environment.

St Thome takes its name from the small but historically important square in which the main Post Office stands. Hall records that public executions were held here as late as 1843 when the 15 Pinto conspirators were

Panaji Church

executed. The Post Office itself was once a tobacco warehouse. On the east side of the square is an attractive house used briefly after 1834 as a Mint, hence its Portuguese name *Casa Moeda*. St Thome church (1849, rebuilt in 1902) is in the corner of the square.

Fontainhas can be approached from several directions. Narrow lanes come down from the St Thome district, while a footbridge leads across the Ourem creek from the new bus stand and the Tourist office straight into the district. A narrow road also runs east past the Church of the Immaculate Conception and the main town square down to the footbridge. However, in some ways the most attractive way to approach is by walking over the Altinho from the Mahalaxmi Temple. This route gives spectacular views from the steep east side of the Altinho, a footpath dropping down into Fontainhas just south of the **San Sebastian Chapel** (1818, rebuilt in 1888) This very attractive little church is in the heart of the Fontainhas district, which retains a quiet charm. Old Portuguese houses with their decorative wrought iron balconies have been

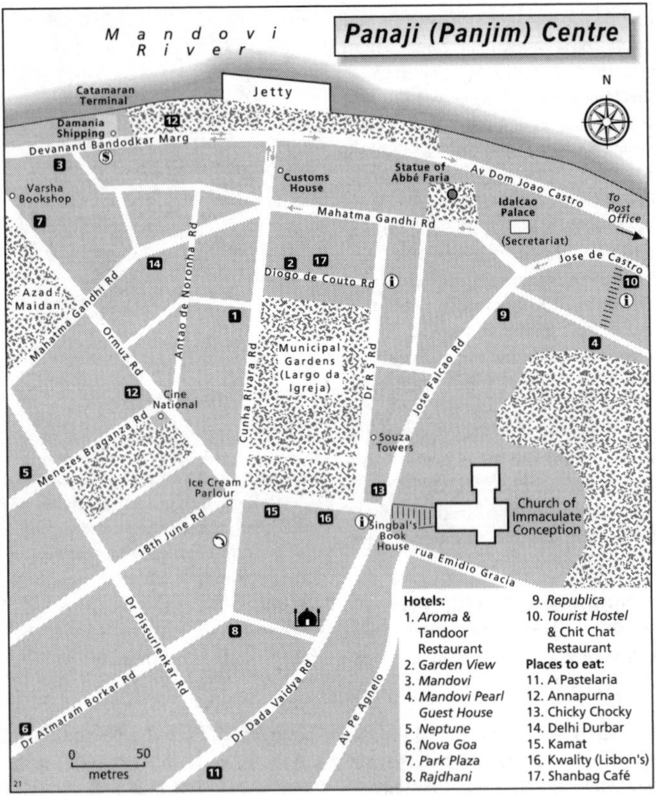

well preserved. The chapel houses the large wooden cross which until 1812 was the crucifix in the Palace of the Inquisition in Old Goa. For 100 years it was housed in the chapel in the Idalcao's palace before being moved to the Chapel of San Sebastian. The church scarcely seems large enough to house the highly ornamented altars, which came originally from a church in Diu.

Fontainhas is also home to the Goa State archives. On the hill behind is the Hindu **Maruti temple** to Hanuman, established towards the end of the Portuguese period without their official approval, and still being extended. During *Shri Hanuman Jatra* (25 February 1998) the deity is carried in a palanquin procession and a big fair is held.

The Campal

The broad avenue running along the sea front from the Idalcao's Palace between the boat jetties on the seaward side and the busy commerical area of town to its south passes through the Campal to Miramar and Dona Paula. Facing across the Mandovi estuary to Reis Magos and Fort Aguada, what is now a pleasingly broad flat park was reclaimed from the sea in 1833. Hall records that its name is an abbreviation of 'Campo de Dom Manuel', Dom Manuel being the Viceroy responsible for clearing and reclaiming the area. While his name is itself a testament to Portuguese rule perhaps the most striking relic of the colonial past is the huge 4m long cannon. The cannon, one of the first to be made in Goa, guarded the crossing from Tiswadi to Ponda at Banastari.

Until independence the broad sweeping road which ran south along the coast to Miramar ended at a huge statue of Albuquerque, now replaced by a statue to Hindu-Christian unity. Today the coast road itself is being extended towards Dona Paula to by-pass the narrower road that runs through the crowded villages.

Markets

Although Panaji is not a traditional Indian market town it none the less has its own bustling Municipal Markets (especially fish and vegetables) just east of the Goa Medical College. They are worth visiting early in the morning for their local colour.

LOCAL INFORMATION

Festivals

In addition to the major festivals:

February: *Mahasivaratri* (25 February 1998) when Siva is honoured. The *Carnival* (3 days preceding Lent in February/March) is somewhat Mediterranean in essence, marked by feasting, colourful processions and floats down streets.

March: *Shigmotsav* (12 March 1998) is a Hindu spring festival held at full moon (celebrated as *Holi* elsewhere in India); colourful floats are taken through the streets often displaying mythological scenes.

March/April: *Feast of Jesus of Nazareth*, is celebrated on the first Sunday after Easter.

November: *Food & Culture Festival* at Miramar Beach (see below).

December: *Feast of Our Lady of Immaculate Conception* (8 December), when a big fair is held.

Mid-range hotels

B ***Mandovi***, D Bandodkar Marg, near the Mahalaxmi Temple overlooking river, T 224405, F 225451, 66 large a/c rooms, good restaurant, popular pastry shop, pleasant terrace bar, exchane, good bookshop, old, part Art Deco, relaxing but lacks great character.

B-C ***Park Plaza***, opposite Azad Maidan, T 222601, F 225635, 37 rooms (power showers!), 28 a/c, a/c bar and restaurant; **B-C** ***Nova Goa***, T 226231, F 224958, 118 good a/c rooms with bath, some have fridge and bath tub, cheaper at rear and in annexe occupied by *Golden Goa*, good a/c restaurant and bar, clean, modern, very clean pool, pleasant staff.

C ***Fidalgo***, 18th June Rd, T 226291, F 225061, once a pleasant hotel, it has very badly deteriorated and so is not recommended but there is a good little bookshop.

D ***Aroma***, Cunha Rivara Rd, T 228310, F 224330, dim public areas, 26 clean rooms some with pleasant outlook, restaurant a/c (Punjabi *Tandoor* recommended for quality and value), bar; **D** ***Blessings***, MG Rd, behind Bhatkar House, T 224770, F 224155, 18 rooms with TV, 2 have huge terraces instead of balconies (some **E** rooms most of the year) overall of rather poor standard for a new hotel, restaurant planned; **D** ***Garden View***, north end of Municipal Garden, T 227844, F 228004, 10 simple rooms, some a/c, unexciting entrance, rooms light, airy, but good views over river and gardens, especially from rooftop restaurant, check-out 0900; **D** ***Keni's***, 18th June Rd, T 224581, F 235227, 38 simple though pleasant rooms, 16 a/c, hot water (0700-0900), room service for meals; **D** ***Orav's Guest House***, 31 Janeiro Rd, T 226128, 16 clean rooms with shower,

Prices: AL Rs 6,000+; **A** Rs 3,000-6,000; **B** Rs1,500-3,000;
C Rs 800-1,500; **D** Rs 400-800; **E** Rs 200-400; **F** Below Rs200

overpriced in season, **E** off-season; **D** *Palacio de Goa*, Gama Pinto Rd, T 221785, F 224155, 7-storey building, 18 simply furnished rooms with phone and TV (not a palace), optional a/c for extra Rs 100, some 4 to 5-bed rooms, dim corridors, restaurant, check-out 0800 (**E** good value, 4 months in off-season); **D** *Panjim Inn*, E212, 31 Janeiro Rd, Fontainhas, T 226523, F 228136, 14 rooms (optional a/c), part in 300-year-old character house kept in traditional style (period furniture, 4-posters), rooms vary – inspect first, dinner overpriced and erratically served, but friendly, relaxed, "no longer as full as it used to be"; new **D** *Panjim Pousada*, nearby, sister hotel of *Panjim Inn*, 7 rooms by 1998, slightly cheaper; **D** *Rajdhani*, Dr Atmaram Borkar Rd, T 235168, 20 good clean rooms with bath, some a/c, in modern Indian business style hotel (extra person Rs 60), good a/c restaurant (Gujarati, Punjabi, Chinese); **D** *Samrat*, Dr Dada Vaidya Rd, T 223318, F 224548, 15 rooms (others occupied 'permanently'), some a/c and some 3-bed, a/c restaurant (Indian, Goan, *Chungwa* for good Chinese), bar, roof-garden; **D** *Sona*, Rua de Ourem, near Patto Bridge and opposite Inter State Bus Terminal, T 222226, F 224425, clean rooms, some a/c and some overlooking Patto river, restaurant next door has unusual car door entrance (more like a theme bar).

D-E *Mayfair and Rohma*, Dr Dada Vaidya Rd, T 223317, F 230068, rooms with shower, some a/c with TV (cheaper in *Mayfair*, **E** non-a/c except around Christmas), Goan and Continental restaurant.

Budget hotels

The more modest hotels may offer to accommodate a third person in a double room with or without a mattress for Rs 50-100.

E *Mandovi Pearl Guest House*, T 223928, 5 rooms, not particularly large, popular if basic, can seem unfriendly; **E** *Neptune*, Malacca Rd, T 224447, 37 rooms, some a/c, big, modern hotel but lacks character, good a/c restaurant, good value; **E** *Republica*, José Falca Rd, T 222638, very basic and not too clean, few refurbished rooms with bath, some overlook river, verandah with views, good meeting place for backpackers; **E** *Tourist Home* (GTDC), Patto Bridge, near the Bus Station, T 225715, 12 large rooms (3 beds), attached bath, **F** dorm, standard government quality, restaurant; **E** *Tourist Hostel* (GTDC), near the Secretariat, overlooking the river, T 227103, 40 rooms with balcony, some a/c but much more expensive, best views from top floor, good open-air restaurant, often full, some complaints about service.

E-F *Park Lane Lodge*, rua de Natal, near St Sebastian Chapel, Fontainhas, T 227154, 8 reasonable rooms (**E** over Christmas period), some with bath, but most use clean common shower-room, rambling old house with character "but run by humourless Christian family", verandahs decorated with birdcages and plants in teapots, mediocre food, gates locked at 2230, popular with backpackers.

F *Frank's Inn*, 83 Menezes Braganza Rd, T 226716, 10 rooms, shared baths, clean; **F** *Venite*, 31 Janeiro Rd, near the Tourist Hostel, T 225537, 3 good-value rooms with a common bath in an old colonial house, usually full throughout the year but is still worth a try, excellent restaurant (see below). Others, on the same road, which are usually rooms belonging to local families, include *Sonia Niwas Guest House*, with 7 rooms, and*Poonam*.

There are several **F** Indian lodges and guest houses in the Fontainhas area although during the high season, finding a room can be very difficult. Prices are usually highly inflated and bargaining fruitless. **F** *Youth Hostel* in Campal (see under 'Miramar Beach' below).

Paying guests: contact Director of Tourism, T 226515, for a list of families.

Places to eat

Most restaurants in Goa serve some alcohol. None in the city have the atmosphere of a Mediterranean café with *al fresco* seating since most are indoors, though there are a few on rooftop terraces.

Bakery: *A Pastelaria*, Dr Dada Vaidya Rd, recommended for good selection; *Mandovi Hotel* has a branch too (side entrance). *Farm Products* outlet, north of Arad Maidan is a "delicatessen".

Chinese: *Chungwa*, in Hotel Samrat, Dr Dada Vaidya Rd, is recommended

Goenchin, off Dr Dada Vaidya Rd, is good but pricey; ***Kwality*** (Lisbon's) with a bar, Church Square, does good, moderately priced Chinese and Indian meals.

Indian: ***Annapurna***, Ormuz Rd, good *dosas* in large, clean eatery with families relaxing over *chai;* ***Kamat***, south of Municipal Gardens (no alcohol), a/c upstairs, recommended for excellent, cheap *masala dosa* and *thali* meals (Rs 30). Also ***Taj Mahal***, MG Rd, opposite the Press, ***Gujarat Lodge***, 18th June Rd, ***Sangeeta***, in Hotel Neptune, Malacca Rd, a/c (Rs 30 meals). ***Vihar***, R José de Costa, also recommended for good South Indian food and is a good local alternative to *Venite*. *Quarter Deck*, east of the Betim ferry jetty does Goan food on the river bank.

Delhi Darbar, MG Rd, T 222544, a/c, mainly North Indian, traditional Mughlai, excellent seafood, very pleasant though fairly expensive (Rs 70-80 for a main dish), good service (clean toilets). ***Shanbag Café***, opposite Municipal Garden Square and ***Sher-e-Punjab***, 18th June Rd, are recommended for good cheap North Indian food; both are popular.

International: ***Chicky Chocky*** near the Church of the Immaculate Conception, good selection of fast foods and '*Sizzle Point*' for speciality sizzlers; ***Eurasia***, Dr Dada Vaidya Rd does Italian, good pizzas (recommended especially when tired of curries!); ***Le Millionaire*** and bar, Padmavati Towers, 18th June Rd, good Indian and Chinese, pleasant atmosphere; ***Mandovi***, D Bandodkar Marg, recommended for seafood and Goan dishes; ***Shalimar***, MG Rd, offers a wide choice; ***Venite***, 31 Janeiro Rd, near the Tourist Hostel, T 225537, 1st floor of old colonial house, arrive early to sit in one of three atmospheric narrow balconies overlooking the street, excellent local Goan food (daily change of menu), good quality, moderately priced, great ambiance, good music, very user-friendly, open 0800-2200 (may close in the afternoon out-of-season) closed Sunday, highly recommended.

At **Alto Porvorim** on the Panaji-Mapusa road: ***O Coqueiro***, near the water tank, with a bar has tables in or out, pleasant ambiance. It serves excellent Goan food, but avoid pork when in gets warm as it is not safe. Opposite it is ***Chinese Garden***, which is recommended. ***Village Nook*** in Church St, east off NH17 beyond the water tank, is a garden pub which serves home-cooked meals. ***Don Pedro*** in a rustic setting, Mexican (and some Goan) food includes *tostadas, fajitas, tortilla* and *chilli* washed down with cocktails for Rs 45.

Entertainment and nightlife

Bars: There is no dearth of bars in the city. Recommended for rooftop views are bars at the *Hotel Mandovi*'s and *Garden View*. *Venite* is a good place for a beer or wine and for meeting other travellers; *Panjim Inn* is becoming expensive but its large verandah is pleasant. For somewhere more modern and off-beat choose the bar next to the *Hotel Sona* (easily spotted with its 'car door' entrance).

Entertainment: A large variety of local drama presentations are performed, many during festivals. **Astronomical Observatory**, 7th floor, Junta House, 18th June Rd (entrance in Vivekananda Rd) open 14 November-31 May, 1900-2100, in clear weather. Rooftop telescope and binoculars, plus enthusiastic volunteers. Worth a visit on a moonless night, and for views over Panaji at sunset.

Museums: The **Archaeological Museum**, is south of the Kadamba Bus Stand, near ADC office, Patto. The **Archives Museum**, Ashirwad Building, 1st floor, Santa Inez, T 46006, 0930-1300, 1400-1730, Monday-Friday; free. The **Central Library** here (1832) the oldest 'public library' in India, has rare books and documents. The **Gallery Experança**, opposite Merces Church, Vadi Merces.

Soccer: Professional matches are played at the stadium; season October-March. Details in local papers.

Watersports: A complex has opened 2 km from Miramar beach. Some of the bigger beach resorts have windsurfing, sailing, water-skiing, parasailing etc. Diving is possible nearby from *Cidade de Goa,* Vainguinim Beach near Dona Paula.

Walking: there are some beautiful walks through the forested areas of Goa. Contact the ***Hiking Assoc of Goa***, 6 Anand Niwas, Swami Vivekenanda Rd or Captain of Ports Office.

Shopping

Mapusa and Margao have better Municipal Markets. There are many shops selling nuts and dried fruit, especially cashew nuts.

Books: *Hotel Fidalgo* shop, past Reception and to the right, has a reasonable selection, also stocks postcards and some foreign newspapers; *Mandovi Hotel* bookshop has a good range, has American news magazines (Time, Newsweek etc), helpful staff; *Varsha*, near Azad Maidan, carries a wide stock in tiny premises, and is especially good for books on Goa, obscure titles are not displayed but ask knowledgeable staff.

Clothes and textiles: *Boutiques*, including a few on 18th June Rd, carry readymades. Some Indian style clothes are sold at the *Government Emporia* where you can also get fabric by the metre; *Khadi Showroom*, Municipal (Communidade) Building, Church Sq, is also good value.

Handicrafts: jewellery (some with a Portuguese hall-mark), particularly malachite set in gold filigree, and clothes, are good buys. The bazars are worth browsing through for pottery and copper goods. Some hotel shops have jewellery, rugs and shell carvings. Goa Government handicrafts shops are at the Tourist Hotels and the Interstate Terminus, which also has the MP Government *Handicrafts Emporium*. Kerala and Kashmir *Emporia* are in Hotel Fidalgo, 18th June Rd. There are other emporia on RS Rd. *Acorn*, is near People's School, Patto Footbridge.

Photography: *Fantasy Studio*, Eldorado; *Souza Paul*, MG Rd; *Central Studio*, Tourist Hostel; *Lisbon Studio*, Church Square.

Local travel

See page 245 under 'Getting Around' for details of prices etc.

Bicycle hire: widely available.

Car hire: **Sai Service** is recommended; 36/1 Alto Porvorim, just north of the Mandovi Bridge, T 217065, F 217064; at Dabolim airport, T 514817; at Panaji T 223901; also from **Hertz**, FS-7 18th June Rd, T 223398, 221840 (Head office, T 022 4965186, F 022 4921172); **Budget**, Porvorim, T 217063; **Wheels**, T 224304, Airport, T 512138.

Motorcyle hire: *Classic Bike Adventure* near New Patto Bridge (see Mapusa), T 0832 273351, F 276124.

Taxis White **Tourist taxis** can be hired from **Goa Tourism**, Trionora Apts, T 223396, about Rs 5.30/km. **Private taxis**: charge similar prices; various outlets include Mrs Satira Dias, T 226969, 225535.

City bus service: from Panaji Bus Stand (Main Terminal) to the city. **Auto-rickshaws** are easily available.

Ferries: flat-bottomed ferries charge a nominal fee to take passengers (and usually vehicles) when rivers are not bridged. *Dona Paula-Mormugao*, fair weather service only, September-May, takes 45 mins. Buses meet the ferry on each side. Important ones include: *Panaji-Betim* (the Nehru bridge over the Mandovi supplements the ferry); *Old Goa-Diwar Island*; *Ribandar-Chorao* for Salim Ali Bird Sanctuary; *Siolim-Chopdem* for Arambol and northern beaches; *Keri-Tiracol* for Tiracol fort.

Long distance travel

NH4A, 17 and 17A pass through Goa. **Delhi** (1,904 km), **Mumbai** (582 km), **Calcutta** (2,114 km), **Chennai** (904 km), **Bangalore** (570 km), **Hyderabad** (712 km), **Mangalore** (371 km), **Pune** (505 km).

Air

Dabolim airport, T 0834 510829, near Vasco, 30 km from Panaji via the Zuari Bridge (twice as far via Ponda). There is a bank counter for exchange and some airlines' desks. **Transport to town**: Indian Airlines coach meets arrivals, Rs 30 pp. Larger hotels and tour companies offer free transfer. The pre-paid taxi counter near the exit shows rates on a board (North Goa Rs 450; South Goa beaches about Rs 250). Local buses run along the main road to Vasco and Panaji; the fare is nominal. See also page 236.

The possible closure of the Zuari Bridge for repairs may greatly increase the transfer time by road from the airport to Panjim and North Goa resulting in a corresponding increase in the cost of transfer by road.

NB Book internal flights to/from Goa, well in advance. Foreigners must pay in foreign currency/exchange. It is usually possible to buy tickets through an agent abroad; ask when you get the international flight to India. Jet Airways have a few of their own offices overseas.

Timetables change so please check with airline. **Air India**, T 224081, **Mumbai**: Monday, 1615, and Thursday, 1300; **Thiruvananthapuram**: Thursday.
Indian Airlines, T 223826, Reservations 1000-1300, 1400-1600, Airport T 512788. Flights to **Bangalore** and **Chennai**: Monday, Tuesday, Thursday, Friday, Saturday; **Delhi**, daily; **Kochi**, daily; **Kozhikode**: Monday, Wednesday, Friday; **Mumbai**, daily.
Jet Airways, T 221472, Airport T 511005. To **Mumbai** daily.
NEPC Skyline, T 223730; to **Mumbai** daily.
Sahara, to **Delhi**: Monday, Wednesday, Friday.

International flights

Direct charter flights for foreigners are available from England, Germany, Holland, Finland and Switzerland from October-April. They offer unbeatable value (especially in November, mid-January to mid-March) with hotel accommodation, and sometimes meals, included. **NB** 'Guest House' or 'Dormitory' style accommodation offered with the cheapest package deals may be unsuitable; ask your travel agent. If this is the case, it would be best to arrange your own hotel on arrival or independently in advance. See also page 234.

Train

Rail Bookings, Kadamba Bus Station, 1st floor, T 225620, 232169, 0930-1300; 1430-1700. The South Central Railway service on the Vasco-Londa/Belgaum sector has now been converted to broad gauge; for details see Transport under Vasco on page 111. See also 'Konkan Railway' box (page 247) and 'Transport' under Margao below.

Road

Share-taxis run on certain routes; available near the the ferry wharves, main hotels and market places (max 5). Mapusa from Panaji, approx Rs 10.

Bus: State Kadamba Transport Corporation (KTC) Luxury and ordinary buses and private buses (often crowded) operate from the Bus Stand in Patto to the east, across the Ourem Creek, T 222634. Booking 0800-1100, 1400-1630. Tourist Information, 0900-1130, 1330-1700; Sunday 0930-1400. The timetable is not strictly adhered to; buses often wait until they are full. The minimum fare (for 3 km) is under a rupee. Frequent service to **Mapusa, Margao, Vasco**; to Old Goa (every 5-10 mins) 20 mins, Rs 2.50, then to Ponda, 1 hour, Rs 6; Calangute direct from Bus Stand 23, 35 mins, Rs 4.50.

Long distance by private 'luxury' or 'sleeper' (with bunks recommended for overnight). Rucksacks and large luggage is usually put into the driver's cabin. Private operators (eg *International Travels*, near Viranis, MG Rd, T 46335, *West Coast Travels*, Old Bus Stand, T 225723, *Laxmi*, T 45745; *Mohan*, T 220142) have daily services from Panaji (and Mapusa and Margao) to Bangalore, Mangalore, Mumbai, Pune. Agents also at beach resorts. To Bangalore Rs 180; Mangalore Rs 150; Mumbai, Rs 400 (sleeper), Rs 250; Pune Rs 300 (sleeper).

Karnataka RTC (Bus Terminus, T 225126), Booking 0800-1100, 1400-1700. **Maharashtra RTC** (Bus Terminus, T 46853), Booking 0800-1100, 1400-1630. **NB** Check times and book in advance at Kadamba Bus Stand.

State buses: to **Bangalore**: 1530-1800 (13 hours), Rs 225; **Belgaum**: 0630-1300 (5 hours); **Hospet**: 0915-1030 (10 hours) Rs 75; **Hubli** many; **Londa**: 4 hours on poor road, Rs 50; **Mangalore**: 0615-2030 (10 hours) Rs 150; **Miraj**: 1030 (10 hours); **Mumbai**: 1530-1700 (15 hours), Rs 200 (a/c Rs 300); **Mysore**, 1530-1830 (17 hours) Rs 200; **Pune**: 0615-1900 (12 hours), Rs 155.

Sea

Mumbai: a fast 'catamaran' service is run by ***Damania Shipping***, T 228711 (Mumbai, T 022374373), between Fisheries Jetty, Panaji (2 km from bus station) and Mumbai. Some find the closed a/c atmosphere and lack of fresh sea air, uncomfortable. See page 228 for details. Departs Panaji, Monday, Wednesday, Friday, 1000; arrives at New Ferry Wharf, Mumbai after 7 hours.

Directory

Airline offices **Air France**, T 226154; **Air India**, 18th June Rd, T 231101-4; **British Airways**, 2 Exelsior Chambers, opposite Mangaldeep, MG Rd, T 224336; **Indian Airlines & Alliance Air**, Dempo House, D Bandodkar Marg, T 224067, 223831. **Gulf**

Air T 226154 & **Jet Airways**, 102 Rizvi Chambers, C Albuquerque Rd, T 221472, Airport T 511005; **Kuwait Airways**, 2 Jesuit House, Dr DR de Souza Rd, Municipal Garden Sq, T 224612.

Banks & money changers Many private agencies change TCs and cash. **Thomas Cook**, D Bandodkar Marg, T 221312, F 221313. Open 1 October-31 March, 0930-1800, Monday-Saturday, 1000-1700 Sunday. Rest of the year (April-September), closed Sunday, but open on most Bank Holidays except 16 January, 1 May, 15 August, 2 October. recommended as the easiest and most efficient money changer in Goa. Also good for Thomas Cook drafts; money transfers from any Thomas Cook office in the world within 24 hours. **Trade Wings**, Naik Building, MG Rd, T 224576; **Wall Street Finance**, MG Rd, opposite Azad Maidan, T 225399.

Amex representative is at Menezes Air Travel, rua de Ourem, but does not cash TCs.

Indian currency against certain credit cards are also given at some banks. **Central Bank**, Nizari Bhavan (against Mastercard); **Andhra Bank**, Dr Atmaram Borkar Rd, opposite EDC House, T 223513, accepts Visa, Mastercard, JCB; **Bank of Baroda**, Azad Maidan, accepts Visa Mastercards and exchanges up to Rs 5,000/day.

Cultural centres **Alliance Française** near Ourem Creek, T 223274; **Indo-Portuguese Institute**, E-4 Gharse Towers, opposite Don Bosco School, MG Rd; **Kala Academy**, D Bandodkar Marg, Campal, T 223288. The modern and architecturally impressive centre designed by Charles Correa was set up to preserve and promote the cultural heritage of Goa. There are exhibition galleries, a library and comfortable indoor and outdoor auditoria where performances are staged. In addition, courses on music and dance are offered. **Renaissance**, Rebello Mansion, 1st floor, behind FLG Garden, Campal, T 225523, across the road from the Kala Academy, is an art gallery with a small café and a handicrafts shop.

High Commissions and consulates Germany Hon Consul, c/o Cosme Matias Menezes Group, rua de Ourem, T 223261, F 43265; **Portugal** 7-B Lake View Colony, Miramar, T 224233, F 224007; **UK** Agnelo Godinho, House No 189, near the GPO, T 226824, F 232828.

Hospitals & medical services *Goa Medical College*, Av PC Lopez, west end of town, T 224566; *CMM Poly Clinic*, Altinho, T 225918; *Sardesai Nursing Home*, near Mahalaxmi Temple off Dada Vaidya Rd, T 223927, clinic 0800-1330, 1500-1630, T 46850; *JMJ Hospital*, Alto Porvorim, T 212130; *Dr Manu Shah's Clinic*, T/4 Shabana Chambers, near El Dourado, T 227083, recommended for acupuncture, osteopathy and naturopathy.

Libraries Some hotels/hostels now run 'book exchanges'; a deposit is usually required.

Post & telecommunications and **Courier services**: *Blue Dart*, FO3 Sukerkar Mansions, T 227768; *DHL*, Alcon Chambers 12, 13, D Bandodkar Marg, T 226487, open 0930-1900, Monday-Saturday; *Skypak*, City Business Centre, Coelho Building, opposite Jama Masjid, T 225199.

GPO: Old Tobacco Exchange, St Thome, towards Patto Bridge, with Poste Restante on left as you enter. Open Monday-Saturday 0930-1730, closed 1300-1400. Many letters are incorrectly pigeon-holed so you can do other travellers a favour by re-sorting any letters you find misplaced.

Telegraph Office: Dr Atmaram Borkar Rd; also has STD, ISD and trunk services. Several private firms offer ISD and fax, including *Haytechs Communications*, 6 Sujay Apartments, 18th June Rd.

Tour companies & travel agents *Citizen World Travels*, F/4 Gomes Building, 2nd floor, C Albuquerque Rd, T 227087, friendly, helpful, efficient; ***Sita***, 101 Rizvi Chambers, 1st floor, C Albuquerque Rd, T 221418; ***Thomas Cook***, 8 Alcon Chambers, D Bandodkar Marg, 'ferociously efficient' if slightly expensive; *TCI*, "Citicentre", 1st floor, 19 Patto Plaza, T 224985.

Tourist offices **Government of India**, Municipal (Communidade) Building, Church Sq, T 223412.

Goa, Directorate, Tourist Home, Patto, T 225583, F 228819, tours can be booked here but **not** GTDC accommdodation; also Information desk at the Tourist Hostel, T 227103, which is chaotic. There are counters at the Kadamba Bus Station, T 225620 and Dabolim airport (near Vasco), T 512644. Goa Tourism Development Corporation (GTDC), Trionora Apartments, Dr Alvares Costa Rd, T 226515, F 223926, for GTDC accommodation.

Andhra Pradesh, near *Hotel Sona*; **Karnataka**, Velho Filhos Building, Municipal Garden Sq, T 224110; **Maharashtra**, near Mahalaxmi Temple. **Tamil Nadu**, Rayu Chambers, Dr AB Rd.

Guides for 4 persons, about Rs 250/4 hours, Rs 350/8 hours; excursion allowance Rs 250, overnight, Rs 800, foreign language supplement, Rs 100.

Useful addresses **Ambulance**: T 223026, T 224601. **Fire**: T 101. **Police**: T 100. **Foreigners' Regional Registration Office**: Police Headquarters. **Wildlife**: Chief Wildlife Warden, Conservator's Office, Junta House, 3rd floor, 18th June Rd, T 224747, and Deputy Conservator of Forests (Wildlife), 4th floor, T 229701, for permits and accommodation in the sanctuaries. World Wildlife Fund, Ground Floor, Block B-2, Hillside Apartments, Fontainhas (off 31 January St), T 226020, will advise on trekking with a guide in the sanctuaries.

Around Panaji in Tiswadi

THERE IS a range of interesting sights immediately around Panaji, from the mangrove reserves of the islands to the churches of Old Goa. The main advantage of the beaches here is that they are very close to Panaji (with frequent buses along the main road) and so offer an easy escape from the bustle and heat of the city.

CHORAO ISLAND M4A2

The island lies opposite Panaji at the confluence of the Mandovi and Mapusa Rivers. 24 ha of the island is being adapted for fish farming. Conservationists succeeded in diverting the planned route of the Konkan Railway which was to cross the island and would have been a threat to the ecosystem.

DR SALIM ALI BIRD SANCTUARY M4B2

The small bird sanctuary occupying under 2 sq km of the western tip of Chorao Island. Best season: November-February. Open 0900-1700. Entry Re 1.

Access

No advance permission is required. The sanctuary is a short walk from the ferry ramp but there are no signs and there seem to be no roads or trails and local people are unaware of its existence.

Wildlife

The banks along the Mandovi River are visited in the winter months by pintails, shovelers, snipes and terns. You may see Blue-winged teals, Maddar ducks, Grey and Purple herons and Adjutant storks. A watchtower provides a vantage point for viewing; Forest Department motor boats carry visitors into the sanctuary. The mangrove forests containing 14 species (*Rhizophora*, *Avicennia*, *Bruguiera*, *Exocaria*, *Sonneratia* etc) form a protective habitat for coastal fauna and in addition to birds it harbours a large colony of flying foxes, crocodiles, turtles and jackals. It is now the focus of a range of conservation measures.

Viewing

The best way to view the sanctuary is by boat. Find a local fisherman to row you along the river for a close look at the mangroves where you are likely to see a variety of birds according to the time of day and the season (best from November to February). Freshwater **crabs** and **mudskippers** are much in evidence. Mudskippers are particularly curious fish that slide out of the water at low tide onto the mud and are able to breathe through the mouth (in addition to their gills when in water). Their moveable eyes on stalks on top of their heads help them to keep a close watch on predators and when necessary 'jump' half a metre! Agree to pay up to Rs 50/hr for the boat.

Getting there Buses along NH4A between Panaji and Ponda stop at the Chorao ferry wharf in Ribandar. Ferry to Chorao every

> **Coloured maps**
>
> The numbers following the town entry refer to the coloured map section. Thus Choroa Island M4A2 will be found on map 4 square A2

15 mins from 0600-2400, taking about 10 mins. Fare Re 1; higher at other times.

CARAMBOLIM LAKE (KARMALI) M4B3

Carambolim Lake, 12 km east of Panaji, near the NH17, is a wide shallow lake, less than 3m deep, lying between the estuaries of the Mandovi and Zuari. Heavily silted up, the lake has been managed for many years, being emptied just before the rains for fishing and re-filled through many drains. The water is auctioned every April for its fish although fish numbers have deteriorated in recent years.

Home to a wide range of varieties of wild rice, it has remarkably rich concentrations of detoxifying algae, some of which are believed to be responsible for the complete absence of mosquitoes in the area around the lake. The Directory of Indian Wetlands records that in winter it is host to the *Coccilellid* predator which feeds on rice pests.

The lake has a wide fauna, including 120 species of migratory and local birds similar to Chorao. Siberian pintail ducks, barbets, herons, woodpeckers, swallows, orioles, drongos and marsh harriers can be seen most of the year. Environmental groups suggest that a large section (nearly 20%) of the wetland may have been reclaimed by the Konkan Railway.

GOA VELHA M4B2

As Richards says, Goa Velha means "old – being already old when the present named Old Goa (Velha Goa), was still young and flourishing". Goa Velha was finally destroyed by the Bahmani Muslims in 1470, although as Gopakapattana or Govapuri it had already suffered from repeated attacks and long term decline. It is difficult now to spot the site of Goa Velha. A faded notice board by a cross standing on a pedestal is the only visible remains.

Procession of all Saints of the Franciscan third order. On the Monday of Holy Week (in 1998 the 30 March) each year there is a procession with all 26 statues of the saints starts from St Andrew's. Dating from the 17th century, it is the only festival of its kind outside Rome. A large fair is held where old fashioned hand-held fans, a local handicraft, are sold. Also actors and musicians perform in villages.

❖ PILAR M4B2

The **Pilar Seminary**, not far from Goa Velha, is on a commanding hilltop site. It was founded by Capuchin monks in 1613, who remained here until 1835. The Carmelites restored it in the mid-19th century, but now it belongs to the Mission Society of St Francis Xavier. The 17th century Church has remains of frescoes in the cloisters and an old Spanish reredos.

The old Convent stands on the site of a Siva temple; relics of a headless *Nandi* bull and a rock carving of a Naga (serpent) among other carvings, were found here. The museum, open 1000-1700, displays some of the finds and the small chapel upstairs has some fine stained glass. The roof top offers good views of the harbour.

Drinks and snacks are available near the church. Buses along the NH17 stop nearby. From there you can walk uphill through the new extension of the seminary.

TALAULIM M4B2

Just north of the Pilar Seminary is the ❖ **Church of St Anna** (Santana) at Talaulim by the River Siridado, a tributary of the Zuari. Built around 1695, its elaborate Baroque façade is similar in design (though smaller) to the great Church of St Augustine at Old Goa, of which only part of one tower remains. Once the parish church with a large congregation, it fell into disrepair when Old Goa nearby declined, and had to be refurbished in 1907.

The 5-storeys provides an interior with great space under a high barrel-vaulted ceiling lit by two upper rows of windows and shows off a profusion of stucco work. The shell-heads to the doors and niches on the lower floor are notable, echoing the design seen on the ornate façade. The church also has the unique feature of hollow side walls through which people secretly went to confession. The wooden image of St Anna above the chancel arch is particularly interesting. She appears as an elderly lady in a hat and carrying a stick, portrayed as she was reported to have appeared in separate visions to a Christian and a Hindu villager during the 17th century. The latter had also been miraculously cured by her and both had said that the lady had requested a home in the village. St Anna is similarly portrayed in the choir grill and the nave.

St Anna's feast day (26 July) is celebrated by both communities who come

Goa – New or Old?

Looking at Godinho's map (oriented with south pointing to the top) you may wonder at the names that the 17th century traveller might have used in what we know as the old heart of Goa. As suggested by Boies Penrose in *Goa of the East*, the old capital shifted from the position of the first settlement, Gopakapattana or Govapuri (GOEM on Godinho's map) on the River Zuari, now **Goa Velha** ('Goa the Old'), to the newer city (marked CIDADE) on the Mandovi across from Divar island which became known as *Goa Nova* ('Goa the New'). Later, the capital (then called *Nova Goa*), moved to the west, closer to the mouth of the estuary, resulting in the earlier new city *Goa Nova* becoming **Velha Goa** (today's Old Goa). The present capital **Panaji** or Panjim is still at that site (marked PANGIN on the map).

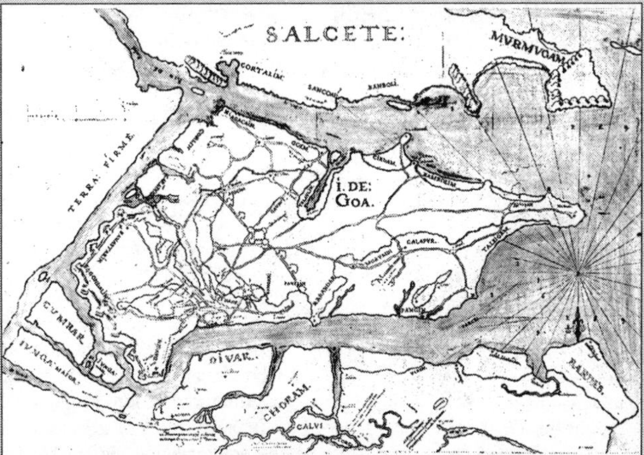

Island of Goa by Manuel Godinho de Erido, c1616

to seek blessing from the mother of the Virgin Mary, whose intervention is traditionally sought by childless couples. It is known popularly as the *Toucheam* (or Cucumber) *Feast* because those who come to pray for a baby boy (*menino*) bring with them a *pepino* (cucumber). Unmarried boys and girls also come to pray for partners bringing with them spoons (*colher*) to plead for wives (*mulher*) and *mung* beans (*urid*) in exchange for husbands (*marido*)!

BEACHES NEAR PANAJI

MIRAMAR

M4B1

Panaji's seafront boulevard runs south for 3 km along the Mandovi estuary. It is a pleasant drive, with good views over the sea but Miramar is very 'urban' in character and the beach is not particularly attractive, so it is not the place for a beach holiday. Although you can wade out a long way, there can be an undertow, and the estuarine waters are polluted.

Inland, the **Taleigao Church** has the image of Our Lady of Loreto. It had been moved there from its original chapel in Vainguinim to the south when it fell into disrepair after the Jesuits were evicted from Goa in 1759.

Festivals

Food & Culture Festival (19-23 November 1997, 18-21 November 1998) at Miramar beach, is organized by the Department of Tourism for 5 days; visitors can sample Goan dishes and watch song and dance performances as well as plays, among other entertainment.

Mid-range hotels

Most of the hotels are on, or just off, the D Bandodkar Marg (DB Marg), the road to Dona Paula which follows the coast. **C-D** ***Solmar***, D Bandodkar Marg (Ave Gaspar Dias), T 230041, 24 a/c rooms and **C** suites, 2 restaurants including *Mughal Mahal* dining bar, exchange, check-out 0900, clean, modern, good value, 2 minutes walk from beach.

D ***Goa International***, Tonca, T 225804, 34 rooms, some with river view, re-opening in December 1997 after renovation; **D-E** ***Bela Goa***, T 224575, 11 simple rooms (2 a/c), restaurant, bar, enthusiastic staff; **D-E** ***London Hotel***, T 226017, 23 rooms, restaurant, bar, travel desk, roof garden; **D-E** ***Miramar Beach Resort*** (formerly ***Yatri Niwas***), close to the beach, T 227754, 60 clean rooms with some a/c, some in new wing to be completed by November 1997, 2-storey blocks by shaded groves, good value, very good fast food restaurant, recommended.

Budget hotels

E ***Riomar Beach Resort***, D Bandodkar Marg, T 226193, 13 non-a/c rooms, clean though basic, balconies are caged and have no views, restaurant and Bar.

F ***Youth Hostel*** away from the beach, T 225433, 2 rooms, dorms, 3 months' notice with 1 day's payment in advance expected, for YHA members and students.

Places to eat

Beach Boogie, Caranzalem Beach, towards Miramar, garden restaurant, varied menu, live music; ***Foodland*** close to the beach; ***Martin's Beach Corner***, Caranzalem, near Blue Bay Hotel, good seafood and Goan dishes in pleasant open air location, recommended; ***Quarterdeck***, near Goa International, is recommended for South Indian fast food.

DONA PAULA

M4B1

A further 4 km south beyond Miramar, the fishing village of Dona Paula has a small palm fringed beach with casuarina groves and is very peaceful. It is thought to be named after Dona Paula de Menezes (the wife of a nobleman, Antonio de Souto Maior, and reputedly a mistress of the Viceroy) who died a young woman, in 1682. A black granite memorial stone is on a wall in the Chapel of Our Lady of Cabo. The

Prices: C Rs 800-1,500; **D** Rs 400-800; **E** Rs 200-400; **F** Below Rs200

family summer house still survives. Others link the village to a Dona Paula who reputedly jumped from the cliffs when refused permission by her father to marry Gaspar Dias, a fisherman. Fisherfolk turned local vendors sell cheap "seaside goods", testifying to Dona Paula's role as a popular Indian picnic spot.

The low laterite cliff forms a head-

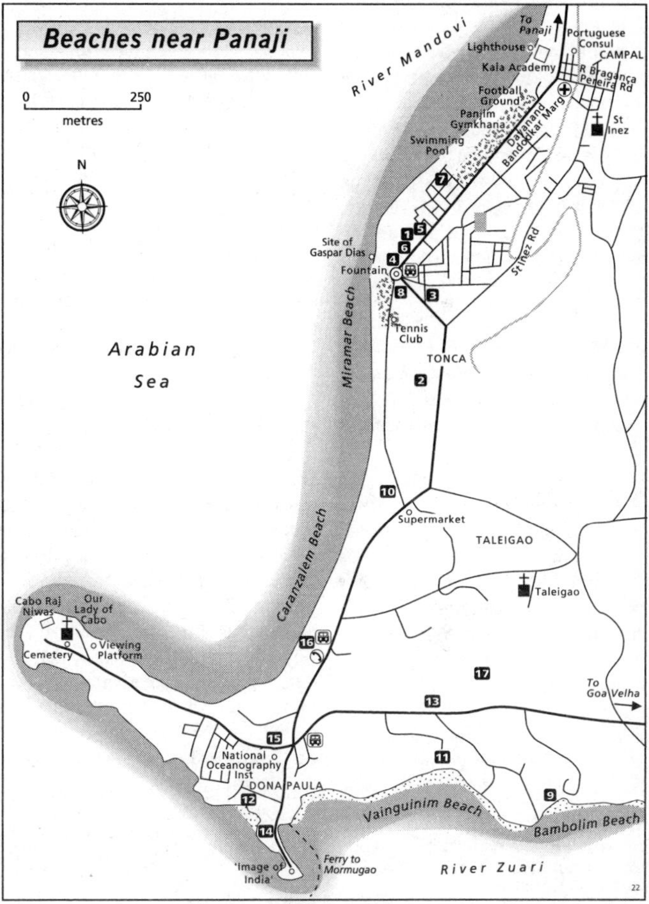

Miramar Hotels:
1. *Bela Goa*
2. *Goa International* & Quarterdeck Restaurant
3. *London Hotel*
4. *Miramar Beach Resort (Yatri Niwas)*
5. *Riomar Beach Resort*
6. *Solmar* & Foodland
7. *Youth Hostel*

Places to eat:
8. Beach Boogie

Caranzalem, Dona Paula & Bambolim Hotels:
9. *Bambolim Beach Resort*
10. *Blue Bay* & Martin's Beach Corner Restaurant
11. *Cidade de Goa*
12. *Dona Paula Beach Resort* & O Pescador Restaurant
13. *Mirabel*
14. *Prainha Cottages*
15. *Sea View*
16. *Swimsea Beach Resort*
17. *Villa Sol*

land joined to the mainland by a short causeway. The platform on the highest point gives pleasant views out to the Arabian Sea and across the bay to Vasco da Gama and the very busy shipping lanes that lead to the port of Mormugao.

A white Pavilion stands on the rocky islet at the end. In 1969, a sculpture by Yrza von Leistner was added to represent 'The Image of India'. The figures of a man and a woman, one looking East (or behind, and the past) and the other West (or forward to the future), with an Asoka *chakra* (wheel) in the middle, speaks not only of India but of Goa. A Sanskrit *sloka* is inscribed below, with a translation in English:

Lead us from Untruth to the Truth,
From Darkness into Light,
From Death to Eternal Life.

A busy passenger ferry crosses over to Vasco from the jetty.

CABO RAJ NIWAS

M4B1

From the roundabout by the National Oceanography Institute a road runs 600m up to Cabo Raj Niwas, now **Raj Bhavan** (the State Governor's House), hence not open to visitors. A platform near the entrance gives superb views over the sweep of the coastline across the Mandovi estuary to Fort Aguada. Marking the site of the Portuguese 'Cabo' fort (of which only 6 cannons and some sections of wall remain between the Raj Bhavan lawns and the cliff), it has a commanding position on the rocky promontory between the two river estuaries.

The first small shrine to **Our Lady of Cabo** was built in 1541 near the area marked out for the future Cabo fort and acted as a landmark for ships at sea and also gave the Fransiscan friars dedicated to preaching, a toehold on the territory. In 1594 the Chapel had a Convent added which was extended in the 17th century. The excavated laterite for building created great hollows which were covered to create useful rain water storage tanks. The Chapel has a simple white façade. Inside, the side altars have unusual 8-point stars (according to some, 'eight' signified regeneration and baptism); the memorial to Dona Paula de Menezes (see Dona Paula above) is in a niche. The door to the Sacristy has carvings similar to Hindu temple art while outside, another ancient heavily carved door leading to the back of the Chapel is thought to have come from a ruined convent in Old Goa. The *Feast* coincides with Independence Day, 15 August.

Documents of 1633 refer to the Chapel and to various buildings of an incomplete Fort and only four guns. During the Napoleonic Wars British troops garrisoned in the fort from 1799-1813 built themselves more buildings which were subsequently demolished by the Portuguese. Several graves in the Cemetery (which still has a gate and four walls), remain as stark reminders. Around 1844, after the religious Orders were abolished, the Archbishop of Goa was given the convent which was refurbished and converted into an impressive residence. This was later acquired by the Governor-General of Goa and, further improved, became the Viceroy's official residence in 1918. Its grand interior was allowed to remain untouched when the Portuguese left in 1961. The Raj Niwas's splendid glassed-in verandah on the seaward side is a special feature

GASPAR DIAS

M4B1

The second line of defence on this side of the estuary was a smaller fort near Miramar Beach. Built to pair with the

Footprint Handbooks

...step inside
a world other travel
guides miss

Win two Iberia flights to Latin America

We want to hear your ideas for further improvements as well as a few details about yourself so that we can better serve your needs as a traveller.

We are offering you the chance to win two Iberia flights to Latin America, currently flying to 25 destinations. Every reader who sends in the completed questionnaire will be entered in the Footprint Prize Draw. 10 runners up will each receive a Handbook of their choice.

Fill in this form using a ball-point pen and return to us as soon as possible.

Mr ☐ Mrs ☐ Miss ☐ Ms ☐ Age

First name

Surname

Permanent Address

Postcode/Zip

Country

Email

Occupation

Title of Handbook

Which region do you intend visiting next?

North America ☐ India/S.Asia ☐ Africa ☐
Latin America ☐ S.E. Asia ☐ Europe ☐
Australia ☐

How did you hear about us?

Recommended ☐ Bookshop ☐
Used before ☐ Media/press article ☐
Library ☐ Internet ☐

There is a complete list of Footprint Handbooks at the back of this book. Which other countries would you like to see us cover?

Offer ends 30 November 1998. Prize winners will be notified by 30 January 1999 and flights are subject to availability.

If you do not wish to receive information from other reputable businesses, please tick box ☐

fort at Reis Magos, it was particularly important in preventing the Dutch from gaining access into the Mandovi. The small **Fortress at the Point of Gaspar Dias**, close to the existing fortification at Cabo, was completed in the early years of the 17th century. The fort had 1.5m thick walls, probably made of laterite blocks, which rose 5m high and provided places for 16 cannons. It saw action when the Dutch attacked repeatedly up to the mid-17th century but its importance waned after the Maratha onslaught. The army decided to abandon Gaspar Dias after it was badly damaged during the mutiny of 1835 and although it housed recuperating soldiers for a time, by the end of the 19th century it fell into disrepair and ultimately crumbled beyond recognition.

All that remains of Gaspar Dias here is the cannon at the circle in present day Miramar, where it marks the possible site of the fort. The other four cannons (of the original 16) that were excavated are to be found at the Directorate of Archives, the Abbé Faria monument and at the Farmagudi roundabout near Ponda.

VAINGUINIM BEACH *M4B1*

The beach to the east of Dona Paula on which the Cidade de Goa stands is backed by a part of Tiswadi which the Jesuits enjoyed as highly productive land. Its rich harvests of tropical fruits complemented the fish, crabs (*culleo*), tortoise and shellfish from the sea. The introduction of canal irrigation also saw a dry-season rice crop – the *vaingon* so the local people began to refer to the area as Culleovaingon or Curlavangni, now simply Vainguinim. After the Jesuits were ordered to leave, the government acquired all Church properties. The coastal area was for a time occupied by British troops sent to protect the Portuguese colony from a threat of attack by the French during the Napoleonic Wars, but they were forced to leave. The beach property was subsequently sold to a private bidder and in 1980 the *Cidade de Goa* was built to occupy the prime site.

There are some watersports on offer near the jetty. Try also *Barracuda Diving* and Hydro Sports Club, *Cidade de Goa*, T 221133. You can change money in the larger hotels; otherwise the State Bank of India, 1000-1400, Monday-Friday, 1000-1200, Sunday, will change TCs.

Luxury hotel

AL-A *Cidade de Goa*, Vainguinim Beach, 1 km east of Dona Paula, T 221133, F 223303, 210 rooms, 26 km airport, 7 km centre, 5 restaurants, sports (including diving) pool (open to non-residents), imaginative development designed by Charles Correa, pleasant and secluded beach but unappealing at low tide

Mid-range

C *Blue Bay*, on Caranzalem Beach, T 228087, 12 neat, modern rooms, some a/c, expensive garden restaurant; **C** *Mirabel*, opposite. Cidade de Goa, T 222038, F 221397, 27 a/c rooms, 2 restaurants, bar, pool, friendly service; **C** *Prainha Cottages*, T 227221, F 229959, 28 rooms in cottages with shower and balcony, some a/c, simple but comfortable and quiet, on a secluded (though not particularly clean) beach, good restaurant, gardens, small pool, recommended; **C** *Swimsea Beach Resort*, Caranzalem Beach, towards Raj Niwas, T 225422, F 224480, 27 a/c small rooms with pleasant breezy balconies, sea facing best, very close to black sandy beach; **C** *Villa Sol*, T 225852, F 224155, 28 a/c rooms with balconies, good restaurant, small pool, built on high ground overlooking Cidade de Goa, a steep hike back from the beach; **C-D** *Dona Paula Beach Resort*, T 227955, F 221371, 21 large pleasant rooms in small buildings around a garden, some a/c and some with sea-facing balcony, quiet, pleasant, small garden restaurant, young friendly management.

Prices: AL over Rs 6,000; **C** Rs 800-1,500; **D** Rs 400-800; **E** Rs 200-400

Budget hotel

E *Sea View*, opposite NIO, T 223327, 12 rooms with TV and balcony, quite basic and no sea views!

Places to eat

Cidade de Goa has several up-market restaurants serving excellent food but at a price. The large sea-front 'coffee house' serves meals all day. ***O Pescador*** at Dona Paula Beach Resort with good views over the jetty, serves seafood specialities. There is also a Punjabi *dhaba*.

BAMBOLIM

M4B2

(8 km from Panaji; *Pop* 5,000) Off the NH17 south, has the site of the Goa University nearby. The dark-sand beach is secluded, free of hawkers and shaded by palms. The *Bambolim Beach Resort* (Rs3,000-6,000) is right on the beach, T 46647, F 46499. 52 a/c rooms, though simple are airy with balcony. Open-air beach-side restaurant (breakfast included), bar, palm shaded terrace, pool, weekly folk entertainment, taxi necessary (usually available), peaceful, isolated spot, recommended. Also, *Palmas de Bambolim*, 1 km from the main road. *Sand & Sea Restaurant*, down the beach will cook any kind of fish dish ordered (watch out for price quoted though). The *Goa Medical College*, T 225727, is located here.

SIRIDAO

M4B2

A short drive from Panaji, Siridao is a small secluded beach often good for shells. The *Feast of Jesus of Nazareth* is held on the first Sunday after Easter.

Old Goa and excursions from Panaji

THE ROAD to Old Goa from Panaji passes over the causeway which was built over a swamp in 1633 by the then Viceroy. It is a very attractive ride in the early morning, especially in the winter when mist often hovers over the still waters of the estuary.

Travel tip

Goa Tourism A visit to Old Goa is included in their *South Goa* and *Pilgrim Tours*.They only spend a short time visiting the sights. It is better to go by bus or share a taxi to give you time to see Old Goa at leisure.

From Panaji, there is a frequent bus service which takes 15-20 mins; fare Rs 2.50. Buses drop you off opposite the Basilica of Bom Jesus; pick up the return bus from east of the MG statue roundabout (no visible Bus Stop sign). Auto rickshaws charge Rs 10, taxis, Rs 100 to Panaji.

If you want to stay in Old Goa, the **D** ***Goa Tourism Hotel*** near MG (Gandhi) Statue Circle roundabout has recently opened. It has 132 beds and a restaurant. There is also a small restaurant near the roundabout which is good, clean and pleasant.

RIBANDAR *M4B2*

At the end of the causeway is the attractive preserved village of Ribandar (pronounced Rai-bunder) or "Royal Harbour", possibly named after the arrival of the Vijaynagar King in the 14th century. The old houses along the road, some substantial and some modest and painted in evocative colours, still conjure up an image of 17th century Portuguese Goa. The **Church to Our Lady of Help**, originally built in 1565, gives thanks to the safe arrival of a Portuguese vessel after a fierce storm at sea. Today the **ferry** is in frequent use for crossing over to Chorao Island for visiting the Salim Ali Bird Sanctuary. It is the shortest route across to Mayem and Bicholim.

❖ OLD GOA *M4B3*

Also known as Velha Goa

When Richard Burton, the explorer, arrived in Goa on sick leave from his Indian army unit in 1850 he described Old Goa as being a place of 'utter desolation' and the people 'as sepulchral looking as the spectacle around them'. The vegetation was dense and he had difficulty reaching the ruins. Today, Old Goa has a melancholy beauty; a city of Baroque churches, now revived by a steady flow of tourists and the great pilgrimage to the tomb of St Francis Xavier in the magnificent Cathedral of Bom Jesus. Visitors are mobbed by hawkers peddling picture postcards and children selling candles.

Old Goa (or Velha Goa) is 8 km from Panaji and may be regarded for Christians as the spiritual heart of the territory. It lies on the south bank of the Mandovi on the crest of a low hill. It owes its origin as Portuguese capital to Afonso de Albuquerque, and some of its early ecclesiastical development to **St Francis Xavier** who was here in the mid-16th century. However, before the Portuguese arrived it was the second capital of the Bijapur Kingdom. All the

Plan of Velha Goa (north oriented downwards)

mosques and fortifications of that period have disappeared; only a fragment of the Sultan's palace walls remain. See also Goa Velha, page 92.

Old Goa was protected by a fortified wall. In the west lay the barracks, mint, foundry and arsenal, hospital and prison. On the banks of the river were the shipyards of Ribeira des Gales and adjacent to these was the administrative and commercial centre. To the east was the market, and the fortress of Adil Shah whilst the true centre of the town was filled with magnificent churches.

All of the churches of Old Goa used the local red laterite as the basic building material. Basalt and fine white limestone were imported from Bassein, for decorative detail. The laterite exteriors were coated with a lime plaster to protect them from the weather which had to be renewed after each monsoon. When maintenance lapsed, the buildings crumbled away.

The Archaeological Survey of India is responsible for the upkeep of the churches.

Further reading: the small inexpensive ASI booklet on the monuments: *Old Goa* by S Rajagopalan, is available from the Archaeological Museum here. The attractive and much more extensive, illustrated books, *Goa: a traveller's historical and architectural guide* by Anthony Hutt, 1988, and Maurice Hall's *Window on Goa*: a history and guide, 2nd ed, 1995, are available from several bookshops in Panaji, Margao and larger resorts.

PLACES OF INTEREST

Holy Hill

As you approach the large central monuments you go over the 'Holy Hill' with a number of churches. The **Chapel of Our Lady of the Rosary** (1526) belongs to the earliest period of church building and is described as Manueline. At the time of the conquest of Goa, Portugal was enjoying a

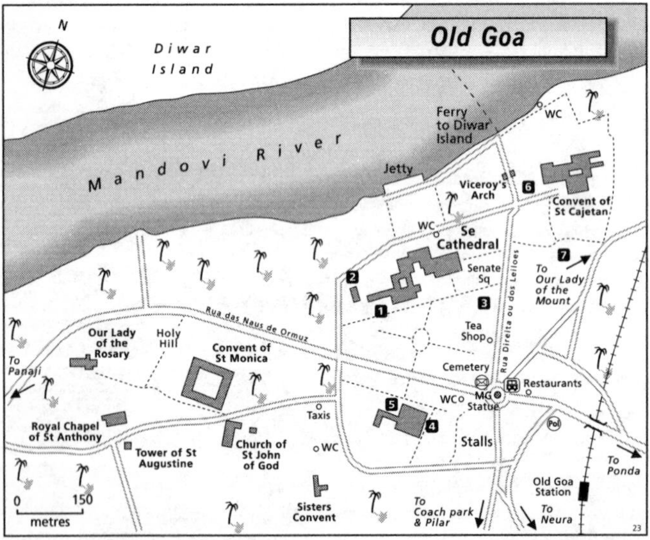

1. Convent of St Francis of Assisi & Archaeological Museum
2. Chapel of St Catherine
3. Place of the Inquisition Tribunal
4. Basilica of Bom Jesus
5. Professed House
6. Gate of Adil Shahi Fortress
7. Ruins of Dominican Monastery

period of prosperity under King Manuel I (r1495-1521), hence the term. The architectural style that evolved borrowed from Iberian decoration, but also included many local naturalistic motifs as well as Islamic elements, seen on the marble cenotaph, owing to the Hindu and Muslim craftsmen employed. The church here has a 2-storey entrance, a single tower and low flanking turrets. From this site Albuquerque directed the battle against the Adil Shahi forces in 1510.

Royal Chapel of St Anthony

The chapel (1543) dedicated to the national saint of Portugal and **Tower of St Augustine** are behind that of Our Lady of the Rosary. Although it is an uphill hike, it is very evocative and well worth the effort. St Anthony's was restored by the Portuguese Government in 1961. St Augustine's is now in ruins, except for the belfry. The building of St Augustine's church, which once boasted eight chapels, a convent and an excellent library was begun in 1572 and was enlarged a few years later to become one of the finest in the kingdom. It was finally abandoned in 1835 because of religious persecution. The vault collapsed in 1842 burying the image, followed by the façade and main tower in 1931. Only one of the original four towers survives. The government has in late 1997 agreed to restore the tower and to make it possible for visitors to climb to the top. They will also place a heritage post box in the tower.

Convent of St Monica (1607-27)

The convent was the first nunnery in India and the largest in Asia. The huge 3-storey square building with the church in the southern part was built around a sunken central courtyard which contained a formal garden. At one time it enjoyed the status of Royal Monastery, now it is the Mater Dei Institute for Nuns, founded in 1964 for theological studies. The only other building on the Holy Hill is the **Church and Convent of St John of God** built in 1685 and abandoned in 1835. Descending from the Holy Hill you enter a broad tree-lined plaza with large buildings on either side. On conducted tours this is where you leave your transport and walk.

❖ Basilica of Bom (the Good) Jesus (1594)

Open 0900-1230, 1500-1830; no photography. The art gallery opens later at 1030 on Sunday and is closed on Fridays and during services. The world renowned church contains the body of **St Francis Xavier**, a former pupil of soldier-turned-saint, Ignatius Loyola, the founder of the Order of Jesuits.

St Francis Xavier's remains form the principal spiritual treasure of the territory (see page 102). The Jesuits began work on their own church in 1594 and by 1605 it was finished and consecrated. The order of Jesuits was suppressed in 1759 and its property confiscated by the

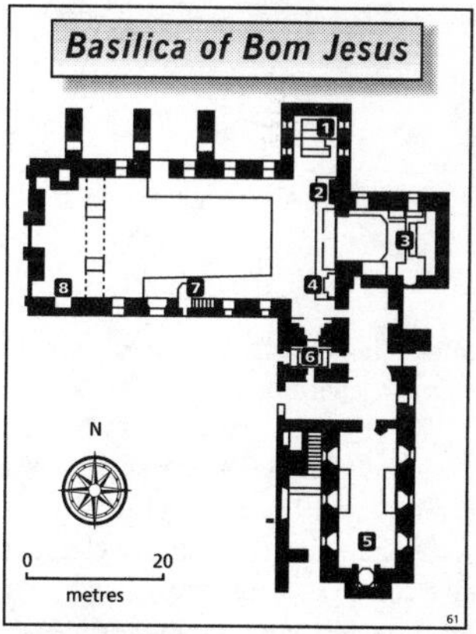

1. Chapel of the Blessed Sacrament
2. Our Lady of Hope
3. Main Altar
4. St Michael
5. Sacristy
6. Chapel of St Francis Xavier
7. Pulpit
8. St Anthony

St Francis Xavier

The 35 year old Spanish Jesuit, Fr Francis Xavier landed in Goa on 6 May 1542, after a journey from Portugal which had taken over a year. Called by Pope Paul III to serve as a missionary in Asia, on his arrival in Goa he agreed to join a newly established seminary as a teacher, where he remained for just under a year. He then moved to South India for two years before following the Portuguese trading route to the Malaccas. While working there he determined to take his missionary work to Japan and returned from the Malaccas to Goa. He spent a short time in Goa before re-embarking for the journey to Japan. Unable to carry out his work there because the Imperial authorities refused him a permit, he set sail to return to Goa but died on 2 December 1552 on Sancian (Chang Cheun), an island off the south Chinese coast near modern Hong Kong. His body was buried in sand and lime was added to hasten decomposition. However, two months later when the grave was opened to transfer the bones, the body appeared fresh and totally unaffected. He was taken to Malacca for a second burial near the church of Our Lady of the Mount. The Viceroy of Goa subsequently had the body returned to Goa in 1554 when it was still found to be in an extraordinary state of preservation. The miraculous body has been venerated ever since by Catholics from all over the world

For Roman Catholics St Francis Xavier's remains form the principal spiritual treasure of the territory. In 1613 the body of St Francis was brought from the College of St Paul in Velha Goa (Old Goa) where it had remained on being returned to Goa in 1554, and placed in the Professed House of Bom Jesus. It was moved into the Church in 1622 after his canonization, and to its present chapel in 1655 where it has remained ever since. St Francis was beautified in 1619 and declared a saint by Pope Gregory XV in 1622. In 1964 Pope Pius XII raised the church to a minor basilica.

Bom Jesus

state. The church, however, was allowed to continue services.

The church was originally lime plastered like the others but this was removed in 1956 to reveal the laterite base. The granite decorative elements have always been unadorned. The façade is the richest in Goa and also the least Goan in character. There are no flanking towers. It appears that the church was modelled on the earlier but now destroyed church of St Paul which in turn was based on the Gesu, the mother church in Rome. There is only one tower in the building and that is placed at the east end, giving it a more Italian look. On the pediment of the façade is a tablet with IHS (Jesus in Greek or *Iaeus Hominum Salvator*). Apart from the elaborate gilded altars, and the twisted Bernini columns, the interior of the church is very simple.

The **Tomb of St Francis Xavier** (1696) was the gift of one of the last of the Medicis, Cosimo III, the Grand Duke of Tuscany, and was carved by the Florentine sculptor Giovanni Batista Foggini. It took 10 years to complete. It comprises three tiers of marble and jasper, the upper tier having panels depicting scenes from the saint's life. The casket containing his remains is silver and has three locks, the keys being held by the Governor, the Archbishop and Convent Administrator.

Exposition Initially after his canonization, St Francis' body was exposed for viewing on each anniversary of his death but this ceased in 1707. Since then only a few special private expositions were held until 1752 when it was again put in public view to dispel rumours that the Jesuits had removed the body. Since 1859, every 10 to 12 years on the anniversary of the saint's death, the holy relics are displayed. In 1953 it was decided that pilgrims should no longer touch the fragile relics so they were placed in a crystal urn. The last exposition was for 6 weeks between November 1994 and January 1995 and the next is scheduled for January 2005. To enable easier viewing by the vast numbers who attend each exposition, the relics are taken to the Se Cathedral during this period. The *Feast Day* is on 3 December.

The body of St Francis has suffered much over the years and has been gradually reduced by the removal of various parts. Soon after his death a "small portion of the knee had been removed to show the captain of the ship on which his body was being carried" its unusually fresh condition. The neck had been broken in the Malaccas by placing the body in a grave which was too short. One devotee is reputed to have bitten off a toe in 1554 and carried it to Lisbon as a relic where it is still supposed to be kept by her family. Part of the arm was sent to Rome in 1615 where it is kept in the Gesu church. Part of the right hand was sent to the Jesuits in Japan in 1619. In 1890 a toe fell off and is displayed in an urn in the Sacristy of the Basilica.

Professed House

Next to the church and connected with it, is the Professed House for Jesuit fathers, a handsome 2-storey building with a typically Mediterranean open courtyard garden. It was built of plaster-coated laterite in 1589, despite much local opposition to the Jesuits. After a fire in 1633 destroyed it, it was only partially rebuilt. It now houses a few Jesuit fathers who run a small college. There is a modern **art gallery** next to the church.

❖ Se Cathedral

Across the square, the Se Cathedral is dedicated to St Catherine on whose day (25 November) Goa was recaptured by Afonso de Albuquerque. The largest church in Old Goa, it is possibly the largest in Asia with a barrel vaulted

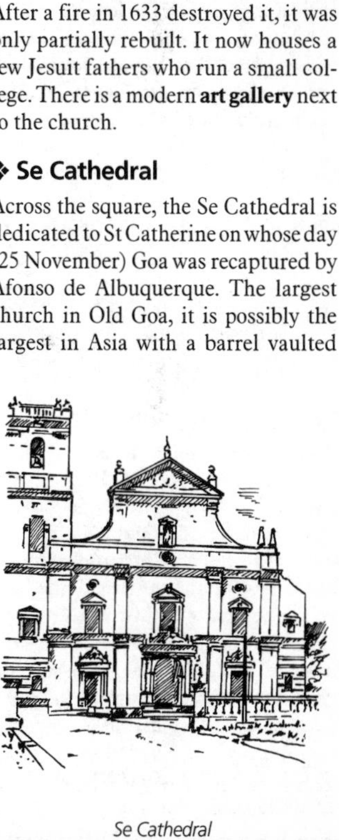

Se Cathedral

ceiling. Built by the Dominicans between 1562-1623 in a Tuscan style on the exterior and Corinthian inside, the main façade faces east with the characteristic twin towers, one of which collapsed in 1776 when it was struck by lightning. The remaining one contains 5 bells including the Golden Bell (rung 0530, the 'Mid-day' Angelus at 1230 and 1830), cast in Cuncolim in 1652. The vast interior is divided into a nave and two side aisles. To your right is the granite baptismal font. On each side of the church are four chapels along the aisles: on the right to St Anthony, St Bernard, The Cross of Miracles and the Holy Spirit, and on the left, starting at the entrance, to Our Lady of Virtues, St Sebastian, The Blessed Sacrament and Our Lady of Life. The main altar is superbly gilded and painted with 6 further altars in the transept. The marble top table in front of the main altar has been used for the exposition of the relics of St Francis Xavier since 1955 in order that the large crowds could be more easily accommodated here. The **Art Gallery** opens 0900-1230 (1030 on Sunday), 1500-1830, closed Friday and during services. Entry free.

Palace of the Inquisition

Southwest of the Cathedral's front door are the ruins of the Palace of the Inquisition. Over 16,000 cases were heard between 1561 and 1774. The Inquisition was finally suppressed in 1814. Beneath the hall were dungeons. In the heyday of Old Goa this was the town centre. Moving back towards the main thoroughfare you can see two churches and a museum in the same complex as the Cathedral.

❖ Church and Convent of St Francis of Assisi

This is a broad vault of a church with two octagonal towers. The floor is paved with tombstones and the walls around the High Altar are decorated with paintings on wood depicting scenes from St Francis' life. The convent was begun by Franciscan friars in 1517, and later restored 1762-5. The style is Portuguese Gothic.

❖ Archaeological Museum and Portrait Gallery

Convent of St Francis of Assisi, T 286133 (1000-1700, closed Sunday). Entry free. The collection of sculptures covers the period from before the arrival of the Portuguese. Many date from the 12th-13th centuries when Goa came under the rule of the Kadamba Dynasty. The exhibits include 'hero stones' commemorating naval battles and 'sati stones' (marking the practice of widow burning). There is also a fine collection of portraits of Portuguese Governors on the 1st floor which provides an interesting study in the evolution of court dress.

St Catherine's Chapel

The chapel was built on the orders of Albuquerque as an act of gratitude at having beaten the forces of Bijapur in 1510. The original church was built of mud and thatch, replaced 2 years later by a stone chapel which in 1539 became the Cathedral. Extended, possibly in 1550 (according to the inscription on the wall), and considerably renovated more recently in 1952, the lime plaster of the simple façade sets off the exposed laterite sections.

Arch of the Viceroys (Ribeira dos Viceroys)

To the northeast of the Cathedral on the road towards the Mandovi River is the arch to commemorate the centenary of Vasco da Gama's discovery of the sea route to India. It was built at the end of the 16th century by his

Arch of the Viceroys

great-grandson, Francisco da Gama who was Viceroy from 1597 to 1600. Built of laterite blocks, it is faced with green granite on the side approached from the river. This was the main gateway to the seat of power and on his arrival by ship, each new viceroy would be handed the keys and enter through this ceremonial archway before taking office. The statue of Vasco da Gama above the arch was originally surmounted by a gilded statue of St Catherine, the patron saint of the city. The latter, however, was removed during the restoration in 1954 (now placed near the Museum), together with the remains of a vaulted room which carried frescoes recording the wars fought by the Portuguese in India. A strange pair of figures appears on the back of the arch. A lady with a sword and book (possibly the Bible) stands above a lying figure of a man (a non-believer) in an awkward posture with his head resting uncomfortably on a bent arm.

❖ Church of St Cajetan (Caetano)

To the east of the arch lies the splendid domed Baroque Convent and Church of St Cajetan. A band of Italian friars of the Theatine order were sent to Golconda near Hyderabad on India's Deccan plateau by Pope Urban III to spread the Gospel but since they were not welcomed there, they moved to Goa to settle, later acquiring land to build this church around 1661. Shaped like a Greek cross, the church was partly modelled on St Peter's in Rome.

The façade with two belfries and tall Corinthian columns has four niches with figures of apostles alongside the three doorways. Inside, four enormous piers decorated with pilasters (one with a carved wooden pulpit), support the high dome above the drum, and create the aisles forming the cross. This is the last remaining domed church in Goa (others which appear domed are not in reality). The vaulted ceiling has coffered floral decoration.

The main altar dedicated to Our Lady of Divine Providence has a free standing reredos which is elaborately decorated (as are the other six side altars) with gilded angels, cherubs, pilasters and scrolls while this rises to shafts of light beneath a golden crown. The oil paintings illustrate the life of St Cajetan whose altar is the larger one on the right. The small niches with the attractive shell motif above, along the walls have carved wooden statues of saints. In the centre, under the dome is a curious platform which is thought to cover a 'well' which may have belonged to a Hindu temple on this site. Some think the device was incorporated into the building to provide the massive

Convent of St Cajetan

structure greater stability in difficult soil conditions!

The crypt below the main altar where the Italian friars were buried, has some sealed lead caskets containing, it is believed, the embalmed bodies of senior Portuguese officials who never returned home.

Beyond is the **Gate of the Adil Shah Palace** comprising a lintel supported on moulded pillars mounted on a plinth, probably built by Sabaji, the ruler of Goa before the Muslim conquest of 1471. The now ruined palace was occupied by Adil Shahi sultans of Bijapur who occupied Goa before the arrival of the Portuguese in 1510. It became the Palace of the Viceroys from 1554 to 1695.

DIVAR ISLAND *M4A3*

The island is approached by ferry from the Old Goa jetty (Arch of the Viceroys) to the south, or the Naroa ferry to the northeast. Divar comprised the 4 villages of Navelim, Goltim, Malar and Naroa.

Once an important Hindu pilgrimage place, a **Ganesh temple** stood on a hill at Navelim in the centre of the island. Afonso de Albuquerque was not thought of as a destroyer of Hindu temples in order to have churches built in the new Portuguese territory (most of the temples in Ilhas were destroyed after his death between 1540 and 1541). The Ganesh Temple, however, was possibly the only exception since documents record the presence of the original Church of Our Lady on the hill which the ailing Albuquerque saw from his ship before he died in 1515.

This is where **Nossa Senhora de Piedade** (Our Lady of Piety), which replaced the the second church to Our Lady of Divar, now stands (the original chapel had been rebuilt and renamed Our Lady of Piety in 1625). There are good views from this hilltop site. The present church dates from 1699-1724 and is ascribed to Fr Frias, a writer and 'architect'. The church with its 'groined' vault with plenty of stucco decoration, has a nave but lacks aisles. There are 6 altars and a highly decorative monumental pulpit. At the top of the main alter is a lovely granite Piet'a set in a niche. The fine interior has been restored, its restrained baroque plaster decoration being highlighted in pastel colours.

The insignificant looking cemetery chapel to the south has an interesting heavily carved stone ceiling and two perforated windows in stone which almost certainly belonged to the Ganesh temple; if locked, ask the resident priest to open it for you. The Ganesh image was initially taken to Khandepar (Ponda), then to Naroa (Bicholim) and finally to its present location in **Candola** in Ponda (see page 120.)

The other place of pilgrimage was the 12th century **Saptakotesvar Temple** to Siva built by the Kadambas which stood in the northeastern corner of the island at Old **Naroa** but was ransacked by Muslim invaders in the mid-14th century. However, like the Ganesh image and many other Hindu deities within Goa, the faceted *dharalinga* made out of 5 metals (*pancha dhatu*) – gold, silver, bronze, copper and iron – was hidden in a field and reinstalled nearby by a Vijayanagar king in 1391. Again, a wave of Portuguese temple destruction around 1540 saw the end of the new temple. The remains of the temple tank can be seen near the small Portuguese Chapel of **Our Lady of Candelaria** (1563) which originally incorporated the ruins of the Siva temple in its unusual circular structure, which was later extended on either side. The Siva linga was subsequently smuggled across the river to Bicholim taluka to be placed in a rock-cut sanctuary in a village which adopted the old name **Naroa** (Narve). The popular pilgrimage was at the same time transferred to the deity's new location. The Saptakotesvar temple, which still attracts a large crowd of worshippers, was renovated in 1668 under instruction from the Maratha leader Sivaji.

Divar was the scene of 'forced' mass baptisms of Hindu islanders to Christianity in 1560 by the Portuguese. Many of the 1,510 new converts continued to make the pilgrimage to the rehoused deity in Naroa in spite of strong attempts by the Portuguese to stop the practice.

The Archaeological Museum in Old Goa has some sections from the two Divar temples in its collection. Some temple parts found their way into Old Goa as in the New Pillory which was put up at the end of the 17th century at the foot of the hill of the Cross of Miracles on the Neura road. Inscriptions discovered by Dr PP Shirodkar in 1983 suggest that the parts probably came from the Saptakotesvar Siva Temple from Divar (1391). A part of the temple's *deepstambha* (which shows places for lighting oil lamps) is under the font in the Church of St Francis of Assisi. The lower section of the lamp tower is at the Archaeological Museum there.

The *Bonderdam Feast*, to mark the harvest is held on the island at Goltim on the last Saturday in August. Before the feast, the villagers process with colourful flags and then hold a mock battle with *fatass* which are imitation guns made out of bamboos.

JUA ISLAND

M4A3

Jua is immediately east of Divar. **Santo Estevam** (St Steven's Church). The rococo style church was built in 1759, again with a false dome and lantern central to its plain façade, flanked by two smaller domes on the towers. The attractive interior shows a lightness of touch; note the fine pulpit and ceiling decorations.

MORMUGAO TALUKA

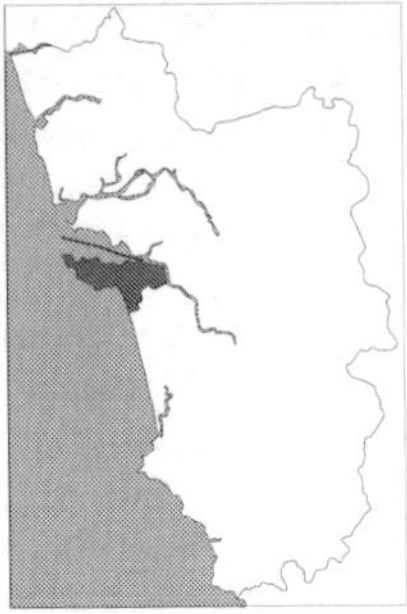

Mormugao taluka, a barren looking laterite projection into the Arabian Sea, is the industrial heart of modern Goa. The passenger terminus of Goa's oldest railway line, the metre gauge line opened in 1888 which connected the state with the interior and the south. The port has grown to become one of the most important on India's west coast. Much of this growth has been a result of the huge increase in iron ore exports from interior Goa, and the ore carriers still form a steady procession coming in and out of the Zuari estuary. In 1950 the population of the town was still under 12,000, but after the opening of the first mines in 1954 growth was rapid.

Although the agricultural potential of the district has always been limited, its coastal position and good natural harbour periodically tempted the Portuguese to move their capital there. According to Richards, at the end of the 17th century the authorities in Lisbon repeatedly told their Goa based representatives to destroy the buildings in Old Goa and to use the stone for building a new capital in Mormugao then a part of Salcete. The attacks of the Marathas made Old Goa increasingly insecure and steps were taken to shift the capital to the more remote and more readily defensible site of Mormugao along with Aguada, Mormugao was the 'throat' through which Goa breathed. A fort was built on the headland and the building of a town started in 1685. In 1703 the Viceroy actually moved there for a few months, but in 1712 the plan to build a new capital in Mormugao was formally abandoned.

The rocky headland and the plateau inland saw little subsequent development until after Independence. The harbour became an important port for the Indian Navy who then developed Dabolim airport on the upland immediately above it. Today that has become the international airport through which all Goa's charter flights arrive, although the airport is still under the control of the Navy and charter flights are only allowed to use it on 4 days a week. A new civilian airport is planned in north Goa.

Today, Vasco da Gama has become Goa's largest town with a population growth of up to 10% a year. Industrial estates have developed rapidly on the plateau above the town and a new export zone at Sancoale is coming into operation. The once barren peninsula is rapidly being converted into the commercial core of the state and over 80% of the population lives in its towns rather than depending on agriculture.

Vasco da Gama

30 km from Panaji; *STD Code* 0834, Mormugao *Population* 91,300

Vasco da Gama (**Vasco**, in short) is the railway terminus of the Central Goa branch line of the South Central Railway. The broad gauge conversion was completed in summer 1997. It has nothing to really offer the tourist, being too industrialised and the surrounding area too bleak.

THE HEADLAND AREA *M4C1*

Mormugao (Marmagoa), the state's principal commercial port is 4 km northwest (as is Dabolim airport, to the southeast). A kilometre before Mormugao is **Pilot Point**, at the base of the ruined fort, which offers excellent views over the harbour, the sea, the Zuari River and Dona Paula beach.

Virtually nothing remains of **Mormugao Fort** on the south headland of Mormugao Bay, and what does is hidden by the industrial development that has taken its place.

Hansa Beach, 4 km, in the Naval area, is safe for swimming (motorcycle taxis charge Rs 15). If you walk, in a cove halfway between the two is a freshwater spring, Suravali.

Warning

Part of Baina Beach, 2 km from Vasco, is the red light district. It is notified as a high risk area for AIDS.

BOGMALO *M4C1*

Bogmalo, the nearest beach to the airport (4 km, and a 10 minutes drive away) – is small, palm fringed and attractive, yet it is sparsely visited. It backs onto the bald upland area of Mormugao peninsula which presents a stark contrast. It is a good base for visiting the rest of Goa or further afield though it can get overrun by sailors when foreign ships are berthed at Mormugao but this is relatively rare. There are plenty of beachside cafés and bars offering excellent value. The ones near *Park Plaza* are dearer but do excellent seafood. *Joet's* is recommended: "very friendly, sun beds on the beach and a couple of hammocks among the palms". There are also numerous gift shops by the beach. Some offer good quality, made-to-measure cotton and silk jackets and shirts at reasonable prices. Try the *Park Plaza* for watersports. A taxi to Vasco costs around Rs 100; half-day hire (eg Panaji and Mapusa market), Rs 600. **NB** For accommodation, see under local information below.

Santra Beach, further south, can be reached by going through the village behind the *Park Plaza*. Boat trips to two small islands are negotiable with local fishermen; costs about Rs 300/boat, which can be shared by a group.

INLAND FROM VASCO

Verna *M4C3*

Verna (the 'Place of fresh air') is actually in Salcete, to the east of the Mormugao taluka. It is surrounded by 7 springs with special healing properties.

Kesarval Springs

Travelling south from Cortalim, immediately north of Verna and just off the NH17, are the Kesarval springs. Named from Quensra-vodd, the springs have medicinal properties and are no longer a 'natural' remote watering place but are very popular with Goans as a picnic spot. From the large car park paths lead past several enclosures through the gently sloping wooded hillside. The covered resting areas for picnics are near the entrance. The path to the springs leads down a short but steep slope into a vertical walled grotto where bathers can stand under the trickling spring water. There is an extraordinary change in the atmosphere from the hot open plateau to the moist, cooler but lush semi-enclosed area surrounding the springs themselves. There is a small hotel and restaurant where you turn off the NH17.

LOCAL INFORMATION

Festivals

The *Vasco Saptaha* (Week) starts on 29 July 1998 with non-stop singing of hymns. Floats showing scenes from legends are taken down the streets in procession.

Luxury hotel at Bogmalo

AL-A *Sarovar Park Plaza Beach Resort* (was *Bogmalo Beach*), T 513291, F 512510, 121 rooms with sea view, 60s style resort hotel (Goa's only multi-storey beach hotel, built before planning regulations), palm-shaded poolside, some watersports, ayurvedic massage therapy, mainly catering for package tourists.

Mid-range hotels: Vasco

C *La Paz Gardens*, Swatantra Path, T 512238, F 513302, 72 immaculate a/c rooms, some around internal 'atrium' or courtyard, very good a/c restaurants including Indian, Chinese, fast food with wide choice, also pleasant bar, free transport to airport and beach, highly recommended.

D *Bismarck*, behind Auto Service, T 512277, 22 clean a/c rooms on 3 floors, some with bath tubs or balcony, small pool and terrace at back with an open-air restaurant, recommended; **D** *Gladstone*, FL Gomes Rd, near the Bus Stand, T 514444, F 510510, 23 rooms, some a/c, restaurant, bar.

D-E *Annapurna*, D Deshpande Rd, T 513735, 33 clean rooms with bath, good veg food; **D-E** *Citadel*, near the Tourist Hotel, Jose Vaz Rd, T 512222, F 513036, 42 comfortable rooms, half a/c, restaurant, bar, good value; **D-E** *Maharaja*, FL Gomes Rd, opposite Hindustan Petroleum, T 513075, F 512559, 40 good, clean rooms, 18 a/c, Gujarati *thalis*, bar, not ideally placed; **D-E** *Rukmini*, D Deshpande Rd, near the MPT Hall, T 512350, good value a/c rooms, restaurant; **D-E** *Tourist Hotel*, off Swatantra Path, T 513119, 64 rooms, some a/c, some 4-6 beds, limited menu canteen (can be noisy), Tourist Office.

Mid-range hotels: Bogmalo

C *Saritas*, T 555965, on the beach, 8 clean new rooms with bath, popular restaurant; **C-D** *Joet's Guest House*, right on the beach, T 555036, 12 small airy rooms with shower, good seafood restaurant, mainly packages.

D *Vinny's Holiday Resort*, overlooking Bay, 1 km uphill from beach, T 555170, 16 spotless rooms, 2 **C** a/c, restaurant, bar, very welcoming family, excellent service, peaceful, regular buses to beach, highly recommended.

Budget hotels

Vasco **E** *Westend*, D Deshpande Rd, T 511574, 25 rooms, some a/c, restaurant, bar. **F** *Rebelo*, opposite Kadamba (new) Bus Stand, on left on entering town, Mundvel, T 512620, 30 rooms.

Bogmalo **E** *El Mar*, set back from the beach, 6 large, basic rooms with shower, seafood available; **E** *Monalise Ashiyana Guest House*, Balli Chali, T 513347.

Places to eat

Adarsh, Swatantra Path, 100m south of railway station, does excellent *masala dosa*, Rs 8; *Ananta* near the Citadel Hotel, Jose Vaz Rd, recommended; *Leads* 300m from station, Indian, Goan, Chinese, no bar but good value; ***Nanking*** off Swatantra Path, good value authentic Chinese.

Shopping
Swatantra Path is the main shopping street. Handicrafts and local wood carvings are sold at shops at the north end; ***Government Emporium*** is at the Tourist Hotel.

Long distance travel
Air
For services from Dabolim airport (4 km), T 512788, see under Panaji above.

Train
Reservations, T 512833. **NB** Broad gauge conversion for the line between **Londa** in Karnataka and **Vasco** was completed in 1997 and now connects with **Belgaum**, **Bangalore**, **Delhi via Agra**, and with **Hospet (for Hampi)** among others.

From **Vasco** to **Londa**: by *Goa Exp 2779*, dep 1330, arr 1740; by *Vasco Bangalore Exp 7310,* dep 2110, arr 0120; both 4¼ hours.

To **Bangalore**: by *Vasco Bangalore Exp 7310,* dep 2110, arr 1240, 15½ hours.

To **Delhi (Nizamuddin)**: *Goa Exp 2779,* dep

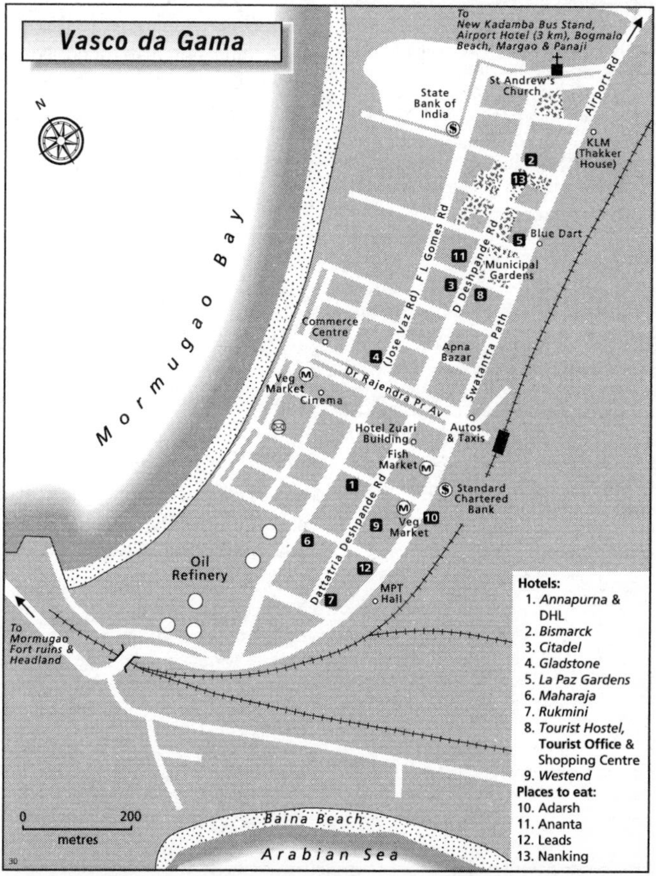

1330, arr 0645 (after 2 nights), 41¾ hours.
To **Hospet (for Hampi)**: *Amravati Exp 7226*, dep 0505 arr 1525, 10¼ hours.
To **Pune** *Goa Exp 2779*, dep 1330, arr 0400, 15½ hours.

Local trains stop at: **Dabolim** (for the airport and Bogmalo), **Cansaulim**, **Seraulim**, **Majorda** (for the beach), **Margao** (for Colva, Benaulim and the southern beaches), **Chandorgoa**, **Sanvordem**, **Calem**, **Colem (Kolamb)**, **Dudhsagar** (for the waterfalls), **Sonauli** and **Caranzol**.

Road

Bus: Kadmaba Bus Stand is 3 km northeast of town; Minibus transfer to town square. Buses to Panaji (every 5 mins) and Margao (every 5-10 mins), Rs 7. Long Distance to **Bangalore** via Hubli: 1645 (15 hours), Rs 230; **Hospet**: 1130 (10 hours) Rs 90; **Hubli** 0745 (6 hours) Rs 60; **Mangalore**: 0730 (10 hours) Rs 140; **Mumbai**: 1445 (16 hours), Rs 230. **NB** Check times in advance.

Taxi to/from Londa, about Rs 1,400.

Sea

From Mormugao, to Dona Paula, passenger launch, Rs 4.

Directory

Hospitals & medical services *Salgaocar Medical Research Centre*, T 512524; *Cottage Hospital*, Chicalim (east of Vasco), T 513864.

Post & telecommunications **Courier**: *Blue Dart*, T 512748; *DHL*, Room 104, Hotel Annapurna, T 513745; *Skypak*, T 512203.

Tour companies & travel agents *Gopi Tours*, 4 Adarsh Building, Swatantra Path, T 514051; *Merces Travels*, 6 Vasco Tower, T 512268; *Travel Corporation of India*, Bismark Hotel, T 512277.

Tourist offices At Tourist Hotel, T 512673.

Useful numbers **Ambulance**: T 512768. **Fire**: T 513840. **Police**: T 512304.

Ponda and the Hindu heartland

PONDA is one of the smallest of Goa's talukas, it is also one of the richest in terms of its Hindu religious architecture. Within 5 km of Ponda town centre are some of Goa's most important temples, including the Shri Shantadurga Temple Quela, and the Nagesh Temple near Bandora.

But it is also home to spice gardens and wonderfully scenic views from the low hills over the sweeping rivers. The Bondla Sanctuary in the east of the taluka, small though it is (and disappointing in terms of its wildlife), is a reminder of the once forest-rich environment typical of the foothills of the Western Ghats.

Today, the drive from Old Goa to Ponda (Rs 7) goes through a prosperous agricultural region with a mixture of beautiful rice paddies on the valley bottoms and a wide variety of tropical palms – coconut and areca being particularly striking.

PONDA TALUKA

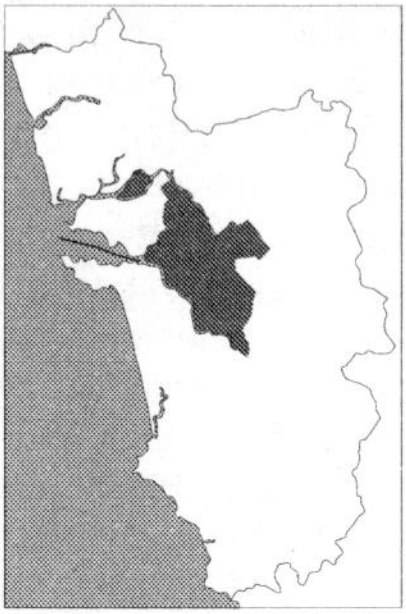

Ponda taluka, officially regarded as in North Goa, is actually right in the centre of the state.

The Zuari, for most of its short course a broad languid and apparently tranquil river, was for 200 years a critically important barrier between the Christianized Old Conquests and the Hindu east. Forming Ponda's southwestern border with Salcete and Mormugao, Hindus fled the Inquisition to the comparative safety across the river, taking some of their most important idols with them. The river provided security.

Before the arrival of the Portuguese, Ponda had been regarded as an area of little use because it had none of the resources which made the coastal region of Tiswadi so well off, and its relative poverty had resulted in an almost total absence of stone built temples. The Zuari provided the defensive moat behind which the unique Hindu temples of contemporary Goa could be established.

Yet the resurgence of Hindusim is not without irony, for during the first two centuries of Portuguese rule in the Old Conquests, Ponda was ruled by the Muslim king of Bijapur. The district had come under Portuguese attack in the first wave of settlement led by Albuquerque. However, the family of Adil Shah, Sultan of Bijapur, fought back and quickly re-took the town and district. They built the Safa Mosque, which today is one of the relatively few significant Muslim buildings left in Goa. The Muslims were defeated by the Maratha Hindu leader Sivaji and Ponda was not re-incorporated into Portuguese Goa until it was ceded by the Hindu King of Sunda in 1763. By this time the Portuguese were less inclined to interfere with local custom and religious belief, and both Muslim and Hindu places of worship were respected.

If Ponda's history has been significantly shaped by the security afforded by the Zuari and the Cumbarjua Creek to its west, it is Goa's other major river, the Mandovi, which separates it from the rapidly industrializing northern district of Bicholim, with its massive open cast iron ores workings. Ponda too now has its share of iron ore and industrial development, as the environmentally controversial plants at Siroda in the south demonstrate.

Its own development has been increased by its newly strategic location on the National Highway, the main route between Panaji and Belgaum. Yet despite the opening of a new bridge across the Zuari at Borim which now gives a direct road link to Margao and the south, many parts of the district are relatively isolated and Ponda also still has extensive areas of almost untouched forest.

PONDA M5B2

Phondya, *Population* 14,700; *STD Code* 0834

Once a centre of culture, music, drama and poetry, the area around the town, with its group of important Hindu temples, was known as *Antruz Mahal*.

Ponda town has little of interest. It has become an important transport intersection, where the main road from Margao via Borim meets the East-West National Highway 4A. Although river transport remains very important, the Zuari and the Mandovi both being vital arteries for the transport of iron ore, the nearby old river port of Durbhat has lost some of its signifiance as road transport has improved.

The Zuari Bridge at Cortalim in Mormugao has been restricted to light vehicles and a ferry service has been re-introduced at that point. If the bridge closes for repairs then passing through Ponda will become a necessary part of the road journey for all routes between north and south Goa.

Places of interest

The **Safa Mosque** (Shahouri Masjid) The Safa Mosque, the largest of 26 mosques in Goa, was built by Ibrahim 'Ali' Adil Shah in 1560. It has a simple rectangular chamber on a low plinth, with a pointed pitched roof, very much in the local architectural style, but the arches are distinctly Bijapuri. Built of laterite, the lower tier has been quite badly eroded. On the south side is a tank for ritual cleansing which has *meherab* designs. The large gardens and fountains here were destroyed during Portuguese rule. Today the mosque is attractively set off by the low rising forest covered hills in the background.

Mid-range hotels

D *Menino*, 100m east of Bus Stand junction, 1st floor, T 313146, F 315026, 20 rooms, some a/c, pleasant, comfortable, good restaurant, totally rebuilt, now an impressive modern hotel, good value. At **Farmagudi**, to the north: **D** *Atish*, T 3132250, F 313239, has 40 comfortable rooms, some a/c.

Places to eat

Good a/c restaurant at the *Menino* Hotel, on the 1st floor with pleasant decor, generous main courses (Rs 60), popular, good service, clean toilet; ***Kirti***, Nirankal Rd, 2 km east of centre, simple but clean a/c room upstairs, cheap, reasonable food.

Directory

Deputy Conservator of Forests (North): T 312095. **Hospital**: T 312115.

HINDU TEMPLES NEAR PONDA

FARMAGUDI M5B2

North of Ponda, as you approach Farmagudi off the NH17, there is a new **Ganesh temple** on the left, opposite a statue of Sivaji which commemorates the Maratha leader's association with the fort. The stone image of Gopal Ganapati was discovered by herdsmen while grazing cattle near the hill and later installed in a small shrine with a thached roof. The temple built by late Shri D Bandodkar, the first Chief Minister of Goa, has the idol, consecrated on April 24, 1966. It is a good specimen of Indian temple architecture synthesizing both ancient and modern styles.

Travel tip

There are seven Hindu temples within 5 km of the centre of Ponda. There is reasonable accommodation in the town and at Farmagudi outside which could be used as an overnight base from which to visit the temples and some of the sites further east. It is also possible to visit two or three of the sights in a day trip from either the northern or the southern beaches.

Ponda fort The fort was built by the Adil Shahi rulers and was destroyed by the Portuguese in 1549. It lay in ruins for over a hundred years before Shivaji conquered the town in 1675 and rebuilt it. The Portuguese Viceroy attempted to re-take it in October 1683 but quickly withdrew, afraid to take on the Maratha King Sambhaji who suddenly appeared with his vast army. The episode is commemorated in Farmagudi.

VELINGA *M5B1*

Goa's only temple to the Lakshmi-Narasimha or Lakshmi-Narayana, Vishnu's fourth *avatar*, is just north of Farmagudi. The small half man-half lion image was originally in a temple in Sancoale (Salcete) which was burnt down and destroyed by the Diogo Rodrigues, the Captain of Rachol Fort in 1567 (who had by then destroyed temples in 58 villages and a mosque in Mormugao). The **Shantadurga temple** shared a similar fate.

The present **Lakshmi-Narasimha Temple** dates from the 18th century and is fairly typical in style though the tower and dome over the sanctuary is somewhat Islamic. Inside there are well-carved wooden pillars in the *mandapa* and elaborate silver work on the screen and shrine. The large spring-fed temple tank has steps down to the water on each side and is enclosed by a niched wall. A tall cosmic pillar with rings stands in the courtyard.

❖ MARDOL *M5B1*

❖ Shri Mangesh Temple

To the northwest of Ponda, on the NH17 leading to Old Goa, the 18th century Sri Mangesh Temple, set on a wooded hill at Priol, is sometimes described as the most important Hindu temple in Goa.

The Mangesh linga was originally in an ancient temple in Kushatali (Cortalim in Salcete taluka) across the river. However, after the Inquisition began in 1561, soldiers set out to destroy Hindu temples throughout Salcete and the deity was carried across the river to Priol. The devotee who saved the linga, named Mukto, has a shrine to his memory in the temple complex. The main linga was initially placed in a small shrine until in the mid-18th century an influential Hindu was able to acquire an estate for the present impressive temple complex. When the Portuguese regained control they exercised a far more liberal policy towards the Hindus and Muslims. Today the temple is supported by a large resident community who serve its various functions.

The temple complex is architecturally typical of the highly distinctive Goan Hindu temple style. It has seen many additions and alterations through the years including pilgrims'

Shri Mangesh – Siva in Goa

The origin of the sanctity of all Hindu sacred sites is explained in mythical stories. Shri Mangesh is no exception. Hall recounts that in one of the stories explaining the origin of the Shri Mangesh temple. Siva had staked everything he posessed on a game of dice against Parvati and lost. He had to leave his home on Mount Kailasa and wandered south and chanced upon a spot in Goa, near Kushatali (present day Cortalim), where he remained to meditate. When Parvati came in search and was lost in a forest she was faced with a fierce tiger and called out for help to her husband. Crying out in her confusion to "Mam Girisha!" which gave rise to yet another name for Siva. The linga which was found in Kushatali was housed in a small temple to Shri Mangesh there.

Shri Mangesh Temple

restrooms, but not always for the better. Sadly the *nagarkhana* (drum tower) over the arched gate which earlier had a pleasing red-tiled pitched roof now is a far poorer structure.

Although there is an arched entrance to the site near the main road, about 1 km from the temple itself, a lane by-passes this arch and leads up to the car park. Pilgrims walk up the path to the drum tower entrance. The farm land of the estate on which the temple depends provides a beautiful setting. Note the attractive temple tank on the left as you approach which is one of the oldest parts of the site. You can get a good view of the temple with its tank in the foreground by climbing the wall into the coconut grove. The tank is surrounded by striking, carefully pointed (mortared) laterite blocks, and on the higher ground behind it rises the lamp tower.

You enter the temple through an arch into the wide open courtyard. The 7-storeyed octagonal *deepmal* or *deepstambha* immediately in front of you, reputed to be

Oracles of Shri Mangesh

The Shri Mangesh temple was famous as a centre for various oracles (fortune tellers). Gomes Pereira records that one such oracle specialised in interpeting cases of crime. He would sit quietly shuffling grains of rice, which he would continue to do when any client came to seek his help in solving a crime. Without asking any questions or being told anything about the case he would simply describe the nature of the crime and then outline the chief characteristics of the perpetrator. Unlike other clairvoyants he never went into a trance but remained conscious and quiet throughout.

Other oracles in the temple practised a form of self-hypnosis called "*bhar*", and clairvoyancy, when dampened petals or leaves were attached to the statue of the village deity, leaves being fixed at 49 pre-determined points. As they dried some fell off, and the question asked by the enquirer is answered by the pattern of the remaining leaves. These practices are still carried out.

the most famous lamp tower in Goa, is a typically stunning white, but around its base are colourful little 'primitif' painted images, red and yellow on a blue background. Lamps are placed in the niches at festivals. The sacred *tulsi vrindavan* (basil enclosure) which is often seen in front of a Hindu home, stands nearby. The highest tower (here 2-storeyed) with an octagonal drum topped by a dome is over the sanctum while the octagonal entrance hall and the two side entrances here too each have dome above. The *mandapa* (assembly hall), has the typical red tiled steeply pitched roof. At the entrance to the shrine itself, where you leave your shoes, is a beautifully carved wooden door. 19th century Belgian glass chandeliers hang from the ceiling of the main hall, usually crowded with pilgrims who make offerings of flowers and coconut bought at the entrance. The *nandi* (Siva's bull) is present, as are the silver *dwarpalas* (guardian deities) and the additional shrines to Parvati and Ganesh. The image of the deity is housed behind a highly decorated silver screen. Inside, it has eight white pillars, approximately 2.5m high, supporting broad arches. The cusped arches above the windows illustrate a Muslim architectural influence.

As in nearly all major temples there are several subsidiary temples or "affiliated deities" – *parivar devtas*. On either side of the screen at the far end of the main temple are shrines to Ganesh on the right and Bhagavati (Parvati) on the left, while Devasharma is near the main temple in the courtyard. Nearby is a *nandi* which is particularly worshipped by the clan of Gaud Saraswat Brahmins who are the temple's *mahajans* (trustees). There are numerous other minor shrines. Behind the main temple are further shrines. Garlands of flowers for offering at entrances are Rs 5. Huge temple cars shelter to the northwest of the temple.

The complex, with its *agrashalas* (Pilgrims' hostel), administrative offices and other rooms set aside for religious ceremonies, is representative of Goan Hindu temple worship.

During *Mangesh Jatra* (11 February in 1998) the *rath* (temple car) with Shri Mangesh is pulled by crowds of attendants.

The Mahalsa Narayani Temple

is 2 km from Shri Mangesh. The deity, originally housed in a "fabulous" temple at Verna in Salcete taluka, was rescued and taken to Mardol around the same time as the Sivalinga of Shri Mangesh found a home nearby. Here *Mahalsa* is a Goan form of Vishnu's consort Lakshmi or according to some, his female form *Mohini* (from the story of the battle between the *Devas* and *Asuras*).

You enter the temple complex through the arch under the *nagarkhana* (drum room). There is a 7-storeyed *deepstambha* and in addition a tall brass Garuda pillar which rests on the back of a turtle (as in Nepal). The half human-half eagle *Garuda*, Vishnu's vehicle, sits on top. The pillar acts as a second lamp tower. The latest renovation and extension to the temple complex was completed in 1995. The improved paving in marble is impressive.

The new *mandapa* (columned hall) is of concrete, its severity hidden somewhat under the red tiling, finely carved columns and a series of brightly painted carvings of the 10 *avatars* (incarnations) of Vishnu (see page 62). The unusual dome above the sanctuary is particularly elegant.

The present *tulsi vrindavana* (basil enclosure), however, sadly replaces an earlier one of massive proportions. The original, which many would argue was worth restoring and preserving, was a fine example of its type, complete with arched niches, columns and balustrade, representing the influence of church architecture in the temple grounds. The large wooden *ratha* (temple car) for the deity can be seen in one corner.

A decorative arched gate at the back leads to the peace and cool of the palm-fringed temple tank. A palanquin procession with the deity marks the *Mardol Jatra* (15-21 February in 1998).

Shri Nagesh Temple lamp tower

BANDORA

M5B1

The ❖ **Nagesh Temple** is 4 km west of Ponda. At Farmagudi junction on the NH17, a fork is signposted to Bandora. A narrow winding lane dips down to the tiny hamlet of Bandora and its temple to Siva as Nagesh (God of Serpents).

The temple's origin can be established at 1413 by an inscribed tablet here though the building was renewed in the 18th century. The temple tank which is well-stocked with carp, is enclosed by white-outlined laterite block wall and surrounded by shady palms. The 5-storey lamp tower near the temple has brightly coloured deities painted in niches just above the base.

The main *mandapa* (assembly hall) has interesting painted woodcarvings illustrating stories from the epics *Ramayana* and *Mahabharata* below the ceiling line, as well as the *Ashtadikpalas*, the 8 Directional Guardians (Indra, Agni, Yama, Nirritti, Varuna,

Vayu, Kubera, Ishana). The principal deity has the usual *nandi* and in addition there are shrines to Ganesh and Laxmi-Narayan and subsidiary shrines with lingas, in the courtyard.

The *Nagesh Jatra* (15 November 1997, 5 November 1998) is celebrated at full moon to commemorate Siva's victory.

South of the Nagesh Temple, the **Mahalakshmi Temple** lies in a valley below the road and is thought to be the original form of the deity of the Shakti cult. Mahalakshmi was worshipped by the Silaharas (chieftains of the Rashtrakutas, 750-1030 AD) and the early Kadamba Kings. The sanctuary has an octagonal tower and dome while the side entrances have shallow domes. The stone slab with the Marathi inscription dating from 1413 on the front of the Nagesh Temple refers to a temple to Mahalakshmi at Bandora. The *sabhamandap* has an impressive gallery of 22 wooden images of Vishnu. The image wears a linga in her head dress, and is considered a peaceful form of Devi.

QUELA

M5B1

Just 3 km southwest from Ponda's town centre bus stand is one of the largest and most famous of Goa's temples dedicated to ❖ **Shri Shantadurga** (1738), the wife of Siva as the Goddess of Peace. The form of Durga was so named because at the request of Brahma she mediated in a great quarrel between Siva (her husband) and Vishnu, and brought back peace in the Universe. Hence, in the sanctuary she stands between the two other deities.

The temple is set in a picturesque forest clearing on a hillside at Quela (Kavale) and was erected around 1738 by Shahu, a grandson of Sivaji, the great Maratha ruler of the West Deccan. The deity. originally from Quelossim (or Quela) had been taken to Ponda 200 years earlier.

Steps lead up to the temple complex which has a very large tank cut into the hillside and a spacious courtyard surrounded by the usual pilgrim hostels and administration offices. The temple has a 6-storey *deepstambha* (lamp tower) and subsidiary shrines. The part-gilded *rath* (car) is housed in the compound. The temple, neo-classical in design, has a tall tower over the sanctum. Its 2-storey octagonal drum, topped by a dome which has a lantern on top, is an example of the strong influence of church architecture on Goan temple design. The interior of polished marble is lit by many chandeliers. Beyond the hall is the sanctum where the principal deity of Shantadurga, flanked by Siva and Vishnu, is housed behind a silver screen.

On a specified date at the end of January, a special ceremony is held to honour the *Mhars* or *Harijans* ("outcastes") who are not otherwise expected to enter temple precincts. The following day the temple goes through a "purification ceremony". *Kavale Jatra* (1 February in 1998) is marked by a procession of devotees accompanying the diety in a palanquin.

Shri Sausthan Goud Padacharya Kavale Math named after the historic seer and exponent of the Advaita system of Vedanta, was established in Salcete between Cortalim and Quelossim (now Mormugao). The Math was destroyed in the 1560s during the inquisition and transferred to Golvan and Chinar outside Goa. After 77 years, in the early 17th century, the Math was re-established here in Quela, the village where the Shantadurga deity (which had also originated in Quelossim) had been reinstalled. There is a temple to Vittala at the Math. There is another Math of the same foundation in Sanquelim.

DURBHAT

M5B1

Southwest from Quela, the road towards the river ends at Durbhat which was once a port on the Zuari. Close by, at **Agapur**, an old Madhavdeo complex of three small shrines found on a low hill is described by KD Sadhale and R Desai. The three cell structural complex built out of laterite with a typical water tank is dated to the 11th century. The period of temple building when carpenters-turned-stone masons continued to imitate wooden constructions is well illustrated here, especially since the mortarless masonry structures have not been covered by later plaster work. The stylized lotus-bud domes of the temples are well preserved and are particularly interesting since inside they are in fact *sikhara* style (as found in towers above sanctuaries of northern temples). Unlike later Goan temple domes which appear to have been influenced by Islamic or Christian architecture, here the corbelled dome is a pure Hindu feature. The condition of the shrines suggest that they had been protected from heavy rain by secondary roofing possibly supported originally on attractively carved wooden columns. The present tiled roof over the ancient structure is, of course, a more recent addition.

SIRODA

M5C2

The **Kamakshi Temple** to the south of Ponda taluka is dedicated to a form of Shantadurga. The image, together with the affiliate deities Raieshwar Siva and Lakshmi Narayana, had been rescued from Raia across the Zuari around 1564, when the original temples were destroyed by the Portuguese. The colourful temple with an unusual sanctuary tower with a tiled roof has four kneeling elephants at its base. The red pyramidal tiled roofs on the *mandapas* and atop the *nagarkhana* over the arched entrance gate are also attractively shaped.

The 16th century **Sivnatha Temple** was founded by a holy man 'Sidha'. The deity is taken out in a palanquin for *Siroda Jatra* on 14 December 1997 (3 December 1998).

AROUND PONDA

A visit to a **spice plantation** at **Savoi Verem** in the northeast of Ponda taluka or the **Pascoal** plantation near Tisk can be very enjoyable and informative. Savoi Verem is best reached via Banastari, north of Ponda and east of Panaji. To the northeast of Ponda is Khandepar where 10th-11th century cave sanctuaries have been found, and beyond it the Bondla Sanctuary.

BANASTARI

M5A1

On the National Highway, Banastari 5 km east of Old Goa, is the site of Albuquerque's hard fought battle of 1512. It is remembered for its clandestine "Night Bazar" which would start trading at midnight on Fridays and continue until midday on Saturday, where stolen Portuguese goods as well as fruit and vegetables were brought. Banastari still holds a traditional local bazar.

MARCELA

M5A1

North of Banastari, Marcela has a number of Hindu temples where most of the deities originally come from *Ilhas* in the Old Conquest territory, in particular from Chorao. The village has several 'wedding halls' so is often busy, especially on auspicious dates of the Hindu calendar.

Shri Devkikrishna - Ravalnath, which has the most important deity in the village, celebrates a festival which coincides with the full moon in January when palanquin processions are taken out.

CANDOLA

M5A1

Nearby, has one of two Ganesh temples in the state. The ancient Ganapati image in the **Ganesh Temple** was originally installed in the Kadamba Temple at Navelim (Divar Island) and was moved to a place of safety when Albuquerque ordered a new church to Our Lady of Divar to be built on the site of the Hindu temple. It appears to have been first taken to Khandepar (Ponda), then to Naroa (Bicholim) and finally brought to Candola. Sections of the ancient temple can still be seen in the centre of Divar Island. See page 106.

Today the old Ganesh image which occupies a subsidiary positiion in the sanctuary has been replaced by a new one. The Kalbhairav image which is also here was found in a house in the village where it had been used as a weight for weighing rice on scales; since the block was a little too heavy a corner was knocked out to make it equal to a *maund*!

Other temples in Candola also house deities which had ancient origins. Shri Ravalnatha came from Jua Island (Ilhas, now Tiswadi) and Shri Bhagvati from Aldona (Bardez).

SAVOI VEREM

M5A2

Outside the village, the **Ananta temple** dedicated to Vishnu as *Sheshashahi Ananta*, stands peacefully in a rural setting. The plain white exterior with pitched tiled roofs contrasts with the brightly coloured carvings on the wooden pillars and supporting beams of the *mandapa*. Visitors are allowed to view the principal deity which is carved on a black stone. The reclining Vishnu with the distinctive conical headdress, rests on the coils of the serpent *Ananta* (or *Shesha*) protected by his hood. He is shown in the period intervening between the creation of one world and the next, when a lotus emerges from his navel supporting Brahma the Creator.

The village's ancient Hindu roots is borne out by the 10th century medieval basalt image of Vishnu showing his 10 incarnations (*avatars*) which was found here and is displayed in Old Goa's Archaeological Museum (No 320).

❖SAVOI SPICE PLANTATION

The plantation, 6 km from Savoi, is focused around a large irrigation tank and covers 40 ha. Half of it is over wetland and half on a hillside, making it possible to grow a very large variety of plants and trees. The families employed on the site are housed on the estate and men, women and the older children can be seen working at different seasonal tasks.

The guided tour, along shady paths, takes about an hour. You will pass grapefruit, areca nut palms (some 150 years old) and coconuts with pepper vines growing up their trunks, tobacco, bay, *papaya*, bread fruit and *cocum*. The last, has a scarlet flesh; once eaten the skin is cut into strips and sun-dried to turn into black *sola* used for flavouring curries. *Bimla*, akin to star fruit, hangs like bunches of large green grapes on branches and is especially good for prawn curries and pickles. You will be shown soft and hard skin jackfruit which can become giants weighing over 20 kg and banana plants which can produce 250 bananas from a single flower (one flower is cut off each plant to be eaten as a vegetable delicacy). The large banyan tree here stands majestically like a benevolent spirit; it is offered prayers along with feni, bread and bananas on Wednesdays and Sundays by the local people who seek its blessing.

On the hillside grow pineapples (200,000 fruit are cut between June and September), bamboo, basil, cocoa, wood-apple, mangoes, and the surprising nutmeg (male and female) which you might mistake for lemons! No space is wasted on this densely cultivated plantation. The staple tuber *suarn* underground can weigh up to 2 kg.

The ubiquitous coconut is not only prized for its fruit which is cut off every 3 months but also the leaves used for thatching and the trunks for building. One of the experts will demonstrate the art of coconut picking by shinning up a tall palm with his feet tied together, cutting fresh green coconuts (which produce a most welcome instant cool drink and a soft succulent kernel) and then gracefully swaying at the crown of one in order to transfer to the top of a neighbouring palm without having to waste any energy climbing down and up again!

The tour concludes with lunch, sampling seasonal produce, and the chance to buy packets of spices which make ideal gifts to take home.

Details of the "Village Tour" which includes Savoi Verem is available from Goa Tourism, Patto.

Pascoal alternatively, a visit to the **spice plantation** here between Ponda (8 km) and Tisk (2 km), well signposted 1.5 km off the NH4A, is highly recommended. Open 0800-1800 daily. Rs 225 for guided tour through a beautiful and fascinating setting. The plantation grows a wide variety of spices and exotic fruit and is pleasantly located by a river. Paddle boats Rs 100/hr. *Glade Bar and Restaurant* (1130-1800) is good but a bit pricey. Spices are available for sale.

KHANDEPAR *M5B2*

4 km northeast of Ponda close to Khandepar (Candepar), just off the NH4A, is the latest and best preserved **cave site**, possibly of Buddhist occupation. Ask for directions to the site which is hidden beyond a wooded area near a tributary of the Mandovi. Carry a torch and beware of snakes.

As described by Hutt, the first three of the four laterite caves have an outer and an inner cell which were possibly used as monks' living quarters. Much more refined than others discovered in Goa, they show clear evidence of schist frames for doors to the inner cells, sockets on which wooden doors would have been hung, pegs carved out of the walls for hanging clothing and niches for storage. The first cave, which Hutt surmises was probably intended for the senior monk, has deep (though rather crude) lotus carvings on the ceiling of the outer cell. The much simpler fourth cave, which is a short distance away and faces the first cave, is only single-celled and was probably used as a prayer room.

The interesting feature in Khandepar is the evidence of a surmounting pyramidal structure in the form of horizontal laterite slabs, placed on top of the cell roofs to give the impression of a Hindu temple *sikhara* (tower). This feature and the carved ceiling (in the style of a *mandapa*) help to date the caves to 10th or 11th centuries, when the Kadambas allowed Buddhism to continue to be practised. Some scholars suggest that the caves were originally carved out of a rocky hillside. They may have had the soil and growth removed and been made free standing at a later stage (around the 10th/11th centuries) and converted to Hindu temples with the addition of the pyramidal roof slabs and carving on the ceiling.

The Archaeological Museum in Panaji has a Krishna imange, a Nandi bull and a 15th century Hanuman image in its collection which were found in Khandepar.

BONDLA SANCTUARY *M5B3*

The smallest of Goa's three wildlife sanctuaries is only 80 sq km in area and is situated in the foothills of the Western

Ghats, which harbours sambar, wild boar, gaur (Indian bison), monkeys and a few migratory elephants which wander in from Karnataka during the summer.

Access

Open mid-September to mid-June; closed Thursdays; 0900-1700. Entry Re 1, Still camera Re 1, video camera Rs 25. 2-wheeler Re 1, 3-wheeler Rs 3, car/jeep Rs 5.

Wildlife

The park has a botanical and rose garden which are well kept in addition to a zoo and deer park (closed for lunch and on Thursdays). The Forestry Department's leaflet describes the zoo as housing 'Goa's wildlife in natural surroundings' but visitors are usually saddened by the condition of the caged animals (which includes an African Lion!), particularly by the inadequate cages and facilities; there is also little information about them. The small and basic Nature Education Centre has the facility to show video films (but is more often used by the staff for watching TV soap operas than wildlife films!). A deer safari is on offer from 1600-1730 with a minimum of 8 people.

Viewing

A 2.4 km nature trail takes you past waterholes, a lake and a tree-top observation tower (about 1 hour on foot). A single metalled road goes some distance into the sanctuary but the chances of seeing many animals is remote. You are most likely to see monkeys and attractive birds, and some deer and Gaur if you are lucky.

Park facilities

The Forest Department advertises simple **F** *Cottages*, mainly built of wood, for 24, and 48 dormitory beds reserved through the Conservator's Office, 3rd floor, Junta House, 18th June Rd, Panaji, T 0832 224747 or DCF, North, Ponda, T 0834 312095. However, on enquiring in mid-1997 these did not appear to be available.

The *Den Cafeteria* near the entrance, serves snacks. A *Restaurant*, a short distance inside the park, charges inflated prices for cold drinks.

Getting there 5 km northeast of Ponda along the NH4A, a left turn (at an insignificant sign) leads to the Bondla Wildlife Sanctuary, 12 km away. After 3 km, go straight over the busy roundabout at Usgao and continue for another 5 km until the road forks. The fork to the right is signposted to the park which is 4 km up a winding and occasionally steep road. **NB** If entering the park with your own transport make sure that you have enough petrol since the nearest petrol pump is at Tisk, 15 km away.

By bus from Ponda via Tisk and Usgaon where taxis and motorcycle taxis are available. KTC buses may run at weekends from Panaji. During the season the Forest Department minibus is supposed to do 2 daily trips (except Thursday) between Bondla and Tisk: from Bondla, 0815, 1745; from Tisk, 1100 (Sunday 1030) and 1900. Check at the Tourist Office first.North Goa.

Salt of the earth

The central and northern coastal districts of Goa have been renowned for salt production, and although this has decreased in importance over the last century, Tiswadi still has over 40 working salt pans, Bardez and Salcete have around 30 each, and Pernem nine.

Salt is produced traditionally in areas reclaimed from mangroves, the period of production being between February and May. Along the raised rural roads close to the sea you may notice a series of shallow rectangular enclosures where salt water is allowed to enter and stand. The water eventually evaporates to leave the crystallized white salt which is piled up in heaps before being transported.

North Goa

IT IS the beaches of Bardez which, more than anything else, give Goa today its reputation as one of the great holiday destinations in the world. The whole coastline of Bardez, one of the 'Old Conquest' talukas, comprises one long stretch of uninterrupted, dune-backed or coconut fringed sand from Fort Aguada in the south to Baga in the north, then beyond the narrow inlet of the Baga River through Anjuna to the rocky headlands and coves of Vagator. Pernem taluka too has fine beaches, though they remain far less visited. North of the Chapora River the largely deserted beaches of Morjim, Mandrem and Arambol lead up to Keri and the Tiracol River with the northernmost outpost of Goa, Tiracol Fort, on a tiny peninsula extension of Maharashtra.

North Goa packs an astonishing range of scenery and landscapes, each area with a distinctive history which has helped to shape sharp contrasts between the four talukas which make it up. The road east to the Western Ghat runs through a region of modern and rapid mineral development and industrialization, then back in time to the densely forested slopes of Bicholim taluka, where ancient Buddhist caves and Hindu temples are tucked away deep in the forested slopes.

BARDEZ & PERNEM TALUKAS

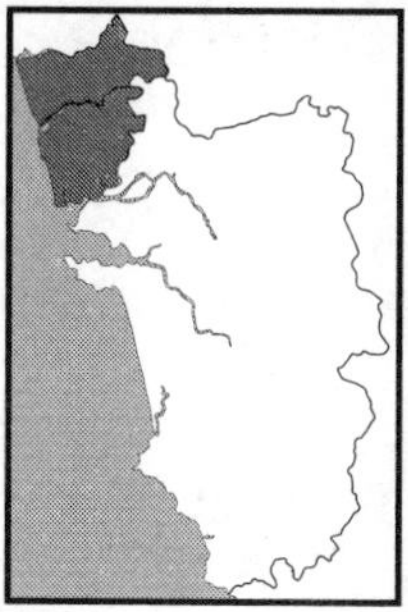

Bardez may have derived its name from *bara desh* (12 'divisions of land') that comprised the district refering to the 12 Brahmin villages that once dominated the region. There are other possible explanations for the name. One popular one is that it refers to 12 *zagors* which were celebrated by the people to ward off evil. Yet another suggests that it is derived from *Bahir des*, meaning 'outside land' – the land beyond the Mandovi River. Whatever the origins of its name Bardez taluka, occupied by the Portuguese as part of their original conquest, bears the greatest direct imprint of their Christianizing influence.

Pernem (Pednem) taluka, sandwiched between the Tiracol and Chapora Rivers and their estuaries, was incorporated into Goa in 1788 as the final part of the New Conquests. Formerly it had been alternately under Hindu and Muslim rule. The Bhonsles of Sawantwadi in modern Maharashtra had been the latest rulers of the hilly district on the northern fringes of Goa before the Portuguese ousted them, and Maratha Hindu influences remain strong throughout the district.

Both the talukas have retained a strong sense of their distinctive identities. Bardez has its own characteristic ecosystem. The beach between Candolim and Baga is backed by a series of sand dunes, stabilized by grasses and casuarina, which form a shelter belt for the flat river-plains inland. The road and settlements all lie to the landward side of this strip. Inland again the short rivers meander across the flood plain between Mapusa and the sea. The Mapusa River itself was once an important transport artery, its banks offering rich and fertile soils for producing vegetables which were then moved to market in Mapusa or down to the Mandovi. Today its banks have been reclaimed for building, its waters abused by urban refuse and sewage, its importance dwindled and its attractiveness largely destroyed.

Interior Bardez and most of Pernem are formed of the rolling laterite hills which extend northwards into southern Maharashtra. More sparsely populated than the coastal fringe the hills are now covered in open forest.

Southern Bardez has some of Goa's *khazan* lands. These saline flood plains, lying below the high tide sea level have been developed and maintained over centuries by an intricate system of sluice gates, keeping saline water out at high tide, allowing surplus fresh water out as the tide recedes. From this complex system has emerged an intricately managed landuse, with salt-tolerant varieties of rice co-existing with aquaculture. *Fish, Curry and Rice* has pointed to the threats which have been posed to the *khazans* by a variety of current practices, including deliberate breaking of the river embankments to allow more intensive aquaculture, and the inadvertent destruction of embankments by the wash of ever larger iron ore carrying barges.

Bardez and Pernem coast

HERE we follow the coast from the north side of the Mandovi Bridge along the estuary of the Mandovi then northwards through Fort Aguada to the northernmost fort of Tiracol. It is a coastline dotted with historic sites interspersed with some of Goa's most beautiful beaches. It is possible to walk virtually uninterrupted along the beach all the way from Aguada to Vagator. The road from Aguada runs about 1 km inland behind the main line of sand dunes, narrow lanes running down at right angles to the sea. There are no private beaches and public access is guaranteed everywhere.

Which beach?

Despite the fact that the sand seems to be one unending stretch from south to north the different beaches do have their own distinctive character. In the **south** there is far less beach shade and the dunes of loose sand are higher and wider. Further north around **Calangute** and northwards to **Baga** the coconut palms come closer to the sea. Some of the villages depend on fishing, and there are clusters of fishing boats at various points along some beaches while others seem deserted. Around Calangute and Baga there are dozens of beach shack restaurants and several night clubs. Beyond the **Anjuna** headland the weekly flea market attracts thousands of visitors during the season, while northwards the beach quickly empties towards **Chapora**, where some of the smaller bays have become home to long term foreign visitors. Into Pernem the impact of tourism is still relatively slight, a few Europeans setting themselves up in the beachside hamlets and motorbike day trippers coming to visit the bays of **Arambol**, but there are very limited facilities and for much of the time the beautiful 2 km of sand of **Keri**, just south of **Tiracol**, Goa's northernmost beach, is almost entirely deserted.

APPROACHING THE NORTH COAST

The NH17 from Dabolim and Panaji crosses the Mandovi bridge to **Porvorim**, which was chosen to become Goa's administrative capital. A left turn in Porvorim goes straight to Calangute via Saligao, but there are several options for reaching the coast. Buses run frequently to Calangute, the central point and busiest town on this coast, but if you have your own transport you can turn left at the north end of the Mandovi Bridge and hug the coast through Reis Magos, then cross to Aguada and up the coast road. In contrast if you go through Porvorim to Mapusa you can go direct to Anjuna or Vagator, or continue northwards to Pernem.

BETIM *M2C2*

Immediately over the Mandovi Birdge on the river bank facing Panaji is the small fishing village of Betim. The attractive country road runs between tightly packed houses and then skirts the

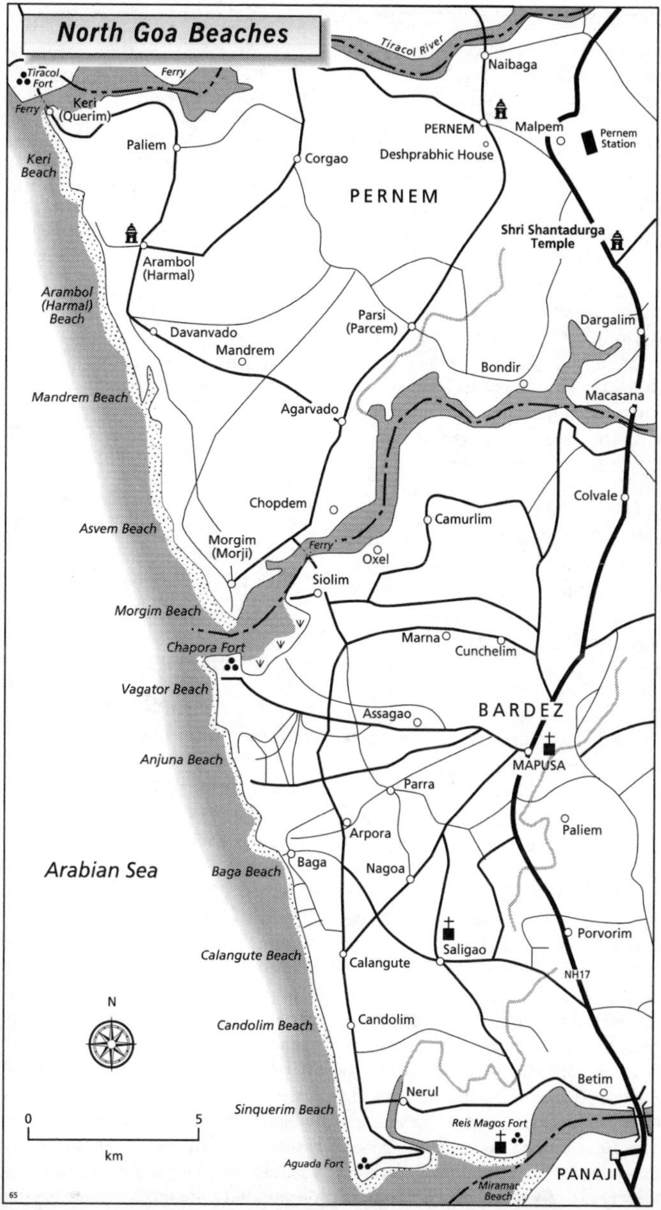
North Goa Beaches
Tiracol River
Tiracol Fort
Ferry
Keri (Querim)
Naibaga
PERNEM
Malpem
Pernem Station
Paliem
Deshprabhic House
Keri Beach
Corgao
PERNEM
Shri Shantadurga Temple
Arambol (Harmal)
Arambol (Harmal) Beach
Parsi (Parcem)
Dargalim
Davanvado
Mandrem
Bondir
Mandrem Beach
Agarvado
Macasana
Chopdem
Colvale
Camurlim
Asvem Beach
Morgim (Morji)
Oxel
Siolim
Morgim Beach
Marna
Cunchelim
Chapora Fort
Vagator Beach
Assagao
BARDEZ
MAPUSA
Anjuna Beach
Parra
Paliem
Arpora
Arabian Sea
Baga
Baga Beach
Nagoa
Saligao
Porvorim
Calangute Beach
Calangute
NH17
N
Candolim Beach
Candolim
Betim
Nerul
Sinquerim Beach
0
5
km
Reis Magos Fort
Aguada Fort
PANAJI
Miramar Beach
65

bay. The **F** *Tourist Complex*, T 227362 has very basic facilities, some beds (Rs 10-30), mattresses (Rs 5) or floor space for students (Rs 3), Tourist Office.

REIS MAGOS

M2C2

Population 7,500

Reis Magos stands appropriately like a watchman facing Panaji across the Mandovi estuary. The small town of some charm (originally called Verem), is most noted for its 'Royal Fort' which was built by Don Alfonso de Noronha between 1551 and 1554. In fact, recognising the site's great srategic importance, Albuquerque had stationed troops on the headland from the outset of Portuguese control. It was intended as a second line of defence should an enemy, notably the Dutch, manage to sail past Aguada and Cabo on the headlands. The first fortification was extended and repaired a few times during the next 50 years. Several underground rooms were excavated which were accessed by going down over 100 steps. Reis Magos, though fairly small, played a vital role in defending the mouth of the Mandovi together with Gaspar Dias but after a new fort was built at Aguada in 1612 its importance waned and it was neglected. In 1703, it was re-erected; 35 years later it had to face the Maratha onslaught on Bardez, and alone with Fort Aguada remained in Portuguese hands.

The **Reis Magos Church** (1555) named after the 'Magi Kings' stands alongside and is one of the early Goan churches which, some believe, was built on the site of a Hindu temple. A Fransiscan friar is believed to have crossed the Mandovi in 1550, arrived in Verem where he put up a temporary altar and celebrated Mass for the first time on Goan territory. Viceroy Noronha had allotted Bardez to the Fransiscans and the church was in a sense a launching pad for the conversion of the district. Dedicated to the three Magi, Gaspar, Melchior and Balthazar, the reredos illustrates the story of the Three Kings with a painted wooden panel showing frankincense, myrrh and gold being offered to the baby Jesus.

The church and the fort stand quite high above water level. The Church façade has a most unusual protruding crown with the Portuguese crest on the gable. It is approached by a flight of steep laterite steps; the granite tiger is thought to have come from a Hindu temple.

Schools and a seminary were attached to the church. The St Jerome Seminary where Konkani was taught alongside philosophy and theology became a prestigious institution. Between 1597 and 1793 many Portuguese dignitaries, including viceroys and governors, en route to or from Old Goa, stayed here as guests of the friars.

It is a fascinating drive to the end of the peninsula beyond Reis Magos, although the road is a dead end and becomes the narrowest of country lanes, winding between palm trees growing in the middle of the road.

Travel tip

From any point on the northern coast between Fort Aguada and Tiracol it is easy to take day trips inland to enjoy something of this diversity. There is plenty in inland Bardez alone to repay a visit; Mapusa, with its market and the Church of Our Lady of Miracles, or the neo-Gothic church of Saligao just inland of Calangute, the southern coastal villages around Reis Magos, or the banks of the Chapora from Siolim to Colvale. Inland Pernem has the magnificent Deshprabhu Mansion, Alorna Fort or the Shri Shantadurga Temple of Dargalim.

Sinquerim Beach

The Festival of Three Kings accompanied by a big fair is celebrated here on the first Sunday in January, as at Chandor on 6 January, each year (see page 183). There is accommodation at the **D** *Bamboo Motels Noah's Ark*, Verem, Reis Magos, T 517321. There are30 rooms facing the pool, restaurant. **NB** The Fort is soon to house a Taj Group *Heritage Hotel*.

NERUL

M2C2

The present temple in Nerul dates from 1910 when special permission was given to return the deity of Shri Shantadurga, which had been removed to Mandrem in Pernem taluka (see page 146). Gomes Pereira records that the present village church of **Our Lady of Remedies** was built in 1569 in place of the destroyed Shantadurga Temple. Workers restoring the parish house in 1893 found a 1m statue of the Hindu deity Betall in the holy well. He suggests that an underground passage which exists in the present church was probably part of the former temple, and that the stone tigers now found decorating the entrance to the church originally also came from it. The big tank in the parish church-house orchard (now in ruins) may have once been the temple tank.

❖ SINQUERIM BEACH

M2C1

Sinquerim (13 km away) is the nearest beach north of Panaji where the Taj Hotel group set up its fabulous *Hermitage Hotel Complex* which dominates the headland around the historic Fort Aguada, partly occupying it. The excellent Taj Sports Complex is open to non-residents. If you want a long beach walk, the firm sand is uninterrupted all the way north to Baga. Although in season there are restaurant shacks at several points along the beach, it is a good idea to take some water as well as a shirt and a hat.

FORT AGUADA

M2C2

On the northern tip of the Mandovi estuary with the Nerul River to the east, Fort Aguada, felt as essential to keep the Dutch Navy at bay, was completed in 1612 through 1% of the revenue raised. It was the strongest of the Portuguese coastal forts and was paired with a channel was excavated to make the headland an island and a platform built to help ships disembark. A large well and a number of springs provided the fort and ships at harbour with drinking water and gave it its name *'aguada'*, meaning watering place (one of the sources of clean mineral water is still there). 200 guns were placed to give the fort all round defensive fire power as well as two magazines, four barracks, two prisons and several residential buildings for the officers. It saw repeated action against the Marathas, was used as a refuge by Goans who fled from Bardez during these attacks and also used to detain prisoners during various revolts. The main fortifications with laterite walls, nearly 5m high and 1.3m thick, are still intact; the buildings lower down form the Central jail.

The motorable road up to the plateau passes the small **Church of St Lawrence** (or Linhares Church, 1630-1643). It has an unusual porch with a terrace and balustrades on the towers and parapets. The *Feast of St Lawrence* (10 August), the patron of sailors, celebrated the natural annual clearing of the sand bars at the mouth of the Mandovi River after the monsoon, which once again allowed ships passage.

A 13m high lighthouse using an oil lamp was added at the top of the fort (84m asl) sometime in the 18th century (records of 1817 refer to its poor condition, in need of repairs). In 1864, a new mechanism allowed a rotating beam to be emitted every 30 seconds (one of the first of its kind in Asia) which was upgraded in 1906. The lighthouse seized to function in 1976. It is supposed to be open from 1030-1730, Rs 2; there are good views from the top. Next to the fort, the new 21m high concrete lighthouse (1975), is open 1600-1730 (Re 1, no photography). Lower down, the smaller

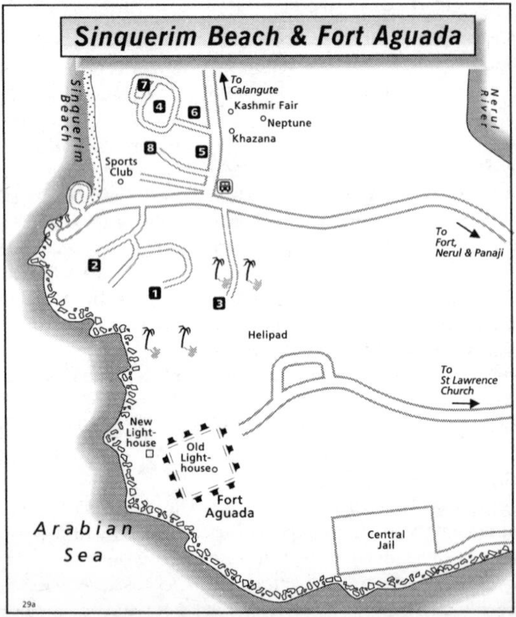

Hotels:
1. *Aguada Hermitage*
2. *Fort Aguada Beach Resort (Taj)*
3. *Marbella*
4. *Taj Holiday Village*
5. *Village Belle*

Places to eat:
6. Banyan Tree
7. Beach House
8. Bon Appetit & Palm Shade

Fort Aguada

circular white Aguada Beacon (1890) emitted a red light.

The government plans to allow the private sector to restore the old fort and set up an amusement park and sports centre for tourists on the Aguada plateau.

Luxury hotels

Prices vary greatly depending on period; peak 21 December-10 January, lowest mid June-end September. At the bottom of the hill, where sections of the fortification jut out to the sea. Taj has 3 superb hotels: **AL** ***Aguada Hermitage***, T 276201, F 276044 (for all 3), exclusive and extremely luxurious, 20 fully serviced 1 or 2 rooms villas (US$ 475 peak season drops to US$135 in low), few some distance away from main building, each with its own spacious tropical garden, nightclub; **AL-A** ***Fort Aguada Beach Resort***, exceptional hotel, superb setting, built into the fort, 120 rooms in 2 wings and some villas with excellent views; separate **AL-A** ***Holiday Village***, 300m away, 144 (most a/c), some well-designed single 'houses', some in less attractive 2-storey blocks further from the sea, imaginative planning, beautiful gardens of bougainvillea and palms, good restaurants (on beach and on dunes), excellent pool with a water bar and hammocks between palms (better than at the *Resort*), informal, helpful efficient staff, highly recommended.

Mid-range hotels

B-C ***Marbella***, lane left off road to *Aguada Beach Resort*, F 276308, 6 very clean, well-decorated rooms (prices vary, best highly recommended) in a large Goan house.

D ***Village Belle***, near the *Taj Holiday Village*, T/F 276153, 10 rooms with bath, restaurant, among palms, 500m from the beach, near the main road, good value out of season.

Places to eat

For something special, try the ***Banyan Tree*** at *Taj Holiday Village* entrance, for excellent Thai food in style. Encircled by a wide verandah, it is in an exotic setting surrounded by a water garden with a great banyan tree; expensive (about Rs 500 for a meal) though not over-priced by Western standards; the ***Beach House*** for the "most lavish and complete dinner, served attentively" is highly recommended. ***Bon Appetit*** and ***Palm Shade*** nearby, are also recommended.

Sports

Taj **Sports Club** (open to non-residents), with a separate access between *Aguada Beach Resort* and *Holiday Village*, provides excellent facilities. Tennis with good markers (Rs 400/hr); squash and badminton (Rs 75-100 for 30 mins); golf (Rs 150). A fine **Health Centre** there offers massage, gym, steam, sauna, all recommended; hairdressers are at hand. **Watersports**: including windsurfing and sailing: hire Rs 300-450/hr, lessons Rs 400-600/hr;.water skiing Rs 450/15 mins and Rs 550/15 mins; also speed boats and parasailing are possible. **Scuba diving** and other watersports are also offered through ***Neptune***, across the main road, behind *Kashmir Fair*, T 276985, open 0930-1730, Monday-Saturday.

Prices: AL Rs 6,000+; **A** Rs 3,000-6,000; **B** Rs1,500-3,000; **C** Rs 800-1,500; **D** Rs 400-800

THE BEACH NORTH OF AGUADA

This section has close to 200 beach shacks open during the season. Candolim has the least developed part of the beach. If you wish to be away from the crowds but within reach of good food, try the beach near *D'Mello's* and *Oceanic*, between Candolim and Calangute. Many shacks hire out sun-beds for around Rs 100 for 2. These are quite unsightly and add to the feeling of overcrowding which is particularly bad at the Baga end.

One visitor counted 131 **fishing boats** varying from under 6m to 9m in length, mainly along Calangute and Baga beaches. They are worth a closer look. Their bases are carved out of solid wood while the sides are made of planks slashed on to the base with ropes, all made waterproof by a dark oil; traditionally using a biproduct of cashew roasting! Many boats are fitted with outboard motors though they still have the old oars. Of particular interest are the distinctive outriggers on one side. During the day you may find the fishermen repairing their nets or engaged in fish-drying, while a growing number are turning to taking out tourists for fishing trips and dolphin watching. Try *John's Boats* in Candolim for 'guaranteed' dolphin watching.

CANDOLIM

M2C1

Population 7,100; *STD Code* 0832

Candolim is a dispersed village, just north of Aguada, which runs into Calangute. It has many new, small hotels but little cheap accommodation. The beach itself is long and straight, backed by scrub-covered dunes but with little shelter. Several of the beach shacks fly Union Jacks, Scottish and English flags and play endless Bob Marley. Sadly, the colourful fruit sellers are rarely seen now. *Traveland*, Laxmi Apartments, T 276773, F 276124, can helpmwith travel requirements.

Mid-range hotels

B *Whispering Palms*, 300m from beach, T 276140,F 276142, 84 rooms (looks like a fortress), restaurant overlooking excellent pool, pleasant garden, good but pricey.

C *Aldeia Santa Rita*, towards Aguada, T 277477, F 276684, 32 rooms with balcony (better upstairs) in colourful 'street' of villas in attractive setting, good restaurant, bar, very small pool, friendly management; **C** *Sunset Beach*, off Fort Aguada Rd, T 276236, 28 rooms, some a/c with balcony, restaurant, no pool, nothing special, overpriced; **C** *Xavier*, opposite the State Bank, spacious well furnished rooms, close to beach.

C-D *Aguada Holiday Resort*, Bamon–vaddo, T 276071, F 276068, 40 good size self-catering apartments, some a/c, expensive restaurant and bar, uncrowded site with some palms (plenty of squirrels), pool, 10 mins from beach; **C-D** *Dona Alcina*, 500m from beach (opposite impressive *Alcon* apartments), T 276266, 300 rooms in several 3-storey blocks, crowded site, lacks style, pool.

D *Alexandra Tourist Centre*, Morodvaddo, in lane opposite the Canara Bank, T 276097, 8 good rooms, some a/c, restaurant; **D** *Casa Sea Shell*, 400m beach, T 276131, 15 simple, well kept rooms, good restaurant, pool; **D** *Costa Nicola*, near the Health Centre (500m from beach), T 276343, F 277343, clean rooms in very pleasant Goan house, some with kitchenette, restaurant and bar, gentle atmosphere, verandah, pretty garden, used by Finnish tour groups, recommended; **D** *Holiday Beach Resort*, short walk to beach, T 276088, F 276235, 20 clean rooms in a rather faded guesthouse, some with balcony, covered terrace restaurant; **D** *Kamal*, towards Aguada, T 276320, 4 large rooms (more in 1998) in attractive new building, *Fiesta* restaurant (some Italian dishes), pleasant garden, charming owner,

Prices: B Rs 1,500-3,000; **C** Rs 800-1,500; **D** Rs 400-800; **E** Rs 200-400

recommended; **D** ***Peravel***, 100m from beach, T 272227, 6 simple rooms, courtyard garden for breakfast among local family houses; **D** ***Sea Shell Inn***, opposite the Canara Bank, Candolim-Aguada Rd, T 276131, 10 spotless, comfortable rooms in 2 blocks (one grafted on to an old colonial house with chapel), poor restaurant; **D** ***Summerville***, T 262681, 15 well kept rooms, breakfast on rooftop, sunbathing terrace, pool planned. On a very quiet part of the beach near unspoilt countryside, 2 pleasant **D-E** guest houses: ***Dona Florina***, Monteiro's Rd, T 277398, F 276878, rooms with shower, and ***D'Mello's Sea View***, behind Dr Monteiro's House, T 277395, 7 rooms and good food.

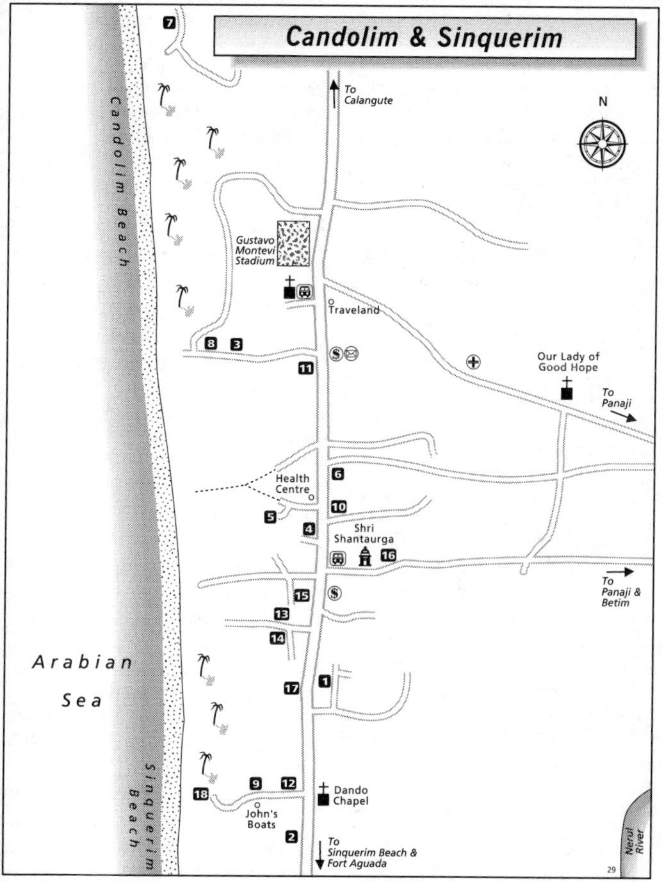

Hotels:
1. *Aguada Holiday Resort*
2. *Aldeia Santa Rita*
3. *Alexandra Tourist Centre*
4. *Casa Sea Shell*
5. *Costa Nicola*
6. *Dona Alcina*
7. *Dona Florina & D'Mello's Sea View*
8. *Holiday Beach Resort*
9. *Peravel*
10. *Peroda de Mar*
11. *Sea Shell Inn*
12. *Summerville*
13. *Sunset Beach*
14. *Whispering Palms*
15. *Xavier*

Places to eat:

16. Coconut Inn
17. Octopus Garden & Kamal
18. Palms 'n Sand

The Sap Tappers

The Portuguese introduced the Western art of distilling when they settled in the palm fringed shores of Goa in 1510. The habit of drinking the spirit of the palm sap, the palm *feni* (and also the *caju feni* derived from the cashew apple) has become an indispensable part of Goan life.

The task of extracting the sap from the crown of the tall palm trees is left in the hands of some 6,000 toddy-tappers who, usually helped by their wives, also process the juice and distil it.

The sap flows when the apex of an unopened flower bunch is 'tapped', by slicing it off and tapping it with a stick to make the cells burst and so the juice to flow which starts in about 3 weeks of the first cut. From then on, successive flower buds are tapped so that the sap can be collected for half a year. Fruit production, of course, stops during this period, but the tapping appears to result in an improved crop of nuts where the yield had been previously poor.

The skillful tapper ties a circle of rope around his ankles and with a cutter in hand, shins up the tall smooth trunk of the palm two or three times a day, to empty the pot of sap.

Traditonally tappers lived as tenants on a landowner's property exchanging the privilege of tapping the palm sap (*toddy*) with performing certain services in the landlords fields and home. The tapper also enjoyed certain hereditary rights so the livelihood and skill was passed on from generation to generation. However, the government's attempts to remove their status as virtual bonded labour has resulted in unforeseen difficulties faced by those whose landlords are refusing to recognize their hereditary rights and privileges. Some tappers have been facing eviction, and with it, their means of earning a living. See also 'Coconut Palms' on page 31.

Places to eat

Coconut Inn, Fort Aguada Rd, by Shantadurga temple, is a typical Goan house with indoor and open-air seating; ***Fisherman's Nook***, Camotinvaddo, good for seafood. In a pleasant area, ***D'Mello's*** beach restaurant has an excellent menu, with tandoori specialities; ***Oceanic*** nearby is also recommended; ***21 Comforts*** (was *21 Coconuts*), further south, is now crowded in with other shacks, does good breakfasts for about Rs 75, snacks (seafood, pancakes) and drinks. ***Octopus Garden***, on the main road towards Aguada, does good food with a wide choice (1000-1500, 1800-2300); ***Palms 'n Sand*** near the beach, does speciality roast piglet (order the day before).

CALANGUTE *M2C1*

Population 11,800; *STD Code* 0832

Calangute, once the remote hippy retreat of the 1960s, is now a busy, rather dirty, commercialized small town. It has experienced dramatic growth since the 1960s when it became the first of the magnets drawing hippies from across the world, and it has now become one of the main centres for package tours. The small centre is very crowded and congested with traffic, especially during the high season.

There is little of architectural merit in the town, though there is an interesting hexagonal "Barbeiria" (barber's shop) near the bus stand at the 'T' junction with the rather unsavoury market. The new fish market next door, however, is quite tidy and pleasant. The Baga road has several streets off it, giving access to the sea. Calangute has a good beach – no rocks and good swimming (but beware of the seaward pulling current). Sun beds can be hired from numerous beach shacks, and hawkers selling sarongs, offering massages or wishing to tell your fortune can be a constant distraction. The affluence of this coastal strip also attracts its fair share of out-of-state beggars.

You will not need to go far to see a large number of fishing boats, tackle and fishermen's huts which have increased in recent years. At weekends the beach near the *Tourist Resort* gets particularly crowded with domestic day trippers (some come in the hope of catching a glimpse of scantily clad foreigners).

Away from the busy beach front, coconut trees still give shade to village houses. However, it somehow feels as if the whole settlement has been taken over by tourism. Licensed shacks line the beach – some offering excellent food and a very pleasant evening atmosphere. Many village homes behind offer private rooms to let, while open space is rapidly being covered by new hotels. The streets of Calangute (and Baga) are lined with shops offering a wide range of goods, mainly souvenirs, metal and leather items, clothes and jewellery from Kashmir and Karnataka.

Away from the town centre, the striking **Church of St Alex** gives one of the best illustrations of Rococo decoration in Goa, while the false dome of the central façade is an excellent example of 18th century architectural development. Note the gold and white scheme and the delicate and restrained handling of the decoration as seen in the remarkable pulpit and the fine reredos.

It is not difficult to see why Calangute is at the centre of the controversy over 'the impact of tourism'. For those with memories stretching back 30 years, it is almost unrecognizable. The huge surge in land values, fuelled by a flow of money from Goans abroad, eager to capitalize on the development opportunity, has seen plots covered in concrete flouting all attempts to control or direct, let alone halt, the building boom. Money has been there to be made, and Calangute is the place to make it.

Yet the area most affected by this transformation of a hippy hideout to a global tourist village is small. Calangute shades rapidly into its neighbouring, and still very different, villages. Candolim to the south, as described above, has more spacious and quiet resort hotels interspersed with modest guest houses and access to a beach which, by European standards at least, is empty. Baga to the north, reached either directly along the beach or along the coconut-shaded road slightly inland, still retains something of its more 'distanced' feel, though even here development has been rapid.

Despite the welcomed growth in income that tourism has brought to Calangute and Baga, it has not been an unmixed blessing. Competition for limited ground water has affected some of the villages just inland, and some see its increasing use as threatening to let sea water into the underground supply, putting local people at risk. Others fear even more the cultural change which mass tourism has brought to this spot. It is here that Goa's nightlife is at its most audible, a transformation that some local people still find hard to accept, and the widespread availability of drugs is both feared and resented by many, just as nude or topless bathing are seen as deeply offensive. Calangute and Baga have become the area of Goa where the tensions between mass tourism and local needs are most exposed. Visitors can help greatly by being aware of the issues and behaving sensitively.

Festivals

The *Youth Fête* (May, 2nd week) attracts Goa's leading musicians and dancers.

Mid-range hotels

B *Paradise Village*, South Calangute, near the beach, T 276351, F 276155, 83 comfortable rooms in 4-room 2-storey chalets, pleasant restaurant (King fish Rs 80, beer Rs 45), large pool, ugly mini golf, excellent service and management, recommended.

B-C *Landscape*, south of St Anthony's Church, T 277230, F 221845, new 2-storey complex, choice of room size, mostly a/c with fridge and neatly furnished, restaurant, somewhat bizarre decor in public areas, pool (with baby pool), away from the beach; **B-C** *Villa Goesa*, Cobravaddo, off Baga Rd, T 277535, T/F 276182, 21 clean rooms, some a/c, some very shaded, excellent restaurant, lush gardens, quiet, secluded, long walk from beach, pool, 20 more rooms (rare in quoting price inclusive of tax and service!), recommended.

C *Falcon*, Calangute-Baga Rd, 1 km from beach, T 277327, F 277330, 26 rooms with heavy, oppressive decor, pool pleasant but shaded; **C** *Goan Heritage*, Gauravaddo, towards Candolim, T 276253, F 276120, 70 large, pleasant rooms, some a/c with fridge (Rs 400 extra, if both are used) with sea view, expensive restaurant (others nearby), nice pool, beautiful garden, close to beach, recommended.

C-D *Arabian Retreat*, Gauravaddo (near *Goan Heritage*), T 279053, F 271467, suites in new 2-storey block with fridge and balcony, some a/c, simply furnished, includes breakfast, 250m from the beach; **C-D** *Varma's Beach Resort*, Meddovaddo, T 276077, F 276022, 12 clean rooms, some a/c with verandahs facing pleasant garden (some noise from bus stand nearby), breakfast only, closed June-September, friendly.

D *Concha Beach Resort*, Umtavaddo, T 276351, F 2662481, 14 rooms, restaurant, windsurfing; **D** *Estrela do Mar*, Calangute-Baga Rd, T 276014, 10 rooms, peaceful, pleasant garden; **D** *Kamat's Holiday Village*, near St Anthony's chapel, 10-min walk from beach, 2 km from centre, T 276430, 132 rooms (some a/c) in 3-storey blocks around pool and lawn, gym, badminton; **D** *Mira*, Umtavaddo, near the Chapel, 10 minutes walk from beach, T 276023, 40 modern, clean rooms (no TV) with shower on 3 floors, courtyard restaurant, near the shops and market; **D** *Tourist Resort* (GTDC), on the beach, near the steps, T 276024, 76 basic rooms, some a/c, in ugly building, some in cottages, dorm, cheap terrace restaurant, bar, can be noisy; **D** *White House*, Gauravaddo (near *Goan Heritage*), T 277938, F 276308, 8 rooms with bath and seaview, very pleasant and small.

Prices: B Rs 1,500-3,000; **C** Rs 800-1,500; **D** Rs 400-800; **E** Rs 200-400

Budget hotels

A small selection: **E** *Calangute Beach Resort*, Umtavaddo, T 276063, 11 rooms, some with bath, restaurant, bar, exchange; **E** *Coco Banana*, 5/139A Umtavaddo, back from Calangute beach, T 276478, 3 good airy rooms in cottage around garden.

Places to eat

Near the *Tourist Resort*: ***Angelina***, near the beach steps, popular, varied menu (Goan, Tandoori, Italian) and ***Cater's***, opposite, raised above the beach, with a large breezy, terrace, are recommended; ***Souza Lobo*** in a large shack on the beach, is still popular for fresh seafood (poor hygiene reported in 1997); ***Lobster Pot*** upstairs in a circular building set back from the beach, has imaginative palm tree decor, good food (Rs 70 main course), some Goan specialities, friendly, unpushy hosts.

Try ***Delhi Darbar***, near the beach, towards Baga, for a candlelit dinner, excellent North Indian and fish dishes, dancing; it's up-market and expensive. ***Johnny's Shack*** does excellent pomfret (Rs 70); ***Palm Court***, near *Goan Heritage* gates is recommended; ***Pedro's*** on the beach behind has authentic, interesting Tibetan dishes to compliment a very smartly printed menu; ***Taste of China*** is on Baga Rd.

Infanteria, near the main crossroads, recommended for breakfast, baked goodies and snacks all day. ***Master Joel Confectioners***, 9 Romano Chambers, opposite the petrol pump, makes good Goan specialities.

Milky Way, inland off Baga Rd, good for health foods, ices during the day, French food (1900-2330), closed off-season; ***Indian Cafe***, behind, serves snacks on a few tables on the verandah of a village home (no fans), pleasant, cheap, also changes money. ***Sip 'n' Dip***, near St Anthony's Church, T 276567, Ashley Gomes, the owner, also has cheap rooms in an old Goan house.

Transport

Bicycles and **motorbikes**: are widely available for hire, among them *JayJays* for bikes. There is a Kinetic Honda repair shop behind *Samir Electricals*, near the petrol station.

Many **buses** from Panaji and Mapusa. **Bus**: to/from Mapusa: frequent service, Rs 2, 20 mins; not all go to Baga.

Taxi: to/from Mapusa about Rs 40-50, bargain hard.

Directory

Banks & money changers: State Bank of India changes some TCs but does not accept Visa; **Bank of Baroda** accepts some credit cards, but get there around 1030 and be prepared to spend at least an hour. Also many private dealers offer a convenient and speedy service but offer a poorer rate.

Shopping: While goods on offer are attractive and varied, it is best to look around first before buying. The asking price in most shops aimed at tourists are highly inflated so be prepared to bargain if you want to pay a realistic price.

Useful addresses: *Kerkar Art Gallery*, Gauravaddo, T 276017, sells paintings, sculpture and crafts; holds open-air cultural show on Tuesday and Saturday, at

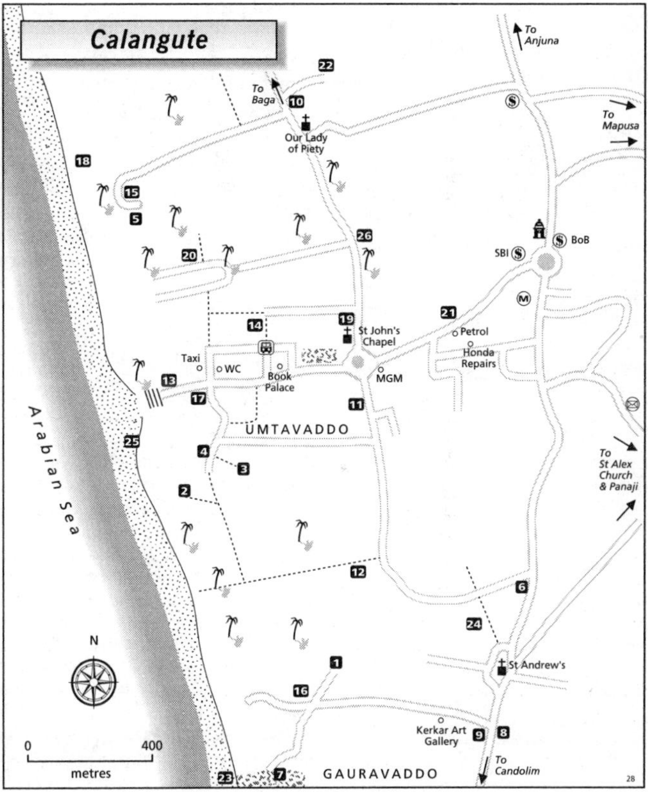

Hotels:
1. *Arabian Retreat*
2. *Calangute Beach Resort*
3. *Coco Banana*
4. *Concha Beach Resort*
5. *Estrela do Mar*
6. *Falcon*
7. *Goan Heritage*
8. *Kamat's*
9. *Landscape*
10. *Martins*
11. *Mira*
12. *Paradise Village*
13. *Tourist Resort & Cater's*
14. *Varma's Beach Resort*
15. *Villa Goesa*
16. *White House*

Places to eat:
17. Angelina & Lobster Pot
18. Delhi Durbar
19. Infanteria
20. Johnny's
21. Master Joel
22. Milky Way & Indian Café
23. Pedro's
24. Sip 'n' Dip
25. Souza Lobo
26. Taste of China

1830, Rs 150; ***Book Palace***, Beach Rd, near the Bus Stand. Several travel agents including ***MGM Travels***, Umtavaddo, T/F 276073.

BAGA

M2C1

Sandwiched between Calangute and Anjuna, Baga (really the north end of Calangute beach) has more character. It has left behind almost completely the hippy past which brought it to prominence and offers some cheap accommodation close to the beach. That is not to say that it is entirely quiet: ***Tito's*** is **the** place for late night drinking and dancing, generally packed from 2300 to 0300, good place to meet people, known for Domingo's Pina Colada, small a/c dance floor inside (techno), entrance free for women, Rs 100 for men. *Bharat* is friendly and a good place for an evening drink.

Hotels:
1. *Alidias Beach Cottages*
2. *Ancona Beach Resort*
3. *Baia Do Sol*
4. *Capt Lobo's Beach Hideaway* & Lafremich
5. *Cavala*
6. *CSM* & Bernard's Place
7. *Jimi's Teepee Village*
8. *Riverside*
9. *Ronil Royale*
10. *Sea View Cottages*
11. *Sunshine Beach Resort*
12. *Venar*

Places to eat:
13. Casa Portuguesa & *Villa Fatima*
14. Electric Cats
15. Indian Impact
16. Nani's & Rani's
17. Nisha
18. St Anthony's & Britto's (Motorbikes)
19. Sunset
20. Two Sisters

Bars:
21. Bharat
22. Tito's

The northern end is quieter and you can wade across the attractive estuary at low tide (with care) for a pleasant 30-min walk round the headland leading to Anjuna beach. The enclosed concrete bridge (possibly one of the ugliest ever built!) across the Baga river adds about 1 km to this walk. Take care when using this bridge at night since it is unlit and not even the full moon can penetrate the excess of concrete. Early risers may see fishermen returning with their catch while at dusk individual fishermen may be seen casting their nets at the mouth of the estuary.

NB Many hotels offer big off-season discounts May-September; some attract package holidays.

Luxury hotel

AL *Nilaya Hermitage*, near Arpora, 3 km inland, T 276793, delightful wooded setting, 8 uniquely furnished rooms, very peaceful, highly exclusive.

Mid-range hotels

C *Capt Lobo's Beach Hideaway*, Cobravaddo, T/F 276103, 10 a/c rooms, "scruffy, depressing and poorly equipped", good restaurant (but service can be slow), bar, pool, nautical theme, nearer to beach than most in its class but crowded site; **C** *CSM Leisure Resort* (Colonia Santa Maria), Cobravaddo, 15 minute walk to centre, T 277447, F 277423, 46 rooms in 10 colonial style villas among palms and bougainvillea, *Banana Grove* tandoori restaurant, bar, pool, beach across dunes.

C-D *Baia Do Sol*, Baga Sq, north end, T 276068, 23 very clean rooms, a/c cottages, good restaurant with views (excellent seafood), watersports, good entertainment, in excellent location, attractive garden setting, recommended.

Prices: AL over Rs 6,000; **C** Rs 800-1,500; **D** Rs 400-800; **E** Rs 200-400

D *Alidia Beach Cottages*, T 276835, F 279014, behind the church, Sauntavaddo, 15 good clean rooms with attached bath, friendly owner, beach 2 minute walk, recommended; **D** ***Cavala***, Sauntavaddo, Baga-Calangute Rd, away from beach, T 276090, F 277340, 25 good rooms with bath, restaurant (very close to road), popular bar, clean, good value, recommended; **D** ***Jimi's Teepee Village***, Baga Hill, just north of bridge, 5 American-Indian style *teepees* with electricity, running water and secure storage, healing massage, recommended for imagination and uniqueness; **D** ***Riverside***, near the bridge, 5 minute walk from beach, T 276062, 18 modern rooms, good restaurant, garden setting, new pool, beautiful location, good value; **D** ***Ronil Royale***, Sauntavaddo, T 276183, F 276001, 20 rooms, some a/c, simple basic but clean, good restaurant (seafood, *tandoori*), coffee shop, pools.

D-E *Venar*, Cobravaddo, clean goodsize rooms; **D-F** *Villa Fatima*, T 277418, Calangute-Baga Rd, Sauntavaddo, 35 rooms (wide range) set round central courtyard, good for meeting people, popular with back packers, recommended.

Budget hotels

You will be overwhelmed by the number on offer. Here is a selection: **E** ***Ancona Beach Resort***, Sauntavaddo, T 276096, 10 rooms, Tibetan restaurant; **E** ***Sea View Cottages***, 16 airy pleasant rooms on the beach; **E** ***Sunshine Beach Resort***, Calangute-Baga Rd, T 276003, 4 attractive rooms around a shady courtyard.

Places to eat

There are plenty of good restaurants here. In hotels: *Baia del Sol*, Capt Lobo's (*Lafremich*), and *Riverside* are recommended. There are also numerous good small cafés along the beach: ***Bernard's Place*** near *CSM*, for Sunday roasts; ***Electric Cats*** for steak; ***Nisha***, good cheap *thalis*.

Indian Impact, Calangute-Baga Rd, is highly recommended for curries – "as good as Bradford"! ***Lotus Garden***, does excellent food but is pricey; ***Casa Portuguesa***, Calangute-Baga Rd, in an old villa with antiques, some tables on verandah, quite exclusive, plenty of atmosphere, great food.

Further north, near the river: ***St Anthony's***, good for Goan and seafood; ***Two Sisters***, recommended for muesli, curd and fruit salad; ***Nani's & Rani's*** across the river, friendly, pleasant, good breakfasts, also STD/ISD and simple rooms (T 276313); ***Sunset*** is further along the path, pleasant for watching the activities of Baga Beach and at the river mouth.

Transport

Bicycles and **motorbikes**: are available for hire; ask outside *Brittos* for motorbikes.

Buses: are fairly frequent to/from Mapusa.

Taxi: to/from Mapusa, about Rs 40 after bargaining.

Directory

Shopping: *Infinite*, north end, British/Indian couple sell original 'designer' creations, cheaply, no pressure. ***Pooja***, on Baga Rd, an environment friendly shop, sells attractive clothes.

Tour companies & travel agents: *Flying Dutchman*, Cobravaddo, Calangute Baga Rd, T 277437, also exhibits works by local and foreign artists, 1000-1300, 1600-2000; ***Lina D'Souza Traveland***, Villa Nova, Sauntavaddo, T 276196, F 276308.

ANJUNA

M2C1

STD Code 0832

Anjuna (pronounced Anzuna) is now one of Goa's most 'popular' coastal villages, though the headland is rather too rocky for comfortable swimming. It took over from Calangute as the centre for hippies but they are long gone leaving '90s 'ravers' and pill-poppers and the season's 'in' crowd, who often stay here on a long-term basis. One recent visitor writes: "If you want to fill your body with stimulants, party all night to Goa Trance, risk harrassment and extortion from the local police ... with the added attraction of warm weather and a tropical setting, then Anjuna is the place for you. The aim, it seems, is to "get off your face, dance until dawn and amuse/bore your friends silly about the previous night's highpoints (those that can be remembered) over breakfast the next morning."

Anjuna's proud past

Few of Anjuna's visitors know anything of its pre-hippy past, yet as Teresa Albuquerque's fascinating profile of the village (available in local bookshops) shows, it has a history of which the local population is very proud. The name gives away part of the secret of its origins. Derived from Hanjuman, a word applying to the Arabs 'Chamber of Commerce', Anjuna was an important Arab trading post from the 10th-12th centuries. But, as was common with many such ports on the west coast of India Arab Muslim traders often formed only a small minority of the population, and Hindu influences were also important, as both the lineage of some of the important Hindu castes and the existence of ancient temples illustrates.

Most traces of such temples have now been obliterated by years of Christianization, for Anjuna, along with the rest of Bardez, was deeply affected by Portuguese determination to convert everyone who lived in its Old Conquest territories. Ceded to the Portuguese by the Bijapur Sultans in 1543, it was allocated to the Franciscans as their sphere of missionary activity. 5 years after the Franciscans began working in Bardez they established the parish of Nagoa, which included modern Anjuna. Local people still talk of the ghosts of this era inhabiting particular groves. According to Teresa Albuquerque between 1546 and 1567, 300 temples were destroyed in Bardez and the income which had previously gone from temple lands to the temples was transferred to Christian education. The Anjuna shrine of Bhumika Devi was moved across into Pernem. The rectorate of Anjuna was established in 1603 when the Church of St Michael was dedicated. It was subsequently re-built on a much grander scale in 1613.

A well-attested story tells how in 1628 a Portuguese Vicar who had told a Hindu woman to have her child baptised was severely attacked by furious villagers. They were found guity of assault and executed. Their houses were confiscated and salt was mixed with the soil on their lands, and as a warning an account was carved in stone on a *padrao* (monument), and set up in the village. Gomes Pereira recounts that many years later the stone fell and broke in two, and that Hindu villagers often light candles on the stone in memory of the victims.

In the course of the next three centuries Anjuna produced a series of notable figures in Goa's history, both in Church and in secular life. The best known cleric was Fr Agnelo Gustav de Souza (1869-1927). Born and brought up in the village, Fr de Souza trained for the priesthood in Mapusa and Rachol before joining the Missionary Society of Pilar. He developed an extraordinary reputation both for his preaching and for his pastoral work. 12 years after his death his body was moved to Pilar and became a place of pilgrimage. In 1986 he was raised by the Pope to the rank of venerable, the final stage towards canonization.

Little of this personal history is evident to casual visitors. However, both from the churches and from some of the splendid houses something of the 400 years of cultural history can be inferred.

Warning Tourism has changed some features of the social face of Anjuna. The church remains strong and community life a powerful force, but the dramatic inflow of money and the wholly different life style of many of the visitors have produced tensions and conflict. The effects of easily available drugs are particularly resented by many in the villages. Incidents of break-ins and mugging have been reported, especially on the beach at night.

During the season, all night beach "parties" continue to attract crowds and even during the day there is a constant roar of motor bikes and scooters along the roads. The easy availability of drugs also attracts local police during the high season. They carry out raids on travellers' houses and harrass partygoers and sometimes innocent motorcyclists, demanding large bribes. Not all international peddlers get away; note that there are several foreigners serving long sentences.

Parts of the beach itself were very dirty at the end of the 1997 season with a lot of visible garbage, and the sand black because of oil pollution. However, the latter problem will probably be resolved by the end of the monsoon.

Close to Our Lady of Piety church on the way into Vagator from Mapusa, the splendid **Albuquerque Mansion** was built in the 1920s by an expatriate Goan who had worked as a doctor in Zanzibar, Dr Manuel F Albuquerque. Honoured by the Sultan of Zanzibar on his retirement he returned home to build what is now affectionately referred to by Teresa Albuquerque as 'the pride of Anjuna'. The house is in fact an exact replica of the Royal Palace

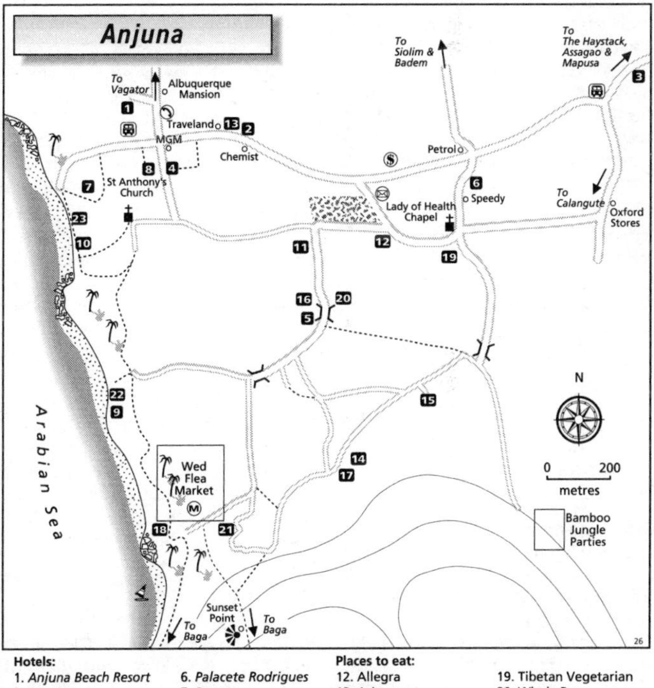

Hotels:
1. *Anjuna Beach Resort*
2. *Don Joao*
3. *Granpa's Inn &* Bougainvillea Restaurant
4. *Manali*
5. *Martha's*
6. *Palacete Rodrigues*
7. *Poonam*
8. *Red Cab Inn*
9. *Rose Garden*
10. *White Negro*
11. *Zebra Lodge*

Places to eat:
12. Allegra
13. Ariana
14. German Bakery
15. Gregory's
16. La Franza
17. Mango Shade
18. Sea Breeze
19. Tibetan Vegetarian
20. Whole Bean Tofu Shop
21. Xavier's
22. Shore Bar
23. Sonic Bar

Travel tip

The Wednesday **Flea Market** is now huge and very popular – some find it colourful and worthwhile for jewellery, souvenirs and ethnic clothes. From its origins as an opportunity for foreign travellers to sell personal possessions in order to get on – or get home – the flea market has become an all-India market. Kashmiris and Rajasthanis set up stall alongside stallholders from much closer to home. Everything is geared gaudily and unashamedly at the tourist. Haircuts and henna "tattoos" are on offer, alongside juggling equipment and chocolate cakes. The best time to visit is the early morning (0800) or just before sunset to avoid the mid-day crowds who jam the approach roads. In the high season the afternoon can get oppressive and it can be difficult to move around but at least the beach provides a handy escape valve. Some visitors are disappointed with the market – "rather full of tourists; Mapusa better for local colour"; still others find it a "gruesome experience", yet many enjoy its hotchpotch business. Many westerners end up at the *Shore Bar* for the Wednesday night rave.

of Zanzibar, so if you never have the chance to visit that African tropical island this is an opportunity to see what the king's home looks like – from the outside. The building was constructed by workers brought specially from Zanzibar.

Mid-range hotels

C ***Don Joao***, Sorranto, T 274325, F 220426, 42 large rooms on 2 floors with balcony and fridge (36 suites with kitchenettes), some a/c, restaurant, exchange, small pool, friendly, good value off-season, away from beach but recommended; **C** ***Grandpa's Inn***, Gaunwadi, Mapusa road, T 273271, F 274370, 10 comfortable rooms with bath in old Goan house, good restaurant, pool.

D ***Palacete Rodrigues***, Mazalvaddo, east of centre, T 273358, rooms and suites in old villa; **D** ***Red Cab Inn***, T 274427, 6 well-designed comfortable rooms, restaurant ('local entertainment', Mondays, 1900), recommended; sister hotel, ***Rose Garden***, north of the market, basic rooms with bath, exchange and ISD/Fax, good sizzlers, tandoori food; **D** *Tamarind*, Kumarvaddo, 3 km from beach, T 274309, 24 rooms, 6 a/c with modern bath in rustic stone cottages, well-managed, excellent restaurant (see below), bar, small pleasant pool, library, pretty garden, 3 dogs and a pet eagle! **D** *Poonam*, near the Bus Stand, T 273247, 23 good size simple, clean rooms with bath, some larger for sharing, restaurant; **D-E** *Martha's*, between bus stand and market, modest guest house, clean rooms, good breakfasts, quiet garden, friendly, recommended.

Budget hotels

Some travellers were robbed when staying in family houses which were not secure; it is safer to choose an approved hotel or guest house. Good padlocks are sold in the a small shop next to the *White Negro Bar* for Rs 150. Most beachside rooms are occupied by long-stay visitors who pay about Rs 2,000/month for the most basic.

E *Anjuna Beach Resort*, DeMello Vaddo, opposite Albuquerque Mansion, T 274433, 17 rooms with bath, balcony, restaurant (breakfast, snacks), bike hire, friendly, secure, quiet, near the beach, good value, recommended; **E** *White Negro*, near the Church, T 273326, rooms with bath, good restaurant and bar, newish, very clean.

F *Manali*, near the bus stand, T 274421, 7 basic rooms, shared bath, restaurant, exchange, library, lockers, reported unfriendly (also rooms in houses to let, Rs 3,000-3,500/month, bucket showers); **F** ***Zebra Lodging***, inland from St Anthony's, 5 rooms, shared facilities, garden, cheap **camping**.

Places to eat

A vegetarian's paradise with plenty of Western and exotic options. ***Allegra*** for Italian dishes; ***Ariana*** for Afghani food; ***Bougainvillea***, at *Grandpa's Inn,* excellent food, bar (wines, imported beer), very pretty garden, bit pricey but

Prices: C Rs 800-1,500; **D** Rs 400-800; **E** Rs 200-400; **F** under Rs 200

recommended; ***German Bakery***, inland from the Flea Market, outdoors, soft lighting, excellent espresso, capuccino, juice and snacks, 2/3 main courses each night (eg lasagna, tofu-burger), recommended; behind this and next to a tennis court is ***Gregory's***, recommended for excellent Continental, especially pizzas (try with prawns), also tennis!

For good seafood: ***La Franza*** restaurant and bar with a large verandah overlooking attractive tropical garden, serves good meals, particularly Continental, recommended. ***Mango Shade***, next to the German Bakery, where party goers on motor bikes hang out afterwards; ***Sea Breeze***, Market area, is busy on Wednesdays; ***Sea Pearl*** is recommended for breakfast and simple snacks; ***Tibetan Vegetarian***, for momos etc (**NB** "Reflexology, massage offered is not recommended for women"); ***Whole Bean Tofu Shop*** offers tofu, tempeh and veg snacks; the upmarket ***Xavier's***, St Michaelvaddo, is along a windy path, east from the market.

Nightlife and entertainment

Bars: *The Haystack*, Arpora, towards Mapusa, offers Goan food and wine, has live music and 'cultural' shows on Friday from 2030; ***Sonic***, is pleasant for a beer at sunset.

Beach parties: near the Wednesday Market; also at ***Bamboo Jungle***, between Baga and Anjuna, recognizable by illuminated trees and luminous wall hangings (**Warning** A serious gang rape occured near here in March 1997; try to go, and leave, in large groups); ***Paradiso***, at the north end of the beach; ***Shore Bar***, north of the Flea market, the place to go on Wednesday evening, where there is a good sound system – a fire jugglers' playground. Several elderly women set up *chai* stalls with cakes and king-size *rizlas* on sale, making a good profit.

Paragliding is possible at the hill top between Anjuna and Baga; 1100-1800, Rs 500 (children are welcome).

Windsurfing boards are available for hire at the south end of the beach; Rs 100/hr, Rs 800/week.

Transport

Frequent **buses** to/from Mapusa; daily from Panaji.

Local **boats** ply from Baga for the Wednesday Market.

Motorcycles are easy to hire; *Classic Bike Adventure* Indo-German company at Casa Tres Amigos, Socol Vado 425, Parra, Assagao, about 5 km east (off the Mapusa road), T 0832 273351, F 262076, recommended for reliable bike hire and tours.

Directory

Banks & money changers: Bank of Baroda, Monday-Wednesday, Friday 0930-1330, Saturday 0930-1130, accepts most TCs, Visa/Mastercard, 1% (min Rs 50); it is better than private dealers closer to town.

Post & telecommunications: Poste Restante at Anjuna Post Office, open 1000-1600, Monday-Saturday; parcels are also accepted without a fuss.

Useful addresses: Chemists opposite Don Joao Resorts; ***Oxford Stores***, for groceries, foreign exchange and photo processing. Petrol is available at *Dinesh Hotel* near the crossroads towards Siolim. Several travel agents include ***MGM***, ***Speedy*** and ***Traveland***, near the bus stand, T 273207, F 217535.

VAGATOR & CHAPORA *M2B1*

STD Code 0832

At the north end of Anjuna village Chapora is an attractive little hamlet with its small bays between rocky headlands shaded by palms. It is quiet and laid back, though it can sometimes get crowded with day-trippers. The beach is particularly pleasant in the early morning, but the sea is not always safe for swimming. Cheaper than Anjuna for rooms and houses, it attracts long-term travellers. Chapora is quite a dirty village compared to others in Goa so it is not surprising that there is very high density of laundries!

Traditional **boat building** is carried out on the riverside, along the estuary mouth at Chapora.

❖ Chapora Fort *M2B1*

The fort commands the hill top at the north end of the bay, only a short but steep walk away, immediately above *Sterling Resorts*. Now in ruins, it stands on the south bank of the Chapora River and dominates the estuary. It was originally built by Adil Shah. Aurangzeb's son Akbar (not Akbar the Great) used it as his headquarters when plotting against his father in a pact with the Mughal's greatest enemies, the Marathas. The Portuguese built it in its present form in 1717 as a secure refuge for the people of Bardez in face of the Maratha attacks as well as a defence of the river mouth. Despite the fact that none of the original buildings have survived the Fort remains superbly atmospheric. The irregular walls, with one major gateway on its eastern side and a series of octagonal battlements was once served by a series of underground tunnels. Views from the sea-facing walls are spectacular. To the north, across the ruffled waters of the Chapora estuary, the stunning blue of the sea meets the fine sand of Morjim beach, curving gracefully northwards towards Mandrem, Arambol and finally Tiracol. To the west a low circular knoll abuts into the sea in front of the fort, while to the south the small coves of Vagator gives way to Anjuna beach. The fort is well worth a visit, but it is quite a climb and normally there are no refreshments save for fruit drinks sold by children at highly inflated prices, so it is worth carrying water.

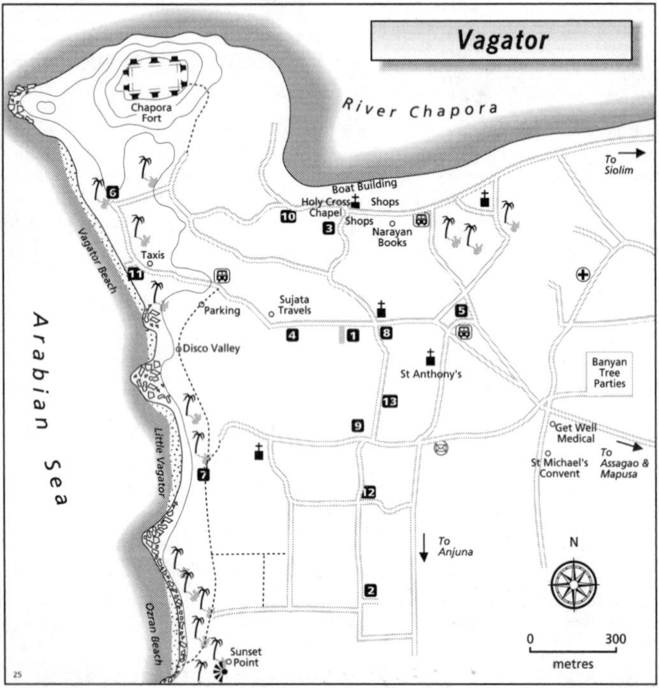

Hotels:
1. *Abu John's*
2. *Hilltop Motel &* Italian Bakery
3. *Noble Nest*
4. *Reshma*
5. *Royal Resort*
6. *Sterling Vagator*
7. *Swami Ram Das*

Places to eat:
8. China Town
9. Day Nite
10. Lonely Planet
11. Mahalaxmi
12. Milky Place
13. Primrose

Goa
N
To Mumbai
MAHARASHTRA
<50m
50-100m
100-300m
+300m
Highway
Main Roads
Railway
After Catherine Lawrence
0
10
km
Tiracol R
Pernem
Naibaga
Alorna Fort
Arambol (Harmal)
NH 17
Dargalim
Parsi
Macasna
Colvale
Siolim
Assonora
Cunchelim
Bicholim
Mapusa
Mapusa R
Maem
Sanquelim
Carambolin -Brahma
Chorao
Arqualem
Calangute
NH 17
Salim Ali Bird Sanctuary
Valpoi
Divar
Kudne R
Caranzol
Aguada Fort
Mandovi R
PANAJI
Old Goa
Banastari
Birondem
Savoi-Verem
Bondla Sanctuary
Pilar
Cambarjua Canal
Mardol
Usgaon
Mormugao
Khandepar
Tisk
Tambdi Surla
Vasco da Gama
Cortalim
Ponda
Sancordem
NH 4A
Molem
Bhagwan Mahaveer Sanctuary
Cansaulim
Loutolim
Zuari R
Borim
Codli
Dudsagar R
Colem
Dudhsagar
Majorda
Rachol
Siroda
Calem
Sanguem R
Margao
Colva
Benaulim
Chandor
Sanvordem
Paroda
Quepem
Sanguem
Arabian Sea
Sal R
Paroda R
Damai
Cuncolim
Zambaulim
Cumbari
Mabor
Bali
Rivona
Curdi
Betul
Fatorpa
Netorli
Pirla
Cabo de Rama Fort
NH 17
Kushavati R
Canacona
Palolem
Cotigao Sanctuary
Talpona R
Partagal Math
Galibag
Mashen
NH 17
To Mangalore
KARNATAKA
Delhi
Calcutta
Mumbai
GOA
Chennai
C
2
3

M2 Bardez & Pernem Taluka

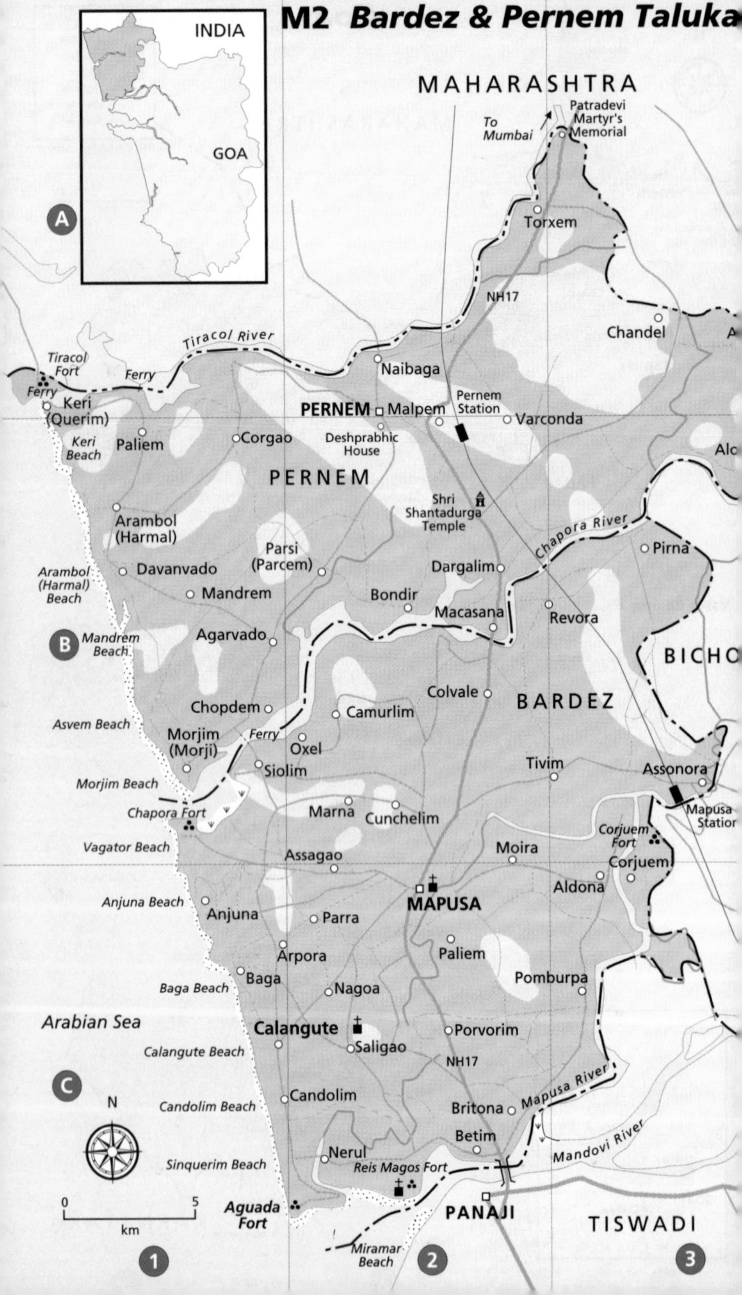
INDIA
GOA
MAHARASHTRA
To Mumbai
Patradevi Martyr's Memorial
Torxem
NH17
Chandel
Tiracol River
Tiracol Fort
Ferry
Ferry
Naibaga
Keri (Querim)
PERNEM
Malpem
Pernem Station
Varconda
Paliem
Corgao
Deshprabhic House
Keri Beach
PERNEM
Shri Shantadurga Temple
Arambol (Harmal)
Chapora River
Pirna
Parsi (Parcem)
Arambol (Harmal) Beach
Davanvado
Dargalim
Mandrem
Bondir
Macasana
Revora
Mandrem Beach
Agarvado
BICHO
Colvale
BARDEZ
Chopdem
Camurlim
Asvem Beach
Morjim (Morji)
Ferry
Oxel
Siolim
Tivim
Assonora
Morjim Beach
Chapora Fort
Marna
Cunchelim
Mapusa Station
Corjuem Fort
Vagator Beach
Assagao
Moira
Corjuem
Aldona
Anjuna Beach
Anjuna
MAPUSA
Parra
Arpora
Paliem
Baga
Pomburpa
Baga Beach
Nagoa
Arabian Sea
Calangute
Porvorim
Saligao
Calangute Beach
NH17
Mapusa River
Candolim
N
Candolim Beach
Britona
Betim
Mandovi River
Nerul
Sinquerim Beach
Reis Magos Fort
0
5
km
Aguada Fort
PANAJI
TISWADI
Miramar Beach
A
B
C
1
2
3

M3 *Bicholim & Satari Talukas*

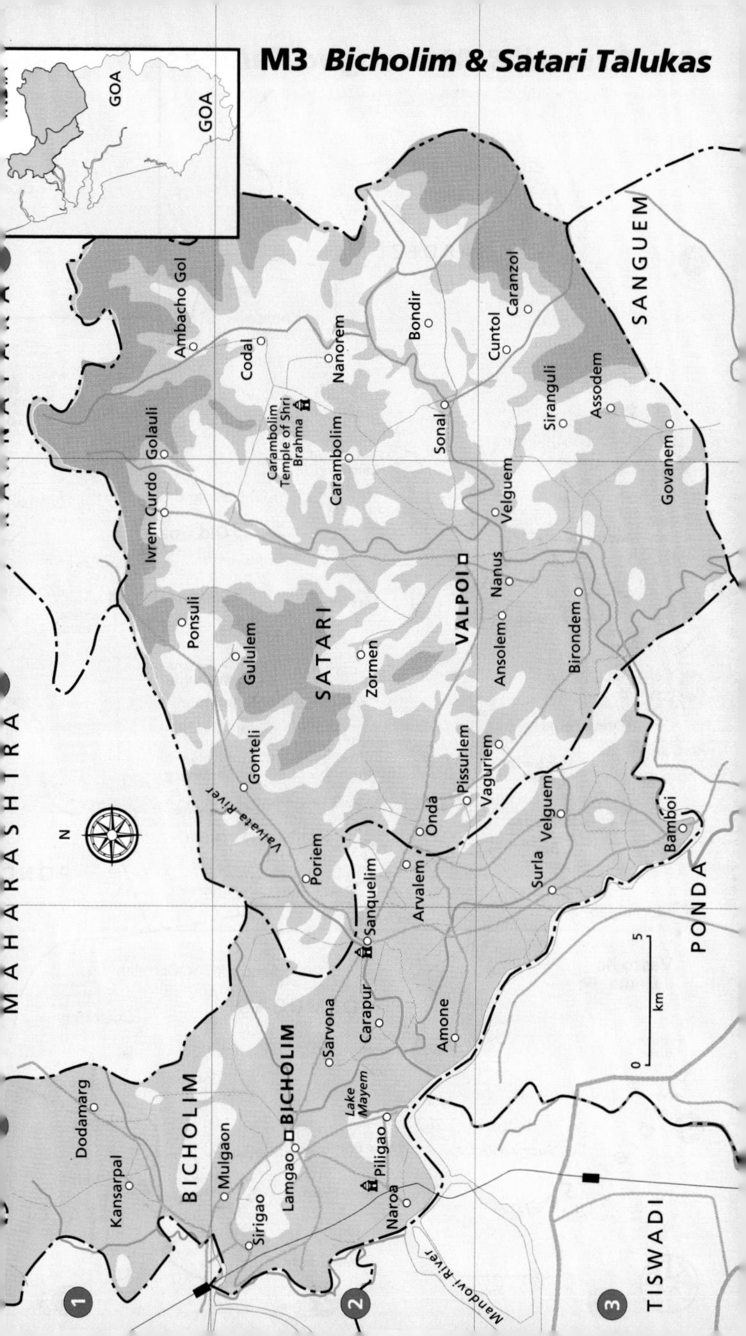

M4 *Tiswadi & Mormugao Talukas*

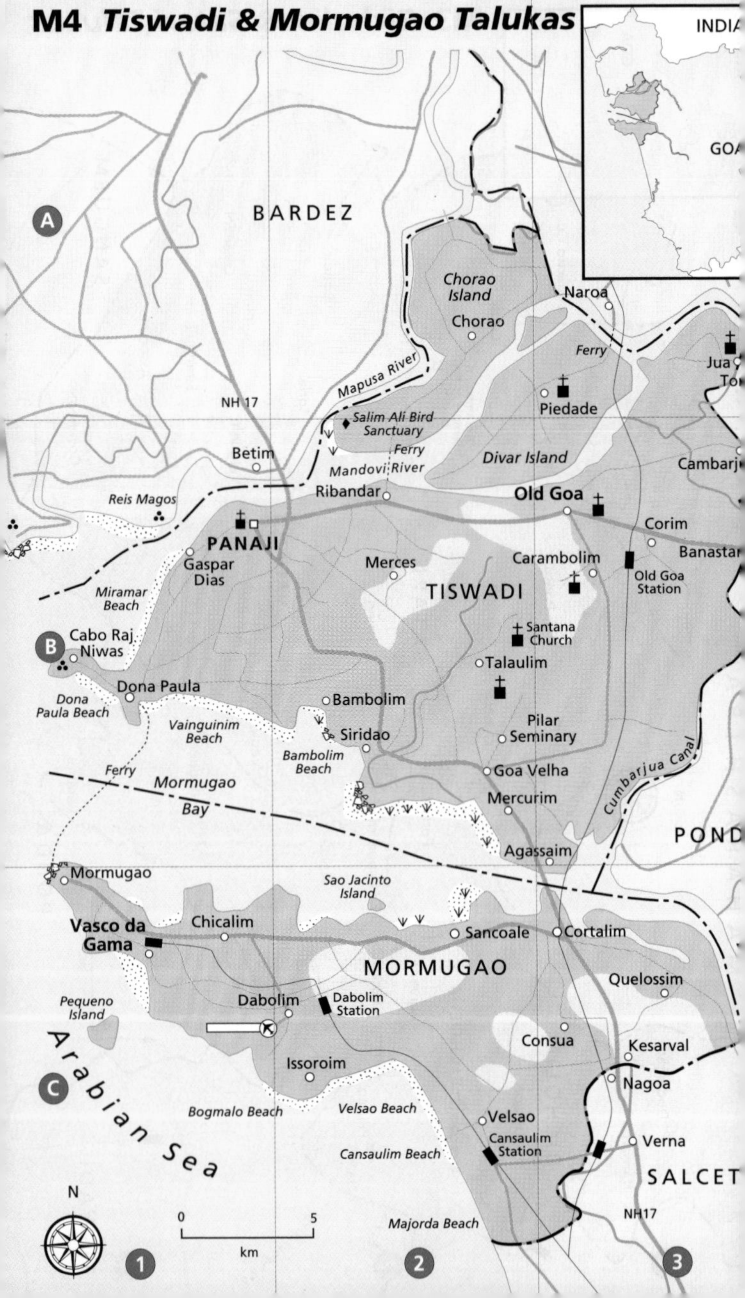

M5 *Ponda Taluka*

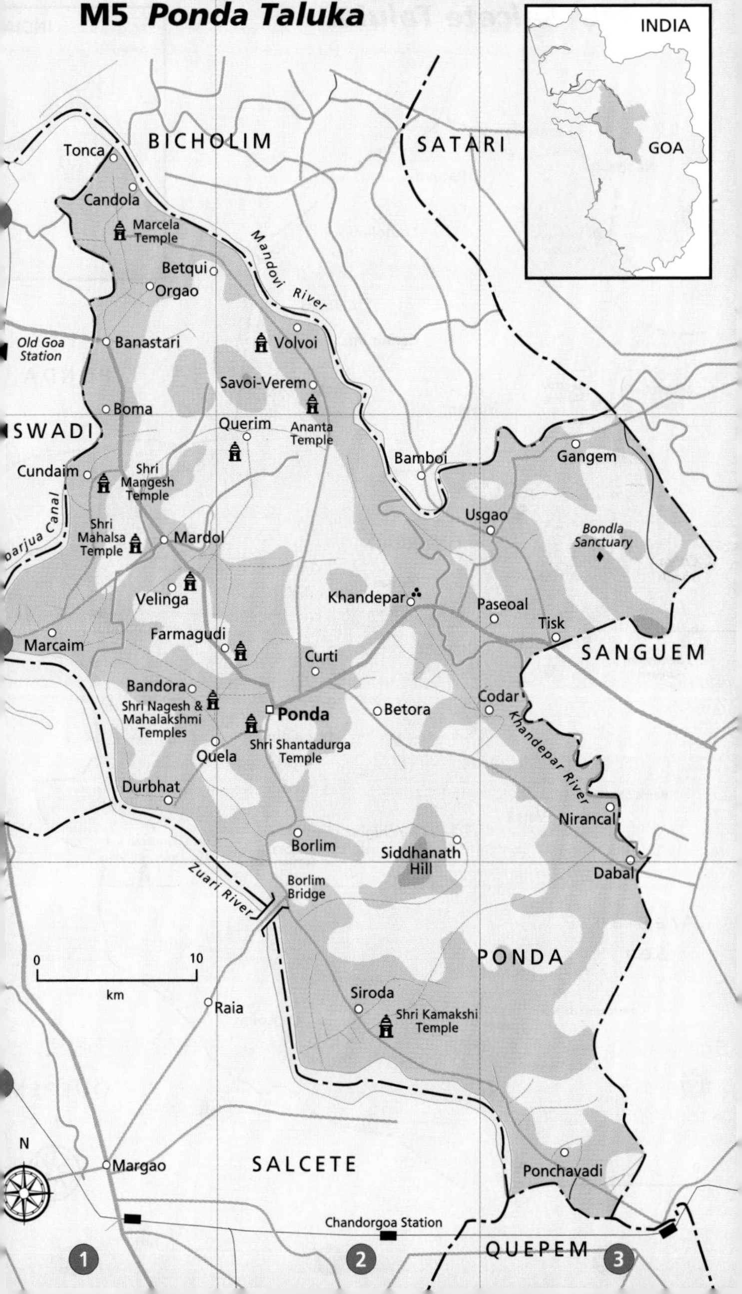

INDIA
GOA
BICHOLIM
SATARI
Tonca
Candola
Marcela Temple
Mandovi River
Betqui
Orgao
Old Goa Station
Banastari
Volvoi
Savoi-Verem
Boma
SWADI
Querim
Ananta Temple
Bamboi
Gangem
Cundaim
Shri Mangesh Temple
Canal
Shri Mahalsa Temple
Mardol
Usgao
Bondla Sanctuary
Velinga
Khandepar
Paseoal
Tisk
Marcaim
Farmagudi
SANGUEM
Curti
Bandora
Shri Nagesh & Mahalakshmi Temples
Ponda
Betora
Codar
Shri Shantadurga Temple
Quela
Khandepar River
Durbhat
Nirancal
Borlim
Siddhanath Hill
Dabal
Zuari River
Borlim Bridge
PONDA
0
10
km
Raia
Siroda
Shri Kamakshi Temple
N
Margao
SALCETE
Ponchavadi
Chandorgoa Station
QUEPEM
1
2
3

M6 *Salcete Taluka*

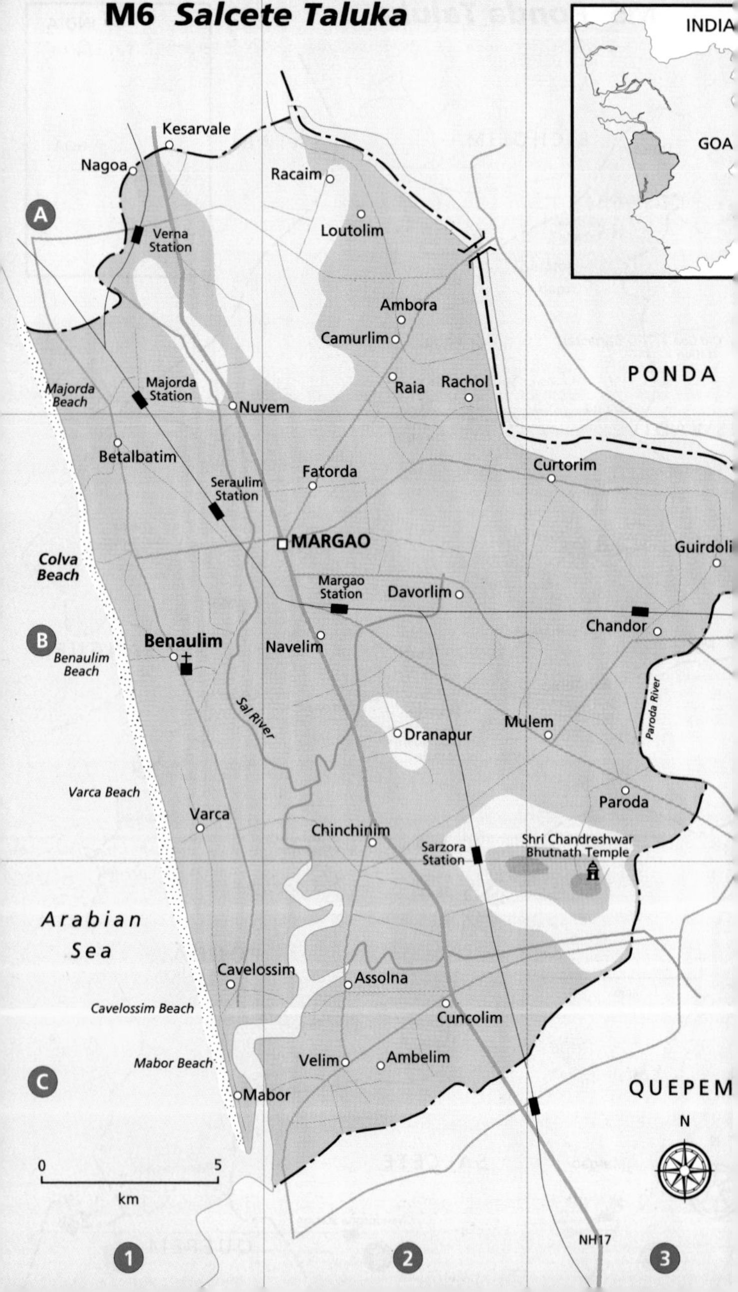

M7 *Sanguem Taluka*

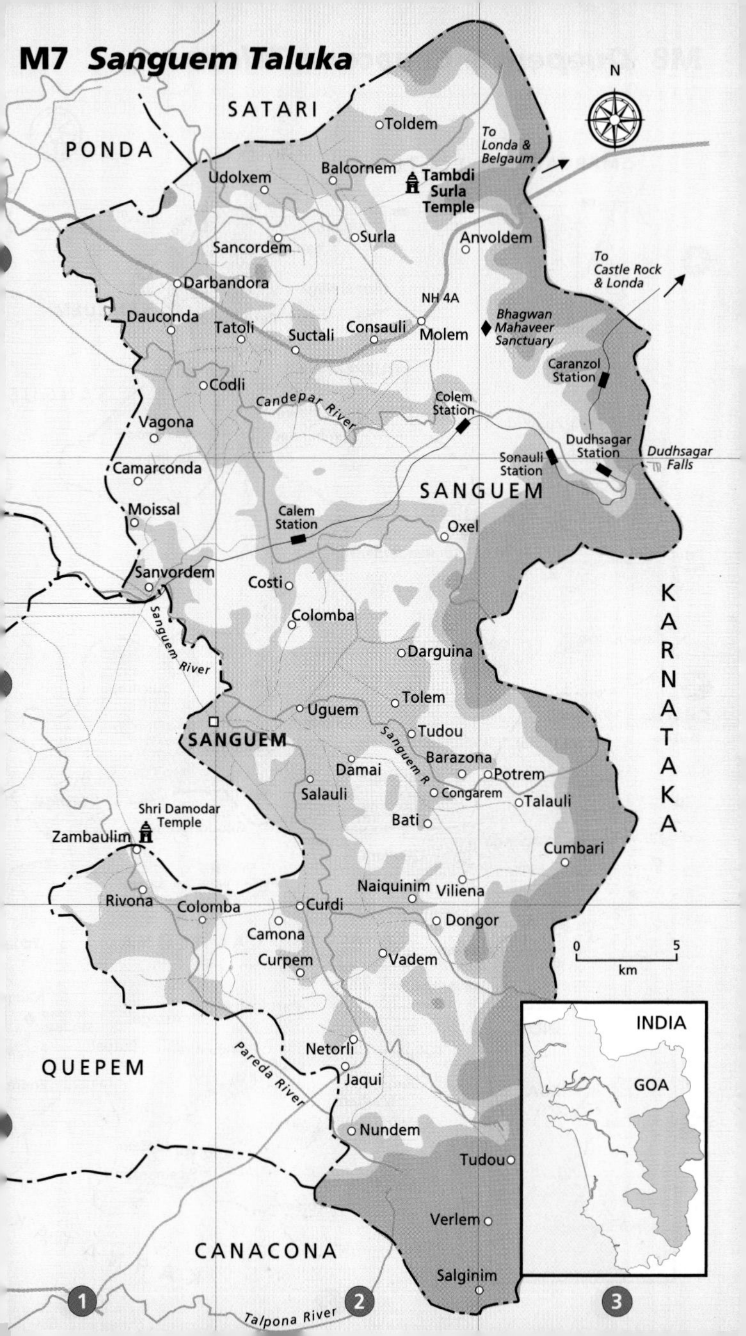

M8 Quepem & Canacona Talukas

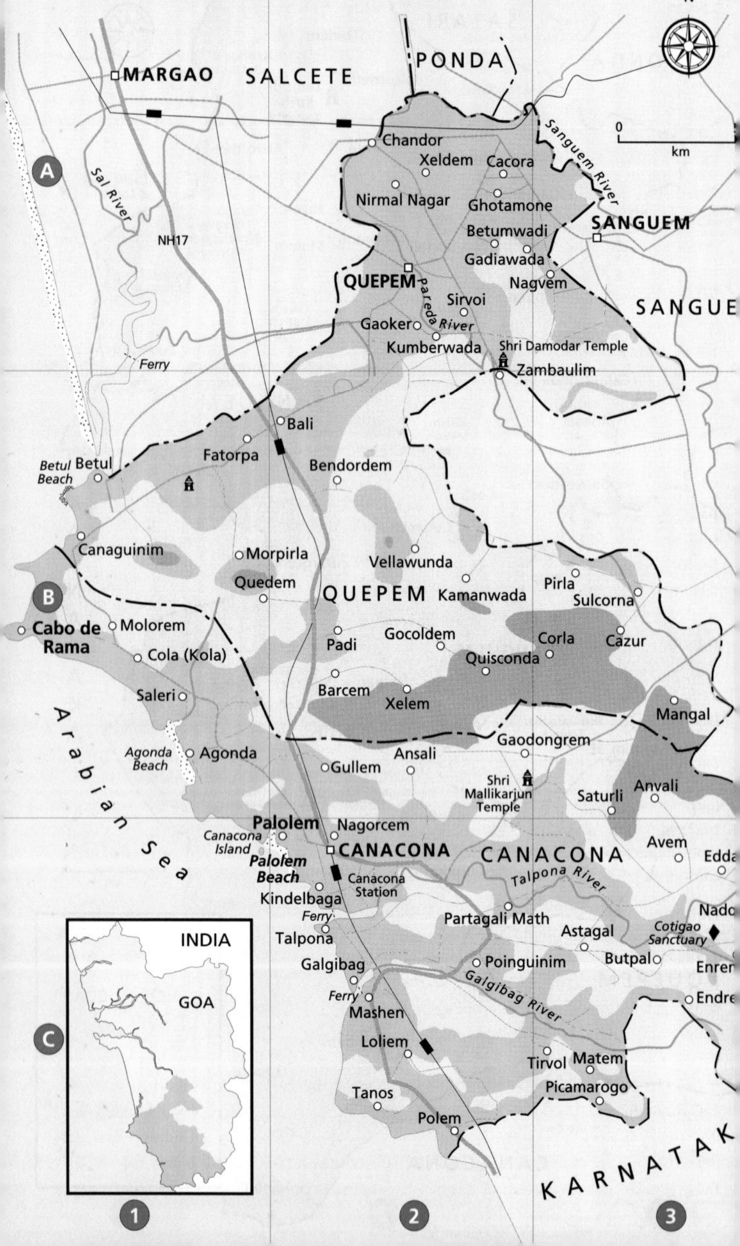
N
km
0
MARGAO
SALCETE
PONDA
Sal River
NH17
Chandor
Xeldem
Cacora
Sanguem River
Nirmal Nagar
Ghotamone
SANGUEM
Betumwadi
Gadiawada
QUEPEM
Pareda River
Nagvem
Sirvoi
SANGUE
Gaoker
Kumberwada
Shri Damodar Temple
Zambaulim
Ferry
Bali
Fatorpa
Betul Beach
Betul
Bendordem
Canaguinim
Morpirla
Vellawunda
Quedem
QUEPEM
Kamanwada
Pirla
Sulcorna
Cabo de Rama
Molorem
Cola (Kola)
Padi
Gocoldem
Corla
Cazur
Quisconda
Saleri
Barcem
Xelem
Mangal
Arabian Sea
Gaodongrem
Agonda Beach
Agonda
Ansali
Gullem
Shri Mallikarjun Temple
Saturli
Anvali
Palolem
Nagorcem
Canacona Island
CANACONA
CANACONA
Avem
Edda
Palolem Beach
Canacona Station
Talpona River
Kindelbaga
Nado
Ferry
Partagali Math
Astagal
Cotigao Sanctuary
Talpona
Galgibag
Poinguinim
Butpal
Enren
Ferry
Galgibag River
Endre
Mashen
Loliem
Tirvol
Matem
Tanos
Picamarogo
Polem
KARNATAK
INDIA
GOA
A
B
C
1
2
3

Travel tip

Day-tourists from Panaji descend on Vagator and Anjuna around 11 o'clock in the morning and start leaving as the heat goes out of the sun in the late afternoon.

North of Chapora, on the Siolim road, **Badem Church** overlooking the estuary is one of the nicest sunset spots.

Little Vagator and Ozran beaches

M2B1

Just south of Vagator Beach which attracts day trippers, there are two other small beaches which are more popular with younger travellers who fancy a change from Anjuna. **Little Vagator** is past the Disco Valley Party spot while a little further along the very attractive **Ozran** beach nestles at the bottom of a palm covered cliff. A steep path leads down to the sands where there is a face sculpture left by one of the original hippies in the 1970s – it is a frisbee hangout.

Getting there From Anjuna, to reach Ozran and Little Vagator Beaches, first take the road towards Siolim and follow it around the hill until you see the sign for the *Alcove Restaurant* and Pub. Turn left here and the rest is obvious. Ozran Beach is recognizable by a small shack on top of the cliff which usually has motorbikes parked outside. Little Vagator is a short distance further. *Sterling Vagator Resort* signs direct you to Vagator and the Chapora Fort.

Mid-range hotels

B-C *Sterling Vagator* (partly time-share), T 273276, F 274376, attractive setting at the foot of the Fort, 30 well maintained cottages, some poolside (uphill) or in peaceful garden setting with shady *jambul* trees near the beach, restaurants (others 10 minutes walk away), quiet, exchange for residents.

C-D *Royal Resort*, T/F 273260, 28 renovated rooms, 10 a/c, 500m from beach, restaurant, bar, pool.

D *Hilltop Motel* has an Italian bakery.

Budget hotels

Chapora Village has a number of very cheap rooms and houses for long term rent; ask locally. Several are along the streets leading to the beach from the bus stops: **E** *Abu John's*, small rooms with bath, good restaurant, garden, pleasant, quiet.

F *Noble Nest*, opposite the Holy Cross Chapel, basic, restaurant. **F** *Mahalaxmi*, on the beach, is basic, cheap and shabby; **F** *Swami Ram Das* restaurant on Little Vagator Beach, allows **camping** (no toilets).

Places to eat

China Town, in the village, with a wide choice is the most upmarket. *Lonely Planet*, offers drinks, snacks and insects aplenty; fly-ridden *Scarlets* does good muesli, ice creams etc, while *Juice Tree* is a popular post-party hangout. In **Vagator**: there are several restaurants along the streets to the beach, some serve good fresh fish including *Mahalaxmi*. *Alcove* does good North Indian. *Milky Place* is good for lassi, yoghurt etc.

Nightlife

Parties at *Disco Valley* between Vagator and Little Vagator beaches and at *Banyan Tree*, east of Vagator. *Primrose* in Vagator has news of "spontaneous" parties.

Transport

Road Daily bus from Panaji, 1¼ hours; frequent from Mapusa to Chapora via Anjuna and Vagator.

Directory

Banks & money changers: No exchange facilities here except at *Sterling Vagator* (for residents only); nearest is at the Bank of Baroda, Anjuna.
Books: *Narayan*, a small bookstall has a selection of books and local newspapers.

SIOLIM

M2B1

Population 9,700, pronounced *Show-lem*

Less than 1 km from the ferry crossing, the **Church of St Anthony** dominates the square. Built in 1606, it replaced an earlier (1568) Franciscan church. St Anthony, the Patron saint of Portugal, is widely venerated throughout the villages of Goa. The high flat-ceilinged church has a narrow balustraded gallery and Belgian glass chandeliers. The attractive and typically gabled west-end has statues of Jesus and St Anthony.

The ferries are half-hourly, but will be made redundant by the new bridge when it opens. The direct route to Arambol and Tiracol passes through Mandrem (see below).

MORJIM

M2B1

Morjim lies on the north side of the Chapora River estuary right at its mouth. After crossing the estuary by ferry to Chopdem the coast road runs as a narrow village lane winding along the edge of the estuary giving beautiful views across to Chapora Fort until it reaches the point where the river meets the sea and the coast turns sharply north. Here the road ends behind the sand dunes, at a picnic spot which is usually deserted, facing a huge expanse of firm sand.

The **Shri Morja Devi Temple** in the village is of special interest because one of its affiliated shrine is dedicated to a Jain guru. This suggests an ancient heritage to the temple, since Jainism was sponsored by both the Chalukyas and the Rashtrakuta dynasties who ruled over the region from the 6th to the 10th centuries AD (see introduction). The principal festival is a month-long *Kalas Utsav* which is celebrated every 3, 5, 7 or 9 years.

Morjim's air of quiet solitude will change if long term plans for a 5-star resort development materialize. At present, only a few beach shacks and some palm umbrellas provide the only shade on this long and wide stretch of sand.

ASVEM

M2B1

There is no coast road up to Mandrem and the road from Morjim cuts inland over the low wooded hills to Mandrem village which lies a few km south of Arambol. Just before you get to the village, a road leads down to Asvem Beach where you can get something to drink and eat at one of the shacks. It is a quiet, attractive palm-fringed beach which has some very cheap beach huts which are snapped up, usually by German travellers.

MANDREM

M2B1

Along the road, the fishing and toddy tapping village occupies a beautifully shaded setting. The beach which is usually deserted, has little shade, but a little to the north is a beautiful little 'island' of sand with coconut palms between the sea and the river.

Mandrem village has the **Shri Bhumika temple** where the image of the deity is believed to be ancient. In the **Shri Purchevo Ravalnatha Temple** there is a particularly striking medieval image of the half eagle-half human Garuda, who acts as the *vahana* (carrier) of Vishnu. It is unusual in that the crouching Garuda is dressed as a soldier with wings protruding from his back.

There are many **F** category village **rooms** for rent, usually indicated by signs, and a number of foreigners rent these for up to 6 months through the winter. Simply ask around in the village. The *Canara Bank* on the main road accepts TCs but has no facilities for card cash.

ARAMBOL

M2B1

STD Code 0832

Arambol (Harmal) is still widely thought of as one of the last idyllically peaceful spots in Goa. A large, strung out village by the sea shore, it is approached by a road which winds across the plateau and down through cashew trees. A sign at the cross roads in the middle of the village near the bus stop points down to the beach, and the road passes a school and village houses sheltering under coconut palms on its 1.5 km route to the sea. Beware of the numerous unmarked speed breakers around the area.

The main beach is a stunning stretch of curving sand. Beach shacks offering a selection of food and drinks are all along the main beach and around the headland towards the smaller beach to the north. They service the growing number of day trippers including motor-cyclists from Anjuna, make their way here.

To the north, a well-made track runs round the headland past a series of tiny bays to the second beach, still more secluded and little used. Unlike the headlands around Anjuna, the rocks which run into the sea here are basalt, the hexagonal columns tilted almost horizontal but eroded into jagged shapes clearly visible for miles along the coast. There are sulphur pits and a lovely fresh water lake which some visitors use for swimming. Paragliding is also arranged from one of the shacks.

If you spend some time in the village you may discover the main village temple, dedicated to the deity **Shri Ravalnath**, though it also has eight affiliated deities. Its priests are Gaud Saraswat Brahmins. Despite the fact that it is in the New Conquests, Arambol also has a Christian community and a church. There are several basic eateries where you can get cheap rice 'plate meals'. The *Welcome Restaurant* is at the end of the road on the sea front. Here too are *Delight Travel* and *Tara Travel*, both will exchange cash and TCs. The small village Post Office is at the 'T' junction 1.5 km from the beach.

A few rooms are springing up in the season although the situation is changing fast. There are plenty of exceptionally cheap rooms to let close to the beach, and in the village; ask at a beach shack. Check security as many rooms are exposed and lack the security of a hotel or guest house compound. The small **F** *Ganesh Rest House*, on the first headland north, 250m from beach, large rooms with bath, good balcony upstairs, restaurant. A little further along, is the tiny **F** *Lakes Paradise* which also serves Goan curry and rice. There is basic, very spartan accommodation in **Waddo**, the small village, near Arambol.

Getting there Until 1997 most people who went to Arambol got there by motorbike though there was a regular bus service to the village from Mapusa. Coming from the south: from Vagator (see above) you can walk to Chapora village to find a local ferry across the estuary (Rs 20 each, Rs 40 for a boat), then take a 2-hr walk north through Morjim and Mandrem along the very attractive coast. Alternatively you can get a bus to Siolim, cross the river by the regular ferry to Chopdem and then pick up a bus or taxi. The main road from Chopdem to Arambol beach is 12 km, the attractive coastal détour via Morjim being slightly longer.

KERI *M2A1*

Keri beach, north of Arambol Beach is a completely unspoilt stretch of sand backed by casuarina trees all the way down to the Arambol highland. It can be reached from the north on foot from the ferry terminal, or from the south by walking round the headland from Arambol. There are dangerous currents near the mouth of the Tiracol estuary so it is best to avoid swimming there; a 5-min walk south along the beach will get you to safe waters. The beach is protected by CRZ regulations from being developed with permanant buildings near the high water mark. **Accommodation** The Forest Department's simple **F** *Keri Forest Rest House*, can be booked through the DCF, North Ponda, T 0834 312095.

❖ TIRACOL

M2A1

Tiracol (Terekhol) is the northernmost tip of Goa, an enclave on the Maharashtra border. The village probably derives its name from *tir-khol* (steep river bank).

The small but strategic **fort** stands above the village on the north side of the Tiracol River estuary on a rugged promontory which gives good views across the water. Its high battlemented walls are clearly visible from the Arambol headland. Built by the Maharaja Khem Sawant Bhonsle in the 17th century, it is protected from attacks from the sea, while the walls on the land side rise from a dry moat. It was captured by the Portuguese Viceroy Dom Pedro Miguel de Almeida (Marques de Alorna) in 1746 who renamed it Holy Trinity and had a chapel built inside (now St Anthony's). Tiracol was only fully and legally incorporated into Goa in 1788. The fort was armed with 22 cannons but saw a bloody massacre in 1835. During a military revolt, a ruthless Commandant, 'Tiger Killer' de Cunha, entered the fort and ordered the beheading of the garrison and civilians who were sheltering there, and went on to exhibit the heads on stakes. Far removed from the centre of administration in Panaji, Tiracol gained a reputation as a spot chosen by Goan freedom fighters to demonstrate their demands from time to time. A group entered the fort on 15 August (Independence Day) 1954 and succeeded in flying the Indian flag there for a day, before being captured and subsequently jailed.

St Anthony's church inside the tiny fort was built in the early 1750s soon after the Portuguese takeover. It has a classic Goan façade and is just large enough to have catered for the small village. In the small courtyard, paved with laterite blocks, stands a modern statue of Christ. Inside, the church has several charming features. The small gallery at the west-end provides space for a harmonium and the choir, while in the body of the church are two old confessional chairs. Too small a church for full scale confessional boxes, two small hinged wooden flaps are pulled out to separate the priest from the penitent, and tucked back against the wall when not in use. There is a typically decorated altar reredos with St Anthony above. Some of the framed paintings on the walls have deteriorated with time. The *Festival of St Anthony* here is held in May (usually on the

Something different

Looking for a place to stay which is really atmospheric and a little bit different? Then try the ***Tiracol Fort Heritage*** T 02366 68248, F 0834 782326. It is one of Goa's most peaceful and romantic places to stay. The 10 converted rooms in the old fort have been sympathetically furnished and have wonderful views. The best are the spacious suites at either end on the first floor (one is particularly good with its own little tiny terrace with a flag pole and is visited by *langur* monkeys). Rooms start at around Rs 1,000-1,500 whilst the suites are likely to be double this but there are discounts from 4 May-3 September. Power cuts can be a problem, especially at mealtimes. The restaurant has a limited menu but the setting must be unique: a reclaimed dry moat lined with laterite slabs. The hotel will arrange boat trips to prawn hatchery as well as scooter hire,

Non-residents can visit between 0900-1800, recommended and then repair to the much cheaper ***Hill Rock***, 1 km from the ferry, T 02366 68264, modern, 8 rooms in a family hotel, restaurant.

second Tuesday) to enable the villagers to attend who would otherwise be away on the conventional festival day of 13 June.

You can explore the fort's battlements and tiny circular turrets which scarcely seem to have been intended for the real business of shooting the enemy. The views from the fort are magnificently atmospheric, looking south to Arambol, Chapora and Fort Aguada. Steps lead down to a terrace on the south side while the north has an open plateau.

Getting there To Tiracol, from **Panaji**, bus leaves at 1130. From **Mapusa**, take a share taxi to Siolim (Rs 8) where you cross the river Chapora by ferry; continue to Keri (Querim) by share taxi, then cross Tiracol river by ferry and walk the remaining 2 km! The **Tiracol ferry** runs every 30 mins, between 0600-2130 (15-min crossing). Both ferries take cars. From **Dabolim Airport**, pre-paid taxi to Tiracol Fort, Rs 700.

SHIRODA

Despite the Fort's romantic setting, modern India and its development needs are near at hand. 3 km to the north the huge industrial complex of the Usha-ISPAT pig iron plant can be seen on the next plateau. The short drive from Tiracol to the Maharashtrian town of Shiroda shows a wholly different face of India, with a landscape wearing the marks of industrialization and heavy lorries filling the roads. Yet the plant has done little to spoil the rural peace of the fort itself and this atmospheric coastal hotel.

Inland from the North coast

THERE are several fascinating one or 2-day excursions from the coastal. It is possible to see not only the churches or forts built during the Portuguese period or remarkable Hindu temples in the interior, but also something of town and rural life in a state undergoing rapid change. Even the most distant site in South Goa is no more than 100 km from here, and can be visited by motorbike or car in a long day though if you want to visit comfortably you should plan for at least one night away. During the high season book accommodation in advance. Most of the interesting towns and villages are far closer, and relatively little time needs to be spent in travelling to enjoy them. The same can be said for visiting the wonderful site of Old Goa or the many temples around Ponda. Sites of interest in Bardez and Pernem are described from south to north, starting just inland from Calangute, and are followed by sites in Bicholim and Satari.

SALIGAO

M2C2

Saligao, just east of Calangute, becomes a familiar crossroads for those who choose to spend some time on one of the beaches nearby. Occupied by Saraswat Brahmins many centuries before the arrival of the Portuguese, Saligao is believed by some to have taken its name from the *sal* trees which were once abundant here. Others suggest it is derived from *sall*, a type of rice cultivated in the heart of this rich agricultural area. Today it is surrounded by coconut palms and the village has several good examples of attractive Goan houses standing in their shady gardens.

The **Our Lady Mother of God** (Mae de Deus Church) in an imposing setting, which is clearly visible from the road, was built in 1873, replacing five earlier chapels. It is an unusual neo-Gothic structure but painted white like the traditional baroque churches in Goa. The prominent horizontal ribbed surface with crennalated parapets and stylized flying buttresses makes it quite unique. Inside, the attractive wooden ceiling with its pierced star design is most unusual. The miraculous statue of the Virgin, originally found in a ruined convent in Dauji Village, Old Goa, was enshrined here when the plague forced the population of Dauji to move out. Saligao also has a minor seminary.

Our Lady of God church, Saligao

POMBURPA

M2C3

Renowned for its hot springs, Pomburpa has one of Goa's more spectacular village churches. The magnificanet painted and gilded wooden reredos in the white painted Church of **Our Lady Mother of God Church** (Mae de Deus Church) bears the hallmarks of the style of the Church of St Catejan in Old Goa, and the ornate decoration in stucco is particularly fine. The annual *Pomburpa Festival* on 4 February draws thousands of visitors and the whole church and village are transformed.

The village also has ancient temples, among the most important being those to **Ravalnath** and **Santeri** (Shantadurga). Although nothing of the ancient buildings survives, the priestly community retains long standing links with the past. Some of the main images of the deities were transferred to Mulgao, just north of Bicholim, to avoid Portuguese destruction.

Getting there Pomburpa can be easily reached by road from Saligao or Porvorim on the NH17 (north of Panaji). Mapusa, on the highway, is a little further north. A ferry to the east crosses the Mapusa River to Chorao Island and the road then runs direct to Bicholim.

MAPUSA

M2C2

Population 31,600; *STD Code* 0832; pronounced *Mahpsa*

Mapusa is the administrative headquarters and main town of Bardez *taluka*. It stands on a long ridge which runs east-west, fertile agricultural land occupying the flat valley floor right up to the edge of the town. It may take its name from these formerly extensive swamps which covered the valley floor - '*maha apsa*' – (great swamps).

Although there is little of architectural merit, **St Jerome's** Church, is interesting. Locally known as Milagres Church, **Our Lady of Miracles**, originally built in 1594, was rebuilt in 1674 and in 1839 after it was destroyed by fire. The small church with its scrolled gable and balconied windows in the façade has a belfry at the rear. The main altar is to Our Lady, and those on the two sides to St John and St Jerome; the retables (shelves behind the altar) were brought here from Daugim, Old Goa. Note also the interesting wooden ceiling. The Church stands near the site of the Shanteri Temple and so is sacred to Hindus as well. Besides, Our Lady of Miracles is believed to have been one of seven Hindu sisters converted to Christianity. Her lotus pattern gold necklace (now stored away) may have also been taken from a Hindu deity which preceded her.

Travel tip

Mapusa has a busy and colourful ❖**Municipal Market**. It is well planned and operates all week except Sundays. The colourful and vibarant 'Friday Market' is a must since vendors come from far and wide and there is a lot of activity right into the evening. There is rarely any backpacker here to be seen selling "ethnic" goods (as you might see in Anjuna). Open from 0800 to 1800 (though some stalls close much earlier). 0730 to 0800 is best for photography when the light is good and you can capture the local stalls being set up. **Warning** Beware of pick-pockets.

When tired of the market stalls you will find the town is small enough to wander around and observe local activity.

Festivals

Feast of our Lady of Miracles (27 April 1998) On the Monday of the 3rd week after Easter, the Nossa Senhora de Milagres image is venerated by Christians as well as Hindus who join together to celebrate the feast day of the Saibin. A huge fair and market is held.

Mid-range hotels

D ***Green Park***, Mapusa-Panaji Rd, Bypass Junction, T 250667, 25 rooms some a/c, modern hotel 2 km from town centre, pool and restaurants; **D** ***Satyaheera***, near Maruti Temple, T 262949, 34 rooms, some with a/c, enclosed rooftop restaurant and bar, friendly, checkout 0900; **D-E** ***Vilena***, opposite the Municipality, T 263115, 14 rooms, 2 a/c, neat, clean, very friendly, roof terrace restaurant, recommended.

Budget hotels

E ***Mandarin***, near Alankar Cinema T 262579, 21 basic rooms with bath, clean rooftop restaurant, check-out 0900; **E-F** ***Shalini***, Taliwada, T 262324, 17 simple rooms, *Moonlight Restaurant* good for lunch; **E** ***Sirsat Lodge***, 2nd Floor, Ramchandra Building, opposite the Taxi Stand, T 262419, 43 rooms, simple and clean, busy area so can be noisy; **E** ***Tourist Hotel*** (GTDC), T 262794, at the roundabout, 49 clean rooms for 2-6, some a/c, good value restaurant, beers. **E** ***Suhas*** (was *Trisul*), opposite the Mapusa Clinic, T 262700, 40 very basic rooms, poor baths, restaurant and bar, roof garden.

Places to eat

Le Pavillon, 1st floor, Aarkay Plaza, Duler, T 201244, 1.5 km north of town centre on the Siolim road, modern, comfortable a/c restaurant with pleasant decor, excellent food, open 1130-1530, 1900-2330, reasonably priced (though a single scoop of icecream costs Rs 40!), recommended. ***Bawarchi***, northwest of Hanuman Temple, behind Police Station, part a/c; ***Mahalaxmi***, Anjuna Rd, a/c, has a South Indian vegetarian restaurant.

Casa Bela, near Coscar Corner, specializes in Goan food; opposite, ***Moonlight***, Shalini Building, 1st Floor, is good for North Indian food at lunchtime, very dark in the evening, used more for drinking than eating. All have **bars**.

Royal-T, Shop 96, near the Shakuntala Fountain, Municipal Market, Goan snacks, sweets and spices; good snacks are also at ***Xavier's***, Municipal Market and ***The Pub***, 1st Floor, Dipti Chambers, opposite the Municipal Market, good for a drink and watch the market activity, friendly owners.

From 1630 until late, carts and stalls near the Alankar Cinema, sell popular meat and seafood dishes.

Local travel

Bus: the Kadamba Bus Stand is near the Market at the centre. Buses to Panaji (every 15 mins). For the northern beaches buses to Calangute (every 20 mins) Rs 3; from there to Aguada or Baga (check before). Also to Vagator and Chapora via Anjuna.

Car hire: *Pink Panther*, T 263180. **Motorcycle hire**: *Classic Bike Adventure* (Indo-German company at Casa Tres Amigos, Socol Vado 425, Parra, Assagao, 4 km west (off the Anjuna road), T 0832 273351, F 276124, recommended for reliable bike hire and tours.

Taxi: Stand, south of the Municipal Gardens: to/from Panaji when shared, Rs 8; Aldona, Rs 4; Chapora, Calangute, Baga, Rs 6; Siolim, Rs 6. **Motorcycle taxi** from opposite the Market: to Anjuna, Rs 20.

Long distance buses

To **Hubli** (KTC) 1130, Rs 52; **Mumbai**: (KTC, MSRTC) 1530-1900, about Rs 225; **Mumbai**: (KTC, MSRTC) 0750-1930, about Rs 180. **NB** Check times in advance.

Directory

Airline offices: NEPC Skyline, T 262694.

Banks & money changers: State Bank of India exchanges cash and TCs; Pink Panther Agency changes Visa and Mastercard Monday-Friday 0900-1700, Saturday 0900-1300.

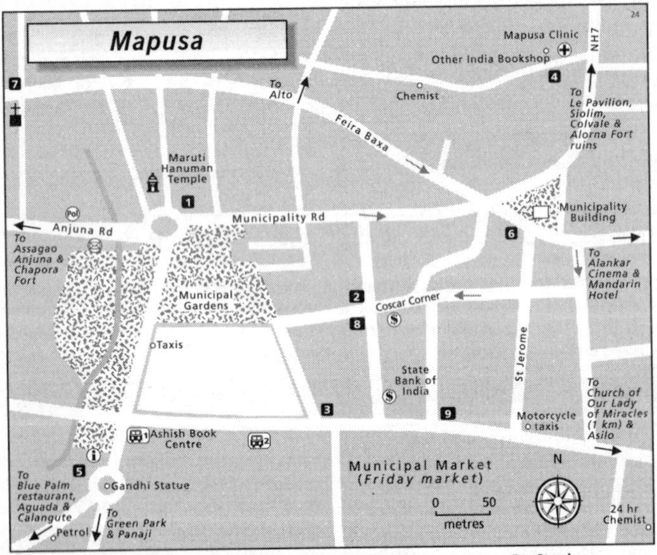

Hotels:
1. *Satyaheera* & Ruchira Restaurant
2. *Shalini* & Moonlight Restaurant
3. *Sirsat Lodge* & Poornima Vegetarian Restaurant
4. *Suhas*
5. *Tourist Hostel* & **Tourist Office**
6. *Vilena*

Places to eat:
7. Bawarchi
8. Casa Bela
9. The Pub

Bus Stands:
1 KTC
2 Private

Hospitals & medical services: *Asilo*, T 262211; There are several pharmacies, including *Drogaria*, near the Swiss Chapel, open 24 hours; *Mapusa Clinic*, T 262350 and *Bardez Bazar Drug Store*.

Post & telecommunications: Telephone & fax: several in town including *JJ Sons*, 13 Garden Centre; another is near the KTC Bus Stand. **Courier**: ***Blue Dart***, T 263208.

Shopping: Books: *Ashish Book Centre*, near the KTC Bus Stand; ***Other India***, 1st floor, St Britto's Apartment, above Mapusa Clinic (opposite *Suhas* Hotel), different and excellent. **Photography**: ***Remy Studios***, Coscar Corner and Shop 8, KTC Bus Stand.

Useful numbers: Ambulance: T 262372; **Fire**: T 262231; **Police**: T 262231; **Tourist Information**: T 262390.

MOIRA

M2B2

Barely 5 km east of Mapusa, Moira is at the heart of a rich agricultural district. The town is certainly ancient though it is impossible to be certain excatly how old. Some claim it goes back to the 6th or 7th century AD. Until the arrival of the Portuguese it seems to have been a Brahmin village, with seven important temples. These were destroyed by the Portuguese during the Inquisition, the idols moved to Bicholim. Moira was one of the villages where mass baptisms were carried out.

Today it is dominated by the **Church of Our Lady of the Immaculate Conception** which has some unusual features to its impressive façade. The square towers are very close to the central feature, a false dome. The balustrades at the top of the first and second floors run right across the building and the central doorways of the ground and first floors have an Islamic appearance given by trefoil arches, in contrast to the Romanesque of the flanking arches. Inside, the crucified Christ image is unusual in having the feet nailed separately instead of together using a single nail.

COLVALE

M2B2

The bridge at Colvale (Kolvale) remains the lowest crossing point of the Chapora River. The first written record of the village goes back to an inscription datd 1011 AD, and the name itself (*Kol*, from Koli, the Konkani name of the local fishing community, and *vale*, meaning 'creek') still describes one of the villages main activities. The area is believed to have come under the influence of Buddhism since a 2nd century (Gautama) Buddha image was found at Mushir near here in the 19th century by a historian, Fr Heras. It is interesting to note that one of the ancient deities of the village is "Gauthama".

Colvale has the attractive **Church of St Francis of Assissi** (originally 1591, the present building dates from 1713). The façade has a rather splendid plaster image of St Francis between two angels, looking down from above, his hands raised in the gesture of blessing. The principal altar inside is dedicated to the Wounds of St Francis. The feast day is 19 September.

Moira's Magic Carpet

Legend has it that the villagers of Moira decided that there was too much space in front of the church and too little behind it. The Moira villagers decided that the answer lay in pushing the church forward. Humouring them, the Sacristan from the neighbouring village of Aldona suggested that they lay out blankets in front of the church to cover the area where they wanted the church to go, and then pushed it from behind until it covered the blankets. This they duly did, but while they were pushing the Sacristan quietly removed the blankets from the front. After a suitable interval he suggested that the villagers come round to the front to view the results of their efforts, as the blankets were now completely covered. They were delighted with the effect!

DARGALIM

M2B2

Dargalim (Dhargal) is 2 km north of Colvale, along the NH17. The **Shri Shantadurga Temple** is invisible from the National Highway itself but the road leading 500m to it is marked by a large yellow and white gateway and is a bare 200m from the Konkan railway line.

The temple's main entrance at the east end leads through a Romanesque arch into a large rectangular, walled and cloistered enclosure. A typical hexagonal lamp tower, *deepstambha*, is near the entrance. The central mandapam and tiled roof are supported by broad, squat round pillars. The *mandapa* (central hall) has a red tiled floor, pink painted pillars and a tiled roof interior.

As you approach the shrine two small tomb-like enclosures house two linga, opening towards the main shrine. The inner sanctum, which is open to all, has pale wooden doors, and a white ceramic tiled wall, interspersed with blue tiles. The entrance steps are black marble, leading into the immaculate white marble flooring of the shrine room. The image is almost invisible in its ornately worked silver fronted *garbagriha*. As with the typical inner shrines of Hindu temples it is cool, pleasant and airy. Worshippers ring one of the bells hanging at the entrance to the shrine to announce their presence to the deity.

The annual festival is in December.

PARSI

M2B2

Parsi (Parchem, Parshem) lies on the road between Agarvaddo and Pernem, an attractive route which climbs steadily up onto the barren laterite plateau. In the tiny hamlet of Parsi, about 6 km southwest of Pernem and 4 km from Chopdem, is the remarkable **Shri Bhagwati Senayan Temple** (rebuilt in the 19th century). The temple has twin *deepstambhas* (lamp towers) in front and five romanesque arches.

In addition to the shrine to Bhagwati, Siva's wife, also known as Parvati, there is a rare minor shrine to Brahma. The very elongated headdresses and the impassively smiling faces carved in the black stone are a remarkable testament to the art of the 7th century AD, for this image, discovered in the

Bhagwati Temple, Parsi

Travel tip

Most guide books and maps show the NH17 running through Pernem and crossing the Tiracol River just to the northwest of the town. This is incorrect. The NH17 bypasses Pernem to its east and then runs northeast along the south bank of the Tiracol River through Torxem (Torchem) and past the Patradevi Martyr's memorial into Maharashtra.

Just to the northeast of Pernem a new road bridge crosses the river to the Usha-ISPAT integrated steel plant, but is only open to company traffic. Immediately to its east is the Konkan Railway Bridge.

undergrowth near the temple, dates from that period. Today it is worshipped in one of the subsidiary shrines.

MALPEM *M2B2*

Just south of Pernem is the small Hindu temple of **Mulvir**. Set in a heavily shaded compound, the low, tile-roofed temple is protected by a large banyan tree at its entrance. Its chief feature is its wall paintings illustrating scenes from the Mahabharata. The main story panel in rather faded, but still clear, colours is the churning of the ocean of milk, the simple figures of people, animals and gods charmingly represented. Sadly the pictures have suffered extensive weathering damage.

PERNEM *M2A2*

STD Code 0832; pronounced *Pedne*

Pernem was ceded to the Portuguese in 1788, among the latest territories to be added to the area under Portuguese control. Today it is a small market town with three major points of interest.

St Joseph's Church In the heart of the town this brightly painted white church on a hill has a statue of Christ in its forecourt and a Latin inscription which reads "Christ reigns over all". The date 1864 is written on the central gable and there are two towers, one the belfry. The interior is plain and largely undecorated.

Shri Bhagwati Temple Below the church immediately to its north, and entered through an ornamental gateway flanked by large dark stone statues of trumpeting elephants, is the green painted 500-year-old temple. The dark *ashtabhuja* (8-armed) image of Bhagwati, is very imposing. Dasara celebrations here attract 25,000 devotees.

❖Deshprabhu House The road which runs north from Pernem to join the NH17, passes the third of Pernem's major landmarks, the great 19th century house belonging to the Deshprabhu family. A huge property with 16 courtyards, despite remaining Hindu the family was honoured by the Portuguese. The temple and museum which have been created in the courtyard can be visited by arrangement with the Tourist Office in Panaji.

TORXEM (TORCHEM) *M2A2*

The northernmost village of Goa is noted for a 15th century sculpture of Mahishasuramardini (Durga slaying the Buffalo Demon) which is now on display at the Panaji Museum. The Shri Mauli Temple has a wide range of affiliated deities including Ravalnath and Bhagvati.

PALIEM VILLAGE *M2B1*

The tiny hamlet of Paliem lies on the edge of the plateau about 5 km north of Arambol just before the road drops down through dense wooded slopes to Keri and the Tiracol ferry. Its Vetal (Betall) Temple has charmingly painted designs of the tree of life on its blue walled exterior.

BICHOLIM AND SATARI TALUKAS

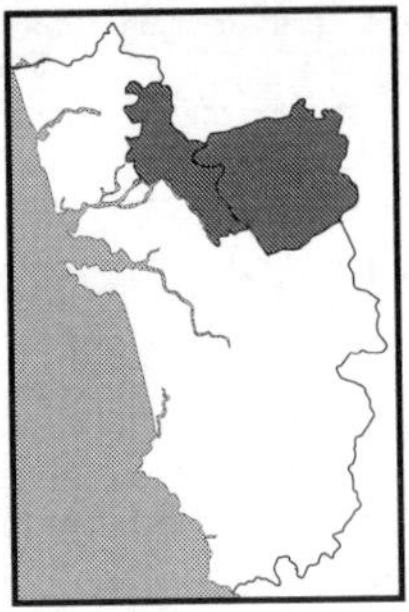

Bicholim, which shares its northern border with the central Indian state of Maharashtra, and Satari which borders both Maharashtra and the south Indian state of Karnataka, are in many senses two of the three most marginal talukas in Goa. Located on the edge of the Western Ghats where the hills rise up sharply to the interior of the Indian Peninsula, they have always been on the margins of political developments elsewhere. Only brought into Goa as part of the New Conquests, they were previously a battle ground in the constantly shifting margins of Hindu and Muslim power for three centuries before.

Difficult terrain, dense forest cover and the lack of any widespread agricultural land meant that population density remained relatively sparse and towns very few. It was to these talukas that Hindus from the Old Conquests often escaped, taking with them the most sacred images and artefacts from the temples of Old Goa and the talukas of the Old Conquests. Even though the distances were short the remoteness of the forested hills of Bicholim and Satari was virtually absolute, protected not only by their own inhospitable character but by the Mandovi River to the south and the Mapusa River to the west.

That pattern of inaccessibility is being changed, and the balance of resources is now fundamentally altered by the discovery of massive iron ore deposits which are being extensively worked in Bicholim. Roads now connect Bicholim with the headquarters of Satari taluka, Valpoi. In turn roads now run south through the dense forest reserves of the Bondla Sanctuary to Tisk or southeast via Tambdi Surla to Molem in Sanguem taluka.

For hundreds of years before the Portuguese arrived however, it seems that these forested hills were also home to Buddhist and Jain communities. Buddhism, which had become possibly India's main religion in the early centuries before Christ, gradually went onto the defensive in following centuries. A resurgent Hinduism, followed by the invasions of Islam, restricted Buddhism to increasingly remote territories, and it remained in these forested hills for some centuries after its elimination from most other parts of India.

The northeast: Bicholim and Satari

ALTHOUGH there are several sites of interest and the journeys through the two talukas offer very attractive scenery, none of them require a lot of time to visit and enjoy. It is possible to make a full day round trip from the coast to Satari via Bicholim and to see a good deal of several sites. There is very little accommodation in either taluka, but it is possible to stay in simple rooms in Tambdi Surla if you want to spend a night away from the coast. It is also possible to take this route from the north coast up to Belgaum or other points on the Indian peninsula via Molem.

BICHOLIM

M3C2

Population 13,700

The taluka headquarters, Bicholim town has little of interest in itself but is the crossroads on the main route between Mapusa and Valpoi and for the route from the south via Divar Island.

NAROA (ÑARVE)

M3C2

The **Shri Saptakoteshwar temple**, across the river from Divar Island, is one of Bicholim's main attractions. Like many in North Goa, the small temple nestles among trees and is shielded from view, almost a miniature. Here again like so many of Goa's temples and small settlements, the deity originated some distance away and was re-established as a result of an enforced move. The faceted *dharalinga* which is the chief image, was moved when the original temple on Divar island was destroyed in order to build a church. The marks on the stone suggest that at one stage it was used as a pulley, probably for drawing water, but was rescued and placed in its present setting as a result of Sivaji's visit in 1668. There is nothing ornate about either the design or the decoration of the temple. The simple and typical red-tiled roof and painted exterior walls house a simple 5-pillared *sabhamandapa* where a black stone *nandi* faces the linga in the small square sanctuary. The *deepstambha* outside with 10 rings is typical of the area. Near it the shrine to Kalabhairav has two rock carvings of sandals. *Mahasivratri* is the special festival here.

The original site on Divar Island is now occupied by the Church of Nossa Senhora de Piedade.

MAYEM LAKE

M3C2

STD Code 0832

The lake is just south of Bicholim and is a very popular local picnic spot. While the pedal boats may not appeal, the setting is very attractive and the Government *Restaurant* on the south

Travel tip

If you are visiting Naroa and the Shri Saptakoteshwar Temple from the coast, or travelling further east to Arvalem, Mayem Lake is a convenient midday rest stop. GTDC has a good restaurant.

Overburdening - Goa's other environmental problem

The south central landscapes of Bicholim (or Dicholi) have been transformed by open-cast iron ore mining. Since the early 1980s Goa has accounted for over 40% of India's iron ore export, mainly to Japan, and Bicholim about 70% of that. The effects are not just the removal of iron ore but the dumping of the waste excavated to get at the ore, known technically as the 'overburden'. In Goa, on average, for every ton of ore mined 6 tons of waste rock is dumped. This has created huge steep-sided hills dominating some of the views and creating major environmental problems. Given the wide availability of restoration techniques in common use in other parts of the world environmental lobbies are pushing Indian companies hard to take measures to reduce the damage that is being done to the environment.

Sesa Goa, one of the mining companies, has been experimenting since the early 1960s in using cashew plantations to restore mined land, a pathbreaking development now being followed by others, but it will be years before the dust and mud which characterize some of the most intensively mined districts are under control. Meanwhile the water table is also dropping and pollution of the ground water is held to be increasing.

Mining near Arvalem

side of the lake serves good food, though the buildings are rather run down. There are clean *sulabh* toilets in the compound.

Budget hotel

E *Lake Resort* (GTDC), T 362144, 18 rooms, few a/c with bath, **F** dorm beds, restaurant.

Transport

From Panaji Bus Stand, buses for Narve pass by the lake. There is also a regular service from Bicholim.

SANQUELIM

M3C2

Population 6,200

Southeast of Bicholim, the town is the 'home' of the Rajput **Ranes tribe** who migrated south from Rajasthan in the late 18th century and spent the next century fighting for the Portuguese as mercenaries, then against them for arrears of pay! In 1895 one of their revolts necessitated the despatch of troops from Portugal.

The **Datta Mandir** (1882) north of the bazar, backed by a hillock covered with dense groves of areca palms, has the *trimurthi* (3-headed) image of Dattaraia which is believed to cure insanity. The temple with an interior of white marble, celebrates its annual festival in December. It is one of two temples in Goa where *Devadasis* (see page 37) play no part and are not permitted to enter (the other is the Ananta Temple in Savoi Verem).

The 14th century **Temple of Vitthala**, to Vishnu, built in the North Indian style, has recently been renovated retaining some of the original carved wooden columns. The annual festival is in April when the temple 'car' is used to transport a Hanuman image. Shri Vitthala is the ancestral deity of the Ranes who still live in the old family house next to the temple.

Getting there One road goes south to Tisk (25 km) at the intersection with the **NH4A**. A longer circuit takes in Arvalem and the Tambdi Surla Temple, joining the NH4A at Molem.

ARVALEM M3B2

2 km east of Sanguelim a turn goes south to this small settlement noted now for its waterfalls and small **Buddhist cave temples**. The latter were subsequently converted for Siva worship, the altars which probably originally supported Buddha images now having Siva lingas set into them. The caves are believed to date from the 3rd-6th centuries AD though a Brahmi inscription found was dated to the 1st century. The two groups of caves were cut out of laterite outcrops, the cells opening out into two pillared porches. No architectural detail survives. Hutt suggests that they were too small ever to be used as living quarters for monks.

In a pleasant shaded site with a temple near their foot, the **waterfalls** are formed at the end of a small gorge, and are impressive during the monsoon when the river is in spate. They are concealed from view until the last moment. Steps lead down from the parking place to the foot of the falls, then a track goes along the river and crosses it by a footbridge, leading a short distance to an open cast mine less than 1 km away.

Next to the falls is the **Shri Rudreshwar Temple**. Although the present building is comparatively modern the temple itself is ancient, although no one knows exactly when it was founded. At the end of February, the *Mahasivaratri festival* (25 February 1998) when devotees honour Siva through the night, is popularly celebrated with processions, singing and theatre performances.

SIRIGAO (SHIRGAUM) M3C2

The **Lairaya Temple**, northwest of Bicholim, is well-known for the **fire-walking** which accompanies the Padvo festivities.

The *Lairaya Jatra* described by Gomes Pereira starts on the 1st day of the Hindu 'New Year' (30 April 1998). A huge pyre is assembled (about 10m square at the base and 6m high) by large numbers of people who gather firewood. Hundreds of *dhonds* who will take part in the ceremony enter the village, recognizable by the piece of coloured cloth they carry on their back and the entwined cane in their hands. During the day, the goddess Lairaya gives *darshan* and is worshipped. Excitement mounts as midnight approaches and a noisy crowd of devotees join the temple priest and the *dhonds* in a procession to the accompaniment of loud music towards the pyre. They first call at a mango tree which is believed to contain an evil spirit that has to be appeased by an offering of red flowers. The pyre is lit by the priest and the *dhonds* continue with their rituals and reach a state of frenzy before preparing to walk on the red hot ashes which the pyre presents. Then at a specified moment, early in the morning, they all jump on to the ashes while some dare to run through tongues of flame. Excitement reaches fever pitch until the last completes the act. If a *dhond* is injured by the flames, he is thought to be impure because he had not prepared himself correctly for the ceremony or because he has a guilty conscience!

KANSARPAL *M3C1*

At the northern end of the taluka, the **Shri Kalikadevi Temple** is about 100 years old. An unusual feature of the structure is that it has two *sabhamandapas* preceding the sanctuary with seven rows of four pillars. One has a sunken section where dance and theatre performances are held during festivals; the *nagarkhana* to seat the musicians is above. The three silver covered temple doors and the sanctuary door are ornately decorated. The inner sanctuary has an image of Devi, the fierce form of Goddess Kali. The goldsmiths who are the temple trustees traditionally set aside the gold dust collected when they make jewellery, to act as the Reserve Fund.

SATARI TALUKA

Satari taluka, the second largest and the second least densely populated taluka in Goa, has always been a largely forested district. The steep hills of the Western Ghats rise to the east and the forests of the Bhagwan Mahaveer Sanctuary are to the south. A government report noted in 1869 that Satari had few properly built temples, the majority "being built of light materials with clay walls and roofs of palm leaves, straw or areca tree leaves." This was put down to the poverty of the district and the fact that the majority of the people lived in scattered settlements, grazing cattle or practising subsistence farming. Part of their poverty was the result of their being effectively bonded labourers for the neighbouring landlords who creamed off any surplus produce.

VALPOI *M3B2*

Population 6,800

Valpoi, Satari's administrative headquarters, is only a small town, which has simple accommodation. The Forest Department's simple **F** *Valpoi Forest Rest House*, can be booked through the Wildlife Office, 3rd floor, Junta House, 18th June Rd, Panaji, T 0832 224747/225926.

CARAMBOLIM *M3A2*

9 km northeast of Valpoi, also called Brahma Carambolim (Cormoli), there is a very unusual **Brahma temple**. The original temple in Carambolim village in the Tiswadi taluka was destroyed during the first Portuguese conquest but the remarkably fine Brahma image (believed to be from the 5th century) was saved and re-installed in Satari taluka in 1541, in its present position. It is one of the most finely worked images in Goa.

Travel tip

If you are visiting Satari from North Goa it is well worth visiting Tambdi Surla, the small but beautifully preserved temple in Sanguem taluka, south of Valpoi (see page 192).

South Goa

THE DIFFERENCE between South and North Goa is more than just a convenient geographical division. The talukas of Salcete, Quepem and Canacona have a wholly different atmosphere from those of the north. The Zuari River acted not only as a great political and cultural divide between Christian Salcete and Hindu Ponda but also as a much wider economic and cultural marker. Some of Goa's finest churches and most magnificent country estates are in the interior of Salcete. Heavily influenced by Portuguese culture, southern Goa has also been drawn towards the southern state of Karnataka. The rising prosperity of Salcete has not created the packaged pop culture of the northern coast. Here the pace is gentler. While Colva acts as the chief beach resort for the population of nearby Margao, long stretches of sand are completely deserted. Inland there is a wide variety of places to explore. Virtually anywhere in the three southern talukas is within reach of a day trip from the coast. Old Goa, and the spice gardens and Hindu temples of Ponda are also within easy reach of a day trip, but it is probably best to plan to spend at least a night if you want to explore the northern beaches.

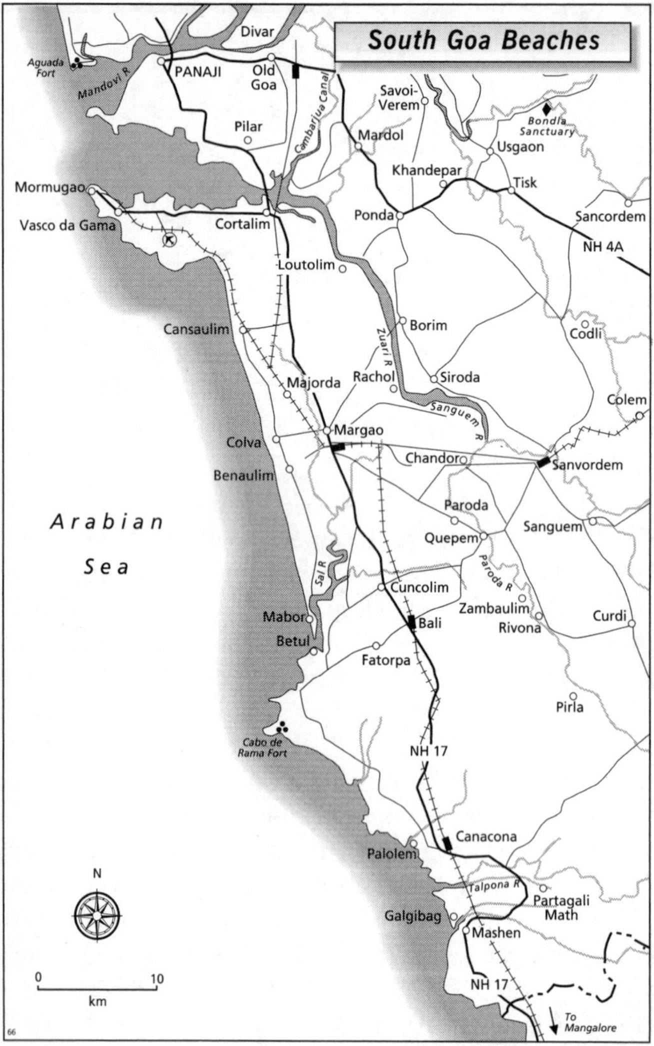
South Goa Beaches
Divar
Aguada Fort
PANAJI
Old Goa
Mandovi R
Cambariua Canal
Savoi-Verem
Bondla Sanctuary
Pilar
Mardol
Usgaon
Khandepar
Tisk
Mormugao
Vasco da Gama
Cortalim
Ponda
Sancordem
NH 4A
Loutolim
Cansaulim
Borim
Codli
Zuari R
Majorda
Rachol
Siroda
Colem
Sanguem R
Margao
Colva
Chandor
Sanvordem
Benaulim
Paroda
Arabian Sea
Quepem
Sanguem
Sal R
Paroda R
Cuncolim
Zambaulim
Mabor
Bali
Rivona
Curdi
Betul
Fatorpa
Pirla
Cabo de Rama Fort
NH 17
Canacona
Palolem
Talpona R
Partagali Math
Galgibag
Mashen
N
0
10
km
NH 17
To Mangalore
66

South Coast Resorts

VIRTUALLY all South Goa's resort beaches are in Salcete, though the southern beach of Palolem in Canacona taluka, one of the most attractive in Goa, is popular with both daytrippers and backpackers.

AROSSIM, UTORDA, MAJORDA

M6A1

STD Code 0834

These three beaches in Salcete are among the least heavily used, broad, flat and open. Around the resort hotels there are clusters of beach shack restaurants, and occasional fishing villages scattered under the coconut palms. Looking northwards up the beach the Mormugao headland is normally clearly in view, though haze sometimes conceals it.

One of the distinctive features of this section of coast is the strip of cultivated land that lies between the main series of villages and the dunes which actually front the sea, used for intensive rice cultivation. The road runs through these villages, set back between 1 and 2 km from the sea, and there is no road that runs along the sea front itself. Old mansions of wealthy families still standing in the villages include **Utorda House** which is known for its well kept gardens. The villages from here southwards to Benaulim

Which beach?

The southern coast comprises two contrasting sections. The whole coastline of Salcete is one unbroken stretch of sand from Velsao to Mabor. From Quepem southwards the coastline changes dramatically. Betul has a rocky headland and a small but inacccessible sandy cove, encapsulated by the laterite cliffs of the Cabo da Rama headland, already in Canacona taluka. The coastline then sweeps southeast with the beaches of Saleri and Agonda providing a prelude to the magnificent and beautifully protected beach of Palolem, the southernmost of the beaches increasingly visited by tourists.

Each section of beach has its own character, depending partly on the villages behind the beach. Unlike the northern beaches, in Salcete virtually the whole coast is lined with village houses scattered beneath the coconut palms, with rice fields immediately behind. The southernmost of the Old Conquests, many of the coastal villages have spectacularly attractive whitewashed village churches.

Salcete has no rocky headlands and the beach at low tide is a wide stretch of firm sand, backed in places by quite high dunes. Only occasionally does settlement come down to the beach itself, as at Colva. The largest beach resorts, some of which have been controversial in Goa, serve largely package tours in the winter and Indian tourists during the monsoon season. Several have excellent facilities and are largely self-contained. Although the south is nowhere near as commercialized as the north several places have at least a few beach shacks serving food, specialising particularly in excellent sea food.

and beyond are noted for the high level of emigration to the Gulf. Some have returned and invested money in new hotels.

Arossim Beach

At the deserted north end of the beach stretch. **B** *Sita Rest Hermitage* opening in October 1997, with 76 rooms, restaurants and pool, aimed to attract package tourists. The only beach shack ***Holy Cross***, run by a charming, friendly couple, has served beer and seafood to the occasional visitor here for the last 4 years.

Utorda Beach

10 minutes walk north of Majorda **A** ***Golden Tulip*** (was *Regency*), T 754185, F 754186, set in large palm-filled gardens, 94 tastefully decorated rooms with balcony, good restaurants, pool (claims to have the largest in Goa!), gym, tennis, watersports, fine white-sand beach.

At Majorda Beach

(pronounced *Mazorda*) is about 18 km from the airport. **A-B** ***Majorda Beach Resort***, 2 minutes walk from the beach, T 730203, F 730212, 108 'rustically furnished' a/c rooms and 10 more expensive individual 'village' suites, 3 restaurants, pools, designed on a grand scale with a rather barn-like public area, covered 'Mediterranean village' street, lush gardens behind. Strangely, small beers are never available in the resort or the beach. **C-D** ***Shangrila***, T 754265, F 754252, some distance from the sea, 12 clean a/c rooms, but overpriced.

BETALBATIM

M6B1

To the south, it was named after the main temple to Betal which once stood here; the deity was moved to Quela (Ponda) for safety. There is a pleasant stretch with some coconut palms and a few casuarinas on the low dunes that separate the seaside from the resort development. Beach bars are 15 minutes walk away.

Hotels at Betalbatim

B-C *Nanu Resorts*, near the beach and open paddy fields, T 734950, F 734428, 72 comfortable and spacious a/c rooms in 2-storey "chalet" complex separated by small patches of green, imaginatively planned and well managed with efficient service, first floor restaurant with verandah facing pool serves good food but occasionally slow service, good pool though little shade in the garden or the beach behind which you reach by crossing a narrow stream, secluded and peaceful (though new time-share blocks are being built alongside), very good value from 1 May-30 September, recommended. 10 minutes walk away, **D** *Alagoa*, 1 km from beach along track, simple, clean rooms, pleasant location, quiet. **E** *Mish Mar*, Dongrim, has 2 rooms.

Getting there: Majorda station is on the Vasco-Margao line. **Road** Buses from Margao (12 km); motorcycle taxis charge about Rs 30. Taxis take 20 mins from the airport, under 15 mins from Margao.

COLVA BEACH

M6B1

Colva (pronounced *Kol-wa*) is one of the most popular beaches in southern Goa, though not as developed or busy as Calangute in the north. It was used as a summer retreat before the monsoon by Margao's elite who would rent fishermen's houses, who in turn would move into shacks. The beachfront of Colva town itself, which is rather dirty, has nothing special to recommend it. However, it is the main evening and weekend day-trip destination for the people of Margao, only 6 km away, so it becomes packed with cars, motorbikes, scooters and pedestrians.

> **Travel tip**
>
> From Dabolim airport it is possible to wind down quite narrow village roads to all of the main resorts in Salcete. For the Mormugao beaches which are no more than 20 mins to half an hour's drive from the airport it is quickest to take the shortest route down off the plateau to Velsao and Cansaulim. For Colva and the resort hotels further south, it can be quicker to join the National Highway and go to Margao before heading for the coast road.

Three rather ugly little concrete bridges cross a muddy stream to the beach, where the original dunes have all been removed to give direct access to the sea. During the season the beach is lined with trinket stalls and a constant succession of beach vendors.

On the road into Colva from Margao you pass the large **Church of Our Lady of Mercy** (Nossa Senhora das Merces, 1630, re-built in the 18th century) The church has a relatively simple façade. Its single tower on the south side of the façade is so short as scarcely to be noticeable, and the strong horizontal lines normally given to Goan churches by 3 of 4 full storeys is broken by a narrow band of shallow semi-circular arches above the second floor.

However, the church is much less famous for its building than for its association with the miraculous Menino Jesus. The Jesuit, Father Bento Ferreira, found the original image in the River Sena, Mozambique, en route to Goa, and brought it to Colva where he took up his position as Rector in 1648. The image was found to have miraculous healing powers and became an object of special veneration. However, when in 1834 religious orders were banned, it was removed to the Rachol Seminary for safe keeping although a diamond ring given as an offering to it

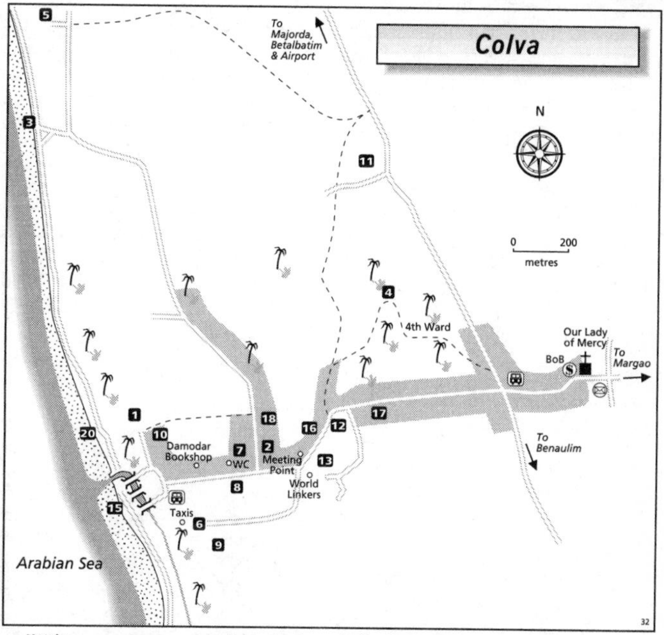

Hotels:
1. *Colmar* & Pasta Hut
2. *Colva Beach Resort*
3. *Fisherman's Cottages*
4. *Garden Cottages*
5. *Longuinhos Beach Resort*
6. *Penthouse Beach Resort*
7. *Sea View Cottages*
8. *Silver Sands & Lactancias*
9. *Sukhsagar Beach Resort*
10. *Tourist Cottages*
11. *Tourist Nest*
12. *Vailankanni*
13. *William's Resort*

Places to eat:
14. Connie M's
15. Joe Con's
16. Johnny Cool
17. Rice Bowl
18. Sea Pearl
19. Splash Bar
20. Zappia's

was left behind. The Church in Colva failed in its attempts to have the statue returned and so installed another figure in 1836 (which is still here today) and put on it the special ring. It was soon found to work miracles, whereas the original statue taken to Rachol ceased to have special powers. The story is celebrated today in the special festival (the Fama of Menino Jesus) in October each year, when thousands of pilgrims flock to see the statue in the hope of witnessing a miracle.

The beach itself, though crowded in peak season, is magnificent with beautiful sand, coconut palms gently swaying in the breeze and blue waters (which can sometimes turn rough and grey-green). Teams of fishermen operate all along the coast from here down to Benaulim further south. Their pitch-boarded catamarans are drawn up on the beach, while motorized craft are anchored offshore. They provide added interest and colour and it is worth waking early to watch them haul in their nets. If you are very early you may even be invited out on a boat. A stream along the seaside is crossed by bridges and there are beachside shack cafés and bars to both north and south.

Festivals

Fama of Menino Jesus (19 October 1998) is celebrated with a colourful procession and a fair. Near the church, specially blessed lengths of string are sold, as well as replicas of limbs which are offered to the image in thanks for cures effected.

Mid-range hotels

Most 6-8 km from Margao railway station.

C *Silver Sands*, T 721645, F 737749, 66 rooms in unimaginative building 2 mins from white-sand beach, some a/c with balcony, pool, package oriented, near cafés, 1997 reports of dirty rooms and pool, poor food and service, expensive massage, poor maintenance; **C-D** ***Colva Beach Resort***, T 721975, T 737753, 24 pleasant, clean rooms, some a/c with balcony, good restaurant, bar, friendly, secure; **C-D** ***Longuinhos Beach Resort***, on the beach, 1 km from resort centre, T 731645, 50 clean rooms with balcony, 6 a/c, no TV (may have in future), good restaurant, boutique, near fishermen's huts; **C-D** ***Penthouse Beach Resort***, near the beach, T 731030, F 733737, 68 rooms in local style cottages, some a/c, exchange, garden dotted with palms, now dirty, badly neglected and greatly deteriorated, not recommended.

Prices: B Rs 1,500-3,000; **C** Rs 800-1,500; **D** Rs 400-800; **E** Rs 200-400

D ***Colmar***, on the beach (little further from Tourist Cottages), T 721253, 45 rooms with hot and cold, and cheap dorm, rooms in cottages with small gardens, good restaurant and bar showing TV sports (popular meeting place), pleasant, more expensive than others nearby but recommended for friendly service; **D** ***Sukhsagar Beach Resort***, behind *Penthouse*, T 721888, 22 rooms with bath, 5 a/c, restaurant, bar; **D-E** ***Tourist Cottages*** (GTDC), near the sea, T 721206, 49 rooms with balcony, few **D** a/c, in 2-storeyed building or cottages, and dorm, restaurant, garden, good value but without character, popular with Indian tourists; **D-E** ***William's Resort***, 500m beach, resort centre, T 721077, F 722852, 36 spotless rooms, some a/c, restaurant, friendly, excellent value.

Budget hotels

Dozens of guest houses too, offer cheaper rooms: **E** ***Garden Cottages***, behind *Johnny Cool's* restaurant, 10 minutes from beach, 4 rooms with bath, private balcony overlooking pleasant surroundings, quiet, clean, friendly, helpful owner, excellent value; **E** ***Sea View Cottages***, opposite *Silver Sands*, 4 rooms with bath; **E** ***Vailankanni***, H No 414/2, 4th Ward, near the crossroads, T 737747, 500m from beach, with 14 fairly clean rooms and bath, friendly family run guest house, good value restaurant.

E-F ***Fisherman's Cottages***, close to the water, rooms with bath and fan, clean, friendly, good value; **F** ***Maria Guest House***, 4th Ward, near the beach, restaurants and shops, 7 rooms, some with bath, very friendly, interesting owners, helpful, will arrange car-hire, popular with backpackers, very good value, highly recommended; **F** ***Tourist Nest***, 2 km from the sea, old Portuguese house, rooms with bath, dorm, good restaurant, bike hire, popular with backpackers.

Places to eat

Several offer cheap Western food and beer. ***China Dragon***, on beach, recommended for good food and friendly service. ***Joe Con's*** and ***Goodman's***, 4th Ward, highly recommended for excellent fresh fish and Goan dishes and value for money; ***Falcon***, on beach near the bridges, does reasonable food. Also ***Connie M's*** has good food; ***Lactancias Music House*** offers limited choice but is good value. Colmar's ***Pasta Hut*** with bar, recommended; ***Zappia's***, on the beach recommended for good food and service.

Rice Bowl, Beach Rd, 750m from the beach, small and a bit pricey but excellent (different from the usual) Chinese and Nepali, wide and varied menu, friendly waiters, quick service, highly recommended; ***Sea Pearl***, 476 4th Ward, Chef (claimed to have worked for the Queen Mother!) produces excellent Western dishes especially roast beef, good desserts, fish pie, arrive early in season (about 1930), food recommended, also has simple **E** rooms with bath; ***Sucorina***, 1 km north, is highly recommended for seafood.

Nightlife

Several hotels on the beach have bars. ***Splash*** is the main place for music, dancing and late drinking, open all night, trendy – popular with English travellers and a few well-off Indians, very busy on Saturdays; during the season it gets full after 2300 on weekdays; serves good cocktails, but poor bar snacks – may not appeal to all.

Local travel

Motorbikes for hire through most hotels, (see also Panaji), Rs 150-200/day (less for long term rental), more for Enfields, bargain hard. **Bicycles** mostly through hotels, Rs 20-25/day (discounts for long term).

Long distance travel

To **Airport**: taxi, Rs 250. To **Margao** (6 km) buses every 30 mins, takes 30 mins, Rs 3; also taxi for 8 people. Last bus to Margao, 1915, from Margao, 2000 (from there to Mangalore, dep 2030 takes 9½ hours, Rs 100); motorcycle taxi, Rs 20-25 (bargain hard), easier in the off-season; auto-rickshaw, Rs 30-40. To **Anjuna** Wednesdays for the Flea Market, bus (through travel agents), dep 0930, return 1730, Rs 85-90.

Directory

Shops: Small square with usual craft shops – Kashmiri papier mâché and Karnataka mirror-work are good value. ***Damodar*** **bookshop**, near the car park and beach, has a good selection of used and new books.

Telecommunications: *WorldLinkers* has 24-hr **ISD/fax**.

Travel company: *Meeting Point*, opposite, T 723338, F 732004, is recommended for very efficient, reliable travel service, Monday-Saturday, 0830-1900 (sometimes even later, if busy).

BENAULIM

M6B1

Population 9,900

Also called Banaley and Bannali ('the place where the arrow fell', referring to the myth of Parashurama and the creation of Goa, see page 61), Benaulim is famous throughout Goa as the birthplace of the Venerable Joseph Vaz, who is commemorated in the Church of the Holy Spirit in Margao. The village was noted for producing carved wooden furniture.

❖ Church of St John the Baptist

This small church, re-built in 1596, is on a hill beyond the village. It is a superb example of Goan Christian architecture. The twin towers are surmounted by shallow domes while the typical scrolls are flanked by crosses. Although the gable façade is striking, the chief beauties of the church are inside. The magnificent altar reredos is uniquely decorated, and there is a wonderful Rococo pulpit which is surmounted by a representation of the Lamb of the Apocalypse from the Book of Revelation. Fr Joseph Vaz, who ultimately died as a missionary to Ceylon, was baptised in the font here in 1651. Note also the very

Benaulim Church

charming St Christopher carrying a child across a river, painted in the nave opposite the baptistry. See Local festival below.

The beach

Benaulim is more tranquil and pleasant than Colva beach. It is easily reached by private transport. Buses go as far as Maria Hall (Dangvaddo), a 1 km walk from the beach. This beach too is a popular destination for weekend and evening visitors from inland so it can get busy and tourists can be plagued by fruit and jewellery vendors as well as drug pushers (to avoid being harassed, be very firm). If you want to escape their constant attention, it is not difficult either to walk, or to hire a bike and cycle some distance south along the beach. Back from the beach is Bank of Baroda, near Maria Hall. There is also a late night chemist, near the main cross-roads. **NB** The road down to the beach is poorly lit after dark and in 1997 several robberies at night were reported, so it is best to walk accompanied.

The 4 km walk or cycle-ride between Colva and Benaulim, through idyllic countryside is recommended.

Dolphin Watching

The trips are scenic and chances of seeing dolphin are high, but it gets very hot (take hat, water and something comfy to sit on). **NB** Groups of dolphins here are usually seen swimming near the surface and don't oblige with performing tricks. Boats from *Café Dominick* (signs on the beach) and several others ask for about Rs 250. Competition in season is intense, so bargain.

Festivals

Feast of St John the Baptist (*Sao Joao*) (24th) A thanksgiving for the arrival of the monsoon. Young men wearing crowns of leaves and fruits tour the area singing for gifts. They also jump into wells to commemorate the movement of St John in his mother's womb when she was visited by Mary, the mother of Jesus!

Mid-range hotels

The massive ***Maynard Goa Beach Resort***, south of *Johncy's*, was built in 1996; **D** *Carina Beach Resort*, T 224050, 14 rooms, some a/c, with shower, pool; **D** *Failaka*, Adsulim Nagar, T 734416, near Maria Hall crossing, pleasant, colourful 3-storeyed house (lit up with fairy lights at night), 16 rooms with shower, very good restaurant, bar, bike hire, very friendly, helpful, recommended; **D** *Palm Grove Cottages*, 1678, Vasvaddo, room facilities vary, some a/c with bath, others cheaper, good restaurant, bar, palm-shaded garden, recommended; **D-E** *Furtado's Beach Resort*, 300m north of main Benaulim beach, cottage on beach 5 basic rooms with fan and bath (cold water),

Prices: C Rs 800-1,500; **D** Rs 400-800; **E** Rs 200-400; **F** under Rs 200

newer **E** *Cottages* at end of track through fields, 30m from beach screened by dunes, 7 rooms with tiny shower, beach restaurant, idyllic location, isolated.

Budget hotels

All along Benaulim Beach Rd, and in the coconut groves on either side, there are numerous rooms available in private houses and "cottages" in the garden, from Rs 50-150 (negotiable); south along the beach from *Johncey's* are some cottages just off the beach where rooms with bath are Rs 80. **D-E** ***L'Amour Beach Resort***, near Benaulim beach, T/F 733720, 20 simple rooms (some a/c) in cottages (overpriced), restaurant, slow service, **NB** take care of possessions.

E ***Caphina***, Beach Rd, past crossroads (2-storey, away from road), very clean rooms, friendly and helpful owners, good value, recommended; **E** ***O'Palmer Beach Cottages***, T 733278, 23 rooms in an isolated square concrete block, rather depressing, no restaurant but close to beach; **E** ***Oshin***, near *Palm Grove*, down a path, good large rooms with bath, breakfast, friendly manager; **E** ***Rosario's Inn***, off Beach Rd, clean rooms (best with bath and own verandah, others in main family house), dorm, breakfast and snacks, popular in spite of off-hand management, recommended for meeting other travellers in a relaxed atmosphere; **E** ***Tansy***, Beach Rd, T 734595, large, very clean rooms with bath in hotel and cottages, friendly, good value, recommended.

F ***Brito's Tourist Corner***, modern building near Maria Hall, 2 km from beach, 10 clean rooms with shower, handy store; **F** ***Libra***, T 403716, 8 rooms, clean, secure, recommended; **F** ***O Mangueiro***, next to *Carina*, 10 minute walk to beach, T 734164, 4 rooms with shower and WC, very clean, kind and helpful, homely atmosphere, nice garden, very safe, reduction for long stay; **F** ***Priti Kunj***, south of Maria Hall crossing, 15m off the main road, behind church, 4 clean, pleasant rooms, 3 with bath, also large 6-bed rooms in family house, meals to order, very kind and helpful owners, highly recommended for homely atmosphere.

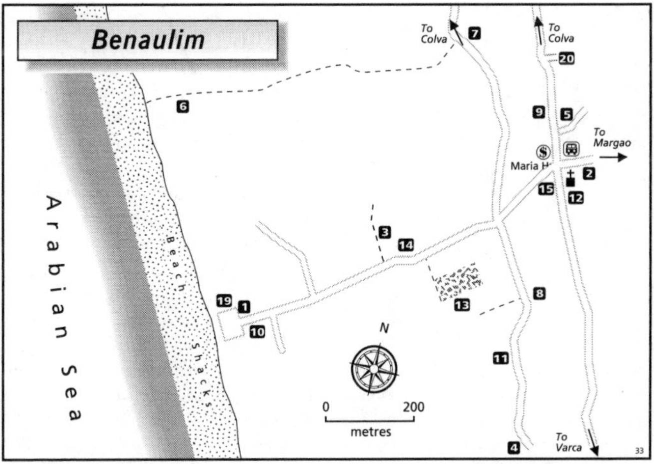

Hotels:
1. *L'Amour Beach Resort*
2. *Brito's Tourist Corner*
3. *Caphina*
4. *Carina Beach Resort & O'Manguiero*
5. *Failaka*
6. *Furtado's Beach Cottages*
7. *Furtado's Beach Resort*
8. *Libra*
9. *Maynard Goa Beach Resort*
10. *O'Palmar Beach Cottages*
11. *Palm Grove Cottages*
12. *Priti Kunj*
13. *Rosario's Inn*
14. *Tansy*

Places to eat:
15. Cacy Rose
16. Dominick's & 'Dolphin Watch' boats
17. Johncey's
18. Karibu
19. Pedro's
20. Tequila

Places to eat

There are over a dozen places along the beach. Many are very slow serving during season. Most close in the monsoons, some May-August. Some find the food disappointing and expensive. Near the bus stand: the popular *Cacy Rose*, just off the main road, is recommended. ***Johncey's***, the most popular (not necessarily the best), varied menu, good seafood, generous portions, *tandoori* recommended (after 1830) but service can be erratic, pleasant atmosphere (backgammon, scrabble); ***Karibu*** is recommended; ***Pedro's***, on beach, imaginative menu, reasonable breakfast but occasionally invaded by flies; ***Tequila***, towards Colva; ***Zumbrai*** south along the beach recommended for seafood.

Local travel

Cycles for hire in village, Rs 25/day.

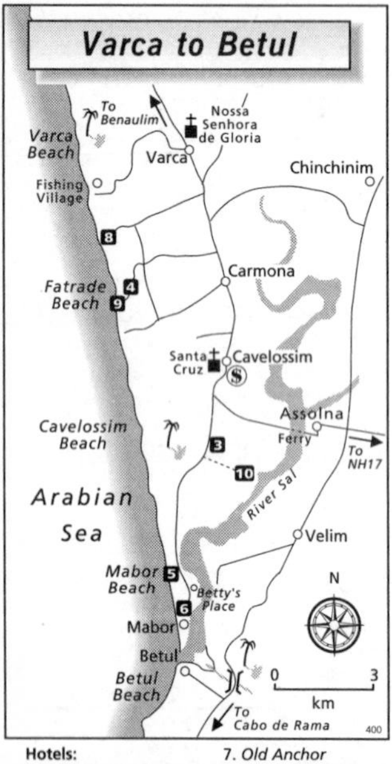

Hotels:
1. *Dona Sa Maria*
2. *Dona Sylvia*
3. *Gaffino's*
4. *Goa Rennaissance*
5. *Holiday Inn*
6. *Leela Beach*
7. *Old Anchor*
8. *Resorte de Goa*
9. *Fatrade Beach*

Places to eat:
10. Goan Village
11. Shallop

Taxis and **auto-rickshaws** are available from the beach esplanade near *Pedro's* and at Maria Hall crossing.

Long distance travel

To or from **Margao**: taxi Rs 70; rickshaw, Rs 50; bus, Rs 2. **Anjuna** Wednesday flea market: bus dep 0930, return 1530, Rs 90; bus, dep 0900, return 1900, Rs 70 (2 hours).

The narrow and attractive road south from Benaulim runs about 1 km inland from the sea through small villages, some with superb white painted churches. Paddy fields and palm groves alternate, and periodically roads run down to the sea, sometimes to small settlements, sometimes to deserted beaches.

VARCA, CAVELOSSIM & MABOR *M6B1/C1*

STD Code 0834

Benaulim beach runs into **Varca** and **Cavelossim** which has some up-market resorts. The beaches here are quieter and cleaner than Colva. The **Nossa Senhora da Gloria Church** at Varca (1700), a short way north of the village, has a particularly striking façade, making use of a fan-like central feature based on the conch shell to give an effect of radiating light. Its twin towers are topped by semi-domes, but doors on the ground floor and the windows on its 2 upper storeys are Romanesque.

Cavelossim's small and relatively simple **Santa Cruz Church** (1763) has a highly decorated altar piece, the gold leaf being set against a turquoise painted Romanesque arch. There is a *Bank of Baroda* near the church which accepts Visa, Mastercard and TCs, helpful staff, open 0930-1330, Monday-Wednesday, Friday, Saturday.

Mabor further south, (or Mobor) lies on the narrow peninsula where the river Sal joins the sea. Some exclusive hotel resorts have been developed, although visually they are quite unobtrusive. The Sal is a busy river and harbour for fishing boats, but it is also very pleasant for boat rides. *Betty's Place*, in a road opposite the Holiday Inn, arranges boat trips for fishing, dolphin viewing as well as trips up River Sal from 1030-1630 (food included) which is recommended.

Varca Church

Luxury hotels

AL *Goa Renaissance Resort*, Fatrade Beach, Varca, T 745208, F 245225, 202 rooms, interesting design by Hawaiian architects, spacious impressive entrance with beams and arches, watersports and 9-hole golf, miles of white sand beach with no rocks, no mosquitoes or flies, high standards but expensive meals and drinks, little else in vicinity, casino open to non-residents; **AL** *Leela Beach*, Mabor, T 746363, F 746352, 194 rooms in villas and pavilions are being completely refurbished in summer 1997 after change of management, all facilities, 3 restaurants, 9-hole golf, for peak season (20 December-10 January) reserve 4 months ahead; **AL-A** *Holiday Inn* (was *Averina*), Mabor, T 746303, F 746333, 144 luxurious rooms (prices vary) with shady balconies around a pool and pleasant, part-shaded gardens, all facilities, health club, tennis, very close to beach, good views of hills.

Mid-range hotels

A *Old Anchor*, 2 km south of Cavelossim, T 746335, F 746336, 238 rooms (part resembles a ship, nautical decor), poorly maintained and not very clean, golf, tennis, not a particularly attractive site, some distance from the beach (compared to the others); **A-B** *Dona Sylvia Resort*, south of Cavelossim, T 746321, F 748320, 176 comfortable rooms, some a/c, low-rise complex has a spacious feeling, nightly entertainment in season, restaurants ("better on beach"), large open-sided café bar serves snacks all day, good pool (also children's pool), the beach is 1.5 km from the entrance, gym, new small golf course, excellent and quick service, highly recommended (closed May-September).

B *Resorte de Goa*, Fatrade Beach, Varca, T 745066, F 745310, 56 rooms and suites in main building and smaller rooms in colourful cottages, remote, idyllic, pleasant pool in large gardens, tennis (good discounts in June-September), palm-dotted dunes on either side, clean deserted beach with some shade.

C-D *Dona Sa Maria*, Tamborim, just north of Cavelossim, T 745672, F 745673, 16 good sized clean rooms, modern (colonial style) villa (opened late 1996), 1 km from deserted beach, pool, family run, very friendly, isolated and 10 mins from the beach but quiet, recommended (closed June-September).

D *Gaffino's*, opposite Dona Sylvia, Mabor, 5 minutes walk from beach, T 746385, 16 clean, simple rooms with bath on 4 floors, 2 a/c, balconies overlook river or sea (far away), bed and breakfast, family run, personal service.

Places to eat

Good, cheap beach restaurants include: ***Goan Village*** lane opposite Dona Sylvia, recommended for *tandoori*; ***Shallop***, near Old Anchor, for Goan dishes and seafood.

Prices: AL Rs 6,000+; **A** Rs 3,000-6,000; **B** Rs1,500-3,000; **C** Rs 800-1,500; **D** Rs 400-800; **E** Rs 200-400; **F** Below Rs200

Roadside cafés near the entrance to the big hotels usually offer Goan dishes and seafood etc are good value. For authentic Goan fish *thali* (Rs 15), try the first house on the left past the church in Cavelossim if heading north. Fishermen sometimes offer to take holidaymakers to Betul where ***River Sal***, and ***Seagull***, on the waterside offer fresh river fish.

Transport

To reach Cavelossim (18 km from Margao) bus journeys are uncomfortably slow; taxis charge Rs 150. **Ferry** Crosses the River Sal (east of Cavelossim); the road goes through Assolna and joins the main road, NH17.

From Cavelossim the shortest route inland and to the south is by the ferry crossing to **Assolna** east of Cavelossim which is signposted. Immediately south of Cavelossim, the road takes a sharp 90° 'S' bend around the church. After crossing the River Sal, a left turn takes you into Assolna village where a turn to the right leads through attractive countryside to the main road towards Betul. The palm-lined road which cuts through open fields before passing old and new village bungalows within shady gardens, is a much quieter alternative to the NH17 for reaching Cabo de Rama and beaches to the south.

Excursions from the Salcete Coast

THE BEACHES in Salcete are within easy reach of enjoyable day trips which give a glimpse of both historic Goa and of modern day village and town life. Goa's second largest town, Margao, is less than 10 km from the beach at Colva and connected directly by road with all the resorts. It is a bustling town with a market that serves the whole of Salcete and beyond. The Konkan railway offers a relatively fast way for visiting either the neighbouring states of Karnataka or Maharashtra, and the modernization of the connections to the interior make possible a wide range of exciting 3-5 day excursions using India's legendary rail network.

In the section below excursions from the south coast resorts are described within each taluka from north to south.

VERNA *M6A1*

The Church here was initially built on the site of the Mahalsa Temple before being transferred. The Jesuits were permitted to work exclusively in Salcete and claimed to have celebrated the first Mass

SALCETE TALUKA

Salcete was named after the 66 (*saashesht*) places that made up the taluka. Unlike Bardez, where the area round Calangute has developed into an almost continuously built up town, Salcete has no coastal town.

The chief focus of economic and cultural life is the taluka headquarters of Margao, but there is a series of large villages and small towns which form a network across the flat plain of the Sal River and its estuary as it drains south, parallel with the coast, from Cansaulim to Mobor.

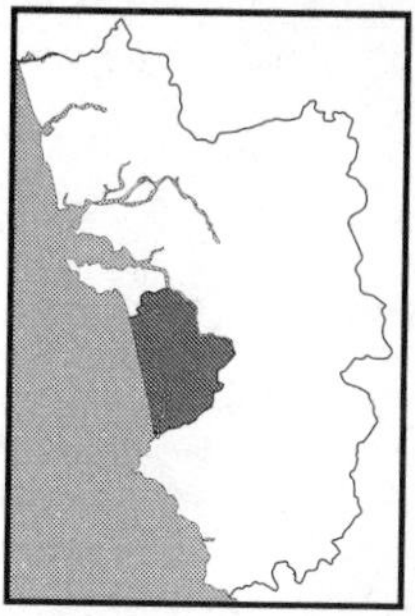

in the territory at **Cortalim** nearby in 1560. However, the Fransiscans had reached Verem (Reis Magos) 10 years earlier.

The original Mahalsa Temple which housed the deity now in Mardol (see page 115), which according to old Portuguese records had some exquisite carvings, was destroyed and marked by the cross to prevent it being re-used for Hindu worship. It had been a sanctuary for widows who did not commit *sati*, and so became known as the 'Temple of Nuns'.

Verna is also the place chosen in 1988 for re-siting the ancient Mother Goddess figure (c5th century BC) from Curdi (Kurdi) in Sanguem, which was threatened by the Selaulim Dam project. Two megalithic sites were found in the area.

❖ MARGAO *M6B2*

Population 72,100 *STD Code* 0834, pronounced *Mudgao*

Also called Madgaon or Margoa, this is the largest commercial centre after Panaji and the capital of the state's richest and most fertile taluka, Salcete. A pleasant provincial town it was given the status of a *vila* (town) by Royal decree in 1778.

Tourism has had little impact on many parts of the town, and you can see old Portuguese domestic architecture and some fine church buildings while also experiencing daily life in a city going about its thriving business.

Margao is at the heart of its district and wider region. As the main station on the new Konkan railway linking Goa with Bombay to the north, and Mangalore and Kerala to the south, and also a major station on the newly widened broad gauge railway which runs from Vasco to central India, Margao will become the hub of Goa's transport connections with the rest of India.

❖ Church of the Holy Spirit

This impressive Baroque church with its classic Goan façade dominates the Old Market (*Feast Day* in June) square, the Largo de Igreja, surrounded by a number of fine town houses. Originally built in 1564 over the ruins of a Hindu temple, it was sacked by Muslims in 1589 and rebuilt in 1675. While the west end is typical white painted plaster, the south wall has extensive exposed laterite. A remarkable pulpit on the north wall has carvings of the Apostles.

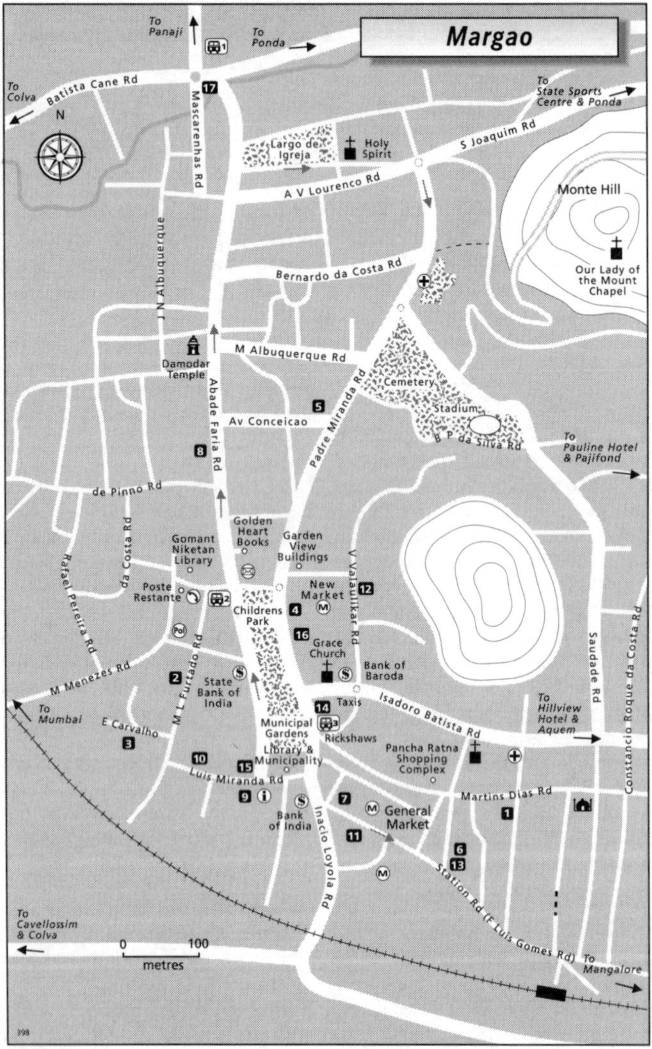

Hotels:
1. *Apsara*
2. *Goa Woodlands*
3. *La Flor*
4. *Mabai*
5. *Metropole*
6. *Milan*
7. *Rukrish*
8. *Twiga Lodge*
9. *Tourist* & **Tourist Office**

Places to eat:
10. Casa Menino
11. Damodar
12. Gaylin Chinese
13. Kamat (Milan)
14. La Marina
15. Longuinhos
16. Marliz Cafeteria

Bus Stands:
1 Kadamba (New)
2 City (Old) for Colva
3 Also for Colva

Margao Cross

The carved reredos is flanked by gold pillars, and there are three Baroque style central pictures. The window arches are in the shape of sea shells while a moulded peacock appears on the north transept wall. There are statues of St Anthony and of the Blessed Joseph Vaz, kept in glass cabinets in the north aisle near the north transept. In the square is a monumental cross with a mango tree beside it.

Abade Faria Street

Many 18th century houses, though dilapidated, can be seen, especially in and around Abade Faria Street. The **de Joao Figueiredo House** has a splendid collection of Goan furniture. The **da Silva House** is a fine example of an impressive town house built around 1790 when Inacio da Silva became the Secretary to the Viceroy. No simple pied-a-terre, it was an impressive mansion; it had a long façade with the roof divided into seven separate cropped 'towers' hence its other name, **Seven Shoulders**. Today, however, only three of these 'towers' remain. The house retains an air of grandeur in its lavishly carved dark rosewood furniture, its gilded mirrors and fine chandeliers. The first floor reception rooms which face the street are lit by large wood and oyster shell windows which are protected by wrought iron balconies. (Unfortunately, the wide 'awning' of corrugated iron which have been added here, as in other fine buildings elsewhere, to shield the rooms from monsoon downpours and strong sunlight, are far from attractive). The chapel screened by wrought ironwork on the first landing is ornately decorated around the altar, quite strikingly set off by a background of blue and gold. The descendants continue to live in a small wing of the diminished house which has the traditional flower-filled courtyard garden at the back.

Market

The covered **Market** is interesting to walk around. The Old Market was rehoused in the 'New' (Municipal) Market in town. The covered Market is not at all touristy although holidaymakers come here from the beaches for their 'shopping trip' to avoid paying inflated prices in the resorts. Monday-Saturday, 0800-1300, 1600-2000.

Other attractions

The pleasant Municipal and Children's **Parks** are near the City Bus Stand. **Monte Hill**, a hillock, has good views over the town and surroundings up to the coastal palms beyond paddy fields ('Motorcycle Taxis' charge Rs 7 for return trip, from centre).

The **Damodar Temple**, 2 km from Kadamba Bus Terminal hosts the winter *Dindi festival* (13 November 1997, 2 November 1998) when there

The burning of a virtuous woman

According to a myth, Sati (Parvati) had been forbidden by her father Daksha to marry Siva but she disobeyed him. Daksha slighted Siva by not inviting him to the special *yagnya* (horse sacrifice) to which every one in the kingdom was to be present. Sati attended the ceremony, against her husband's wishes, but on hearing her father grossly abusing Siva she threw herself into the sacrificial fire. The act gave rise to the term **sati** (or *suttee*) meaning simply a good or virtuous woman. In another story, Krishna's eight wives too are remembered for having followed their husband to be burnt on his funeral pyre.

Recorded in the Vedas, the self immolation of a 'virtuous woman', often out of a sense of duty, probably became accepted practice until the early centuries BC and even then it was mainly restricted to the *Kshatriya* caste. There are references to the mimed ceremony in which the widow symbolically joined her dead husband on the pyre but was led away before the pyre was set alight. The burning of widows was resumed by around the 6th century AD, mainly along the River Ganga, and in Bengal and Rajasthan. If a woman refused she would have been considered to have brought dishonour to her husband's family. She would then be deprived of all means of support and was sometimes forced into prostitution.

In Goa, Afonso de Albuquerque forbade the practice of widow burning which was prevalent among the Hindus when the Portuguese arrived. In 1550, a further order meant that anyone reported to have "assisted" a widow to commit *sati* would be taken into custody and his property divided between the person who denounced him and the work of the Church of St Thomas. The pressure to abandon the customary *sati* led to widows being prevented from remarriage by insisting that they shave their heads and stop wearing jewellery (thus removing the means of making herself attractive) and also adopt a restricted diet. These observances also were attacked by the colonial rulers during the 16th and early 17th centuries. There are some *sati* stones (and *hero* stones) in the the Old Goa Archaeological Museum.

The Bengali religious leader and social reformer Raja Rammohan Roy made great efforts to abolish sati and allow widow remarriage in the early 19th century and the act was made illegal in 1829. The practice however, continued and even today, cases are reported where family pressure has a led a woman to her husband's funeral pyre.

is a palanquin procession along with singing of devotional hymns.

The town also boasts Goa's largest football stadium of international standard which can seat 40,000.

NB Traffic congestion has worsened due to disruption caused by the building of the new railway line. The single overbridge, however, may well fall short of the demand and the traffic chaos at the south entrance to the town may not be solved.

Excursions

A fascinating trip from the coast can take in two of the most important Christian sites in Salcete, a glimpse of both past and present village life. Loutolim and Rachol can both be reached by taking the main Ponda road out of Margao, Loutolim being just to the north of the road and Rachol 6 km to the south (it is also a well-signposted turn off to the left, 4.5 km east of Margao for those combining this trip with a visit to Chandor).

Mid-range Hotels

Holiday-makers usually head for the beaches, using Margao for an overnight stop for making travel connections. It will be the main point of access to Goa for travellers on the new Konkan railway. **NB** Station Road is still universally called by that name, though the road signs give it its official name of Francisco Luis Gomes Rd.

D ***Goa Woodlands***, ML Furtado Rd, opposite City Bus Stand, T 721121, 46 rooms, 18 a/c, clean and spacious with bath, restaurant, bar, popular with business travellers; **D** ***Hillview***, Aquem Alto, T 735212, 22 rooms, some a/c; **D** ***La Flor***, E Carvalho St, T 731402, 34 rooms, 15 a/c, restaurant; **D** ***Metropole***, Avenida Conceicao, T 721556, 50 rooms, some a/c, restaurant, bar, pool, roof garden; **D-E** ***Tourist Hotel*** (GTDC), behind the Municipality, T 731996, 69 acceptable rooms, some a/c, simple restaurant (good veg vindaloo).

Budget hotels

Some like *Gold Star* and *Green View* don't accept foreign visitors. **E** ***Apsara*** (was *Neptune*), Martins Dias Rd, 3rd Floor, T 731491, 20 rooms, some a/c, now run down and tatty; **E** ***Mabai***, Praca Dr George Barreto, T 721658, 20 rooms (9 a/c) just about all right for a single night's stop – "roof garden" is an expanse of concrete with no plant or chair in sight; **E** ***Milan***, Station Rd, T 722715, useful if arriving late by train, good Indian veg restaurant; **E** ***Twiga Lodge***, 413 Abade Faria Rd, T 720049, 4 pleasant rooms, good value; **E-F** ***Rukrish***, Station Rd, T 721709, 17 clean rooms, some with balconies.

F ***Paulino***, Saudade Rd, Pajifond, T 220615, 14 rooms.

Places to eat

Pork is not usually available. ***Café Madgaon*** is good for South Indian snacks; ***Casa Menino*** (part a/c) with bar, Luis Miranda Rd (LIC Building); a/c ***Gaylin***, 1 Varde Valaulikar Rd, for Chinese; Four Indian veg ***Kamat*** restaurants, clean and good value, try a/c *Milan Kamat* on Station Rd; ***La Marina*** near the Taxi Stand; ***Longuinhos Food Affair*** near the Municipality, open all day, North Indian; ***Maria Luiza Bakers*** near the Municipal Garden and ***Souza Bakery***, towards Kadamba Bus terminal, do reasonable cakes and breads (no bebinca anywhere!).

Prices: C Rs 800-1,500; **D** Rs 400-800; **E** Rs 200-400; **F** under Rs 200

Local travel

Local Bus Stand is by the Municipal Gardens. You can usually board buses near the *Kamat Hotel*, southeast of the Gardens.

Car hire: Rs 650-900/day or Rs 5,500/week with driver from *Sai Service*, T 735772, recommended.

Motorcycle Taxis and City bus service.

Long distance travel

Train Enquiries, T 732255. **NB** The Konkan Railway will have *Shatabdi Exp* and an *Overnight Exp* between Mumbai and Mangalore via Margao, ultimately reducing the Mumbai-Margao and the Margao-Mangalore journeys to less than 8 hours. A daily passenger train began running between Margao and Mangalore at the beginning of August. The new station will be 500m south of the old station.

The broad gauge conversion of the line between Vasco and **Londa** in Karnataka which runs through Margao and Dudhsagar Falls, was completed in 1997 and now connects stations on the line with **Belgaum**. There are services to **Bangalore**, **Delhi via Agra**, and **Hospet (Hampi)** among others. See Transport under Vasco above on page 111.

Bus: the **Kadamba (New) Bus Stand** is 2 km north of town (City buses to the centre, Re 1 or Motorcycle Taxi Rs 8); buses arriving before 1000 and after 1900, proceed to the centre.

Services to **Benaulim**, Rs 2; **Cabo da Rama**: 0730 (2 hours) Rs 10; **Colva**: every hour, Rs 3.**KTC buses** to: **Panaji**: frequent (1½ hours), Rs 6; **Vasco**: hourly, Rs 5.

Private buses: to **Bangalore**: 1700 (15 hours) Rs 275; **Mangalore**: 1800, 2130 (8-10 hours) Rs 140; **Mumbai (Dadar/VT)**: 1400, 1700 (16 hours) Rs 600 (sleeper), 400; **Pune**: 1700 (13 hours), Rs 450 (sleeper).

Auto-rickshaw: to **Colva**, Rs 25; beach, Rs 35-50. **Bus**: to beach, Rs 2. **Taxi**: **Panaji**, about Rs 300; **Colva**, Rs 60. **Travel tip** Avoid **Tourist Taxis which can be 5 times the price.**

Directory

Banks & money changers: State Bank of India, west of the Municipal Gardens; **Bank of Baroda**, east of Gardens, behind Grace Church. **NB** It is important to get exchange before visiting beaches to the south.

Hospital & medical services: *JJ Costa Hospital*, Fatorda, T 722586; *Hospicio*, T 722164. *Holy Spirit Pharmacy*, open 24 hours.

Post & telecommunications: GPO, north of Children's Park, Poste Restante, near the Telegraph Office, down lane west of Park. **Courier**: *Skypak*, T 724777 and *Rau Raje Desprabhu*, near Hotel Mayur, Old Market. **Telephones**: STD (and sometimes Fax) facilities at several places in town, including the New Market near the Post Office and Taxi Stand.

Shopping: Books: *Golden Heart*, Confident Building, off Abbé Faria Rd, behind the GPO, T 726339 (closed 1300-1500), is the biggest bookshop in Goa, wide collection, a bit like a warehouse but very helpful staff. **Handicrafts**: Tourist Hotel shop; ***AJ Mavany***, Grace Estate. **Photography**: ***Lorenz***, opposite the Municipality, ***Wonder Colour Lab***, Garden View Building. **Textiles**: ***MS Caro***, Caro Corner, has been in business since 1860, and has an extensive range including 'suiting', and will advise on tailors who can make up garments to order, in a few days; some will make near perfect copies of a sample. **Tailor**: ***J Vaz***, Martires Dias Rd, near Hari Mandir, T 720086, good quality reliable men's tailor.

Tourist offices: At the Tourist Hotel, T 722513.

Useful addresses: Ambulance: 722722; **Fire:** T 722175; **Police**: T 722175. Damania Shipping for catamaran to Mumbai, *Tourist Hotel*, T 731966.

LOUTOLIM *M6A2*

The small village of Loutolim (Lutolim) has several interesting Goan country houses around it, including **Miranda House**. The Mirandas became wealthy as owners of areca plantations. The garden still has specimen palms as reminders. Their fine country house built around 1700 is at the end of a rough track which starts near the church square, approached through impressive iron gates. The main door is to one side instead of being central to the front of the house. The house, though, is typical in having a garden courtyard at the back around which runs the family rooms and bedrooms (note the attractive panelled wood ceilings) protected by shady verandahs. There is also the family chapel (described by Hall, as now having a brightly painted door and ceiling) with the kitchen and servants' quarters at the far end. The formal reception rooms are to the front lit by equally formal dark wood windows. The grand dining hall upstairs is accessed from the front hall, which in turn leads to the large library. The bedroom suite on the other side once offered sanctuary to the Ranes in the 19th century (see page 158), and a defensive gun hole in the wall by a door still serves as a reminder of those uncertain years. The house retains little of the original furniture but more recently acquired pieces of period artefacts are now set off by imaginative furnishings in some of the rooms. Ask at the Tourist Office if the house is open to visitors.

Another fine house in its private compound is the **Salvador Costa House**, now shared by two descendants. Here too, the household revolved around a central courtyard at the back, but unlike the Miranda House, a wide welcoming verandah greeted the visitor. Some fine features of its grand past are still evident in the original beautifully carved furniture, grand chandeliers and mirrors in one part of the house.

The village has recently started attracting visitors to ❖ **Ancestral Goa**, a privately developed open-air site designed to illustrate Goa's traditional past. Entry Rs 20, open 0900-1800 daily. A visit is highly recommeded.

The 'museum' was conceived by Maendra Alvares an artist/sculptor who has devoted considerable time and energy (and finance) to create a unique centre.

The 'model village' built on a slope behind his own home has examples of old town and village houses and artisans' huts and traces the evolution of buildings. Great care and research have gone into constructing authentic replicas with an eye to detail when fitting them out with appropriate tools, utensils and artefacts, and providing a sympathetic setting.

The tour takes you through the changing styles of structures from the humblest to the most comfortable, and at the same time illustrates interesting details of day-to-day life:

The **fisherman's** shack: a simple shelter made out of palm fronds and bamboo with sand and shells on the ground .

The **farmer's** single-room home is built of mud and laterite blocks, with distinctive small clay tiles on the verandah roof. There is a stone fireplace and clay benches.

The **Taverna** progresses to being partly white-washed, with larger terracotta "Mangalore tiles" on the roof, a layer of cowdung covers the mud floor and it has a long verandah with benches made of wood and clay.

The **landowner's** impressive house shows Portuguese influence in its raised balcao (verandah), plastered walls built of laterite and mortar, clay floor tiles, red cement seats, the family altar, and the use of decorative ceramic wall tiles, slatted wood ceilings and oyster-shell windows. See page 56.

Various interesting village activities are illustrated from the distillation of the feni liqour from cashew apples in a *bhati*, to the potter and the village violin master. Of particular interest are structures like the Boca da Vaca (the Cow's Mouth') spring which supplied a community with water, *Sant Kuris* (the wayside Holy Cross), where an annual feast is celebrated, *dhone* (pairs of pillars), which were found on roadsides (which the owner interprets as rests for heavy loads carried long distances), and the travellers' "safe passage" *racondar* lamps found under trees at significant points on a route. Brightly painted models of human figures may appear a little strange in the rustic surroundings but it is hoped that they will be supplemented by real artisans since live demonstrations of some crafts may be possible in the peak season.

Set on a hill side in very attractive surroundings, visitors are given a guided tour by well-informed guides who lead you through a socio-historical journey. Parts of the trail now have protection from the sun while a cooling mist of water provides a welcome escape from the mid-day heat during the hotter months. Take a hat, never-the-less.

An added attraction is a chance to see a range of Goa's spices and fruit trees recently planted here which will

A typical Goan house

The banquet of the Mharus

According to Almeida Alvares the rite of Reddebhogvoll goes back to a story involving one of the affiliated deities of Betall, who used to be provoked by an evil spirit, or *mharu*. The mharu would enter the temple and slap him. On the advice of another deity from a nearby village, Betall succeeded in making the evil spirit slip and fall down, and thus kept him under foot, where he still remains.

This event is celebrated in the sacrifice of animals in his honour. Pereira goes on to say: "When the date has been fixed one man from the class of *devdasis* goes on its eve, at nighttime, to convoke the spirits (*mharus* and *bhuts*), in the boundaries of the village, in the streets and around the trees where they dwell.

On the following night the Mhars, carpenters, ironsmiths, washermen and other Sudra artisans gather in the temple. They take inside two buffaloes (which they overwork on purpose) and three goats. The doors are then closed and there remain only twelve persons and the caller who sits down and embraces Betall, blindfolded.

At midnight, when all of them are in a rave, amidst cries which express the joy of the spirits and at the sound of drums, they cut the heads of the buffaloes and the goats and sprinkle their blood on a heap of boiled rice at the feet of Betall.

This is the banquet of the Mharus. The caller then leaves hold of Betall who would have fallen if he had not been caught and who is seen rocking at the time when the Mharu comes out from below his feet and goes with others to take part in the banquet.

The Mhars of the village then take the animals to an isolated palm grove and eat them there."

become more productive as they mature. At the top of the site is "Natural Harmony", a sculpture of Sant Mirabai singing a devotional song accompanied by her one-string instrument *ektara*, carved out of a single horizontal block of laterite (15m x 5m). Maendra Alvares' single-handed achievement has entered the Limca Book of World Records for its size. A little further up is the *Big Foot*, designed as a dance floor for wedding parties and other functions; each toe forms a platform for the band!

At the end of the tour, visitors are invited to have a glass of "fresh lime" (not bottled water but safe to drink) and visit a small gift shop with local hand made crafts, pottery, ceramics and paintings.

A bakery about 500m away in a private house sells exceedingly mouth-watering *melting moments* macaroons made with ground cashew nuts. Ask for directions.

❖ RACHOL

M6A2

Rachol (pronounced *Rashol*) is set in a fertile valley, vivid green during the wet season and into the New Year, but burnt brown in the summer heat. A stone archway crosses the road marking the entrance, the road coming to an abrupt end in a hamlet by the river bank. The seminary is well worth a visit. Its white painted buildings are scattered on the left around a garden court.

The Fort

There is little evidence of one of Goa's early important forts save a gateway and parts of some walls. Originally Muslim, it was captured by the forces of the Hindu Vijayanagar King in 1520 who then handed it over to the Portuguese who, they hoped, would in turn keep the Muslims at bay. During the Maratha Wars of 1737-9 and the siege that followed the fort was badly damaged. Having lost the northern provinces the Portuguese paid a huge indemnity to keep the southern forts. The one in Rachol was repaired by the Marquis of Alorna in 1745. With the threat of aggression removed, the 100 cannons here were dispersed and most of the buildings gradually disintegrated over the ensuing years.

❖ Rachol Seminary

This is open to visitors even during term time, though quiet is requested. An attendant will show you round the church and the seminary between 0900-1300, 1430-1700; entry free. There is a daily service at 0700 to which visitors are welcome. The seminary was established here in 1580 (after the earlier one at Margao was destroyed by Muslims the previous year) since the site had the protection of the fort. Originally known as the College of All Saints, it was rededicated to **Ignatius Loyola** in 1622. The Rachol complex, principally an ecclesiastical college, also includes a hospital, a primary school, an early printing press which printed the Bible in Konkani, is nearly a self-sufficient community. The Seminary was under the Jesuits from 1610 until 1759 when they were expelled, and the 'Oratorians' installed in their place. However, in 1835, when all religious orders lost favour in Portugal they too were removed and the Seminary became the responsibility of the Diocesan Clergy of Goa.

For successive generations the seminary has been the most prestigious centre of education in Goa, producing some of Goa's secular as well as religious leaders and indeed many have served in remote corners of the world. The Seminary now is a forward-looking institution which trains clergy able to meet the challenges of society today. The vast stone structure of the seminary is built round a large courtyard; the exterior is lime-washed but inside the courtyard the walls are pink. There is an underground cistern which some suggest belonged to an ancient Siva temple here which was destroyed and an underground passage from the courtyard conjures up images of an escape route through the fort in the precarious years of the 17th and 18th centuries. The seminary also contains large galleries and a famous library of rare books.

Rachol Seminary

The Church

The Church here, dating from 1609, was rebuilt in 1622. The impressive interior, beautifully restored and rich with gilding, has nine altars including one to St Constantine containing his relics, and one with the celebrated Menino Jesus statue (which was considered miraculous when it had been installed in Colva, see page 165). There are many murals in the Seminary and Church including several portraits of saints.

❖ Museum of Christian Art

It is attached to the seminary but run independently by the Department of Archaeology, is open 0930-1300, 1400-1700, Rs 5, closed Monday. The small, well-kept museum houses exhibits of Indo-Portuguese sacred art mainly from Goa's churches, convents and Christian homes, and was opened in January 1994 with funding from the Fundaçao Calouste Gulbenkian, Lisbon and Indian institutions. The 155 precious items reflect a wealth of workmanship in wood, ivory, silver and gold.

Church of Our Lady of the Snows

(Nossa Senhora das Neves), now the Parish Church, is a short distance away on the riverside.

CURTORIM M6B3

9 km from Margao and southeast of Rachol, Curtorim (Kurhtori) is a straddling village on the left (south) bank of the Zuari. The **Church of St Alex** (1597) possibly on the site of a Hindu temple, was rebuilt 50 years later and further renovated 200 years ago. Its siting away from the village centre is unusual. Here it stands in an attractive open setting, with its huge square facing a tranquil tank edged by shady palms. The large ornamental piazza cross resembles the monumental cross in front of Margao's Church of the Holy Spirit. The church towers illustrate the influence of Hindu design in 18th century Goan churches. The octagonal drums topped by domes and lanterns recall the principal tower over the *garbagriha* of the Shri Mangesh Temple at Mardol. The interior with its five altars is profusely and elaborately decorated with some very fine detail.

> **Travel tip**
>
> A long day's excursion from one of Salcete's beaches can also include Chandor and Chandranath Hill.

❖ CHANDOR M6B3

About 13 km east of Margao (and south of Curtorim), on the site of the 11th century Kadamba capital of Chandrapur, Chandor is an interesting village. The once navigable tributaries of the Zuari river here allowed trade to flourish with distant Arab ports as early as the 7th century and even earlier, a 4th century Bhoja king's copper-plate inscription dates the existence of an ancient fort which once stood at Chandrapur nearby, taking advantage of the natural defensive moat the two rivers provided. In addition to the fort walls, brick foundations of a 7th century Siva temple was found in 1929, near the sign on the roadside which marks the site of the old capital. The massive body of a *nandi* bull too was discovered which must have come from the Siva temple.

Today, Chandor is very much a backwater. Succeeding Muslim and Christian rulers destroyed much of Chandor's Hindu past. The **Church of Our Lady of Bethlehem** built in 1645, replaced the principal *Sapta Matrika* (Seven Mothers) temple which was demolished in the previous century.

❖ Three Kings Festival

Crowds gather on 6th January each year, for the Three Kings Festival at Epiphany, which is similarly celebrated at Reis Magos where there is a big fair, and at Cansaulim (Quelim) in southern Goa. The three villages of Chandor (Cavorim, Guirdolim and Chandor) come together to put on a grand show. Boys chosen from the the villages dress up as the Three Kings and appear on horse back carrying gifts of gold, frankincense and myrrh. They process through the village before arriving at the church where a large congregation gathers.

❖ Menezes Braganza House

Chandor also retains several fine Portuguese mansions, among them the enormous Braganza family house.which faces one side of the large Church square, about 400m from the railway station, and receives visitors right through the year. **Luis de Menezes Braganza** was an influential journalist and politician (1878-1938) who not only campaigned for freedom from colonial rule but also became a champion of the less privileged sections of Goan society. The part-late 16th century mansion he inherited (extended in the 18th and 19th), shows the opulent lifestyle of the old Portuguese families who established great plantation estates, still complete with all furniture and effects. The central staircase which divides the house into two halves, leads upstairs to the public reception rooms in the front and the private rooms at the back. The kitchen and servants quarters were downstairs at the back around the courtyard. Typically, the reception rooms at the front are lit by large glazed windows. You will be shown the impressive *drawing room* containing many of the family's prized posessions, the cherished library with about 5,000 volumes in several languages, a small study which still retains its oyster shell window, a grand Ball Room with Belgian chandeliers and mirrors, Italian marble floor and gilded door frames, the Dining Room with an impressive collection of porcelain. Goa's trading links with Portuguese Macau and China are well illustrated by the range of Chinese artefacts, while family portraits and porcelain carrying the ancestral coat-of-arms speak of bygone days lived in grand style. Visitors may also be shown the section which is occupied by the family and view the orchards that belong to this fine house.

Visit the better maintained half owned by Aida de Menezes Bragança. The guided tour by this elderly member of the family who resides here, is fascinating. She has recently completely restored the teak ceiling of the 250-year-old library gallery to return it to its original state; the old *mareta* wood floor survives since this native Goan wood can withstand water. In the Dining Room, the original polished *argamassa* floor has been replaced by new mosaic though a small section of old tiles have been retained near a window, as an example. The original ceiling of the grand salon (Ball Room) has been cleverly refurbished with patterned fibreglass to imitate the original American zinc panels. Donations of Rs 50 per visitor is appreciated. The house is usually open 0900-1800 everyday but it is best to confirm by phone (T 784201). You will find the front door open; go up the stairs and knock on the door on the left.

PARODA *M6B3*

Paroda, 15 km southeast of Margao (and about 4 km northwest of Quepem), is at the start of the climb up the 350m high Chandranath Hill (only signposted in Hindi) which has the **Chandresvar**

Bhutnath Temple at the top. The temple was referred to in copper plate inscriptions as early as the 5th or 6th century AD. The final climb on foot is up rough steps to bring you to a superb open site for the brilliant white temple dedicated to Siva as the Lord of the Moon. Water is believed to ooze from the rock linga which has a face carved on it, when it is touched by moonlight at each full moon; the temple was reputedly designed to make this possible. The Moon was worshipped by Bhoja kings who ruled South Goa from the pre-Christian era up to the mid-8th century. There is a separate shrine to Siva Bhutnath, an unadorned tall linga. An enclosure houses two wooden temple chariots; the older one has some good carvings. There are distant views from the hilltop, particularly at sunset, across to the sea. It is also believed that the hill is one of the 180 holy ancient pilgrimage centres for Hindus, the *tirthas*.

A second temple in the village, dedicated to Raibondkaranchem Deul, which has ancient sculpted images, is visited regularly by pilgrims from Ribandar in Tiswadi.

CUNCOLIM *M6C2*

Population 15,000

To the south of the taluka, and on the NH17, Cuncolim saw the destruction of its three principal Hindu temples (including the Shantadurga) when the Jesuits were Christianizing the area and later built churches and chapels on their sites. The annual Shantadurga *jatra* takes place in December-January (6 January 1998, 29 December 1998) when thousands accompany the image, in procession from Fatorpa to Cuncolim.

According to Souza's account, Cuncolim was also the scene of the massacre of five Jesuits and several converts by local Hindu 'rebels' who had been incensed by the repeated destruction of temples and defilement of temple tanks. Most of them were subsequently captured by the Captain of Rachol fort and 15 were killed by his soldiers. The Christian 'martyrs of Cuncolim' were initially buried in Rachol but were transferred to Old Goa where their relics are lodged in the Se Cathedral. The Golden Bell, the largest in Goa which hangs in the remaining single tower of the same cathedral, was cast here in 1652.

Cuncolim is also one of the few places in the area to have a **petrol station**.

CACORA *M8A2*

This tiny hamlet in north Quepem, on the road between Sanvordem and Chandor, is noted for its **Shri Mahadeva Temple**. Although the temple is unremarkable in appearance it has some very unusual features. One is that among its affiliated deities is a shrine in the precincts to a Muslim *Pir* (saint) which Gomes Pereira notes is served by a Muslim who is permanently employed by the temple. Even more remarkable is the annual ritual during which a buffalo is sacrificed in a ceremony known as '*Reddebhogvoll*', not uncommon in Maratha and Sudra villages.

QUEPEM *M8A2*

Population 12,000

Quepem is 15 km southeast of Margao. The Forest Department's simple **F** *Quepem Forest Rest House*, can be booked through the Wildlife Office, 3rd floor, Junta House, 18th June Rd, Panaji, T 0832 224747/225926.

To go to **Cabo de Rama**, from Margao or Quepem, travel via **Bali** on the NH 17, through Fatorpa.

FATORPA

M8B1

Fatorpa is no more than a tiny hamlet on the road from Bali to Cabo de Rama. Leaving the NH17 in Bali the road runs to a junction at Fatorpa, dropping down to the **Shri Shantadurga Temple** partially concealed in its shallow valley. There are 14 affiliated deities. The image of Shantadurga, originally from **Cuncolim** in Salcete, was brought to Fatorpa (with several others) in 1583. The modern concrete temple has no trace of the original structure, although the diety is still lodged in her sanctuary behind a silver screen.

The annual *jatra* (once held on 20th day of *Phalgun*) now takes place in December-January (6 January 1998, 29 December 1998), when the deity is taken in procession by a large number of pilgrims. They travel from Fatorpa to the site of the original temple in Cuncolim, where the Chapel of the Sacred Heart stands. The *Fatorpa Gulal* (18 March 1998) is similar to *Holi* when people throw coloured powder and water on each other.

Old Shantadurga Temple

Quepem and Canacona Coast

BETUL

M8B1

Betul in Quepem taluka is an important fishing village in an idyllic setting. Just after the bridge which crosses the mouth of the river a narrow road zigzags through the village along the south side of the Sal estuary. It is well worth the walk. The village, depending on fishing, coir production and labouring, is delightfully shaded by coconut palms, jackfruit, papaya and banana, and the track goes along the water's edge overlooking the wide estuary between Betul and the southernmost tip of Mabor Beach. A sand bar traps the estuary into a wide and protected lagoon. Cool breezes from the sea moderate the temperatures of the plateau above so that even in the hottest season it is perfectly bearable.

A walk along the 'jetty' past dozens of many-coloured fishing boats will reveal busy fisherfolk loading fish into baskets or their catch of tiny silvery fish glistening in the sun trapped under spread out nets on the bank.

The road to the south from Betul village climbs steeply from the lush tropical valley to the searing heat of the bare plateau. It passes a new development by IPSEN for the Oil and Natural Gas Commission of India, after 2.6 km reaching a crossroads. From the crossing a road goes to northeast (left) to **Bali**, 9 km, passing Shakti Bauxite

QUEPEM AND CANACONA TALUKAS

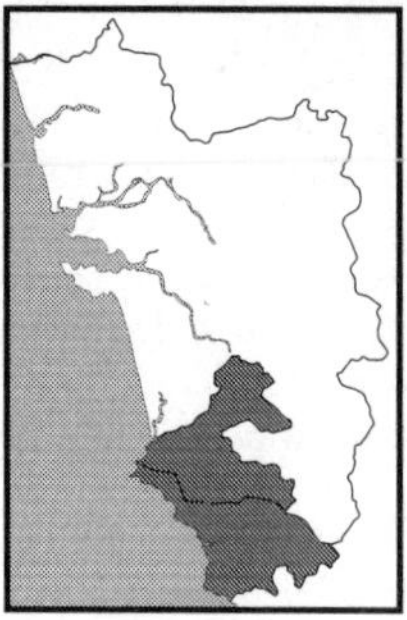

Quepem and Canacona are the two southernmost New Conquest talukas. Towards the south of Goa and into northern Karnataka the Western Ghats get closer to the sea, rising as a clearly visible range of hills even from the coastal road in the south. They are thus the only talukas that have both hill ranges and a coastline, but they share some of the geographical features of the talukas to the north. Low laterite plateaus continue to alternate with wooded valleys, but the forest comes closer to the sea here in the south than anywhere else in Goa. Hence Canacona's small Cotigao Sanctuary is a bare 15 km from the sea, easily reached from Palolem but also within reach of a day trip from Salcete.

The chief attractions in Canacona taluka are on the coast, Cabo de Rama and Palolem, but each has its share of Hindu temples inland and some very attractive scenery.

mines on the plateau. Workers' tent-like huts made of grey thatch are set in a stark landscape. The road southwestwards from the crossroads towards **Cabo de Rama** first has coconuts growing in the valleys with breadfruit trees, then it traverses a really bleak landscape, dominated in the dry season by almost black laterite which is enlivened during the rains by patches of green cultivation. After passing the High School, 1.6 km from the junction, there is an extraordinary landscape of meticulously reclaimed land, tiny rectangles of levelled plots with little laterite block bunds built to trap the rain. You wind down into the valley for 1 km, where a minor road forks off to the right to Cabo de Rama (the sign to Cabo de Rama may be almost invisible), while the left leads to the southernmost beaches of Goa. Heading for the fort, you pass through beautiful lightly wooded countryside, dominated by cashew trees, and there are magnificent sweeping views. A small village below the fort has seized the opportunity to cater for visitors to this corner of Goa.

❖ CABO DE RAMA *M8B1*

Cape Rama is named after the hero of the Hindu epic the *Ramayana*, who is said to have lived there with his wife Sita during their period of exile. The Cape was an obvious site for a fort to any power whose interests might be threatened from the sea. Its origins pre-date the arrival of the Portuguese who captured it in 1763 and used it as a prison too.

The road runs through the small village, with the amazingly brightly painted *Fernandes Corner Restaurant* about 500m from the car park at the Fort's entrance followed by *Pinto's Bar*, near the entrance to Fort; *Zina Bar*, next door. These offer meals, drinks and some very basic rooms.

The fruit and nut case of cashew

The cashew or (*kazu*) tree which you will see in many parts of Goa, particularly in Bardez, Bicholim and Satari talukas, produce the 'apple' which turns yellow or red when ripe and is then harvested between March and June (see page 29). The tree, which is one of the principal and dependable 'plantation crops', is often not formally planted in separate orchards, but grows productively without much attention of fertlizers or irrigation. Cashew was introduced by the Portuguese in the early days of colonization, principally to conserve soil, but later better varieties were introduced (including those from South America) which would yield high quality nut.

The cashew nut, which is enjoyed all around the world, is obtained from roasting the lower part of the fruit in large wood-fired kilns until charred, and then painstakingly cracked open (often by village women) to reveal the pale nut. The dried nut is sometimes roasted and salted before packing. The charred nut-case produces a valued waterproof 'paint' which is used to seal wooden boats.

The "apple" takes a different route. Traditionally, the juice was squeezed out by crushing the fruit under foot in the village *bhati* (distillery) in the same way as grapes are treated in traditional wineries, but now there are modern distilleries. The juice is then strained to produce a delicious sweet drink *niro*, which needs to be kept cool to avoid fermenting. However, most of the juice extracted is allowed to ferment for 15 days; this is then boiled in large earthen pots and distilled to first yield the low alcohol *urak*. Further distillates produce the stronger *cashew feni*..

The Fort

The gatehouse, which has been restored, looks rather quaint, with narrow firing slits irregularly spaced like a miniature design by Le Corbusier. The main entrance seems far from impregnable, considering the scale of the fortifications, but note the strategically positioned hole in the wall, pointing straight at the door, behind which a cannon could be stationed.

The outer ramparts are excellently preserved, with several cannons still scattered along their length. Despite the absence of buildings, other than the church, the magnificence of the site gives it an extraordinary atmosphere. There are stunning views from several of its major bastions, and you can walk virtually the entire outer length of the fort. From two of the gates it is possible to scramble down to the sea, but great care is needed on the crumbly laterite paths. The most dramatic of the walls is on the landward side, where it rises 10-15m above the floor of the moat which was dug both to provide laterite blocks from which the fort is constructed and to create the moat itself.

The gatehouse is at the lowest point of the whole fort, the ground rising to its highest in the southwest. The view is particularly good to the south in the evening light, across bays stretching down past Palolem to Karnataka easily visible on a clear day. From the highest point and observation post (where a modern but disused and run-down building has been built) there is a 360° view, and the wall then drops down to the north. At its lowest it is only 20m or so above the sea. At this point of the compound, deeply wooded now, is the source of the Fort's water supply. A huge tank was excavated to a depth of about 10m, and even today it has water right through the dry season. There are two springs, one of which gives out water through two spouts at different temperatures.

The whole atmosphere of the Fort, untroubled by more than a handful of visitors, creates a sense of history and drama to which only the most unimaginative could fail to respond.

Getting there From Margao, the bus departs at 0730 from southeast corner of the Municipal Gardens (Rs 10, 2 hours), return at 1200 or later. From Betul or Palolem, hire a motorcycle. followed by a few others.

After retracing your steps along the road from Cabo de Rama to the junction you can either return along the Betul/Bali road or take the road south, the coast road to Agonda and Palolem (although there are no signs to tell you this). It is a very attractive alternative to the National Highway.

❖ PALOLEM *M8C2*

STD Code 0834

Further south on the coast (40 km from Margao via Cuncolim), Palolem has a beautiful curve of palm fringed golden sand beach, 2 km off the National Highway – the best beach by far. It is becoming increasingly popular as people search for the remaining unspoilt idyll and are travelling further to find one. As a result Palolem is no longer a deserted bay but has a line of beach shacks serving food and drink in the seaseon while the range of accommodation inreases with demand. It does not have a bank so arrive with enough funds but the small **Post Office** in the village can arrange poste restante. There is a good clothes shop near the Beach Resort; the friendly woman owner "is not pushy ... unlike some men"!

The fairly narrow strip of beach has rather strange rocky outcrops at each end which are locally referred to as 'Pandava's drums' and 'footprints'. An added attraction here is the fresh water stream to the north, as well as the small Canacona Island which can be reached by a short swim or by wading across at low tide. Nudism is not welcomed by the local people. **Dolphin watching** and **fishing** trips are offered by fishermen; mornings between 0830-1230 best. One contact is Dattu Pagi, Boat No 520, 4 people for about Rs 600 for 1½ hour trip. **NB** Take sun-block, shirt, hat and drinking water. You may be able to see some dolphins from the headland to the south of Palolem, just before sunset.

Many visitors just visit for the day, especially from beaches further north though two of Goa's most innovative 'hotels' have recently encouraged some to stay a while. **NB** The beach can sometimes have a bit of a 'heavy atmosphere' (heroin usage was reported in early 1997).

Mid-range hotels

D-E *Bhakti Kutir*, at the southern end, 18 tents of varying sizes in natural environment emphasising peace and meditation, all tents have mosquito nets, common bath and organic toilets (a neutralizing compound is added after use instead of water for flushing); also 3 **C** *cottages* made entirely from natural materials (local stones, slate, palm leaves and wood), imaginatively and sympathetically built, all are away from the beach and very quiet, highly recommended; **D-E** *Tonrick's Royal Cottages*, 200m from beach, T 643239, 7 comfortable rooms with shower and toilet, some with small kitchen, very clean and modern, well-maintained, friendly, recommended.

Budget hotels

E *Cocohuts*, towards the southern end, T 737457, 25 rooms expected in 1998, the breezy, shaded huts are built among palm trees on bamboo stilts and palm leaves about 3m above the ground, each divided into 2 rooms with 2 beds, with electricity and fan, shared toilets, right on the beach (since the structures are removed during the monsoon,

Prices: **C** Rs 800-1,500; **D** Rs 400-800; **E** Rs 200-400; **F** under Rs 200

200m building regulations don't apply), imaginative development by local doctor, very popular for their novelty, beachside restaurant, recommended; **E *Palolem Beach Resort***, T 643054, 11 basic cottages with shower and toilet, 11 simple tents (in season) with shower block, camping (Rs 150/tent), ISD phones, clean, very quiet shaded site, friendly, often full, book at least a week ahead; **E *L'Allegro Holiday Resort***, T 643173, immediately north of the resort, 4 tiny rooms, basic and fairly bleak but right on the beach, often full.

F rooms: A few beach bars and village houses take in guests but toilet facilities are very basic ('pig' toilets, unconnected to sewers, are raised on a platform where pigs do the necessary 'cleaning out' below).

Places to eat

In addition to the ones above, several simple bars and eating places on the beach and in

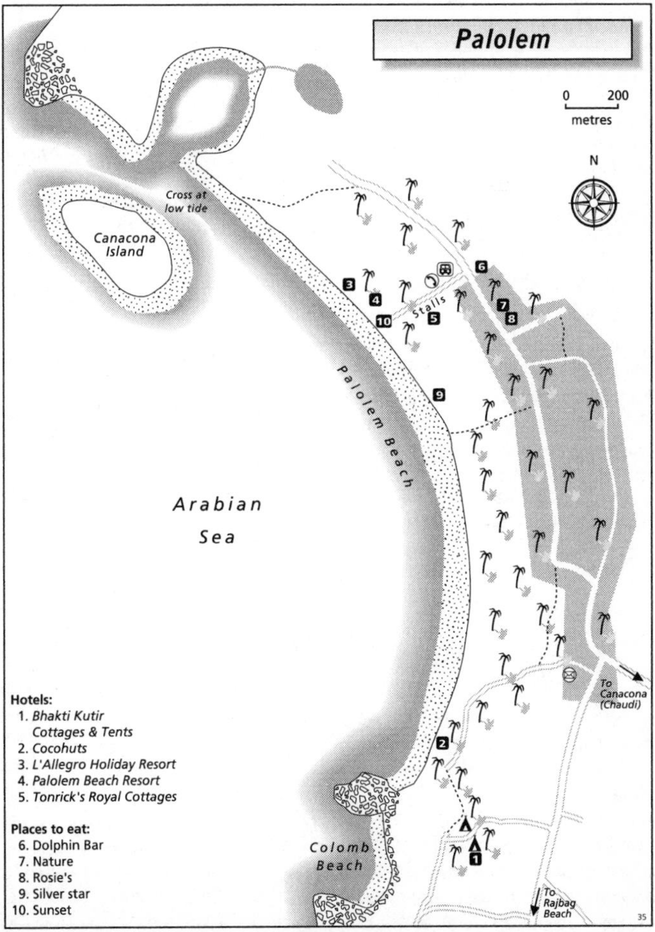

the village. ***Silver Star*** with hammocks in the shade; ***Sun & Moon*** on main Palolem Rd, good food and atmosphere, very friendly; ***Sunset*** on the beach and ***Rosie's***, near the main road, are recommended.

Transport

Bicycle: several outlets in the village hire them out for Rs 3/hr or Rs 25/day.

Train: The Konkan Railway's Margao-Mangalore sector started operating in August 1997, with a stop at Canacona Station, about 3 km away.

Bus: There are 6 daily direct buses between Margao and Palolem, 1 hour, Rs 9; from Palolem, dep are at 0645, 0730, 0930, 1415, 1515, 1630. From Margao, buses to Karwar (Karnataka) go via Canacona; from Canacona, taxis and auto-rickshaws charge Rs 25 to Palolem beach. Alternatively, get off the bus at Canacona Junction (before Canacona village) and walk 2 km to the beach.

COLOMB AND RAJBAG BEACHES

M8C2

South of Palolem, a walk along the shore over rocky outcrops gives access to attractive sandy coves of Colomb Beach with huts of the fishing community nearby; some take in guests. Further south after wading across a stream (possible before the monsoon) you reach the unspoilt Rajbag Beach backed by dunes and casuarinas, remains virtually unvisited and provides excellent swimming. All this will change in 1999 when the **A** *Bharat-Hilton Resort* with 280 rooms and all the usual facilities is expected to open.

At **Kindlebaga**, 2 km from Canacona, is the isolated and somewhat surprising **D-E** *Molyma*, off NH17, west from the cross roads, T 643028, F 643081, 43 modern, large rooms, airy restaurant with limited menu, bar, friendly service, good value though rather deserted, set among trees within 15 minutes walk to a good beach beyond dunes.

GALGIBAG

M8C2

South of the Talpona River, which has a ferry crossing, a short strip of land juts out to sea. Galgibag is a change from the fishing villages across the river as it has well-built houses belonging to the townspeople. There are lucrative casuarina plantations in addition to the ubiquitous palms.

CANACONA

M8C2

Population 10,400; locally pronounced *Kannkonn*

Canacona , sometimes called Chaudi (Chauri) is a crossroads settlement on the NH17 between Panaji and Karwar in Karnataka. 'Chaudi' refers to the town's main square, where the bus and auto stands are, while the large church and high school of **St Tereza of Jesus** (1962) are on the northern edge of town. The rail link on the Konkan railway line has naturally brought the idyllic beaches nearby to the attention of developers.

Shri Malikarjuna Temple with 60 auxiliary deities is believed to date from the mid-16th century and was renovated in the year 1778. The *mandapa* has substantial carved wooden pillars. The temple 'car' festival *Rathasaptami* in February and *Shigmo* in April attract large crowds.

There is not much in the way of facilities at the moment. Accommodation is confined to the Forest Department's simple **F** *Canacona Forest Rest House*, nearby, can be booked through, DCF. South Margao, T 0834 735361. *Canacona Palace*, 50m east of the crossroads, serves good Udupi vegetarian food. The State Bank of India, next to Canacona Palace, has no foreign exchange facility. The Pai Chemists is 100m east of the crossroads. Post Office is a further 100m down the NH towards

Karnataka. Petrol is available from the small house opposite the big tree about 1 km north of the village.

Getting there **Trains** on the new Konkan railway line from Margao to Mangalore stop at Canacona/Chaudi. See page 247. The section of line between Margao and Sawantwadi should be open by the end of October to enable trains from Mumbai to run the full distance to Mangalore. **Buses** run to Palolem and Margao.

The NH17 continues south to the Karnataka border through some beautiful countryside and unspoilt villages. There is a border checkpost with a barrier across the border to stop vehicles. **NB** Motorcyclists must carry all documentation. See page 251.

PARTAGALI

M8C2

Close to the Cotigao Wildlife Sanctuary and just east of the NH17, the **Shri Sausthan Gokarn Partagali Jeevotam Math** at Partagali Village is on the banks of the river Kushavati. The followers who were originally Saivites were converted and became a Vaishnav sect and a *math* (religious establishment) was set up in 1475 AD at Margao. However, during the period of Portuguese Christianization (1560-68), the foundation was moved to Bhatkal (northern Karnataka). After a time, the 6th Swami (who was also responsible for the temple to Rama, Lakshman, Sita and Hanuman here), re-established at Partagali where it has continued uninterrupted. The symbol representing the spiritual movement which is over 500 years old is an ancient *Vatavriksha*'(Banyan tree) which spreads over an area of about 65m x 70m. Known as '*Bramhasthan*' it has been a place for meditation, and the sacred tree with the Ishwarlinga in front of it is believed to have drawn worshippers from the surrounding area for over 1,000 years. Partagali has been developed into a centre of culture and learning, while continuing with its ancient traditions. The temple which also has a typical tall Garuda pillar, celebrates its festival in March/April.

COTIGAO WILDLIFE SANCTUARY

M8C3

The second largest of Goa's wildlife sanctuaries, Cotigao, established in 1969, is about 80 km south of Panaji. One of the most densely forested areas of the state, the 105 sq km sanctuary is in part hilly to the south and east. The vegetation is mostly moist deciduous with some semi-evergreen and evergreen forest cover. The Talpona river flows through the park. There are several small settlements of *Velip* and *Kunbis* who are forest-dwelling groups existing on subsistence farming so it offers a good opportunity to observe traditional rural life. Some regret that their hunting and wood-gathering activities have been curbed with the establishment of the Sanctuary. The villagers grow chillies and harvest cashew from the forest to take to the market in Cotigao. There have been attempts to introduce sugarcane, rubber and eucalypts by some agencies but environmentalists argue that this would lead to clearing of trees and change the nature of the forest.

There is a Nature Interpretation Centre with a small refrence library at the entrance.

Access

7 km south of Canacona, a 1.5 km road along a left turn (east) off the NH17 between Canacona and Poinguinim leads to the Cotigao Sanctuary. Entry Re 1. Still camera Re 1; Video Rs 25. 2-wheeler Rs 1.50, 3-wheeler Rs 3, car/jeep Rs 5. Buses run from Canacona. Open 0800-1800.

Wildlife

The sanctuary claims to harbour a wide range of mammals (including panther, sloth bear and hyena) and several reptiles but you are really only likely to see wild boar, the odd deer and gaur and many monkeys on a visit although bird spotting is more rewarding. Birds not easily seen elsewhere in Goa include rufous woodpecker, Malabar crested lark and white-eyed eagle.

Viewing

The Department's jeep is available to go around the sanctuary along the network of metalled and unmetalled roads within the sanctuary with a free guide. Contact the Range Forest Officer whose office is by the Interpretation Centre at the entrance. There is a viewing platform up a tall tree at Bhutpal 9 km from the entrance and waterholes at Tulsimol and Dhantali but there are no signposts so you will have to be taken by a guide. Unfortunately day visitors may only enter after 0800 by which time it is often warm enough to reduce animal activity to a minimum.

Park information

Visitors usually come for a day trip. Those wishing to stay close by, choose to stay in Palolem or at *Molyma* at Kindlebaga. Overnight stay in the forest is possible, with permission. Three ***tents*** with concrete floors are available free but only the hardiest of campers could endure a night here, made even more difficult by the rich insect life. The tree-platform is the other alternative. A room is available at the simple **F *Forest Rest House*, Poinguinim**. Contact the Conservator's Office, 3rd floor, Junta House, 18th June Rd, Panaji, T 0832 224747. **NB** No food or refreshments are available at the park entrance or inside the santuary.

The Goa-Karnataka border is further south, just under a 1 hour bus ride. Across the border there is a marked improvement in the road surface. It no longer winds through the forest but is relatively wide and straight as it runs along the Karnataka coast.

The Interior Hills

❖ TAMBDI SURLA *M7A2*

From the crossroads at Molem on the NH4A, the road north through dense forest goes to Tambdi Surla (not always signposted); ask local people or follow signs for the *Shanti Nature Resort*. It is also possible to reach the site along minor roads from Valpoi in Satari to the north.

The **Mahadeva Temple** is a beautifully preserved miniature example of early Hindu temple architecture from the Kadamba-Yadava period. Tucked into the forested foothills, it is the only major remaining example of pre-Portuguese Hindu architecture in Goa. It may well have been saved from destruction by its very remoteness. The place is often deserted, though the compound is well maintained by the Archaeology Department. The entrance to the temple is a short walk from the car park.

The 12th-13th century black basalt temple stands on a platform with three plain mouldings. The stone used must have been transported some distance as basalt is not available locally. The exterior walls have little decoration save for the breaks provided by the vertical pilasters. However, there are good miniature reliefs and sculptures on the shikara above the *garbagriha*, showing deities including Brahma with Swarasvati above, Siva with Uma-Mahesh above, and Vishnu with Kumarashakti above. The low wall near the open sided entrance hall has finely carved lozenge-with-rosette motifs which still appear crisp.

Aligned east-west, the entrance/main hall (*sabhmandapa*), middle hall (*antaralaya*) and sanctuary (*garbagriha*) are on the same east-west axis. The 10 pillars, each different, are relatively plain, but four monolithic pillars which support the stone ceiling with a very fine example of the conventional floral design, are deeply incised. Hutt suggests that the carving showing an elephant trampling a horse (on the lower section of the first pillar on the right) may have political significance, since horses were the favoured animals of war of the Muslim invaders, in contrast to the elephants used by Hindu kings.

The *shikharas* of the four niches in the *mandapa* which contain images including *Nagas*, throw light on how the original temple must have looked with its tower over the *garbagriha* complete. A *Naga* with two hoods appears on a separate slab.

Something different

About 500m from the temple is the ***Shanti Nature Resort*** which comes highly recommended for its location and eco-friendly approach. 9 large mud huts with palm-thatched roofs, electricity and running water, are set in a natural forest setting. Emphasis is on rest and meditation. Yoga and rejuvenating natural therapies are available. The restaurant caters for all tastes including herbal foods and excursions to the forest and local villages can be arranged. Expect to pay around Rs 400. Contact Passive-Active Tourism, *Hotel 4 Pillars*, Rua de Ourem, Panaji, T 225240, F 229463, for further details.

MOLEM *M7A2*

Molem, 12 km south, is the start of hikes and treks in December/January. Popular routes lead to Dudhsagar (17 km), the Sanctuary and Atoll Gad, 12 km, Matkonda Hill, 10 km and Tambdi Surla. Contact the Hiking Assoc, 6 Anand Niwas, Swami Vivekenanda Rd, Panaji. Molem is also a stop on the bus route between Panaji and Belgaum and the truck stop atmosphere is redeemed

Tambdi Surla temple

by the presence of a section of the National Park which is easily accessible (see below) –"very pleasant though you are unlikely to see any wildlife other than monkeys". **E *Tourist Complex*** (GTDC), 300m east of Police Check Post, about 500m from the temple, T 0834 600238, 23 simple but well maintained, clean rooms, some a/c, dorm, checkout 1200, giving time for a morning visit to Tambdi Surla, uninspired North Indian food and beer. The Forest Department's simple **F *Molem Forest Rest House***, can be booked through the Conservator's Office, 3rd floor, Junta House, 18th June Rd, Panaji, T 0832 224747. ***Chai*** stalls serve snacks and breakfast omlettes.

BHAGWAN MAHAVEER SANCTUARY

M7A3

Access

Tickets are available at the Nature Interpretation Centre, 100m from the police checkpost, Molem. The entrance to the Molem National Park, within the Sanctuary, 100m east of the Tourist Complex, is clearly signed but the 14 km of tracks are not mapped. Open 0900-1700.

Wildlife

The 240 sq km Sanctuary contains a herd of gaur (*Bos gaurus* – often called Indian Bison), deer, monkeys and rich birdlife. Occasionally elephants and tigers wander in from neighbouring Karnataka during the summer months, the tigers remaining on higher ground favoured by the few black panthers in the sanctuary but these are rarely spotted.

The magnificently attractive Dudhsagar Falls, are in the southeast corner. The **Devil's Canyon** which is an impressive river gorge, can be visited after getting permission from the Interpretation Centre where you can get directions. The river is believed to have crocodiles.

Within the Sanctuary, Forest Department jeeps are available; contact the Range Forest Officer (Wildlife), Molem. Motorbikes can manage the rough track, outside the monsoon period, but not a scooter.

Colem is a busy small town which has seen a lot of activity recently during the rail gauge conversion. The station is the best point to connect with the Dudhsagar train for those touring Goa by car. Jeeps are also available for the trip to the Falls (see Transport below).

❖ Dudhsagar Falls

M7A3

The spectacular falls on the border between Goa and Karnataka, which are the highest in India, measure a total drop of about 600m. The name, 'the sea of milk', is derived from the white foam that the force of the water creates as it drops in stages, forming pools along the way. They are best seen just after the monsoon, between October and December, but right up to April there is enough water to make a visit worthwhile.

To experience the delights of a beautiful part of the forested Western Ghats, most people visit Dudhsagar by rail which from 1997 has been converted to broad gauge; the line runs across about the mid-point of the vertical drop of the cascades. The small Dudhsagar railway station allows you to step down and then walk back to the opening between the two train tunnels. A rough, steep path takes you down to a viewing area which allows you a better appreciation of their falls' grandeur, and to a beautifully fresh pool which is lovely for a swim (take your costume and towel). There are further pools below but you need to be surefooted. **NB** The final section of the journey is a scramble on foot across

SANGUEM TALUKA

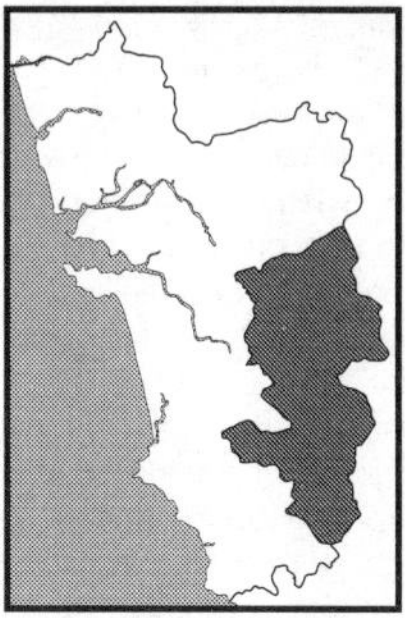

Like Satari to its north, Sanguem covers Goa's eastern hill borderland with the South Indian state of Karnataka. The still-forested hills, populated until recently by tribal peoples practising shifting cultivation rise to Goa's highest points. Just on the Goan side of the border with Karnataka are the Dudhsagar Falls, some of India's highest waterfalls, where the River, which ultimately flows into the Mandovi, cascades dramatically down the hillside. It is one of the great monsoon sights of Goa but even in the dry season is a very attractive place. Much of the southeastern part of the taluka is inaccessible and there are no places to stay, but some places on the district roads can be reached in a day trip from the coast, including Dudhsagar itself.

The north of Sanguem taluka is more accessible, traversed by the NH4A which runs from Ponda to Molem before passing into Karnataka. Both the Bhagwan Mahaveer Sanctuary and the beautiful small Tambdi Surla temple can be reached in a day from the coast (about 2 hrs from Panaji).

stream beds with boulders; it is a difficult task for anyone but the most athletic. The really fit and adventerous may wish to make the arduous climb up to the head of the falls with a guide, which is well worth the effort. Allow 3 hours, plus some time to rest at the top, and make sure of returning before the train you will need to catch.

For those on a motorbike (but not a scooter), for the start of the trail to the falls, from Molem crossroads take the road south towards Colem. From there it is a 17 km rough track with at least 2 river crossings (not recommended after a long period of heavy rain). The ride through the forest is very attractive and leads to the spectacular reward at the end, even in the dry season. A swim in the pool at the Falls is particularly refreshing after a hot and dusty ride. Guides are available but the track is easy to follow even without one.

Dudhsagar Falls

Park information

There is no accommodation inside the sanctuary; carry provisions. The nearest GTDC accommodation is the *Tourist Complex* in Molem, see above.

Transport

Train: Gauge conversion from metre to broad was completed in mid-1997 so trains on the Margao-Londa line are expected to make a visit to the falls possible by train again; the stops before the Falls are at Colem (6 km away), Sonauli and then Dudhsagar. From the southern beaches, you can get on the train at Vasco (over 2 hours' journey to the Falls), Cansaulim, Majorda or Margao.

Road: Those approaching the Sanctuary by car can pick up the train at Colem (the stop after Calem) to visit the Falls. If coming from the south, travel via Sanguem. The road from Sanvordem to the NH17 passes through mining country and is therefore badly pot-holed and has heavy lorry traffic.

Buses: between Panaji, Ponda or Margao, and Belgaum/Bangalore, stop at Molem; from Molem (and Colem) shared jeeps are available for the return journey through the sanctuary to the Falls, for about Rs 1,200 for 6.

From **Molem**, a road to the south off the NH4A leads through the forested hills of Sanguem taluka to Colem and **Calem** railway stations and then south to **Sanguem**. From there, a minor road northwest goes to **San Vordem** and then turns west to **Chandor**.

SANGUEM

M7B1

Population 6,200

20 km from Molem, Sanguem is the headquarters of the largest taluka in Goa. Although inland it has the 'backwaters' feel. The 19th century Jama Masjid was renovated in 1959. The Forest Department's simple **F *Sanguem Forest Rest House*,** can be booked through the Conservator's Office, 3rd floor, Junta House, 18th June Rd, Panaji, T 0832 224747.

ZAMBAULIM

M7B1

Zambaulim, 22 km southeast of Margao, has the **Damodar Temple** which is attractively set along the banks of the Kushavati (Panti) River. According to Hall, the deity originally from Margao was transferred here in 1567 but the temple structure is fairly modern dating mainly from the 1950s to the 1970s. The water of the river here is believed to be especially blessed and have medicinal properties so attracts pilgrims from both the Hindu and Christian communities.

Zambaulim Gulal is celebrated like *Holi* (24 March 1998). Festivities continue for a week with much feasting, cultural shows and a big fair.

The area around had also came under the influence of Buddhism. Punna, a monk, is believed to have lived in the village and preached the doctrine of Buddhism. A statue of the Buddha was found in Rivona nearby (see below).

CURDI

M7C2

Curdi (Kurdi), 8 km south of Sanguem, is known as a megalithic site where a 2.5m laterite Mother Goddess statue (c5th century BC) was excavated. This is also where sections of a Kadamba Temple to Siva (c11th century), described by R Gomes Pereira as built of laterite and granite and consisting of a *garbagriha* and a pyramidal *shikhara*, were discovered. The Mahadeva Temple was threatened by the Salauli Irrigation Project and was resited in the new settlement. A short distance away rockcut steps led down to a stream where a small rockshelter was also found with two statues of Siva. The shelter is now under water.

The Mother Goddess statue was taken to Verna (also a megalithic site) by the Directorate of Archaeology and re-sited on the spot where an old Mahalsa temple stood until 1560.

RIVONA

M7B1

Hall suggests that the name is derived from *Rishi-vana* (Forest of Saints), recalling a period around the 7th century when groups of Buddhist monks are believed to have established cave retreats in this part of Goa. Ask for directions in the village and carry a torch; beware of snakes.

The rock-cut **cave sites**, where a statue of the Buddha was found, are referred to as the Pandava Caves locally. The headless stone statue, described by R Gomes Periera as belonging to the 7th century and missing the left arm, was found seated on a throne with three lions in front; it is now in the Archaeological Museum, Panaji. The caves were later taken over by Hindus who left carvings on stones including a stylized long-tailed Hanuman holding a tree in one hand.

Just south of the bazar along the main road through the village, a dirt path opposite the water pump leads to the first cave site in about 100m. The small set of excavated cells, which Hutt suggests were used as a monastery, is approached by steps that lead down to a vestibule with a well which has a funnel shaped hole channelled through to the surface to provide light and air. Another entrance porch, facing a pool also gave access to the cells within through the vestibule. Natural springs supplied water which was stored in tanks. While most of the caves were excavated, Hutt suggests that part is structural, being built out of stone blocks.

To find the second cave site return to the main road, and follow a path for about 400m down to the river and along it. The cave shelter near the valley bottom, which is more open, has a platform at the back. Here too, there was no shortage of water. The hole to the right of the cave entrance is believed to have been the start of a tunnel to Curdi, some 8 km away.

The road to Curdi, first passes through Colomba.

Colomba has the Shantadurga Temple, one of only a few places in India where Brahma is worshipped, here as an affiliate deity.

Excursions outside Goa

WITHIN EASY reach of the coast and just beyond Goa's borders are fascinating glimpses of the India beyond the old Portuguese enclave. Both the physical and the cultural contrasts are immediate, and 2 or 3-day excursions from the beaches of Goa allow you to see at least something of peninsular India beyond the steamy coastal fringes of the Western Ghats. To the south in coastal Karnataka the ancient Hindu pilgrimage site of Gokarna is rapidly gaining a reputation as the most recent of India's 'dropping out' beaches, becoming the third point of the Goa-Gokarna-Hampi triangle.

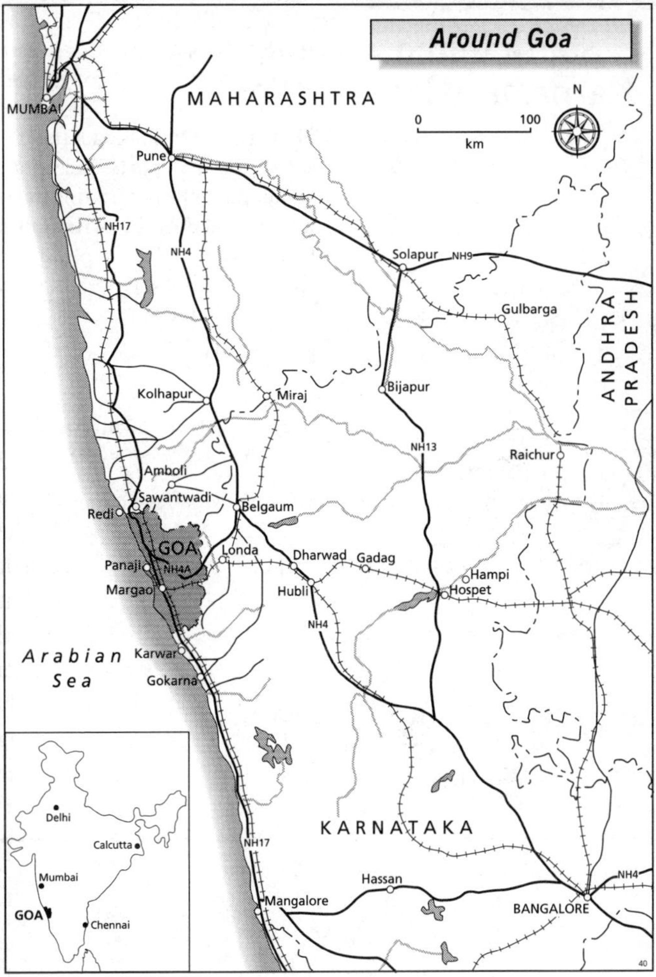
Around Goa
MAHARASHTRA
0
100
km
N
MUMBAI
Pune
NH17
NH4
Solapur
NH9
Gulbarga
ANDHRA PRADESH
Bijapur
Kolhapur
Miraj
NH13
Raichur
Amboli
Sawantwadi
Belgaum
Redi
GOA
Londa
Dharwad
Gadag
Panaji
NH4A
Hampi
Hospet
Margao
Hubli
NH4
Arabian Sea
Karwar
Gokarna
Delhi
Calcutta
Mumbai
GOA
Chennai
KARNATAKA
NH17
Hassan
NH4
Mangalore
BANGALORE
40

South to the Karnataka Coast

JUST ACROSS the southern border of Goa the National Highway enters the coastal lands of northern Karnataka. Broad estuaries and long stretches of golden sand mark the coastline, while inland low wooded hills rise rapidly into the Western Ghats. The Konkan railway now cuts through this landscape to the port of Mangalore. On the coast itself is a string of small ports, once a part of the chain of Arab trading posts which linked Arabia with South East Asia. Many retain a significant Muslim population and cultural identity.

GOKARNA

STD Code 08386

The narrow streets, traditional houses and temples together with its long wide expanse of beach, lure growing numbers of backpackers moving on from

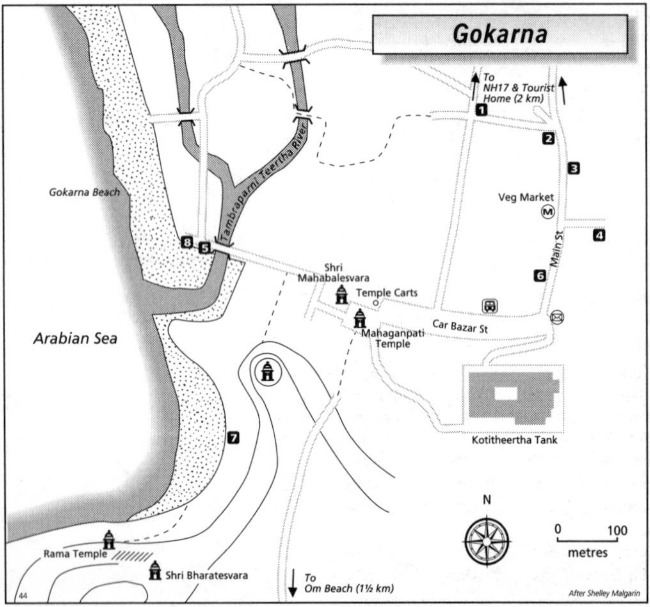

Hotels:
1. *Green's OM*
2. *Ramdev Lodge*
3. *Shastri's Guest House*
4. *Vaibhav Nivas*

Places to eat:
5. Little Fast Food
6. Pai
7. Seashore
8. Vishwa

Goa. There is a somewhat curious mixture of Hindu pilgrims and castaways from the hippy era here. You may also notice tribal women wearing a simple cloth held at the neck by bead necklaces, their only piece of jewellery. The specially sanctified **temple** at Gokarna is famous for its Atmalinga, which **Ganesh** is believed to have tricked **Ravana** into putting down on this spot. As Ravana was unable to lift the linga up again, it is called *Mahabala* (the strong one). The Tambraparni Teertha is regarded as particularly sacred for casting the ashes of the dead. Today Gokarna is a centre of Sanskrit learning.

The walk down to Gokarna beach is flanked by pilgrims and *sadhus* begging for alms so come prepared with small change. Walk northwards if you are searching for a quiet stretch. The superb, secluded **Om Beach**, 2 km south, can be reached by a path from the town temple or by walking over the cliffs. Popular with younger travellers, the beach has picturesque views of paddy fields and the Western Ghats.

Budget hotels

E-F *Green's 'Om'*, 6-min walk from bus stand, T 46445, 16 rooms with bath, 2 a/c, restaurant, beer, not very friendly.

F *Nimmu Guest House*, near Temple, 6 cleanish rooms with shared Indian WC, roof terrace for overspill; **F** *Ramdev Lodge*, 4 simple rooms with bath, cheap; **F** *Shastri's Guest House*, Dasanamath, T 46220, 24 cleanish rooms with bath (some 3/4-bed), set back from road, quiet, short walk uphill behind gives superb views of town and sunset, good value, recommended; **F** *Tourist Home* (Karnataka Tourism), 2 km north on hilltop facing the sea, T 46236, 3 good value rooms, dining room, garden, helpful staff, but a trek; **F** *Vaibhav Nivas*, Ganjigadde off Main St (5-min walk from bazar), T 46714, family guest house, small rooms, few with bath (Indian WC), meals ("pain cakes and forage" for breakfast, sums up the food), taxi, full of travellers from nearby beaches.

Prices: C Rs 800-1,500; **D** Rs 400-800; **E** Rs 200-400; **F** under Rs 200

Places to eat

Cheap veg *thalis* are available near the bus stand and along Main St. ***Pai***, near Veg Market does good *masala dosa*; ***Seashore***, on beach, South Indian *thalis*; ***Vishwa***, on beach, Nepali run, varied menu including Tibetan, large helpings. Great ice cream parlours abound – try *'gudbad'* (with nuts and fruit) – near the beach. ***Little Fast Food*** does cheap drinks and snacks.

Transport

No auto rickshaws here! KSRTC **buses** provide a good service: **Karwar (and Ankola)** frequent (1½ hours); **Hospet** 0700, 1425 (10 hours); **Jog Falls** 0700; **Mangalore via Udipi** 0645 (7 hours); **Panaji** 0800 (5 hours).

Excursion North of Goa

FROM North Goa southern Maharashtra offers Maratha coastal forts, almost totally unvisited beaches, and even the minor "hill station" of Amboli. All these can be seen en route to the important former Muslim capital of Belgaum.

Further afield, but still accessible by train, bus, car or motorbike, and also offered as a tour by travel companies, Hampi, the capital of the Vijayanagar Empire, is one of India's most atmospheric historic sites.

AMBOLI: A MINOR HILL STATION

From the northern coastal beaches the minor hill station of Amboli in southern Maharashtra is within easy reach by motorbike or car. Crossing the Tiracol River by the Keri ferry the road crosses into Maharashtra. The deserted but atmospheric Reddi Fort, one of Sivaji's major coastal forts, is immediately behind a beautiful stretch of deserted beach and lagoon. The ghats rise steeply inland of Sawantwadi, the road winding its way up to a height of nearly 700m. Amboli, a popular tiny holiday resort with Indians during the monsoon, when it is either shrouded in mist or experiencing torrential rain, is set in hilly wooded countryside. The route up through the southernmost corner of Maharashtra has a quite different feel to it from Goa.

It is easy to make a simple return trip to Amboli or to continue to Belgaum and return via Londa to Goa.

REDI BEACH AND VENGURLA

Redi beach is a delightful picnic spot less than 10 km from Tiracol fort. It can easily be visited on the way to Amboli. In the coastal belt there are many salt pans which provide an important source of income in the district.

Redi Beach and Fort

Just 3 km north of the Goa border and Tiracol, a turn off from NH17 south of Shiroda, leads to Redi Village and beach 4 km further on. An old Maratha Fort (now in ruins but interesting to wander round), dominates the view over a stunning and almost unvisited bay. There are no facilities or shops at Redi so you must carry water and food. There are tiny villages on the way, some with small markets.

VENGURLA AND SAWANTWADI

Vengurla was a trading settlement on an island, now joined to the land. It is reached by returning to the NH17 from Redi Beach and continuing north, passing through the small market town of Shiroda. A left turn at the cross roads goes to Vengurla, the right turn going to Sawantwadi. Sawantwadi was the capital of the Bhonsle kings of southern Maharashtra who were constantly trying to extend their territory into Goa. Today it is a large market town, centred on the big tank and palace buildings (not open to the public). Sawantwadi now has a railway station on the Konkan railway and is connected by frequent buses to Panaji, about 1½ hours away.

AMBOLI

Altitude 690m

The route up to Amboli climbs the Sahyadri Ranges of the Western Ghats, giving superb views over the coastal plains out towards the sea. Set on the flat topped heights of the Western Ghats overlooking the coastal plain below, Amboli is a quiet and little-visited resort. There are attractive walks and several waterfalls. Bauxite mines (10 km) can also be visited. It is quite far though from the coastal towns of Ratnagiri (210 km) and Vengurla (50 km) so you will probably need to stay overnight. Accommodation is available at **D** *JRD International*, Vengurla-Belgaon Road, 1 km from bus stand, which has 30 pleasant clean rooms, a few 'cottages', and a reasonable Indian restaurant with a permit room. Alternatively the **E** *Resort* (MTDC), offers a reasonably comfortable base.

Getting there Take the train to Kolhapur or Belgaum, then by local bus.

BELGAUM

Population 420,000; *Altitude* 770m; *STD Code* 0831

Today a large Indian city, Belgaum has none of the tourist influences which contribute to the character of modern coastal Goa, and it is a fascinating and relaxing contrast to the much more westernised coastal resorts. For a glimpse of a contemporary Indian town, rooted in tradition but still responding to rapid economic and social change, Belgaum is the nearest large centre to Goa's borders.

Easily accessible, the crowded market in the centre gives a glimpse of India beyond the influence of foreign travellers. With its strategic position in the Deccan plateau, the town had been ruled by many dynasties including the Chalukyas, Rattas, Vijaynagaras, Bahmanis and the Marathas. Most of the monuments date from the early 13th century. The **Fort** (currently being renovated), though pre-Muslim was rebuilt by Yusuf Adil Shah, the Sultan of Bijapur, in 1481. Inside the **Masjid-i-Sata** (1519), the best of the numerous mosques in Belgaum was built by a captain in the Bijapur army, Azad Khan. Belgaum is also noted for its Jain architecture and sculpture. The late Chalukyan **Kamala Basti** with typical beautifully lathe-turned pillars and a black stone Neminatha sculpture, stands within the fort walls. To the south of the Fort and about 800m north of the *Hotel Sanman* on the Mumbai-Bangalore by-pass, is a beautifully sculpted Jain temple, which according to an inscription, was built by Malikaryuna. Along the entrance wall are well carved sculptures of musicians.

Burgess has described a further Jain temple which stands in the former Government store yard. The temple has "massive square pillars ... but relieved by floral ornamentations". He comments on the care taken in carving the door leading from the central mandapam. "On the centre of the lintel is a Tirthankar, and above the cornice are four squat human figures." Outside, **Kapileswara**, the oldest Hindu temple is worth visiting.

Mid-range Hotels

D *Adarsha Palace*, College Rd, T 435777, F 431022, small modern and 'personal' hotel, friendly management, recommended; **D** *Milan*, Club Rd (4 km rly), T 425555, F 423535, 45 rooms with bath (hot shower), some a/c, veg restaurant, good value; **D** *Sanman*, College Rd, T 430777, 2 km bus stand and station.

Budget hotels

E *Mayura Malaprabha* (KSTDC), Ashok Nagar, HUDCO Complex, T 433781, simple clean rooms in cottages, restaurant, bar, Tourist Office; **E-F** *Sheetal*, Khade Bazar near bus station, T 429222, rooms with bath (prices vary), veg restaurant, Indian style, noisy hotel in busy and quite entertaining bazar street, recommended.

Transport

Train The railway station is about 4 km from the centre. **Bangalore**: *Miraj Bangalore Exp 6590*, 1845, $13\frac{3}{4}$ hours. **Mumbai (VT) via Miraj and Pune**: (change at Miraj) *Hubli Miraj Pass/Mahalaxmi Exp 305/1012*, 1655, $15\frac{1}{2}$ hours (50 minute wait at Miraj) and for Pune $10\frac{1}{2}$ hours. **Goa**: the conversion to broad gauge was completed in 1997, and now connects Vasco in the west of Goa with **Belgaum, Bangalore, Delhi via Agra,** and **Hampi** among others.

Road There are frequent buses through Belgaum, between Mumbai and Bangalore. Panaji is approximately 5 hours by bus. From Panaji, buses for **Belgaum** dep 0630-1300.

Excursion East of Goa

FURTHER afield, but still accessible by train, bus, car or motorbike, and also offered as a tour by travel companies from Goa, Hampi, the capital of the Vijayanagar Empire, is one of India's most atmospheric historic sites.

HOSPET

Population 135,000; *Altitude* 480m; *STD Code* 08394

Hospet is used as a base by many visitors to **Hampi** since it offers a variety of accommodation and has the nearest railway station. The remains at Hampi are very scattered and need at least one whole day, and two to see more fully.

The Main Bazar in Hospet is interesting to walk down, with old houses and character. There is a significant Muslim population and *Muharram* is celebrated with vigour with *firewalkers* walking across burning embers along with noisy celebrations, a custom which may go back to long before Islam arrived. Villagers still celebrate events such as the beginning or end of migrations to seasonal feeding grounds, with huge bonfires. Cattle are driven through such fires to protect them from disease. The archaeologists Allchin and Allchin suggest that Neolithic ash mounds around

Hospet could have resulted from similar celebrations over 5,000 years ago.

Excursions

The Tungabhadra Dam (6 km) The 2 km Dam is 49m high and offers panoramic views. One of the largest masonry dams in the country it was completed in 1953 after 8 years of construction work to provide electricity for irrigation in the surrounding districts. **Accommodation** **E** *Vaikunta Guest House*, Tungabhadra Dam, T 44241, beautiful hill-top site, but out of town above the dam so own transport needed, usually occupied by officials, book 15 days in advance. At Munirabad, 5 km north of Dam: **F** *Indrabhavan* and **F** *Lake View Guest House*, difficult to reserve. **Transport** Tourist Office coach tours including a visit to the Dam but several local bus services daily do the trip (¼ hour).

Tours

KSTDC tours from Hospet to Hampi and Tungabhadra Dam, Rs 60. English speaking guide but rather rushed.

Mid-range hotels

Station Rd has been renamed Mahatma Gandhi Rd (MG Rd). **D** ***Malligi Tourist Home***, 6/143 Jambunatha Rd, T 58101, F 47038, 118 large mosquito-ridden rooms, 2 a/c with bath, good veg restaurant (personal attention), garden restaurant with bar, exchange (limited hours, poor rate), travel (bus reservations, eg to Panaji, Rs 20 fee), reports of unsatisfactory service, poorly maintained annexe and tip-seeking staff.

Budget hotels

E *Mayura Vijayanagara* (KSTDC), TB Dam

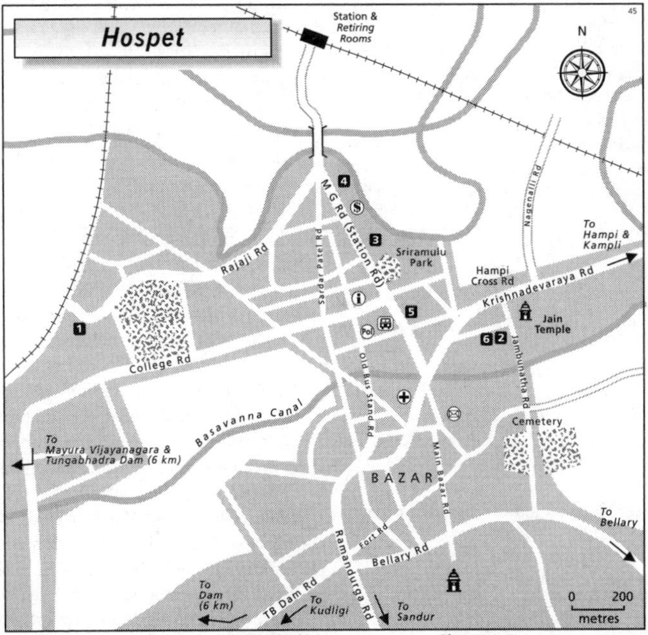

Hotels:
1. *Inspection Bungalow*
2. *Malligi Tourist Home* & Restaurant
3. *Priyadarshini*
4. *Sudarshan*
5. *Vishwa* & Shanthi Restaurant

Places to eat:
6. Eagle Garden Restaurant

Rd, 3 km west of centre, T 48270, basic with fans, mosquito nets and bath, simple dining hall, good *thalis*; **E** ***Priyadarshini***, V/45 MG Rd, near bus station, T 48838, some dearer a/c rooms, extra bed Rs 35, good restaurants, recommended; **E** ***Sudarshan***, MG Rd, T 48574, few a/c rooms with bath. **F** ***Railway Retiring Rooms***, T 48360.

Places to eat

Malligi's veg restaurant is recommended; ***Eagle*** next door, open-air with bar, pleasant but not too clean; two at ***Priyadarshini*** (with a bar) for good veg *thalis*; good South Indian meals near bus station.

Local travel

From Hospet to/from **Hampi**, travel via Kamalapuram, especially in the rainy season when the slower road to Hampi Bazar which winds through villages, is barely passable.

Bus: frequent buses to Hampi's 2 entry points (via Kamalapuram and Museum, Rs 3.50 and via Hampi Bazar, 30 mins, Rs 3), from 0630; last return around 2000. Also from Tungabhadra Dam, 45 mins.

Cycle-rickshaws: from Rly station to Bus Stand about Rs 10.

Cycles: are very useful as the site is spread out though some paths are too rough to ride on. May not be available in Hampi itself; hire in Hospet but check condition carefully.

Taxi: also for sharing.

Long distance travel

Train: Margao *Amravati Exp 7227*, approx 10 hours. **Bangalore** via Guntakal, *Hampi Exp, 6591*, 2030, 10½ hours. **Guntakal**: *Vijaynagara Exp, 7310*, 1905, 2½ hours; *Hampi Exp, 6591*, 2030, 2½ hours. **Secunderabad via Guntakal**: *Vijaynagara/Venkatadri Exp, 7310/7598/7604*, 1905, 14½ hours (2½ hour wait in Guntakal).

Bus: (*Express*) to/from **Bangalore**, several from 0700, 10 hours; **Mysore**, 1830, 10½ hours (*Exp* buses to Belur/Halebid from both). Services to other sites, eg **Badami** (6 hours) and **Bijapur** (6 hours). Overnight Karnataka Tourism luxury coaches to various towns.

Direct buses to **Panaji** (Goa) – *Luxury*, 0630 (10½ hours), State bus, 0830 (reserve a seat in advance); others involve a change in Hubli (4½ hours). From Panaji to **Hospet**: 0915-1030 (10 hours) Rs 75.

Directory

Banks & money changers: State Bank of India, next to Tourist Office, does not exchange TCs but will change cash (US$ and £ sterling); **State Bank of Mysore** may oblige. *Monica Travel*, near Bus Station, changes TCs (3% charge).

Post & telecommunications: Post office: opposite vegetable market. **Telegraph office**: in *Hotel Sudarshan*. **Fax and ISD**: *Essar Area Fax*, beside New Bus Stand, Station Rd.

Tourist offices: Karnataka, MG Rd, Taluka offices, near Bus Stand. Free map and leaflets, and sometimes guides for the sites.

❖ HAMPI

Altitude 467m; *STD Code* 08394; *Best season* October-March. Known as the 'The town of victory', **Vijayanagara**, is 13 km northeast of Hospet town.

Hampi-Vijayanagar is one of India's most remarkable former capital city sites. The rocky outcrops of the peninsula provided the 14th century Vijayanagar kings with an apparently impregnable hill fortress in which they built a stupendous range of palaces and temples. Although now largely in ruins the site is till hugely impressive. Within range of a 3-5 day excursion from Goa, it offers a chance to see something of the wealth of India's past.

Hampi was once the seat of the Vijayanagara Empire and a great centre of Hindu rule for 200 years from its foundation in 1336, although there may have been a settlement in the area as early as 1,000 years before then.

The city was enormously wealthy, 'greater than Rome', with a market full of jewels and palaces plated with gold, having held a monopoly of trade in spices and cotton. It was very well fortified and defended by a large army. With the defeat in 1565 at Talikota at the hands of the Deccan Sultans, the city was largely destroyed. Today the stark and barren area of 26 sq km on the right bank of the river Tungabhadra has the ruins of the great empire strewn across it.

The site for the capital was chosen for strategic reasons but the craftsmen adopted an ingenious style to blend in their architectural masterpieces with the barren and rocky landscape. Most of the site is early 16th century, built during the 20 year reign of Krishna Deva Raya (1509-1529) with the citadel standing on the bank of the river. Excavations undertaken by the Archaeological Survey of India are still in progress. You enter the area from the west at *Hampi Bazar* or from the south at *Kamalapuram*. The **Tourist office** is located here on the approach to Virupaksha Temple.

Sacred Centre

The road from the west comes over **Hemakuta Hill**, overlooking the sacred centre of Vijayanagara, the Virupaksha Temple and the Tungabhadra River to its north. On the Hill are two large Ganesh monolithic sculptures and some small temples. Good views at sunset. Climb **Matanga Parvat**, over the road, early in the morning (around 0530) for a spectacular sunrise. **Warning** Go in a group and don't carry valuables as muggings have been reported.

The road runs down to the village, the once world-famous **Market Place**. You can now only see the wide pathway running east from the towering **Virupaksha** (*Pampapati*) **Temple** with its 9-storey *gopuram*, to where the bazar hummed with activity. Before entering the precinct, foreigners are expected to register police office on the left. Rs 2. 0800-1230; 1500-1830. The temple is still in use; note the interesting paintings on the *mandapam* ceiling. The monkeys here can be aggressive.

You can walk along the river bank (1.5 km) to the famous Vitthala Temple. The path is easy and passes several interesting ruins including small 'cave' temples (worthwhile with a guide). Alternatively, a motorable road skirts the Royal Enclosure to the south, and goes all the way to the Vitthala Temple. On the way back you can visit the **Raghunatha Temple**, on a hill top, for its Dravidian style, quiet atmosphere and excellent view from the rocks above, especially at sunset.

After passing **Achyuta Bazar**, which leads to the Tiruvengalanatha Temple 400m to the south, the riverside path goes near **Sugriva's Cave**, where it is said that Sita's jewels, dropped as she was abducted by the demon Ravana, were hidden by Sugriva. There are good views of the ancient ruined bridge to the east, and nearby the path continues past the only early period Vaishnavite shrine, the 14th century **Narasimha Temple**. The **King's balance** is at the end of the path as it approaches the Vitthala Temple. It is said that the rulers were weighed against gold, jewels and food, which were then distributed to Brahmins.

The **Vitthala Temple**, a World Heritage Monument, is dedicated to Vishnu. It stands in a rectangular

> **Travel tip**
>
> Hampi is becoming increasingly popular with "western spiritual wanderers" (many moving on from Goa) for whom the demands of the spirit don't preclude a search for the material, notably in actively seeking financial support for their meditation. **WARNING** Police are warning visitors to take special care, especially at night, as muggings have been reported. Photos of "undesirables" are displayed in hotels and the bus station in Hospet.

courtyard, enclosed within high walls. Probably built in the mid-15th century, it is one of the oldest and most intricately carved, with its *gopurams* and *mandapas*. The *Dolotsava mandapa* has 56 superbly sculpted slender pillars which can be struck to produce different musical notes. It has elephants on the balustrades and horses at the entrance. The other two ceremonial mandapas, though less finely carved have some interesting carved pillars, eg *Krishna* hiding in a tree from the *gopis*, a woman using a serpent twisted around a stick to churn a pot of buttermilk. In the courtyard is a superb chariot carved out of granite, the wheels raised off the ground so that they could be revolved!

On the road between the Virupaksha bazar and the Citadel, you pass **Krishnapura**, Hampi's earliest Vaishnava township with a Chariot St 50m

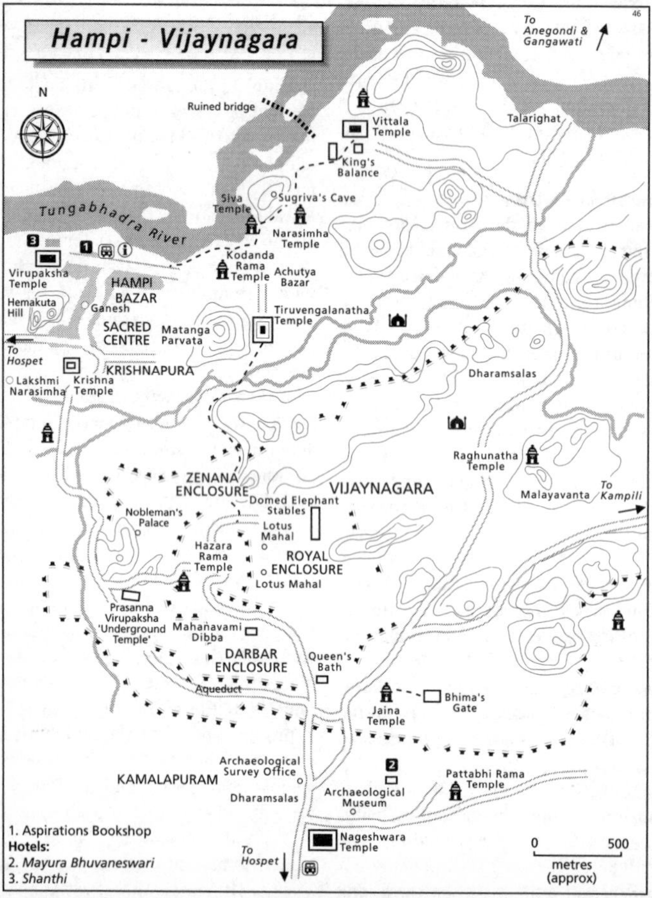

wide and 0.6 km long, which is now a cultivated field. The **Krishna temple** has a very impressive gateway to the east. Just southwest of the Krishna temple is the colossal monolithic statue of Lakshmi Narasimha in the form of a 4-armed man-lion with fearsome bulging eyes sheltered under a 7-headed serpent, *Ananta*. It is over 6m high but sadly damaged. The road south towards the Royal Enclosure passes the excavated **Prasanna Virupaksha** (misleadingly named "underground") and interesting watchtowers.

Royal Enclosure

At the heart of the Metropolis is the small **Hazara Rama Temple**, the Vaishanava 'chapel royal' (*hazara* meaning 1,000). The outer enclosure wall to the north has five rows of carved friezes while the outer walls of the *mandapa* has three. The episodes from the epic *Ramayana* are told in great detail, starting with the bottom row of the north end of the west *mandapa* wall. The 2-storeyed **Lotus Mahal** is in the **Zenana** or ladies' quarter, screened off by its high walls. The watch tower is in ruins but you can see the domed **stables** for 10 elephants with a pavilion in the centre and the guardhouse. Each stable had a wooden beamed ceiling from which chains were attached to the elephants' back and neck. In the **Durbar Enclosure** is the specially built decorated platform of the **Mahanavami Dibba**, from which the royal family watched the pageants and tournaments during the 9 nights of *nava ratri* festivities. The 8m high square platform originally had a covering of bricks, timber and metal but what remains still shows superb carvings of hunting and battle scenes, as well as dancers and musicians.

The exceptional skill of water engineering is displayed in the newly excavated system of aqueducts, tanks, sluices and canals, which could function today. The 22m square **Pushkarini** is the attractive stepped tank at the centre of the enclosure. The road towards Kamalapuram passes the **Queen's Bath**, in the open air, surrounded by a narrow moat which had scented water fill the bath from lotus shaped fountains. It measures about 15m by 2m and has interesting stucco work around it.

Further reading Longhurst's *Hampi Ruins* recommended; Settar's *Hampi* (both at *Aspirations Bookshop*, Hampi Bazar, which has an interesting selection of books as well as postcards, crafts from Aurobindo Ashram, Pondicherry and soft drinks.

Museums

The **Archaeological Museum** at Kamalapuram has a collection of sculpture, paintings, copper plates and coins. Archaeological Survey booklet is on sale; a scale model of Hampi in the courtyard. 1000-1700, closed Friday.

Festivals

January-February: Virupaksha *Temple Car festival*. Also annual Purandaradasa Aradhana *Music festival* at Vithala Temple.

Budget Hotels

Travellers planning to spend more than a day may prefer to stay near the complex.

Hampi Bazar has plenty of character; several basic lodges and more being built. **F** *Shanti Guest House*, T 51368, down path to the right of the temple, 23 rooms around courtyard, common shower, very clean and friendly, cycle hire.

Kamalapuram: **D-E** *Mayura Bhuvaneswari* (KSTDC), 2 km from site, T 51374, 27 clean rooms, some a/c, reasonable restaurant, cycle hire. **F** *Hampi Power Station Inspection Bungalow*, 3 km climb from Kamalauram, T 48272, pleasant spot but basic rooms, meals to order, contact Supt Engineer, HES, Tungabhadra Dam, Hospet.

Places to eat

Hampi Bazar: ***Sambhu*** opposite *Shanti*, for fresh pasta/noodles and espresso plus all the usual; also bus/train tickets for small commission (better than trying in Hospet), recommended. ***Suresh***, 30m from *Shanti*, down a small alley, very friendly family, made to order so takes a while, but well worth the wait; ***Ganesh*** in main street and ***Raju*** behind *Shanti recommended* especially for *parathas*; ***Gopi*** for good simple, cheap *thalis*. Simple places serving veg meals near the Bus Stand including open-sided ***Krishna*** and ***Trisul***. ***Shanti*** does good carrot/apple/banana/chocolate cakes.

Kamalapuram: ***Mayura Bhuvaneswari***, does good meals; snacks are available near the bus stand.

Local travel

From Hampi to/from **Hospet**, travel via Kamalapuram, especially in the rainy season when the slower road to Hampi Bazar which winds through villages, is barely passable.

Bus: frequent buses from Hampi's 2 entry points (via Kamalapuram and Museum, Rs 3.50 and via Hampi Bazar, 30 mins, Rs 3), from 0700 until about 2000. Also from Tungabhadra Dam, 45 mins.

Cycles: are very useful as the site is spread out though some paths are too rough to ride on. May not be available in Hampi itself; hire in Hospet but check condition carefully.

Taxi: also for sharing. For Long Distance transport see Hospet above.

Mumbai (Bombay)

MUMBAI IS ONE of India's most remarkable cities. The commercial hub of the Indian economy for over 150 years, it remains uniquely open to the rest of the world and is yet a city shaped by India's diverse cultures. There is plenty to see in a short visit, including the maginificent Elephanta caves which, within less than an hour's boat ride across the harbour, illustrate the superb artistry of India's ancient craftsmen.

Population: 12.57 million; *STD Code*: 022; *Languages*: Marathi, Gujarati, Hindi and English. There is also a sizeable Tamil speaking population.

History

The modern name of Mumbai is derived from the local name for the goddess Parvati and Hinduism had made its mark on Mumbai long before the Portuguese and then the British transformed it into one of India's great cities. The caves on the island of Elephanta were excavated under the Kalachauris (500-600 AD). From well before that until the arrival of the Portuguese, Arab dhows traded down the coast, but less than 350 years ago the area occupied by this great metropolis comprised seven islands inhabited by Koli fishermen (from whom we have the word 'coolies') and their families.

The British acquired these marshy and malarial islands as part of the marriage dowry paid by the Portuguese when Catherine of Braganza married Charles II in 1661. Some suggest that Bombay took its English name from the Portuguese Bom Bahia, or 'good harbour'. 4 years later, the British took possession of the remaining islands and neighbouring mainland and in 1668 the East India Company leased the whole area from the crown for £10 sterling per year, which was paid for nearly 50 years.

Today Mumbai has become the hub of India's commercial activity. It is the home of India's main stock exchange and headquarters for many national and international companies. It is also a major industrial centre.

With population pressure in the surrounding agricultural hinterland, Mumbai is still growing fast. One third of the population live in its desperately squalid *chawls* of cramped, makeshift and miserable hovels. There are also many thousands of pavement dwellers, yet despite the extreme poverty Mumbai remains a city of hope for millions.

APOLLO BUNDER AND THE GATEWAY OF INDIA

The Indo-Saracenic style Gateway of India (1927), designed by George Wittet to commemorate the visit of George V and Queen Mary in 1911, is modelled in honey-coloured basalt on 16th century Gujarati work. The great gateway comprises an archway with halls on each side capable of seating 600 at important receptions. The arch replaced an earlier, lighter building. It was the point from which the last British regiment serving in India signalled the end of the Empire when it left on 28 February 1948. The area around the Gateway is popular among Mumbaiites for evening strolls and is a pleasant place to visit at sundown. A short distance behind the Gateway is an impressive statue of **Sivaji**, erected in 1960.

> **Travel tip**
>
> Daily flights from many parts of the world make Mumbai a very attractive alternative to the normal charters which carry most tourists into Goa. It gives you a chance to see something of India's largest city as well as some of India's countryside on the way to and from Goa. The opening of the Konkan railway, reducing a tortuous 18-hour train or bus journey to under 8 hours. There is also a high speed catamaran as an alternative by sea during the season, while motorbike or car allow you to explore something of the Konkan coastline or the Peninsula on the way south.

❖Taj Mahal Hotel

The original red-domed hotel has been adjoined by a modern skyscraper (the *Taj Mahal Inter-Continental*). Jamshedji Tata, a Mumbai Parsi, was behind the enterprise; designed by W Chambers, it is now one of the world's leading hotels. **Warning** Drug addicts, drunks and prostitutes frequent the area behind the hotel; exercise caution.

Bombay Natural History Society (BNHS), Hornbill House on SB Singh Marg, opposite Regal Cinema, founded over 100 years ago, is dedicated to the conservation of Indian's flora and fauna. It has a knowledgeable PR officer, a shop, wildlife collection and library.

COLABA

South of the Gateway of India is the crowded southern section of Shahid (lit. 'martyr') Bhagat Singh Marg (Marine

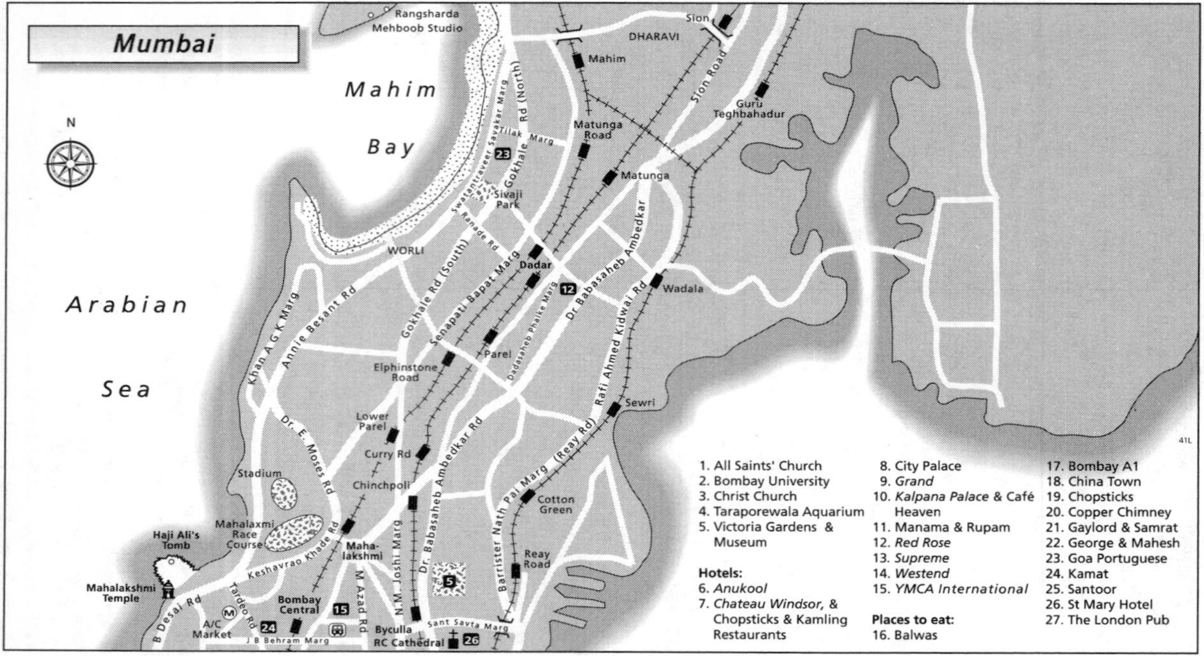
Mumbai
N
Mahim Bay
Arabian Sea
Rangsharda
Mehboob Studio
DHARAVI
Sion
Mahim
Sion Road
Guru Teghbahadur
Matunga Road
Matunga
Tilak Marg
Swatantraveer Savakar Marg
Gokhale Rd (North)
Sivaji Park
Ranade Rd
WORLI
Dadar
Wadala
Dr Babasaheb Ambedkar
Gokhale Rd (South)
Senapati Bapat Marg
Dadasaheb Phalke Marg
Rafi Ahmed Kidwai Rd
Parel
Elphinstone Road
Khan A G K Marg
Annie Besant Rd
Sewri
Lower Parel
Curry Rd
Dr. E. Moses Rd
Dr. Babasaheb Ambedkar Rd
Barrister Nath Pai Marg (Reay Rd)
Cotton Green
Stadium
Chinchpoli
Mahalaxmi Race Course
Haji Ali's Tomb
Keshavrao Khade Rd
Maha-lakshmi
N.M. Joshi Marg
M Azad Rd
Reay Road
Mahalakshmi Temple
B Desai Rd
Tardeo Rd
A/C Market
Bombay Central
J B Behram Marg
Byculla
RC Cathedral
Sant Savta Marg
41L
1. All Saints' Church
2. Bombay University
3. Christ Church
4. Taraporewala Aquarium
5. Victoria Gardens & Museum
Hotels:
6. Anukool
7. Chateau Windsor, & Chopsticks & Kamling Restaurants
8. City Palace
9. Grand
10. Kalpana Palace & Café Heaven
11. Manama & Rupam
12. Red Rose
13. Supreme
14. Westend
15. YMCA International
Places to eat:
16. Balwas
17. Bombay A1
18. China Town
19. Chopsticks
20. Copper Chimney
21. Gaylord & Samrat
22. George & Mahesh
23. Goa Portuguese
24. Kamat
25. Santoor
26. St Mary Hotel
27. The London Pub

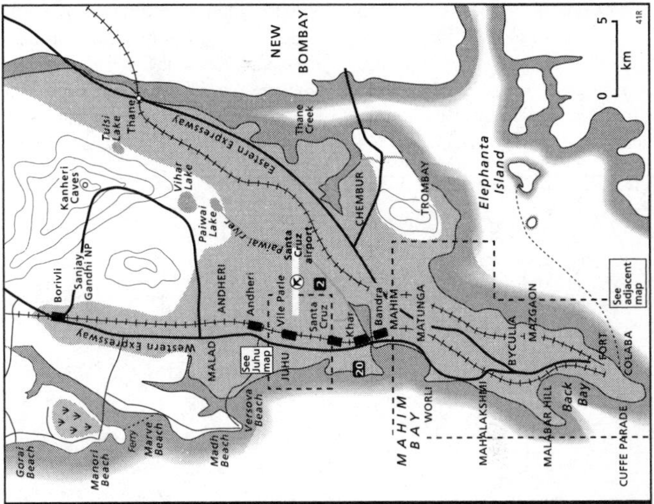

NEW BOMBAY
Gorai Beach
Manori Beach
Ferry
Marve Beach
Madh Beach
Versova Beach
MALAD
See Juhu map
JUHU
Borivli
Sanjay Gandhi NP
Kanheri Caves
Tulsi Lake
Thane
Vihar Lake
Paiwai Lake
Paiwai river
ANDHERI
Andheri
Vile Parle
Santa Cruz airport
Santa Cruz
Khar
Bandra
MAHIM
MATUNGA
Western Expressway
Eastern Expressway
Thane Creek
CHEMBUR
TROMBAY
Elephanta Island
MAHIM BAY
WORLI
MAHALAKSHMI
BYCULLA
MAZGAON
See adjacent map
FORT
COLABA
MALABAR HILL
Back Bay
CUFFE PARADE
0 km 5

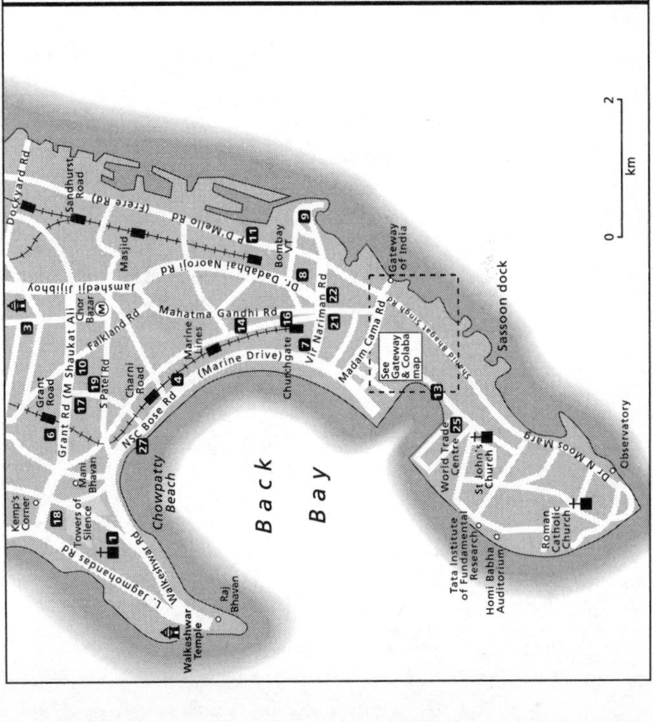

Walkeshwar Temple
Raj Bhavan
L. Jagmohandas Rd
Walkeshwar Rd
Towers of Silence
Kemp's Corner
Chowpatty Beach
Mani Bhavan
Grant Rd (M Shaukat Ali
Grant Road
NSC Bose Rd
Charni Road
S Patel Rd
(Marine Drive)
Marine Lines
Falkland Rd
Chor Bazar
Mahatma Gandhi Rd
Jamshedji Jijibhoy
Masjid
Dr. Dadabhai Naoroji Rd
Sandhurst Road
Dockyard Rd
P D'Mello Rd (Frere Rd)
Bombay VT
Churchgate
Vir Nariman Rd
Madam Cama Rd
See Gateway & Colaba map
Gateway of India
Shahid Bhagat Singh Rd
Sassoon dock
Back Bay
World Trade Centre
St John's Church
Dr N Moos Marg
Observatory
Roman Catholic Church
Tata Institute of Fundamental Research
Homi Babha Auditorium
0 km 2

St) which leads to Colaba. The Afghan Memorial **Church of St John the Baptist** (1847-58) is at the northern edge of Colaba itself. Early English in style, with a 58m spire, it was built to commemorate the soldiers who died in the First Afghan War. Fishermen still unload their catch early in the morning at **Sassoon Dock**, the first wet dock in India; photography is prohibited. Beyond the church near the tip of the Colaba promontory lie the **Observatory** and **Old**

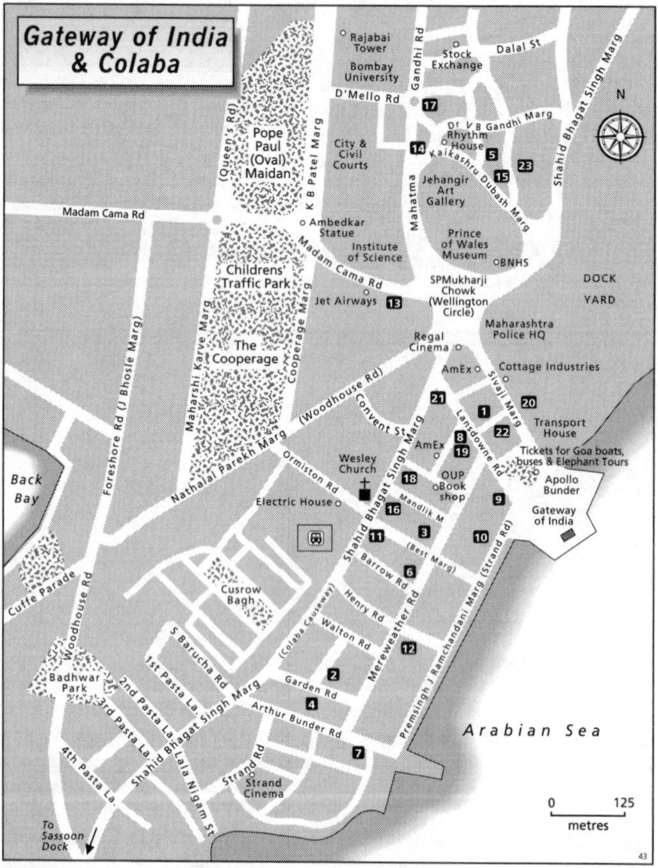

Hotels:

1. *Apollo*
2. *Bentley's*
3. *Diplomat & Regent*
4. *Godwin*
5. *Lawrence*
6. *Salvation Army Red Shield Guesthouse*
7. *Seashore*
8. *Suba Palace*
9. *Taj Intercontinental*
10. *Taj Mahal*
11. *Volga*
12. *Whalley's Guesthouse*
13. *YWCA International Guesthouse & YWCA*

Places to eat:

14. Chetana & Books
15. Copper Chimney
16. Food Inn
17. Khyber
18. Leopold & Waghela Fax
19. Ling's Pavilion
20. Mandarin & Hongkong
21. Mondegar
22. Nanking
23. Trishna

European cemetery in the naval colony (permission needed to enter; try week day). Frequent buses ply this route.

CENTRAL MUMBAI

The area stretching north from Colaba Causeway to Victoria Terminus, the heart of British Mumbai, dates from after 1862, when Sir Bartle Frere became Governor (1862-7). Under his enthusiastic guidance Mumbai became a great civic centre and an extravaganza of Victorian Gothic architecture, modified by the Indo-Saracenic influences.

Just behind the Prince of Wales Museum in Shahid Bhagat Singh Marg is **St Andrew's Kirk** (1819), a simple neoclassical church. The steeple, irreparably damaged by lightning in 1826, was rebuilt a year later. Next door there used to be a circular building (1840) for storing imported American ice. Local ice plants appeared in the 1880s. At the south end of Mahatma Gandhi (MG) Rd is the Renaissance style **Institute of Science** (1911) designed by George Wittet. The Institute, which includes a scientific library, a public hall and examination halls, was built with gifts from the Parsi and Jewish communities.

❖ Pope Paul Maidan

On the east side of the Pope Paul (Oval) Maidan, is a series of striking buildings, bringing together a range of European styles from the early English Gothic to the Romanesque. From south to north they are the old Secretariat, the University Library and Rajabai Clocktower, the High Court and the Public Works Office.

The Venetian Gothic style old **Secretariat** (1874) is 143m long, with a façade of arcaded verandahs and porticos faced in buff-coloured Porbander stone from Gujarat. Decorated with red and blue basalt, the carvings are in white Hemnagar stone. The University **Convocation Hall** (1874) to its north was designed by Sir George Gilbert Scott in a 15th century French decorated style. Scott also designed the adjacent University **Library** and the 79m high **Rajabai Clocktower** (1870s) next door, based on Giotto's campanile in Florence. The sculpted figures in niches on the exterior walls of the tower were designed to represent the castes of India. Originally the clock could chime 12 tunes such as Rule Britannia.

The **High Court** (1871-9), in Early English Gothic style, has a 57m high central tower flanked by lower octagonal towers topped by the figures of Justice and Mercy. The Venetian Gothic **Public Works Office** (1869-72) is to its north. Opposite, and with its main façade to Vir Nariman Rd, is the former General Post Office (1869-72). Now called the **Telegraph Office**, it stands next to the original Telegraph Office adding Romanesque to the extraordinary mixture of European architectural styles. Both buildings are in honey-coloured sandstone from Kurla.

NB The old buildings of the centre are floodlit after 1900.

Horniman Circle

Turn right at the Flora (or Frere) Fountain (1869), now known as **Hutatma Chowk**, along Vir Nariman Rd to the Old Custom House, Town Hall and Mint on the imposing Horniman (Elphinstone) Circle. The **Custom House** is believed to incorporate a Portuguese barrack block of 1665. Over the entrance is the crest of the East India Company. Parts of the old Portuguese fort's walls can be seen; more exist in the Naval Dockyards (inaccessible to tourists). Many Malabar teak

'EastIndiamen' ships were built here.

The Mint (1824-9), built on the Fort rubbish dump, has Ionic columns and a water tank in front of it. The **Town Hall** (1820-3) has been widely admired as one of the best neo-classical buildings in India. The Doric columns that give the Town Hall its grandeur were shipped from England. The original idea of paired columns was abandoned as being too monumental and half the imported columns were used at Christ Church, Byculla. The Corinthian interior houses the Assembly Rooms and the Bombay Asiatic Society.

Horniman Circle was laid out in 1860. On the west edge are the Venetian Gothic **Elphinstone Buildings** (1870) in brown sandstone. The **Cathedral Church of St Thomas** was begun in 1672, opened in 1718, and subject to a number of later additions. Inside are a number of monuments forming a heroic 'who's who of India'.

Behind Horniman Circle on the water's edge lies the **Old Castle**. Entry is not permitted. Going north to Victoria Terminus you pass the **Port Trust Office** on your right, while a little farther on, to your right by the station is the **General Post Office** (1909), based on the architecture of Bijapur (Karnataka) in the Indo-Saracenic style.

THE VICTORIA TERMINUS AREA

The ❖ **Victoria Terminus** (1878-87), the most remarkable example of Victorian Gothic architecture in India, was opened during Queen Victoria's Golden Jubilee year. The first train in India had left from this terminus for Thane in April 1853. Known today as **'VT'**, over half a million commuters use the station every day.

The frontage is symmetrical with a large central dome flanked by two wings. The dome is capped by a 4m statue of Progress by Thomas Earp, who also carved the Imperial lion and Indian tiger on the gate piers, nearly all executed by the Bombay School of Art. The Booking Hall with its arcades, stained glass and glazed tiles was inspired by London's St Pancras station.

The station was built at a time when fierce debate was taking place among British architects working in India as to the most appropriate style to develop for the buildings. One view held that the British should restrict themselves to models derived from the best in western tradition. Others argued that architects should draw on Indian models, trying to bring out the best of Indian tradition and encourage its development. By and large, the former were dominant, but as Tillotson argues, the introduction of Gothic allowed a blending of western traditions with Indian (often Islamic Indian) motifs, which became known as the Indo-Saracenic style.

MARINE DRIVE AND MALABAR HILL

You can do an interesting half-day trip from Churchgate Station, along Marine Drive to the Taraporewala Aquarium, Mani Bhavan (Gandhi Museum), the Babulnath Temple, past the Parsi Towers of Silence to Kamla Nehru Park, the Hanging Gardens and the Jain Temple. If you wish you can go further towards Malabar Point to get a glimpse of Raj Bhavan and the Walkeshwar Temple, before returning via the Mahalaxmi Temple and Haji Ali's tomb.

The **Towers of Silence** are in secluded gardens 500m west of Mani Bhavan. This very private place is not accessible to tourists but it can be glimpsed from the road. Sir Jamshetji Jeejeebhoy gave a large area of land around the towers, thus affording them privacy and allowing the creation of a tranquil garden. Parsis believe that the elements of water, fire and earth must not be polluted by the dead, so they lay their 'vestments of flesh and bone' out on the top of the towers to be picked clean by vultures. Some guides claim that the reason the Hanging Gardens were created was to protect Mumbai's water supply from being polluted by half-eaten corpses dropped by vultures. There is no truth in this.

The **Hanging Gardens** (Pherozeshah Mehta Gardens) immediately south of the Towers of Silence, in the centre of a low hill, are so named since they are located on top of a series of tanks that supply water to Mumbai. These formal gardens have some interesting animal topiary and good views over the city.

Nearby is the Church of North India **All Saints' Church** (1882). Across the road from the Hanging Gardens is the **Kamla Nehru Park** (1952), named after the wife of India's first Prime Minister. There are very good views over Back Bay especially from the top terrace.

MUSEUMS

❖**Mahatma Gandhi Museum** (**Mani Bhavan**) 0930-1800. Rs 3. This private house, at 19 Laburnum Rd, where Mahatma Gandhi used to stay on visits to Mumbai, is now a memorial museum and research library with 20,000 volumes. Not easy to find (taxi drivers often don't know it) but well worth a visit. Display on top floor very good, especially diorama depicting important scenes from Gandhi's life – slides (without mount) are available (Rs 100). Cards, pamphlets etc at the door. Allow 1 hour.

❖**Victoria and Albert Museum** (Bhav Daji Lad Museum) north of Byculla station. Monday, Tuesday, Thursday, Friday, Saturday 1030-1700, Sunday 0830-1645, closed Wednesday; Rs 2. Inspired by the Victoria & Albert Museum in London and financed by public subscription, it was built in 1872 in a Palladian style. Sir George Birdwood, a noted physician and authority on Indian crafts, became its first curator. The collection covers the history of Mumbai and contains prints, maps and models.

In front of the Museum is a **Clocktower** (1865) with four faces (morning, noon, evening, night), and a stone statue of an elephant found by the Portuguese in the harbour. Elephanta Island was named after it. The **Victoria Gardens** are very attractive. A list at the entrance shows which trees are in blossom.

❖**Prince of Wales Museum** South end of MG Rd. Closed Monday. 1015-1730 (October-February), 1015-1800 (July-September), 1015-1830 (March-June). Rs 5. Camera fee Rs 15 (no flash or tripods). Good guide books, pamphlets, cards and reproductions on sale. Citywide bus connections; ask at Inspectors' booth outside. Designed by George Wittet to commemorate the visit of the Prince of Wales (later King George V) to India in 1905. A bronze statue of the king stands outside and an equestrian statue of Edward VII on the other, all set in a landscaped garden. The dome of glazed tiles has a very Persian and Central Asian flavour. The whole is Indo-Saracenic, and thus in keeping with the Gateway of India which was built at the same time.

There are three sections. The archaeological section has three main groups: Brahminical, Buddhist and Jain, Prehistoric and Foreign. The Indus Valley section is well displayed. The art section includes an excellent collection of Indian miniatures and well displayed *tankhas*. There are also works by Gainsborough, Poussin and Titian as well as Indian silver, jade and tapestries and a collection of arms. The **Natural History** section is based on the collection of the Bombay Natural History Society founded in 1833 and includes dioramas.

Jehangir Art Gallery (in the Prince of Wales Museum complex). Open 1030-1900, closed Monday. Mumbai's principal art gallery. The '*Samovar*' café is good for a snack and a drink including chilled beer; terrace overlooks museum gardens. Phones and toilets. Temporary members may use the library and attend lectures. **Gallery Chemould** on 1st flr. **National Gallery of Modern Art**, Sir Cowasji Jehangir Hall, opposite Prince of Wales Museum.

❖ELEPHANTA CAVES

More than 1,200 **cave sites** have been discovered across India. The vast majority of these were purpose-built as temples and monasteries and were excavated over the period from 3rd century BC to the 10th century AD. Jain, Buddhist and Hindu caves often stand side by side in the same rock formation.

The setting of the Elephanta caves is symbolically significant; the sea is the ocean of life, a world of change (*Samsara*) in which is set an island of spiritual and physical refuge. The journey to it was also important. In the rough seas of the monsoon it could be both difficult and dangerous. It was therefore a voyage of determination as well as discovery.

The caves are 10 km by boat from the Gateway of India. An earlier name for the island was Gharapuri – city of forts – but the Portuguese renamed it after the colossal sculpted elephants when they captured Mumbai from the Sultan of Gujarat in 1535. It is an extremely popular day trip for Mumbaiites so avoid the weekend rush. It is quite a stiff climb of about 125 sloping steps from the old landing place on the south of the island; palanquins available. Today boats normally land in the northwest, about 400m from the caves, which are at a height of 75m. The island is formed of two parallel ridges separated by a valley; the highest point is 173m. About 1,500 people live on the island and there are several restaurants.

NB Maharashtra Tourism normally organizes a *Festival of classical music and dance* on the island in the 3rd week of February.

The temple cave on Elephanta island, dedicated to Siva, was probably excavated during the 8th century by the Rashtrakuta Dynasty which ruled the Deccan from 757 to 973 AD. The Portuguese stationed a batallion on Elephanta who reportedly used the main pillared cave as a shooting gallery. They are also believed to have removed an important stone panel which probably gave more precise information on the cave's excavation and ornamentation. Muslim rulers and the British were not blameless either. The Archaeological Survey of India is doing its best to preserve the site, though most of the caves are damp, moss-covered and full of bats.

The Entrance

Originally there were three entrances and 28 pillars, eight of which have been destroyed or collapsed. The two side entrances on the east and west have subsidiary shrines which may have been excavated and used for different ceremonies. The main entrance now is from the north. At dawn the rising sun casts its rays on the approach to the main shrine (*garbagriha*), housed in a square structure at the west end of the main hall. On your right as you enter is a carving of Siva as Nataraj (see page 44). On the left

Mumbai tours

City sightseeing

Several tour operators offer city sightseeing. The **City Tour** usually includes visits to The Gateway of India, Aquarium (except Monday), the Prince of Wales Museum (closed Monday), Jain temple, Hanging Gardens, Kamla Nehru Park and Mani Bhavan (Gandhi Museum). Some tours stop during the monsoon. The **Suburban Tour** includes Juhu Beach, Tulsi Lake National Park, Kanheri Caves and Lion Safari Park (closed Monday). Some visitors have described the tour as 'awful'.

ITDC, Nirmal Bldg, Nariman Pt, T 2026679. Booking also at 123 Maharshi Karve Rd, T 213144. **City Tour**: daily except Monday, 0900-1300 and 1345-1745, Rs 40. ***Maharashtra Tourism***, Madam Cama Rd, opposite LIC Building, T 2026713. **City Tour**: daily except Monday, 0900-1300 and 1400-1800, Rs 60. **Suburban Tour**: 0915-1815, Rs 145. Approved guides from the India Tourist Office, T 2036854.

Film Studio Tours

As the capital of India's film industry it is sometimes possible to see the Mumbai film makers at work. One which may offer tours is *Film City*, Goregaon, T 6801535.

Elephanta Caves

Tours by *Elephanta Jal-Vahatuk Sahakari Sanstha Maryadit*, Gateway of India. Hourly boat, 0900-1415, Rs 35-50; reserve at Apollo Bunder, T 2026364. If you wish to sightsee

is a badly damaged carving of Siva as Lakulisa. Seated on a lotus, the symbol of the unconscious mind and enlightenment, the figure has a Buddha-like feel. From the steps at the entrance you can see the *yoni-linga*, the symbol of the creative power of the deity.

The Main Hall

The pillars in the main hall, in a cruciform pattern, have a square base from which rises a thick ribbed column topped by a capital. Between 5 and 6m high, they have no structural importance. At the corner of each pillar is a dwarf signifying the earth spirit (*gana*) and the occasional figure of Ganesh (Ganapati). To the right, the main **Linga Shrine**, 6m square and 1m above the floor of the temple, has four entrances, each corresponding to a cardinal point guarded by a *dwarpala*. The interior of the sanctum is bare, drawing attention more firmly to the *yoni-lingam* which the devotee must walk around, clockwise.

The wall panels

To the north of the *garbha-griha* is **Bhairava killing the demon Andhakasura**. This extraordinarily vivid carving shows Siva at his most fearsome, with a necklace of skulls and a skull and cobra on his head, crushing the power of Andhaka, the chief of darkness. It was held that if he was wounded each drop of his blood would create a new demon. So Siva impaled him and collected his blood with a cup which he then offered to his wife Shakti. In winter the best time to see this panel is in the early afternoon.

Opposite, on the south side of the *garbha-griha* is the badly damaged panel of the **Marriage of Siva and Parvati**. Siva stands with Parvati on his right, just before their wedding (normally a Hindu wife stands on her husband's left). She looks down shyly, but her body is drawn to him. Behind

Parvati stands her father Himalaya and to his left is Chandramas, the god of the moon, carrying a pot of *soma*, the food of the gods, as a gift. On Siva's left is Vishnu and below is Brahma.

At the extreme west end of the temple are **Siva as Nataraja** (left) and **Siva as the Yogi** (right). The former shows a beautifully executed figure of Ganesh above and Parvati on his left. All the other gods watch him. Above his right shoulder is the 4-headed god of creation and intellect, Brahma. Below Brahma is the elephant-headed god Ganesh.

On the south wall, opposite the entrance are three panels. **The Descent of the Ganga** is on the west. The holy Ganga (Bhagirathi) flowed only in heaven but was brought to earth by her father King Bhagiratha (kneeling at Siva's right foot). Here, Ganga is shown in the centre and her two tributaries, Yamuna and Saraswati on either side. These three rivers are believed to meet at Allahabad.

To the left of the Descent of the Ganga is the centre piece of the whole temple, the remarkable Trimurti sculpture of the **triple-headed Siva** as Lord of the Universe (*Maheshwara*). Nearly 6m high, he unites all the functions of creation, preservation and destruction. Some have seen the head on the left (your right) as representing Vishnu the **Creator**, while others suggest that it shows a more feminine aspect of Siva and may be that of Uma. To his right is **Rudra** or Bhairava. He has snakes in his hair, a skull to represent ageing from which only Siva is free, and has a look of anger and vengefulness. The central face is Siva as his true self, balancing out creation and destruction – **Siva Swarupa**. In this mode he is passive and serene radiating peace and wisdom. His right hand is held up in a calming gesture and in his left hand is a lotus bud.

The panel to the left has the 5m tall carving of **Siva as Ardhanarisvara**. This depicts Siva as the embodiment of male and female, representing wholeness and the harmony of opposites. In the rock sculpture the female half is relaxed and gentle, the mirror in the hand symbolizing the woman reflecting the man. Siva has his vehicle, Nandi on the right.

To the east, opposite the *garbha-griha* was probably the original entrance. On the south is **Siva and Parvati on Mt Kailash**. Siva is the faceless figure with Parvati on his left. They are shown playing at dice. Parvati has lost and is sulking but her playful husband persuades her to return to the game. They are surrounded by Nandi, Siva's bull, celestial figures above an attendant carrying a child and an ascetic with his begging bowl.

On the north is **Ravana Shaking Mt Kailash** on which Siva is seated, supported by two attendants. Siva is calm and unperturbed by Ravana's show of brute strength and reassures the frightened Parvati. He pins down Ravana with his toe, who fails to move the mountain, begs Siva's forgiveness and receives it.

The Subsidiary Shrines

The larger shrine on the east side has a lingam. There are also damaged images of Karttikeya, Ganesh and the Matrikas.

Getting there *Maharashtra Tourism* launches with good guides leave the Gateway of India, every 30 mins from 0900 (last return dep Elephanta 1730) journey 1½ hour, Rs 50; not during monsoons (June-September); Reservations, T 2026384. Faster catamarans may be available. Small private boats without guides continue during the monsoon when the seas can be very rough.

LOCAL INFORMATION

Accommodation & places to eat

Most hotels are concentrated in the central area (Marine Drive, Nariman Pt, Apollo Bunder and Colaba) and in Juhu out of town. Prices are much higher than elsewhere in India, but there are some moderately priced hotels immediately behind the Taj.

Juhu and Vile Parle are convenient for the airport especially early morning departures. Here the **B** and **C** category hotels are strictly functional. Juhu Beach used to be quite an attractive and relaxed seaside area. The sea is now polluted but there is a lot happening on Sunday evenings when the beach has a fairground atmosphere. For services in **AL**, **A** and **B** hotels, see page 241. **Hotlink**, India's first on-line reservation system, links 300 medium to top class hotels, T 6152394.

Paying Guest accommodation Contact Govt of India Tourist Office, 123 M Karve Rd, T 2033144.

NB Accommodation in Mumbai is usually heavily booked. Whenever possible make reservations in advance. If you have not, arrive as early in the day as possible.

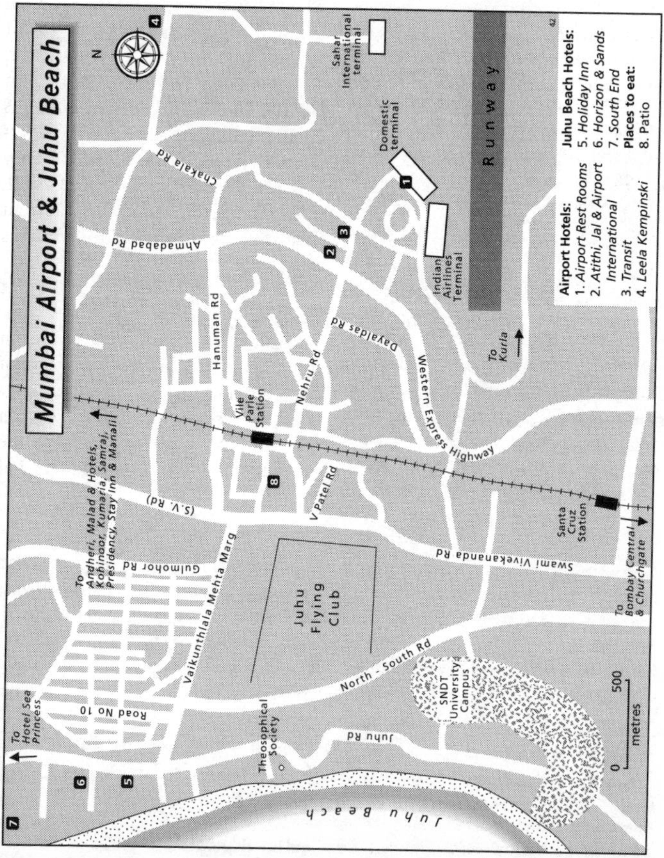

Street names: Dr Annie Besant Rd is AB Rd; Bhulabhai Desai (Warden) Rd is B Desai Rd; Dr Dadabhai Naoroji Rd is Dr DN Rd; Mahatma Gandhi Rd is MG Rd; Sardar Vallabh Bhai Patel (Linking) Rd is VB Patel Rd.

Airport and Juhu Beach

Virtually all hotels in these areas are less than 10 km from the airport and about 20-25 km from the centre; most are close to a suburban railway station. Many down to **D** category offer free coach transfer to/from airport. The Tourist Information Counter will assist with bookings ('Vile Parle' is pronounced 'Veelay Parlay').

Airport hotels:

AL *Leela Kempinski*, Sahar (near International Terminal), T 86363636, F 86360606, 460 rooms, excellent restaurants, good sports facilities, pricey but excellent.

B-C *Atithi*, 77A Nehru Rd, Vile Parle, T 6116124, F 6111998, 47 rooms, functional, clean, 5 minutes walk domestic terminal, good value, heavily booked.

C *Airport International*, 5/6, Nehru Rd, Vile Parle (E), T 6122891, F 6141773, near domestic terminal, 27 rooms, modern business hotel, clean, comfortable; **C** *Transit*, off Nehru Rd, Vile Parle (E), T 6105812, F 6105785, 54 rooms, modern, reasonable "overnight halt" for airport.

D *Airport Rest Rooms*, old Domestic Terminal, Santa Cruz, for passengers with connecting flights within 24 hours of arrival, comfortable, clean, but often full, ask at Airport Enquiries; **D** *Stay Inn*, 247 Sher-e-Punjab Soc, Chokshi Hospital Lane, Mahakali Caves Rd, Andheri, shuttle to airport, newly renovated, clean rooms, some a/c, convenient.

Places to eat

Manjit da Dhaba, corner of West and Main Ave, opposite Grindlays Bank, Linking Rd, Santa Cruz – eating around a mango tree on rush seats round simple wooden tables, authentic North Indian dishes, many served in *handis*, quite expensive, reservations essential, popular with the young; *Patio*, Vile Parle (W), modern, Indian/Chinese recommended.

Juhu Beach

AL *Holiday Inn*, Balraj Sahani Marg, T 6204444, F 6204452, 190 rooms, 2 pools, courtesy coach to town, reliable.

B *Horizon*, 37 Juhu Beach, T 6117979, F 6116715, 161 rooms, facilities including disco, good but no sea view; **B** *Juhu Hotel*, Juhu Tara Rd, T 6146122, spacious comfortable room, cottage style, large seafacing lawns, good restaurant (esp Mughlai and seafood), bar, soundproofed disco; **B-C** *Sands*, 39/2 Juhu Beach, T 6204511, F 6205268, 40 rooms, excellent restaurant, recommended.

Budget hotel:
D-E *South End*, 11 Juhu Tara Rd, T 6125213, 38 rooms, some a/c, light refreshments.

Dadar, Mumbai Central & Grant Rd area

(See map, page 212); Dadar can be a good option to stay – plenty of restaurants and good trains to Churchgate and VT.

C-D *Red Rose*, Gokuldas Pasta Rd (behind Chitra Cinema) Dadar E, T 4137843, 31 rooms, some a/c, mostly shared but clean baths, flexible checkout, friendly – "welcoming at 0530 with no booking", recommended.

D *Anukool*, 292-8 Maulana Saukat Ali Rd, T 392401, 23 rooms, some a/c, good value; **D** *Kalpana Palace*, 181 P Bapurao Marg, opposite Daulat Cinema, Grant Rd, T 3000846, 30 decent rooms, some a/c; **D** *Railway Retiring Rooms*, Mumbai Central, T 3077292, some a/c with bath.

Budget hotels:

E *YMCA International House and Programme Centre*, 18 YMCA Rd, near Mumbai Central, T 3091191, shared bath, meals included, temp membership – Rs 40, very good value, often booked up 3 months ahead.

Places to eat

Chinese: *Chinatown*, 99 August Kranti Marg, Kemps Corner, upstairs more comfortable, Szechwan, Cantonese and Mandarin dishes, 27 soups to choose from.

Indian: *Bombay A1*, 7 Vadilal A Patel Marg

> **Travel tip**
>
> Town hotels are clustered into four main areas, between 25-30 km from airport: around **Dadar and Mumbai Central Stations** (Mumbai map); near **Churchgate, Nariman Point and Marine Drive** (Central Mumbai map), near **Victoria Terminus** (Central Mumbai map), and around **Colaba** (Gateway of India and Colaba map).

(Grant Rd Junc), cheerful, varied Parsi cuisine, including *Patrani Machli*; ***Copper Chimney***, Dr AB Rd, Worli, T 4924488, window into kitchen, excellent food from extensive menu, reasonable prices, undiscovered by tourists; ***Goa Portuguesa***, THK Rd, Mahim, authentic dishes, taverna style with guitarist, try *sungto* (prawn) served between *papads*, *kalwa* (oyster), *teesryo* (shell) and clams, lobsters cooked with tomatoes, onions and spices and *bebinca* to end the meal; ***Heaven***, corner of Grant Rd/P Bapurao Marg, very cheap, friendly (eg alu matar Rs 6); ***Kamat***, Navrose Mansion, Tardeo Rd, very inexpensive *thalis* and veg snacks; ***Rajdhani***, Mangaldas Rd, opposite Crawford Market, an a/c oasis, excellent lunch *thali*, very friendly welcome, recommended; ***St Mary Hotel***, 120 St Mary Rd, Mazgaon, T 868475, Goan, small inexpensive upstairs restaurant, chutney fish fry and beef tongue specialities.

Churchgate, Nariman Point and Marine Drive

B-C *West End*, 45 New Marine Lines, T 2039121, F 2057506, 80 small, pleasant suites but need refurbishing, good restaurant, excellent service, very efficient front desk, well located, good value, highly recommended.

C-D *Chateau Windsor Guest House*, 86 Vir Nariman Rd, T 2043376, F 2851415, 36 rooms (some a/c) vary, some very small and dark, 24-hr coffee house, friendly, clean, good value.

D *Supreme*, 4 Pandey Rd, T 215623, clean rooms with bath, good service but a little noisy.

Places to eat

Chinese: ***Chopsticks***, 90A Vir Nariman Rd, Churchgate, good Schezwan, moderately priced, offering unusual dishes eg taro nest, date pancakes and toffee bananas (also at Jewel Mahal a/c Shopping Complex and 7 Bungalows, Versova); ***Golden Gate***, Madam Cama Rd; ***Kamling***, 82 Vir Nariman Rd, Cantonese, seafood, simple but good, often busy, lots of ice creams.

Fast food: ***Akbarally's Snack Bar***, Vir Nariman Rd; ***Croissant***, Vir Nariman Rd, opposite Eros Cinema, burgers, sandwiches, hot croissants, ice cream, lively atmosphere; ***Pizzeria*** 143 Marine Drive (corner of Churchgate), to satisfy a craving, good sea views; ***Rasna***, near KC College, Churchgate, garden café, Indian, Chinese and veg, packed lunches, closed Sunday.

Indian: ***Balwas***, Maker Bhavan, 3 Sir Vithaldas Thackersey Marg, inexpensive, well-prepared food; ***Gaylord***, Vir Nariman Rd, good food (huge portions), tables inside and out, barbecue, pleasant, good bar; ***Samrat***, Prem Court, J Tata Rd, Churchgate, large Gujarati *thalis*; ***Santoor***, Maker Arcade, Cuffe Parade, south of Back Bay near *President Hotel*, small, Mughlai and Kashmiri specialities, chicken *malai* chop (with cream), *chana* Peshawari (*puri* with chickpeas), Kashmiri soda made with salt and pepper recommended; ***Satkar***, Indian Express Bldg, Churchgate, delicious food, a/c section more expensive.

Victoria Terminus

Mumbai map 212

C *Grand*, 17 Sprott Rd, Ballard Estate, T 2618211, F 2626581, 73 a/c rooms, exchange, bookshop, old fashioned, built around a central courtyard but relaxing.

D *City Palace*, 121 City Terrace (Nagar Chowk), opposite VT Main Gate, T 2615515, F 2676897, tiny though spotless, rooms (some without window), with bath (Indian WC), some a/c, renovated, modern, room service, good value, highly recommended.

Budget hotels

E *Manama*, 221 P D'Mello Rd, T 2613412, reasonable rooms, popular; **E** *Rupam*, 239 P D'Mello Rd, T 2618298, 37 rooms, some a/c with phone, clean, friendly, comfortable beds.

Places to eat

Bharat, 317 SB Singh Marg, opposite Fort Market, excellent seafood and crab as well as *naans* and *rotis*, recommended; ***George***, 20 Apollo St (near Horniman Circle), pleasant quiet atmosphere, faded colonial feel, good service, lunchtime *biriyanis* and *thalis* good value; ***Mahesh Lunch Home***, Sir PM Rd, Fort, excellent for Mangalorean, Goan and *tandoori* sea food, a/c, bar, inexpensive, very popular.

Gateway of India and Colaba

See map, page 214

AL ***Taj Mahal***, the original, with great style and character, 294 rooms, and ***Taj Mahal Intercontinental***, Apollo Bunder, T 2023366, F 2872711, 306 rooms, excellent shopping parade and pastry shop, excellent restaurants (no shorts), very good Indian dance performance (evenings) open to non-residents, Rs 50, 1 hour; check bill for minor errors before leaving especially at night when international flight departures signal large exodus of aircrews.

C ***Apollo***, 22 Lansdowne Rd, Colaba, behind *Taj*, T 2020223, F 2871592, 39 rooms, some a/c, best with sea view, excellent, helpful, friendly service; **C** ***Diplomat***, 24-26 BK Bonam Behram Marg (behind *Taj*), T 2021661, F 2830000, 52 a/c rooms, restaurant, exchange, quiet and homely, good value, recommended; **C** ***Godwin***, 41 Garden Rd, T 2841226, F 2871592, 48 large, clean a/c rooms (some on upper floors have better views), rooftop garden, helpful management, recommended; **C** ***Regent***, 8 Ormiston Rd (Best Marg), T 2871854, well furnished a/c rooms, no restaurant but good room service; **C** ***Suba Palace***, Apollo Bunder, T 2020636, F 2020812, just behind *Taj*, clean, modern, well run, recommended.

D ***Bentley's***, 17 Oliver Rd, offGarden Rd, T 2841474, F 2871846, 37 rooms, 4 a/c, breakfast included, good value; **E** ***Whalley's***, 41 Mereweather Rd, T 2834206, 25 rooms (inspect first), some good a/c with balcony and bath, including breakfast, accepts TCs, old-fashioned; **D** ***YWCA International Guest House*** (for men and women), 18 Madam Cama Rd (entrance on side), Fort, T 2020445, F 2822057, 34 clean, pleasant rooms with bath, breakfast included, temp membership – Rs 25-50, deposit with advance reservations in writing, recommended.

Budget hotels

Few left in the area charging under Rs 400. **E** ***Lawrence***, Rope Walk La, behind Prince of Wales Museum, T 2843618, 9 rooms, usually full, very good value; **E** ***Seashore***, 4th Flr, 1/49 Kamal Mansion, Arthur Bunder Rd, T 2874237, has good room facing sea.

Many **F** category are clustered around the *Taj Mahal Hotel*. ***Salvation Army Red Shield Hostel***, 30 Mereweather Rd, T 2841824, mostly dorm (Rs 75 including breakfast, Rs 100 including meals), some double rooms (Rs 320, all meals included), lockers Rs 25/item 0800-2200, showers Rs 25, check out 0900, book in advance or arrive early, check in as others check out, recommended as convenient, friendly, best value; ***India*** and ***Gateway Guest Houses***. ***Volga***, above Citywalk Shoes, Colaba Causeway, simple but acceptable, and ***Volga II***, a few shops down near Leopold, very small, basic rooms, shared bath, clean but rather expensive.

Places to eat

Cafés: serving chilled beer are the craze but some have suffered for their popularity, prices have gone up and waiters care too much for a large tip from groups of foreigners: ***Leopold's***, Colaba, still full of young backpackers for western food and drink but getting expensive; ***Mondegar***, near Regal Cinema, is similar but a little cheaper; ***Food-Inn*** 50m from Leopold's makes a pleasant change (a/c upstairs), reasonably priced, mainly Indian (some western) snacks, friendly service, recommended; this and other similar cafés nearby are far better value than *Leopold's*. ***Churchill***, 103B Colaba Causeway, wide selection (pizzas, pastas, fish dishes, even beef steaks!) Rs 30-70, delicious sundaes.

Chinese: ***Ling's Pavilion***, 19/21 KC College Hostel Bldg, off Colaba Causeway (behind *Taj* & Regal Cinema), T 2850023, stylish decor, good atmosphere and delightful service, colourful menu, seafood specials, generous helpings, highly recommended; ***Ming Palace***, Apsara Bldg, Colaba Causeway, 'Shanghai potatoes' recommended; ***Nanking***,

Apollo Bunder, good choice of very good Cantonese dishes, expensive, try fish ball soup, Pomfret Nanking, Pickled fish, and Beef with watercress. *Mandarin* and *Hongkong* are opposite.

Fast food: ***Sheekh Kebab Stall*** on Tulloch Rd, behind *Taj Mahal Hotel*, does excellent Muslim snacks, opens 1900.

Indian: ***Bagdadi***, Tullock Rd (behind Taj Hotel), one of cheapest for first class food, fragrant biryani, delicious chicken (Rs30), crowded but clean; ***Chetana***, 34 K Dubash Marg, opposite Jahangir Gallery, T 2844968, excellent veg *thalis* (also small religious bookshop); ***Copper Chimney***, 18 K Dubash Marg, T 2041661, subdued lighting and quietly tasteful, excellent North Indian dishes, must reserve; ***Khyber***, 145 MG Rd, Kala Ghoda, Fort, T 2143229, for an enjoyable evening in beautiful surroundings (traditional carved furniture, paintings by Hussain, AE Menon), excellent food, especially lobster and *reshmi* chicken kebabs, try *paya* soup (goat's trotters!), outstanding restaurant, reserve; ***New Indian Coffee Shop***, Kittridge Rd, Sassoon Dock, good Kerala breakfast; Parsi ***Paradise***, Sindh Chambers, Colaba Causeway, closed Monday, not a/c, spotless, excellent *dhansak* but also serves other cuisines – try *Sali boti* (mutton and 'chips'); ***Pathuk's***, near Stock Exchange, very good veg and non-veg, a/c, bar, friendly owner; ***Trishna***, 7 Rope Walk Lane, behind Kala Ghoda, by Old Synagogue, good seafood, particularly crab, "swinging, crowded and fun", highly recommended.

Shopping

Most shops are open 1000-1900 weekdays; the bazars sometimes staying open as late as 2100. Best buys in Mumbai are textiles, particularly tie-and-dye from Gujarat, handblock printed cottons, Aurangabad and 'Patola' silks, and gold bordered saris from Surat and Khambat. Wood carving, brass ware and handicrafts make good gifts. Jewellery and leather goods also attract the Western shopper. The top hotel arcade shops often stock a good selection of high quality goods but prices are usually higher than elsewhere in the city. Even then, Mumbai prices are often higher than in other Indian cities.

Bazars: ***Crawford Market***, MR Ambedkar Rd (fun for bargain hunting). For a different experience try ***Chor (Thieves') Bazar***, on Maulana Shaukat Ali Rd in central Mumbai, full of finds – from Raj left-overs to precious jewellery. Some claim that the infamous name is unjustified since the original was 'Shor' (noisy) bazar! On Fridays 'junk' carts sell less expensive 'antiques' and fakes.

Books: the bookshop at the Airport Domestic Terminal (not the shop near the entrance) is very good and cheap. ***Crossword***, 22 B Desai Rd (near Mahalakshmi Temple), smart, spacious, good selection, some imported pricey, recommended; ***Danai***, 14th Khar Danda Rd and *Centaur Hotels*, good for books and music; ***Nalanda***, *Taj Mahal Hotel*, one of the best for art books; *Oberoi* bookshop charges higher prices. ***New Secondhand Bookstore***, Kalbadevi and ***Strand Books***, off Sir PM Rd near HMV, excellent selection, arranges shipping (reliable), 20% discount on airfreight. Religious books at ***Chetana***, 34 K Dubash Marg.

For **Antiquarian** books and prints try ***Jimmy Ollia***, Cumballa Chambers (1st Flr), Cumballa Hill Rd. Along Churchgate St and near the University are lines of **second-hand** book stalls.

Clothes: B Desai Rd, Dr DN Rd, Colaba Causeway shops starting near the *Taj Mahal Hotel*. Cheapest at **Fashion St** opposite Mumbai Gymkhana, S Bhagat Singh Marg, but check quality (often export surplus) and bargain vigorously.

Men's: ***Cotton World***, Mandlik Rd, Colaba and ***Raymonds***, B Desai Rd (also tailoring) are recommended.

Handicrafts: Government emporia sell good handicrafts and textiles at fixed prices. ***Bihar Emporium***, Dhun Nur, Sir PM Rd; ***Black Partridge*** (Haryana), Air India Bldg, Nariman Pt; ***Central Cottage Industries Emporium***, Apollo Bunder, represents a nationwide selection, especially Kashmiri embroidery, South Indian handicrafts and Rajasthani textiles; most representative of the region is ***Gurjari***, 27 Khaitan Bhavan, J Tata Rd, particularly good for textiles, furnishings, wood carving and brassware; ***Handloom House***, Dr DN Rd; ***Kairali***, Nirmal, Nariman Pt; ***Kashmir Govt Arts Emporium***, Co-op

Insurance Bldg, Sir PM Rd; ***UP Emporium***, Sir PM Rd for silks, cottons and brocades; ***Gangotri*** (UP), ***Mrignayanee*** (MP) and ***Phulkari***, ***Shikha*** and ***Trimurti*** (Maharashtra) are all at World Trade Centre, Cuffe Parade; ***Khadi and Village Industries***, Dr DN Rd. ***Sadak Ali***, behind *Taj* hotel, good range, prices not fixed.

Jewellery: you can buy silver by weight at the ***silver bazar***, Mumbadevi, and gold jewellery at ***Zaveri Bazar***.

Leather: try ***Dhaboo St bazar*** for bargains, or pay higher prices at arcade shops in top hotels. *Oberoi* shopping centre will make you a jacket in 1-2 days. 'Bhendi Bazar' (ask taxi driver) for good quality and wide selection at a fraction of the price. ***Rasulbhai Adamji***, Colaba Causeway, behind *Taj* has excellent handbags, cases, wallets.

For shoes: *Oberoi* Centre and Colaba Causeway.

Music: ***Rhythm House***, North of Jehangir Gallery; ***Hiro***, SP Mehta St, good Indian classical CDs (Rs 400), helpful advice, recommended.

Silks & Saris: ***Kala Niketan***, MG Rd and Juhu Reclamation; ***Vama***, in Kanchenjunga (Peddar Rd, next to Kemp's Corner), tailoring possible.

Local travel

Auto-rickshaws: not available in central area. Metered charge about Rs 6 for first 1.6 km, revised tariff card held by the driver (x5, in suburbs). **Victorias** (horse-drawn carriages), available at Mumbai Central, Chowpatty and Gateway of India. Rates negotiable.

Buses: Red BEST (Bombay Electrical Supply Co) buses are available in most parts of Greater Mumbai, T 4128725. Within the Central Business Dist, buses are marked 'CBD'.

A **Car with driver** (including fuel) may be hired for varying numbers of hours with a specified km allowance, eg 4 hours/50 km, 8 hours/80 km, 12 hours/120 km.

City sightseeing If you exceed the km allowance shown, there is an 'extra km' charge depending on the type of car hired. If you are late returning the car there is an 'extra hour' charge. A typical rate chart is given as a guide The charge in Mumbai, Delhi and Madras is higher than in other cities.

Out-of-town: a 'kilometre rate' applies when a car is hired for out-of-town journeys. In addition there is a driver charge of Rs 160 and a 'night halt' charge. For example, an Economy car taken out for 1 night and covering 200 km would cost Rs 1,920.

Self-drive cars are also available but are not recommended for anyone who is unaccustomed to Indian road conditions. An Economy car (fuel extra) would cost Rs 3,000 for 3 days.

Many operators quote competitive rates for hire. **Auto Hirers**, 7 Commerce Centre, Tardeo, T 4942006; **Blaze**, Colaba, T 2020073; **Budget**, T 4942644; **Hertz**, T 4965186, F 4921172, charges are higher; **Sai**, Phoenix Mill Compound, Senapati Bapat Marg, Lower Parel, T 4942644, F 4937524, recommended; **Wheels**, T 4948168. Holiday **Caravans** with driver, T 2024627.

Taxis (yellow top): easily available. Metered charge about Rs 10 for first 1.6 km. Pay according to revised tariff card (meter x 11). Taxis called by hotel doormen often arrive with meter registering Rs 10, so better to hail one on the street.

Train Suburban electric trains are economical. They start from Churchgate for the western suburbs and Victoria Terminus (VT) for the eastern suburbs but are often desperately crowded (Stay near the door or you may miss your stop!); there are 'Ladies' cars. Trains leaving Mumbai Central often have seats at the terminus but soon fill up.

NB Avoid the rush hour, and keep a tight hold on valuables. The difference between 1st and 2nd class is not always obvious although 1st class is 10 times as expensive. Inspectors fine people for travelling in the wrong class.

Long distance travel

Mumbai is connected by good motorable roads to all major regional tourist and business centres: **Pune** (163 km), **Mahabaleswar** (239 km), **Aurangabad** (392 km), **Panaji** (Goa – 597 km).

Air

The **International** (Sahar) terminal is 30 km from Nariman Pt. There can be long queues at immigration; 24 hour Thomas Cook exchange offers good rate. **Left Luggage** counter, International airport, is a long walk (across the drive from end of Departure terminal), Rs 35/item. New counter planned.

The **Domestic terminals** (Santa Cruz) are a little closer to the centre of town. The **new** domestic terminal, exclusively for Indian Airlines, is about 400m from the **old** domestic terminal used by all other domestic airlines.

NB It is often difficult to get reasonable **accommodation** in Mumbai, particularly late in the evening. Touts are very pushy at both the international and domestic terminals, but the hotels they recommend are often appalling. It is worth making your own telephone call to hotels of your choice from the airport. The *Rest Rooms* in the **Old** domestic terminal are clean, comfortable (room Rs 480, dorm Rs 180); available for those flying within 24 hours, but are often full. Apply to the Airport Manager.

International Departure Tax Rs 750 (Rs 150 within South Asia).

Indian Airlines: Air India Bldg, Nariman Pt, T 2023031, Airport T 142 and **Jet Airways** fly daily to **Goa** and many cities across India;

Getting to the airport

Buses EATS (Ex-servicemen's) and red BEST buses connect both terminals with the city (Rs 38-45 plus baggage). Drop-off and pick-up points in town are Air India and Indian Airlines offices, *Taj Mahal Hotel* and Prince of Wales Museum. From the airports every 2 hours (odd hours); **from the city**, the bus starts from Air India, Nariman Pt, at the following times: 0415, 0815, 1015, 1130, 1315, 1415, 1545, 1730, 1915, 2115, 2315, 0030, cost Rs 44 plus Rs 7 for luggage.

Pre-paid taxis into town, from counter at the International terminal, recommended. Retain your receipt as the driver requires this at the end of the journey. Small additional charge for luggage. To Nariman Pt or Gateway, about Rs 250, 1 hour. **NB** During rush hour it can take 2 hours.

Train: Outside the 'rush hour' and if travelling light, between Churchgate/ Dadar and Santa Cruz (Domestic)/Andheri (International), the train is a good option – at Andheri, use 'E' side; plenty of good restaurants to pass the time when waiting for a late night flight.

Train

Mumbai is the HQ of the Central and Western Railways. **Enquiries**: Central Railway, T 134/135. **Reservations**: VT (Victoria Terminus), T 2623535, 0800-1230, 1300-1630 (Foreigners' Counter opens 0900); Western Railway, Churchgate, and Mumbai Central, T 2038016 (for foreigners, Ext 4577); 0800-1345, 1445-2000. All for 1st Class bookings and Indrail Passes. **Foreign tourists**: Tourist Quota counter on mezzanine floor above Tourist Office opposite Churchgate Station; foreign currency payment only. Otherwise, queue downstairs at Reservations. Railway Tourist Guides at VT and Churchgate can assist.

NB For all trains, book as early as possible; sometimes sleeper reservations are possible for same-day travel. VT has TV screens showing availability of seats 3 days in advance.

For **Goa**: The new Konkan Railway makes train travel relatively quick and easy; a *Shatabdi Exp* and an *Overnight Exp* are expected to operate between Mumbai and Mangalore via Margao by the end of 1997. The service from Mumbai Central to the Goa-Maharashtra border (Sawantwadi station) was available in early 1997.

The Mumbai-Sawantwadi section was opened in early 1997. From September the journey was lengthened to 11 hours, with stops at Dadar and Thane.

Buses connect for transfer to Panaji; from Panaji, depart 1600 from Kadamba Bus Stand; Rs 23 for semi-luxury, or Rs 14 ordinary.

The section between Margao and Mangalore in Karnataka with a stop at Canacona opened at the beginning of August 1997 with a daily service.

Patil Tours & Travels are collaborating with 'Wagon-Lits' to introduce a "luxury tourist train" daily between Mumbai and Goa (Rs 1,500). The a/c chair car train with business facilities will depart from Mumbai (VT) at 0600, and arrive at Margao at 1300 with a stop at Mapusa Road station; return from Margao 1500, arriving in Mumbai at 2200.

Road

Bus: Maharashtra RTC operates bus services to all the major centres and District HQs in the state as well as to Ahmadabad, Bangalore, Goa, Mangalore, Indore, Vadodara and Hyderabad in other states. Information on services from MRTC, Central Bus Stand, Mumbai Central, T 3076622, or Parel Depot, T 4229905. Private buses also travel long distance routes. Some long distance buses also leave from Dadar where there are many travel agents. Information and tickets from Dadar Tourist Centre, just outside the station, T 4113398.

Ferry

To **Goa**: fast 'catamaran' services between Mumbai, DSIL, Terminal 2, New Ferry Wharf (ask for *Bhaucha Dhakka*) and Fisheries Jetty at Panaji. Tuesday, Thursday, 1000; Friday, Saturday, Sunday, 2230 (dep Panjim Monday, Wednesday, Friday, 1000), 7 hours, but suspended in bad weather and monsoons. Two classes (about US$40 each way, Indians Rs 1,100); lower class non-reclining seats, but comfortable a/c (though can get warm in sun), light meal included, excellent service, recommended. **NB** Heavily booked at Christmas so reserve early, direct with ***Damania Shipping***, Mallet Bunder Rd, T 3731855, F 3743740 (Panjim T 0832 228711). Otherwise, travel agents around Apollo Bunder sometimes have tickets, same day.

Directory

Airline offices: Santa Cruz Airport, T 6144433, 6113300. Sahar Airport, enquiries, T 6329090, 8366700.

Domestic: **Gujarat Airways**, T 6177063; **Indian Airlines**, Air India Bldg, Nariman Pt, T 2023031, Airport T 6114433; **Jet Airways**, B1 Amarchand Mans, Madam Cama Rd, T 2875086 (T 8386111: 24 hours), Airport, T 6102772; **NEPC**, T 6107068, Airport T 6113545; **Sahara**, T 2832446.

International: **Air India**, 1st Flr, Nariman Pt (Counters also at Taj Mahal Hotel, Centaur Hotel and Santa Cruz), T 2024142, Airport T 8366767; **Aeroflot**, 241-2, Nirmal Bldg, Nariman Pt, T 2821682; **Air Canada**, Oberoi Towers Hotel, Nariman Pt, T 2027632, Airport T 6045653; **Air France**, Maker Chamber VI, Nariman Pt, T 2025021, Airport T 8328070; **Alitalia**, 206 Nariman Pt, T 2045018; **British Airways**, 202-B Vir Nariman Rd, T 2820888; **Continental**, **Eastern**, **Iberia** and **MAS**, STIC Travels, 6 Maker Arcade, Cuffe Parade, T 2181431; **Delta**, Taj Mahal Hotel, T 2837314; **Egypt Air**, 7 J Tata Rd, T 2824088; **Emirates**, Mittal Chamber, Nariman Pt, T 2871649; **Gulf Air**, Maker Chambers, 5 Nariman Pt, T 2021777.

Japan, 1/2 Raheja Centre, Nariman Pt, T 2874936; **KLM**, 198 J Tata Rd, T 2833338; **Lufthansa**, Express Towers, Nariman Pt, T 2875264; **PIA**, 7 Stadium House, Vir Nariman Rd, T 2021373; **Qantas**, 42 Sakhar Bhavan, Nariman Pt, T 2020343; **Royal Jordanian**, 199 J Tata Rd, T 224580; **Saudia**, Express Tower, Nariman Pt, T 2020199; **SAS**, 15 World Trade Centre, Cuffe Parade; **Singapore Airlines**, Taj Intercontinental, T 2022747; **Swissair**, Maker Chamber VI, 220 Nariman Pt, T 2872210.

Banks & money changers: Most are open 1000-1400, Monday-Friday, 1000-1200, Saturday. Closed on Sunday, holidays, 30 June, 31 December. Best to change money at the airport, at Bureau de Change (upstairs) in Air India Bldg, Nariman Pt or at **Thomas Cook**, Dr DN Rd, 64, Bajaj Bhavan, Nariman Pt, A/2 Silver Arch, JB Nagar, Andheri.

ATMs for Visa card holders using their usual PIN have opened at **British Bank** (16 Vir Nariman Rd); **Citibank** (Air India Bldg, Nariman Pt, 293 Dr DN Rd); **Hongkong Bank** (52/60 MG Rd, Fort); **Standard Chartered** (81 Ismaili Bldg, Dr DN Rd, 264 Annie Besant

Car hire rental rates

MUMBAI	ECONOMY	REGULAR A/C	PREMIUM A/C	LUXURY A/C
Car with driver	**Maruti 800 Ambassador**	**Maruti 800 Ambassador**	**Maruti 1000 Contessa**	**Esteem Opel etc**
8 hrs/80 km	Rs 800	Rs 1,000	Rs 1,500	Rs 2,000
Extra km	Rs 8	Rs 10	Rs 15	Rs 18
Extra hour	Rs 50	Rs 60	Rs 80	Rs 100
Out-of-town				
Per km	Rs 8	Rs 10	Rs 15	Rs 20
Night halt	Rs 160	Rs 200	Rs 250	Rs 250

Train timetable

Train	Number	Departs	Arrives	Journey Time
Mumbai-Sawantwadi Exp	*KR111*	*Mumbai Central* at 2230	Sawantwadi at 0940	$11\frac{1}{4}$ hrs
Mumbai-Sawantwadi Exp	KR112	Sawantwadi at 1855	Mumbai Central at 0635	$11\frac{1}{4}$ hrs

Rd). Also available at other branches across the city.

State Bank of India, Bombay Samachar Marg (at *Centaur Airport Hotel* until 2200) and Churchgate, behind India Tourist Office, among others. Other foreign and Indian banks have several branches.

Credit Cards: **American Express**, Majithia Chambers, 276 Dr DN Rd; **Diners Club**, Raheka Chambers, 213 Nariman Pt; **Mastercard**, Bank of America, Express Towers; **Visa**, ANZ Grindlays Bank, 90 MG Rd.

Embassies & consulates: Australia, Maker Tower E, 16th Flr, Cuffe Parade, T 2181071; **Austria**, 206-210 Balram Bldg, Bandra (E), T 6442291; **Belgium**, Morena, 11 Dahanukar Marg, T 4929261; **France**, Datta Prasad, NG Cross Rd, T 4950918; **Germany**, 10th Flr, Hoechst House, Nariman Pt, T 2832422; **Indonesia**, 19 Altamount Rd, T 3868678; **Israel**, 50 Deshmukh Marg, Kailas, T 3862794; **Italy**, Kanchenjunga, 72G Deshmukh Rd, T 3874071; **Japan**, 1 ML Dahanukar Marg, T 4934310; **Malaysia**, Rahimtoola House, Homji St, T 2860056; **Netherlands**, 1 Marine Lines Cross Rd, Churchgate, T 2016750; **Philippines**, 116 Free Press House, Nariman Pt, T 2020375; **Russia**, 42 Napean Sea Rd, T 3633627; **Spain**, 6 K Dubash Marg, T 2874787; **Sri Lanka**, 34 Homi Modi St, T 2045861; **Sweden**, 85 Sayani Rd, Prabhadevi, T 4360493; **Switzerland**, 102 Maker Chamber IV, 10th Flr, Nariman Pt, T 2043550; **Thailand** 43 B Desai Rd, T 3831404; **UK**, Maker Chamber IV, Nariman Pt, T 2830517; **USA**, Lincoln House, B Desai Rd, T 3633611.

Hospitals & medical services: The larger hotels usually have a house doctor, the others invariably have a doctor on call. Ask hotel staff for prompt action. The telephone directory lists hospitals and General Practitioners. *Prince Aly Khan Hospital,* Nesbit Rd near the harbour, T 3754343, is recommended.

Chemists: several open day/night especially near hospitals. *Kemps*, *Taj Mahal Hotel*, Apollo Bunder open until late; *Wordell*, Stadium House, Churchgate; *New Royal*, New Marine Lines; *Karnik's*, opposite RN Cooper Hospital, Gulmohar Rd, JVPD Scheme, Vile Parle (W); *Gohil*, Vile Parle (E); *Badri*, Khara Tank Rd.

Post & telecommunications: Usually open 1000-1700. Sahar Airport 24 hours. Post Offices all over the city and most 5-star hotels.

GPO: Nagar Chowk. Monday-Saturday, 0900-2000 (*Poste Restante* facilities 0900-1800) and Sunday 1000-1730; parcels from 1st Flr, rear of building, 1000-1700 (Monday-Saturday); cheap 'parcelling' service on pavement outside.

Central telegraph office: Hutatma Chowk, Churchgate PO, 'A' Rd. Colaba PO, Colaba Bus Station and also at Mandlik Rd, behind *Taj Mahal Hotel*. Foreign PO, Ballard Pier. Counter at Santa Cruz.

Couriers: *EMS Speedboat*, GPO, T 2621671; *DHL*, Maker Chambers V, Nariman Pt, T 2044055; *Skypak*, Marol, Andheri E, T 6368181; *Infotek*, Express Towers, Nariman Pt, T 223092 have international phone, fax, telex and other business services under one roof.

Shipping offices: Damania Shipping, T 3743737, F 3743740 with catamarans to Goa (see Ferry below); **Shipping Corp of India**, Madame Cama Rd, T 2026666.

Tour companies & travel agents: Some well established agents: ***American Express***, Regal Cinema Bldg, Colaba, T 2048278; ***Cox and Kings***, 270-271 Dr DN Rd, T 2043065; ***Everett***, 1 Regent Chambers, Nariman Pt, T 2845339; ***Mercury***, 70VB Gandhi Rd, T 2024785; ***MS Travels***, 7/10 Botawala Bldg, 3rd Flr Horniman Circle, T 266 3995; ***Sita***, 8 Atlanta, Nariman Pt, T 2835289; ***Thomas Cook***, Cooks Bldg, Dr DN Rd, T 2048556; ***Trade Wings***, 30 K Dubash Marg, T 2844334; ***Space Travels***, 4th Flr, Sir PM Rd, T 2864773, offer discounted flights and special offers for students, Monday-Friday, 1000-1700, Saturday 1030-1500; ***Orient Express***, 359 Dr DN Rd, T 2871047; ***Peerless Travels***, Churchgate Chambers, 5 New Marine Lines, T/F 2666400; ***TCI***, Chandermukhi, Nariman Pt, T 2021881.

Tourist offices: Govt of India, 123 M Karve Rd, opposite Churchgate, T 2033144, F 2014496, Monday-Saturday 0830-1730 (closed 2nd Saturday of month from 1230). Counters open 24 hours at both airports, and at *Taj Mahal Hotel*, Monday-Saturday 0830-1530 (closed 2nd Saturday from 1230). Helpful staff who can also issue Liquor Permits (essential for Gujarat). **Maharashtra**: CDO Hutments, opposite LIC Bldg, Madam Cama Rd, T 2026713; Express Towers, 9th Flr, Nariman Pt, T 2024482; Information and Booking counters at international and domestic terminals. Also at Koh-i-Noor Rd, near *Pritam Hotel*, Dadar T 4143200; VT Rly Station, T 2622859; C Sivaji Rd, Gateway of India, T 241877.

Goa, Mumbai Central Station, T 3086288; **Gujarat**, Dhanraj Mahal, Apollo Bunder, T 2024925; **Madhya Pradesh**, 74 World Centre, Cuffe Parade, Colaba, T 2187603; **Rajasthan**, 230 Dr DN Rd, T 2044162.

Useful numbers and addresses: Police Emergency: T 100. **Fire**: T 101. **Ambulance**: T 102. **Foreigners' Regional Registration Office**: Annex 2, Police Commissioner's Office, Dr DN Rd, near Phule Market, T 268111. **Passport Emigration Office**: T 4931731.

Section 4

Information for travellers

BEFORE TRAVELLING

VISAS AND PERMITS

The Government of India has changed the rules regarding visas frequently over the last 3 years. They may change again, so it is essential to check details and costs. Prices vary according to nationality. In late-1997 the following visa rules applied to British Passport holders:

Transit visa. Fee £3.

Tourist visa – 6 months. **NB** Valid for 6 months from the date of issue. Multiple entry. Fee £26.

Business visa up to 1 year validity from the date of issue. Fee £32. A letter from company explaining nature of business is required.

Visa up to 5 years validity (Indian origin only; proof must be shown). Fee £64. **NB** All those who have or have held Indian passports, their spouses and children may apply.

Student visa up to 1 year validity from the date of issue. Fee £32. (You must send a letter of acceptance from Indian educational institution. Allow up to 3 months for approval.)

You will need to fill in one form and enclose 3 passport photos. Some High Commissions, Embassies and Consulates will issue visas by post. Applications must be made on the prescribed form and the passport must be valid to cover the period of visit. Transit visas are issued to those passing through India en route to another country. Nationals of Bhutan and Nepal do not require a visa – they only need a suitable means of identification. Arrangements for visa application and collection vary from office to office, and should be confirmed by phone. Tourists from countries which do not have Indian representatives may apply to resident British representatives, or enquire at the Air India Office.

Visa extensions

Applications should be made to the Foreigners' Regional Registration Office at Mumbai, or an office of the Superintendent of Police in the District Headquarters.

Income tax clearance

All foreign visitors who stay in India for more than 180 days are required to get an income tax clearance exemption certificate from the Foreign Section of the Income Tax Dept in Delhi, Mumbai, Calcutta or Chennai.

HEALTH

Health facilities are reasonably good in the main cities and details of chemists and hospitals are given town by town. Government hospitals are often overcrowded. Modern private clinics can, on the other hand, be fairly expensive. Most hotels will call a local English-speaking doctor in an emergency.

MONEY

Currency

Indian currency is the Rupee. New notes are printed in denominations of Rs 500, 100, 50, 20, 10, 5, 2, though some Re 1 notes are still in circulation. The Rupee is divided into 100 Paise. Coins are minted in denominations of Rs 5, 2, 1, and 50, 25, 20, 10 and 5 Paise, though 10 and 5 Paise coins are virtually never seen. It is useful to keep a supply of small denomination notes, especially for tipping.

Warning It can be difficult to use torn or very worn currency notes. Check notes carefully when you are given them and refuse any that are damaged. In rural areas many people treat the Rs 5 and Rs 2 coins with suspicion.

Credit cards

Major credit cards are increasingly acceptable in the main centres, though in smaller cities and towns it is still rare to be able to pay by credit card. Payment by credit card can sometimes be more expensive than payment by cash. However, shopping by credit card for items such as handicrafts, clothing, and carpets from larger dealers doesn't mean that you have to accept the first price asked. Bargaining is still expected and essential.

American Express cardholders can use their cards to get either cash or TCs in Goa, Mumbai and other major cities. Diners, Master Card and Visa are widely used. There is no consistency as to which credit cards will be accepted from place to place or bank to bank, so it is worth carrying more than one. Remember that it often takes a long time to check authorization. Automatic Telling Machines (ATMs) that accept foreign cards are still very rare, though this is beginning to change. Railway Reservation centres in some major cities are now accepting Visa card.

Money changing

It is best to get cash on arrival at the airport bank or the Thomas Cook exchange counter while you wait for your luggage to be unloaded. This is generally far easier and less time consuming than using banks in the city. Banks often give a substantially better rate of exchange than hotels but may mean a longer wait. Large hotels and resorts change money 24 hrs a day. **NB** If you cash sterling, always make certain that you have been given Rupees at the **sterling** and not at the **dollar** rate.

Encashment certificate Some banks can be reluctant to give you the free encashment certificates – ask for it. It allows you to change Indian Rupees back to your own currency (you may only take a limited amount of Rupees out of India). It also enables you to use Rupees to pay hotel and other bills for which payment in foreign exchange may occasionally be required.

Black market Premiums on the currency black market are very small and highly risky.

WARNING Changing money through unauthorized dealers is illegal.

Travellers' cheques (TCs)

Most TCs are accepted without difficulty, but some organizations, like Indian Airlines, only accept TCs from certain companies. If you are travelling widely and off the beaten track it can be useful to have TCs from well known companies, eg Thomas Cook and American Express, and in different currencies. A traveller warns that replacement of lost AmEx TCs may take weeks.

Travellers' Cheques nearly always have to be exchanged in banks or hotels, and can only very rarely be used directly for payment. Identification documents (eg passport) need to be shown. Except in hotels, encashing TCs nearly always takes up to 30 mins or longer, so it is worth taking larger denomination TCs and changing enough money to last for some days. Hotels will normally only cash TCs for resident guests, but the rate is often poorer than in banks. Most banks, but not all, will accept US$ TCs. Many will also accept sterling. Other major currency TCs are also accepted in some larger cities.

Transferring money to India

Thomas Cook, American Express and ANZ Grindlays can make instant transfers to their offices in India but charge a high fee (about 8%). State Bank of India branches abroad charge less but can take 2-3 days. A bank draft (up to US$1,000) which you can post yourself (3-5 days by Speedpost) is the cheapest option (Lloyds Bank charge about 1.5%).

Cost of living

The Indian cost of living remains well below that in the industrialized world. Most food, accommodation and public transport, especially rail and bus, are exceptionally cheap. Even the expensive hotels and restaurants in Goa are less expensive than their counterparts in Europe, Japan or the United States. There is a widening range of moderately priced but clean hotels and guest houses and good, inexpensive beach restaurants, making it possible to get a great deal for your money. Budget travellers (sharing a room) can expect to spend about Rs 350-400 (about US$12-13 or £7-8) a day to cover cost of accommodation, food and travel. Those planning to stay in fairly comfortable hotels and use taxis for travelling to sights should expect to spend at least Rs 2,000 (US$65 or £40) a day. You will need to allow a lot of money in Mumbai, however.

NB Prices in the *Handbook* are quoted in Rupees as these are used exclusively throughout India. Very few people are familiar with international currencies, including dollars, apart from currency touts on city street corners. Visitors do best to think in Rupee terms.

WHAT TO TAKE

It is always best to keep luggage to a minimum. Laundry services are generally cheap and speedy. A sturdy rucksack or a hybrid backpack/suitcase, rather than a rigid suitcase, covers most eventualities and survives bus boot, roof rack and plane/ship hold with ease.

Light cotton clothes are useful in Goa at any time of year. It is a good idea to have some very lightweight long sleeve cotton shirts and trousers for evenings, preferably light in colour, as they also give some protection against mosquitoes. Some find open shoes or sandals best in hot weather, with or without light cotton socks, but it is also important to guard against blisters, cuts and bruises which are common problems with unprotected feet. Comfortable canvas shoes or trainers are good options. Modest dress for women is advisable; also take a sunhat and headscarf. **NB** It is worth shopping locally for cotton items as these are very good value.

Checklist:

Air cushions for hard seating
Bumbag
Contact lens cleaning equipment – not readily available in South Asia
Earplugs – hotel rooms can be very noisy
Eye mask
Insect repellent and/or mosquito net, electric mosquito mats, coils
Neck pillow
International driving licence
Photocopies of essential documents
Short wave radio
Socks: take a thick pair for visiting temples and mosques, where stone floors get baking hot
Spare passport photographs
Sun hat
Sun protection cream – factor 10 plus
Sunglasses
Swiss Army knife
Tissues/toilet paper
Torch and spare batteries
Umbrella (excellent protection from sun, rain and unfriendly dogs)
Wipes (*Damp Ones* or equivalent)
Zip-lock bags

Those intending to stay in budget accommodation might also include:
Cotton sheet sleeping bag
Money belt
Mosquito net (impregnated)

Padlock with chain (for hotel room and pack)
Plastic sheet to protect against bed bugs on mattresses
Soap
Student card (ISIC)
Towel
Toilet paper
Universal bath plug

Health kit:
Antacid tablets
Anti-diarrhoea tablets
Anti-malaria tablets
Anti-infective ointment
Condoms/Contraceptives
Dusting powder for feet
First aid kit and disposable needles
Flea powder
Sachets of rehydration salts
Tampons
Travel sickness pills
Water sterilizing tablets

GETTING THERE

AIR

Charters to Goa

Access to Goa by air is restricted to charter flights which arrive at the airport at Dabolim. An increasing number of tour operators from UK (eg *Inspirations, Manos, Somak, Thomson, Tropical Places*) as well as a few from Finland, Germany, Holland and Switzerland, offer good value package holidays between October and April. Flights are only allowed to land in daylight and on certain days of the week; over 21 charter arrivals are expected in the 1997-98 season. See also page 88.

To Mumbai

From Europe There is a very wide choice of flights from many cities, including: Amsterdam, Frankfurt, Geneva, London Heathrow, Paris, Rome and Zurich.

From USA and Canada From New York (JFK): LA via JFK; San Francisco via Frankfurt; and Toronto.

From Australasia Brisbane and Cairns via Singapore; Melbourne, Perth and Sydney.

From the Far East Many flights on all main routes. From Bangkok; Hong Kong; Kuala Lumpur; Singapore; and Tokyo.

From the Middle East Bahrain.

NB Airline schedules change frequently, so it is essential to check with a travel agent well before making travel arrangements.

Discounts

It is possible to obtain significant discounts, especially outside European holiday times, most notably from London, even on non-stop flights. Mid-July to mid-August and Christmas and New Year are peak periods and most expensive. Shop around and book early. It is also possible to get discounts from Australasia, South-east Asia and Japan. Some Middle Eastern, Central European and Central Asian airlines offer highly discounted fares.

Stop-overs and round the world tickets

You can arrange several stop-overs in South Asia on round the world and other longer distance tickets. RTW tickets allow you to fly in to one and out from another international airport.

Ticket agents

Many ticket agents that offer discounted tickets advertise in the European and American press. Trailfinders of London, one of the world's biggest agencies, has a range of discounted deals, T 0171 938 3939. Competitive rates are quoted by STA with over 100 offices worldwide (in London, T 0171 937 9962). Campus Travel too offer good discounts to students and have offices in several University cities. General Sales Agents (GSAs) for specific airlines can sometimes offer excellent deals. Jet Airways, 188 Hammersmith Rd, London W6 7DJ, T 0181 970 1500, Manchester T 0161 643 9700, is GSA for Gulf Air, Kuwait Airways among others; Welcome Travel 55/57 Wells St London W1P 3RA, T 0171 439 3627 is GSA for Air India.

It is also possible to get good air travel arrangements for some internal flights using international carriers. In 1997, **Air India** flights from Europe to any of 12 Indian destinations were offered at the same price, with stopovers in India for a small extra charge. See Getting Around below.

International air tickets can be bought in India though payment must be made in foreign exchange. Discounts are available on some routes.

Airline security
International airlines vary in their arrangements and requirements for security, in particular the carrying of equipment like radios, tape-recorders, lap-top computers and batteries. It is advisable to ring the airline in advance to confirm what their current regulations are. **NB Internal airlines often have different rules from the international carriers**. You are strongly advised not to pack valuables in your luggage (there have been several reports of vandalism and theft from luggage, particularly on Air India) and avoid having to repack at the airport.

ON ARRIVAL

CUSTOMS

Duty free allowance
Tourists are allowed to bring in all personal effects 'which may reasonably be required', without charge. The official customs allowance includes 200 cigarettes or 50 cigars, 0.95 litres of alcohol, a camera with 5 rolls of film, a pair of binoculars. You may be asked to register valuable personal effects or professional equipment on a Tourist Baggage Re-Export Form (TBRE), including jewellery, special camera equipment and lenses, lap-top computers, sound and video recorders. These forms require the serial numbers of such equipment. It saves considerable frustration if you know the numbers in advance and are ready to show the serial numbers on the equipment. In addition to the forms, details of imported equipment may be entered into your passport. Save time by completing the formalities while waiting for your baggage. It is essential to keep these forms for showing to the customs when leaving India, otherwise considerable delays are very likely at the time of departure.

Duty free shopping
Duty free shops in Goa and Mumbai are extremely limited.

Currency regulations
There are no restrictions on the amount of foreign currency or TCs a tourist may bring into India. If you were carrying more than US$10,000 or its equivalent in cash or TCs in 1997 you had to fill in a currency declaration form. This could change with a relaxation in the currency regulations.

Money changing
It is possible to change money at the airport banks. See **Warning** on page 232.

Prohibited items
NB The import of dangerous drugs, live plants, gold coins, gold and silver bullion and silver coins not in current use are either banned or subject to strict regulation. It is illegal to import firearms into India without special permission. Enquire at Consular offices abroad for details.

Export restrictions
Export of gold jewellery purchased in India is allowed up to a value of Rs 2,000 and other jewellery (including settings with precious stones) up to a value of Rs 10,000.

WARNING Export of antiquities and art objects over 100 years old is restricted. Ivory, skins of all animals, snake skin and articles made from them are banned.

DOCUMENTATION AND TAX

Arrival Arrival can be a slow process. Disembarkation cards, with an attached customs declaration, are handed out to passengers during the inward flight. The immigration form should be handed in at the immigration counter on arrival. The customs slip will be returned, for handing

TRANSPORT FROM THE AIRPORT

There is a pre-paid taxi counter immediately outside the airport terminal. There is a list of fares to 58 destinations across Goa. Sample prices in mid 1997 were Anjuna Rs 488. Calangute or Mapusa Rs 420, Candolim Rs 430, Colva Rs 225, Majorda Rs 186, Margao Rs 264, Mobor Rs 390, Panaji Rs 312, Ponda Rs 340, Tiracol Rs 702, Vagator Rs 507, Vasco Rs 50.

There was only one direct bus per day from the airport to Panaji, departing at 1330, but some airlines have their own bus, and major hotels organise their own pickups. The cheapest and most reliable way to reach many destinations is to take a taxi to the Vasco bus stand, which is directly connected to many other centres. See also page 88.

over to the customs on leaving the baggage collection hall. **NB** The immigration formalities at Mumbai can be very slow. You may well find that there are delays of over an hour in processing other passengers passing through immigration who need help with filling forms.

Departure tax

From September 1997 the tax was raised to **Rs 750** which is payable for all international departures other than those to neighbouring SAARC countries, when the tax is Rs 150. This must be paid in Rupees before checking-in at the counter; it is worth setting the amount aside for when you leave.

ESSENTIAL INFORMATION

Conduct

Courtesy and appearance Cleanliness and modesty are appreciated even in informal situations. Nudity is not permitted on beaches in India and although there are some places where this ban is ignored, it causes widespread offence. Displays of intimacy are not considered suitable in public and will probably draw unwanted attention.

Most travellers experience great warmth and hospitality, but with it comes an open curiosity about personal matters. You should not be surprised by total strangers on a train, for example, asking details of your job, income and family circumstances.

Religious sites Visitors to churches and Hindu temples should observe customary courtesy, especially in clothing.

Shoes must always be removed outside (and leather items outside Jain temples). Take thick socks for protection when walking on sun-baked stone floors.

NB Non-Hindus are sometimes not permitted into the inner sanctum of Hindu temples and occasionally even into the temple itself. Look for signs or ask. Offering boxes are provided for those who wish to make donations which should not normally be handed to priests or monks since they may be forbidden to touch money. It is also not customary to shake hands with a priest or monk.

Social behaviour Use your right hand for giving, taking, eating or shaking hands as the left is considered to be unclean. Women do not shake hands with men as this form of contact is not traditionally acceptable between acquaintances. Do not photograph women without permission.

The **greeting** when meeting or parting used universally among the Hindus across India is the palms joined together as in prayer, sometimes accompanied with the word *Namaste*, translated as 'I salute all divine qualities in you.' "Thank you" is often expressed by a smile and occasionally with the somewhat formal *dhannyabad* or *shukriya* (N and W).

Electricity

220-240 volts AC. Some top hotels have transformers to enable visitors to use their appliances. There may be pronounced variations in the voltage, and power cuts are common. Socket sizes vary so take a universal adaptor (available at airports). **NB** Many hotels even in the highest categories don't have electric razor sockets. It is difficult to get shaver adaptors for Indian sockets in shops outside India, so a battery operated shaver is recommended. During power cuts, diesel generators, are becoming increasingly common in the medium and higher category hotels, to provide power for essential equipment to function, but this may not always cover air-conditioning.

Hours of business

Banks: Monday-Friday 1030-1430, Saturday 1030-1230. Top hotels sometimes have a 24-hr service.

Post Offices Usually 1000-1700 Monday-Friday, Saturday mornings.

Government offices Monday-Friday 0930-1700, Saturday 0930-1300 (some open on alternate Saturday only).

Shops Monday-Saturday 0930-1800 (some take a mid-afternoon break of upto 3 hrs from 1200-1500). Bazars keep longer hours.

NB There are regional variations.

Official time

GMT + 5½ hrs. Conception of time is different in India, being rather vague. Unpunctuality is common so patience is needed.

Photography

It is advisable to take rolls of films and any specialist camera batteries although colour and black and white films are available cheaply at major tourist centres.

Safety

Goa is still a very safe place compared to European and American holiday destinations. About a ¼ of a million foreign tourists visit the state each year and over 99% of them enjoy a carefree and crimefree holiday in the sun. However, thefts and physical assaults have been increasing on certain beaches especially in dimly lit stretches within the tourist belt.

Some cases of late night robbery attacks on tourists were reported in 1997 in the Benaulim and Colva beach roads. It is best to leave valuables and important documents in a hotel safe (many have them) but remember to get a detailed receipt. Travellers have also been robbed immediately after obtaining cash from banks or money changers in the daytime. Cheap accommodation without adequate security is another target; foreign currency, cameras and music systems being the usual draw. Use a good padlock and be "beachwise" in Goa, as you would be "streetwise" at home.

Even after taking all reasonable precautions people do have valuables stolen. This can cause great inconvenience. You can minimize this by keeping a record of vital documents, including your passport number and TC numbers in a completely separate place from the documents themselves. If you have items stolen, they should be reported to the police as soon as possible. Larger hotels will be able to assist in contacting and dealing with the police.

Personal security In general the threats to personal security for travellers in Goa are remarkably small. However, care is necessary in some places, and basic common sense needs to be used with respect to looking after valuables.

In the great majority of areas in India visited by tourists violent crime and personal attacks are extremely rare. Goa is becoming an exception to this rule, where incidents of petty theft and violence directed specifically at tourists have been on the increase, and the police have also been involved in extorting money from tourists.

Theft is not uncommon. It is essential to take good care of personal valuables both when you are carrying them, and when you have to leave them anywhere. **You cannot regard hotel rooms as automatically safe**; even hotel safes do not guarantee secure storage. Avoid leaving valuables near open windows. It is best to keep TCs, passports and valuables with you at all times. **Money belts worn under clothing** are one of the safest options although you should keep some cash easily accessible in a purse.

Security on trains It can be difficult to protect your valuables if travelling alone by train. 1st class a/c and 1st class compartments are self-contained and normally completely secure, although nothing of value should be left close to open train windows. Two-tier a/c compartments, which have much to recommend them especially in the summer, are larger, allowing more movement of passengers and are not so secure. Attendants may take little notice of what is going on, and luggage should be chained to a seat for security overnight. Locks and chains are easily available at main stations and bazars.

Travelling bags and cases should be made of tough material, if possible not easily cut, and external pockets (both on bags and on clothing) should never be used for carrying either money or important documents. Strong locks for travelling cases are invaluable. Use a leather strap around a case for extra securtiy. Pickpockets and other thieves do operate in the big cities. Crowded areas are particularly high risk, and it is impossible to travel far on railways without being in crowded areas from time to time. Keep valuables as close to the body as possible. Women may prefer to use compartments reserved for them. See section on Women travellers below.

Drugs These are widely available from local and foreign dealers at most resorts in Goa, especially at the northern beaches of Anjuna and Chapora. All night beach "parties" are heavily involved with drug-taking. Some police have been suspected of planting drugs on likely looking travellers and then arresting them, hoping for substantial bribes for their release. Usually, 'stop and search' tactics are carried out at entrance and exit roads to the all night parties. Police are also known to search cheap accommodation, particularly in the Anjuna to Chapora area. The bribe demanded may run into hundreds of dollars and some foreigners are detained in local police cells until the necessary funds are raised.

WARNING Anyone charged with the illegal posession of drugs risks facing a fine of Rs 100,000 and 10 years imprisonment. In the 18 months after 25 November 1995 over 50 were imprisoned for drugs related offences, 21 among them were foreigners.

Police Dealings with the police can be very difficult. The paper work involved in reporting losses can be time consuming and irritating, and your own documentation (eg passport and visas) may be demanded. The police themselves sometimes demand bribes, though tourists should not assume, however, that if procedures move slowly they are automatically being expected to offer a bribe. The **traffic police** are tightening up very hard on traffic offences. They have the right to make on-the-spot fines for speeding, illegal parking or crossing traffic lights on the red, and for failing to carry the correct documents. It is essential to ensure that you have a valid international driving licence and insurance papers and ownership papers with you when driving a car or motorbike. If you face a demand for a fine, insist on a receipt. If you have to go to a police station, try to take someone with you. If you face really serious problems, for example in connection with a driving accident, you should contact your consular office as quickly as possible. However difficult it may seem, if you are faced with unlawful detention by the police the best policy is to keep calm and patient. Insist on seeing the senior officer and on reporting the matter to the Chief of Police.

Confidence tricksters These are particularly common where people are on the move, notably around railway stations or places where budget tourists gather. A common plea is some sudden and desperate calamity; sometimes a letter will be produced in English to back up the claim. The demands are likely to increase sharply if sympathy is shown.

It is also essential to take care that credit cards are not run off more than once when making a purchase.

Shopping

Bazars (the local markets), are often a great experience, but you must be prepared to bargain. It pays to first look around. Street hawkers often pass off fake marble, ivory, silver, semi-precious stones, coral etc, as real. Taxi drivers and couriers sometimes insist on recommending certain shops where they expect a commission and prices are likely to be inflated. Export of certain items such as **antiquities, ivory, furs and skins is controlled or banned**, so it is essential to get a certificate of legitimate sale and permission for export. You can get excellent examples of the handicrafts of different states from the government handicrafts emporia. They are generally the safest bet for guaranteed quality at reasonable prices; there is no bargaining. In private shops and markets bargaining is normally essential.

Some shops offer to pack and post your purchases. Many small private shops cannot be trusted. Unless you have a specific recommendation from a person you know well, only make such arrangements in Government emporia or a large store.

NB See departure regulations above for items that are prohibited for export.

Tipping

In the largest hotels a tip of Rs 10 per piece of luggage carried by staff, would be appropriate.

Tour companies sometimes make recommendations for 'suitable tips' for coach drivers and guides. Some of the figures may seem modest by non-Indian standards but are very inflated if compared with normal Indian earnings. Some tour operators recommend a tip of Rs 50/day for drivers and guides. This can safely be regarded as generous, though some will try to persuade you otherwise.

The more expensive hotels and restaurants frequently add a service charge to the bill. Otherwise 10% is the usual amount to leave in expensive hotels, less elsewhere.

Taxi drivers do not expect to be tipped but a small extra amount over the fare is welcomed and particularly if a large amount of luggage is being carried.

Porters at airports and railway stations often have a fixed rate displayed but will usually press for more. Ask fellow passengers what the fair rate is – they will nearly always advise.

Weights and measures

India now uses the metric system for weights and measures. It has come into universal use in the cities. In remote rural areas local measures are sometimes used. The more common are listed in the glossary at the end of the Handbook, where a conversion table is also provided.

Women Travellers

Compared with many other countries it is relatively easy and safe for women to travel around India, even on their own, though most people find it an advantage to travel with at least one companion. There are some problems to watch out for and some simple precautions to take which make it possible to avoid both personal harassment and giving offence.

In Goa (and in major cities and tourist centres) travellers have increasingly reported harassment from local men who follow and touch them or behave indecently. Remember, what may be considered to be normal, innocent friendliness in a Western context may be misinterpreted by some Indian men (especially the sexually frustrated). Cases of rape have been reported especially after beach parties so it is best to walk in large groups at night.

- Modest dress for women is always advisable: loose-fitting non see-through clothes, covering the shoulders, and skirts, dresses or shorts (at least knee-length).

- Unaccompanied women may find problems of harassment – local men may follow and touch them. Women are most vulnerable in major cities, crowded bazars, beach resorts and tourist centres. Buses in many Indian cities warn against "Eve teasing", the euphemism for physical harassment. Seats for women are set aside in buses, while separate compartments in trains try and get around the problem. If you suffer harassment and identify the person responsible, it can be effective to make a scene. As one woman traveller wrote, "they should not get away with it, and in many public places other people will quickly take your side."
- We have had several letters from women travellers complaining of being molested while being measured for clothing in tailors' shops, especially in North India. If possible, be accompanied by a friend when having a fitting.
- It is always best to be accompanied when travelling by night, especially travelling by rickshaw or taxi in towns. Be prepared to raise an alarm if anything unpleasant threatens.
- See health section on page 260 for special health issues.

WHERE TO STAY

Hotels

Like the rest of India, Goa has a wide range of accommodation. You can stay safely and very cheaply by western standards in resorts, towns and villages. There are also high quality hotels, offering a full range of personal and business facilities, though some find their food rather bland. Prices for the top luxury resorts are sometimes comparable with the West.

In the peak season (October to April) bookings can be extremely heavy so it is best to reserve accommodation well in advance which you can do by fax either from abroad or in India itself. However, double check reconfirmation details, and always try to arrive as early as possible in the day, or your reservation may be cancelled. If you travel out from the major centres (eg spending a night away from your booked hotel, when touring) be prepared to accept much more modest accommodation.

NB In some hotels, room boys will enter your room without knocking or without waiting for any response to a knock. Both for security and privacy, it can be a good idea to lock your door when you are in the room.

Prices & categories

The price for each category is a guide to what you would pay for the best standard double room, remembering that taxes can sometimes add considerably to the basic price. When prices range between categories, it is indicated by two letters, eg **C-D**.

The first six categories used in this Handbook are based on prices of the best double rooms, in late 1997. They are not star ratings, and individual facilities vary considerably. Normally the following facilities will be found as standard in the given classes.

Travel tips Many hotels are prepared to **discount** their listed price by at least 10-15% to independent travellers who ask for it since the hotel would be otherwise be paying the commission to any agency. Outside the peak season, further discounts apply.

Most **AL** and some **A** category hotels charge foreigners, except those working in India, and NRIs (non-resident Indians), a 'dollar price', about 50% more than the 'rupee price'. All hotels in Class **C** and above, and some below, accept payment by credit card.

In many towns the best hotel is in the **C** category, but they are not necessarily the best value. Some charge higher prices for a flash reception area rather than better rooms. Most large towns will have at least one **D** category hotel, often offering very good value, and often with cheaper rooms than the average for the category.

Budget hotels There are some excellent value hotels in the **E** and **F** categories, though they can vary in quality.

Many **F** hotels (and some **D** or **E**) have rooms for Rs 80 or less and/or dormitory beds for around Rs 50. These are always very basic, but can be clean and adequate; occasionally dormitories have only 4 or 6 beds and are very good value. There is a **Youth hostel** at Miramar near Panaji. Long-stay visitors often rent cheap rooms on a monthly basis.

NB Noise can be a problem in cheaper hotels, as many are in busy parts of town. An **extra bed** in a room is usually available at an attractive rate. A lower **extra person** charge often means that only a mattress will be provided, and sometimes not even that. Clarify when reserving.

Railway Retiring Rooms For people travelling off the beaten track outside Goa there are several cheap options. Railway stations often have *Retiring Rooms* or 'Rest Rooms'. These may be hired for periods of between 1 and 24 hrs by anyone holding a onward train ticket. They are cheap and usually provide a bed and a fan. Some stations have a couple of a/c rooms, but they are often very heavily booked. They can be very convenient for short stops if travelling extensively by train, although some can be very noisy. The old Domestic **airport** at Mumbai has similar facilities.

Taxes In Goa, a range of taxes (including Business Turnover Tax or BTT) apply to different categories of hotels. In the cheapest hotels no extra tax is normally chargeable. A tax of 5% is charged on rooms costing up to Rs 500; 10% for Rs 800, rising to 15% over Rs 800. An additional 10% service charge may apply. From September 1997 the central government announced a further tax of about 3% to be imposed on Tourism related activities (other than air travel).

When a **Luxury tax** applies in the higher category hotels in India, these are added to bills presented at the end of your stay which usually includes meals. **Tip** To avoid the extra charge, if you eat in the hotel restaurant, it is worth paying the meals bill separately to ensure that tax is not added to food as well as room charges.

WARNING Some visitors have complained of **incorrect bills**, even in the most expensive hotels. The problem particularly afflicts those who are part of groups, when last-minute extras sometimes appear mysteriously on some guests' bills. Check at the desk the **evening before departure**, and keep all **receipts**. It is essential to check carefully again when paying your bill.

Hotel facilities and irritations

Air-conditioning Few hotels in Goa have central air-conditioning as most resort hotels have spacious areas open to sea

Hotel classifications

AL Rs 6,000+ (about US$170+; higher in Mumbai) – Luxury hotel. All facilities for business and leisure travellers to the highest international standard.

A Rs 3,000-6,000 (about US$85-170) – Central a/c, attached baths, phone, TV, business centre, multicuisine restaurants, bar, 24-hr room service, exchange, shops, laundry, travel counter, swimming pool, sports.

B Rs 1,500-3,000 (about US$45-85) – Most of the facilities of **A** but perhaps not business centre, swimming pool, sports or luxury.

C Rs 800-1,500 (about US$25-45) – Usually central a/c, often good value restaurant, exchange, travel.

D Rs 400-800 (about US$12-25) – Some a/c with bath, TV, restaurant.

E Rs 200-400 (about US$6-12) – Simple room with fan, shower, often shared toilet facilities. May not have restaurant, cheapest without bedlinen and towels.

F Below Rs 200 (about US$6) – Very basic, shared toilet facilities (often 'squat'), variable cleanliness and hygiene.

breezes. Rooms are usually cooled by individual units and occasionally large 'air-coolers'. Sometimes, these can be noisy and unreliable. When they fail to operate tell the management as it is often possible to get a rapid repair, or to transfer to a room where the unit is working. Fans are provided in all but the cheapest of hotels.

Checkout time In most places you will be required to leave your room by 1200 on the last day, though you may usually ask to leave your bags at the Reception for some time after that if you wish. Some hotels expect you to vacate your room by 0900 (ask at the time of checking in), while others operate a convenient 24-hr checkout system, meaning you can stay 24 hrs from the time of check-in.

Insects In cheap hotels you need to be prepared for a wider range of insect life, including ants, flies, cockroaches (extremely difficult to eradicate) and harmless spiders and geckos (house lizards). Poisonous insects, including scorpions, are uncommon. Hotel managements are nearly always prepared with insecticide sprays, and will come and spray rooms if asked.

Mosquitoes Mosquitoes may penetrate even the best hotels, though they are less common immediately on the coast. Dusk and early evening are the worst times for mosquitoes. Remember to shut windows and doors after dusk. Trousers and long-sleeved shirts are advisable, especially out of doors. At night fans can be very effective in keeping mosquitoes off. Electrical devices, used with insecticide pellets, are now widely available, as are 'mosquito coils' which burn slowly to emit a 'scented' smoke. Many small hotels in mosquito-prone areas have mosquito nets. It is worth taking your own repellent devices (and impregnated mosquito net) if you are planning to travel in remote areas.

Seasons Many hotels in Goa charge the highest room-rate over Christmas and New Year (between mid-December to mid-January), but also offer up to discount from mid-June to Mid-September.

In the low season, after April, when foreign package tours cease with the last charter flight out, some of the larger resort hotels turn their attention to attracting Indian business conventions and conferences. These hotels take on quite a different character. Some hotels offer 3-4 day special weekend bargains for Indian tourists which throw in a few excursions, a complimentary massage, a bottle of wine etc, and are often not great value. You may prefer to take advantage of a genuine discount of 20%-50% on the room price. During the low-season, hotel restaurants may offer a different menu with more spicy dishes, to suit the change in clientele.

Some hotels and restaurants close for a period between June-September. Certainly the beach assumes a deserted look as the shacks disappear one by one.

Toilet facilities Apart from the **AL** and **A** categories, 'baths' do not necessarily refer to bathrooms with Western bathtubs. Other hotels may provide a bathroom with a toilet, basin and a shower. In the lower priced hotels and outside large towns, a bucket and tap may replace the shower, and an Indian 'squat' toilet instead of a Western WC. Even medium sized hotels which are clean and pleasant do not always provide towels, soap and toilet paper.

Water supply In some areas water supply is rationed periodically (especially in the dry season), occasionally even in the better hotels. **NB** For details on drinking water see page 244 under food and drink.

FOOD AND DRINK

Food

Most visitors are surprised – and often delighted – at the enormous variety of delicious food on offer, some bearing little relation to the various 'curries' available outside India. Furthermore, there is a remarkable range of delicious savoury snacks and sweets. Restaurants and beach cafés in the main tourist centres offer Goan food as well as a good range of dishes from other parts of India. To suit the unaccustomed palate, they also have some Western, Chinese and sometimes even Thai and Tibetan options.

Goan food

Although Goan food has similarities with that in the rest of India – rice, vegetable curries and *dal* are common, for example – there are many local specialities. See also page 267.

Common ingredients in Goan cooking include rice, coconut and cashew (*cazu*) nuts, pork and a wide variety of seafood. Not surprisingly, the food in this region is hot, making full use of the small bird's-eye chillies that are grown locally. Chilli was only introduced to Goa by the Portuguese, adding just one more ingredient to the already richly flavoured and spiced diet. One recipe for the popular *sorpotel* suggests that in addition to other spices you should use 20 dry chillies for $1\frac{1}{2}$ kg pork plus liver and heart, with four green chillies thrown in for good measure!

Goa's Christians had no qualms about using pork (not eaten by Muslims and most Hindus). A state dominated by its coastline, Goa freely uses the harvest from its seas. The standard "fish curry and rice", the common Goan meal, has become a catch phrase. Most beach shacks offer a good choice (depending on the day's catch), and will usually include preparations of kingfish, tuna, mackerel, prawns and shark. You will find lobsters, baked oysters, boiled clams and stuffed crabs as specialities.

Vegetarians are well provided for in Goa. South Indian Brahmin food is wholly distinctive, tamarind and coconut being typical ingredients. Three of its snacks – *dosai*, *idli* and *vadai* – are good vegetarian options.

North Indian cooking is often called *Mughlai*, hinting at the Muslim influence on North Indian diet over the last six centuries. Cream and *ghee* are favourite cooking mediums, and spices, herbs, nuts and fruit are all ingredients added to dishes which usually have meat as the main focus of the meal. Several different kinds of *kebab*, meat balls and minced meat preparations are served alongside *biriyani* or *pulao*. *Tandoori* dishes, marinated meat cooked in a special earthen oven, come from the far northwest, but are widely popular.

One of the intriguing features right across the country is ***paan***, which rounds off a main meal. The *paan* leaf is the vehicle for a succession of pastes and spices, the making of which is regarded as an art. Areca nuts, lime, tobacco and a number of sweetened and scented ingredients will go into the bright green leaf, to be carefully folded and then chewed, seemingly endlessly.

A **thali** is a complete meal served on a plate or stainless steel tray, or more traditionally, on a banana leaf. Several preparations, placed in small bowls, surround the central serving of wholewheat *puris* and rice. A vegetarian *thali* would basically include chapati, rice, *daal*, two vegetable curries and poppadum, although there are regional variations. Fish, mutton or chicken curries are popular non-vegetarian dishes which can be quite hot and spicy. A variety of sweet and hot pickles are offered – mango and lime are two of the most popular. These can be exceptionally hot, and are designed to be taken in minute quantities alongside the main dishes. Plain *dahi* (yoghurt) is usually included which acts as a bland cooling dish to accompany highly spiced food. You may wish to order a sweet to end the meal.

Western food Many hotel restaurants and beach cafés offer 'European' options, eg toasted sandwiches, stuffed pancakes, apple pies, crumbles and cheese cakes. Italian favourites (eg pizzas and pastas) are well established, while Mexican and Jewish dishes are newcomers. Western confectionery, in general, is disappointing. Ice-creams, on the other hand, can be exceptionally good (eg *Cadbury's*, *Dollops*,

Kwality's, Walls).

Fruit and nuts Home of one of India's most famous mangoes, the *alfonso*, Goa has a wide range of fruit. Some are highly seasonal – mangoes in the hot season, for example – while others (eg bananas) are available throughout the year. The extremely rich *jackfruit* is common, as are papaya and watermelons. Cashew nuts and pineapples (brought from South America) and papaya (brought from the Philippines), were introduced to Goa by the Portuguese.

See Eating out: food and menus on page 267.

Drink

Drinking water used to be regarded as one of India's biggest hazards. It is still true that water from the taps or wells should never be regarded as safe to drink. Public water supplies are nearly always polluted and unsafe. Bottled mineral water is now widely available although not all bottled water is mineral water; some is simply purified water from an urban supply. Buy from a shop or stall, check the seal carefully (some are now double sealed) and avoid street hawkers; when disposing bottles, puncture the neck which prevents misuse but allows recycling for storage. Always carry plenty with you when travelling. Water sterilisation tablets can be bought from many chemists outside India. **NB** It is important to use pure water for cleaning teeth.

Beverages Tea and coffee are safe and widely available. If you wish to order it 'black' say 'no sugar', 'no milk' when ordering. At a roadside stall, however, *chai* or *chaa* is milky and sweet. *Nescafe, espresso* and *capuccino* coffee are sometimes on offer but may not turn out as you would expect in the West.

Soft drinks There is a huge variety of bottled soft drinks, including well known international brands (eg *Coca-Cola, Pepsi, Fanta*), which are perfectly safe. Popular and safe Indian brands include *Limca* or *Teem* (lime and lemon), *Thums Up* (cola) and *Mirinda* (orangeade), but some find them too sweet. Fruit juice is available in cartons, including mango, pineapple and apple; the best known brands are *Frooti* and *Jumpin'*. Prices of pre-packed drinks range from Rs 8-15.

Fresh fruit juice (prepared hygienically) is a better option; fresh lime-soda (plain, sweet or salty) is popular. Cool and refreshing fruit-flavoured milk-shakes and yoghurt based *lassis* cost around Rs 20-25. Plain *lassi* is cheaper at about Rs 10.

NB Don't add ice cubes to any drink as the water from which the ice is made may be contaminated.

Alcoholic drinks A wide range of alcoholic drinks is available in Goa including some foreign brands in the major centres. Despite recent price increases, drinks in Goa remain relatively cheap compared to elsewhere in India. The increase in alcoholism (especially among Goan men) have led certain groups to call for prohibition.

Feni The fermented juice of cashew apples, distilled for the local brew *cazu feni* (*fen*, froth) which is strong and potent. Coconut or *palm feni* is made from the sap of the coconut palm. *Feni* is an acquired taste so it is often mixed with soda. It can also be taken "on the rocks" (poured on ice), as a cocktail mixed with fruit juice (bottle, about Rs 25) or pre-flavoured (eg with ginger). **Tip** Don't drink this on an empty stomach. Sip slowly and avoid taking more than a couple of 'tots' when you are new to it.

Beer is usually available in three popular brands – *Kingfisher, Kings Pilsner* (brewed with imported German hops) and the stronger *Arlem* (brewed on the outskirts of Margao). All three come in large bottles (650 ml) and cost Rs 30-40; the latter two also come in half-size bottles and cost Rs 15-25. Another lager, *Belho*, is sold in half-litre cans and two strengths, 'strong' and 'extra strong'.

Goan **wines** tend to be of the fortified variety and are sweet. 'Port' (a legacy of Portuguese rule), a very sweet red wine with an alcohol content of around 14%.

A cup of chai!

Not long ago, when you stopped at a road side tea stall nearly anywhere in India and asked for a cup of *chai*, the steaming hot sweet tea would be poured out into your very own, finely handthrown, beautifully shaped, clay cup! Similarly, whenever a train drew into a railway station, almost any time of day or night, and you heard the familiar loud call of "*chai* garam, garam *chai!*" go past your window, you could have the tea served to you in your own porous clay cup.

True, it made the tea taste rather earthy but it added to the romance of travelling. Best of all, when you had done with it, you threw it away and it would shatter to bits on the road side (or down on the railway track) – returning 'earth to earth'. It was the eco-friendly "disposable" cup of old – no question of an unwashed cup which someone else had drunk out of, hence unpolluted and 'clean'. And, of course, it was good business for the potter.

But, time moves on, and we have now advanced to tea stalls that prefer thick glass tumblers (which leave you anxious when you glance down at the murky rinsing water). A step ahead – those catering for the transient customer, now offer the welcome hot *chai* in an understandably convenient, light, hygienic, easy-to-stack, thin plastic cup which one gets the world over, sadly lacking the biodegradability of the earthen pot. With the fast disappearing terracotta cup we will lose a tiny bit of the magic of travelling in India.

Some cheaper brands resemble sweet sherry, although the better ports are very easy to drink in quantity! A good bottle sells for Rs 50-60 in a wine shop, though beach shacks will charge Rs 40-80 depending on quality, or Rs 60 for a large peg, and quarter bottles for Rs 20-25. Dark rum is cheap (eg *Old Monk*, Rs 80 a bottle) and *Honey Bee* brandy is popular.

GETTING AROUND

AIR

In addition to **Indian Airlines** (the nationalized carrier) there are several private airlines, some serving Goa (eg **Jet Airways** which has an excellent record of service, and NEPC). It is essential to book as early as possible, especially in the peak season. All the major airline offices are connected to the central reservation system. The more you can get done before you leave home, the better. Buying tickets on Indian Airlines can be time consuming and frustrating so it is advisable to use a reputable travel agent. Jet Airways is very efficient. Details of flights are given in the Panaji and Mumbai section of the *Handbook*.

Air ticket pricing

Foreigners buying air tickets in India must use foreign exchange and pay the 'Dollar rate'. Competing airlines charge virtually the same price. Major credit cards, TCs and cash (with encashment certificate) are accepted. Indian Airlines offer a 25% discount for passengers under 30 years of age.

Delays

Be prepared for delays especially on Indian Airlines. For long journeys flying saves time – but often not as much as you may hope! Despite the improvements in air travel it can be a very frustrating experience.

Reserving internal flights abroad

Some travel agents will confirm Indian Airlines reservations if the main ticket is with Air India or some other major airline. If flying with others, confirmation can take weeks.

Jet Airways internal flights may be booked through their offices from any part of the world. In London, T 0181 9701533. Indian Airlines tickets can be booked through Save Time Travel, T 0181 9038777.

Air travel tips

- If you do not have a confirmed booking it pays to arrive early at the airport and to be persistent in enquiring about your position in the queue.
- Indian Airlines do not permit batteries in hand luggage or on your person. Confiscated batteries may not be returned. However, rules change, so check. You need to collect small tags from the check-in desk for cabin baggage which are stamped after the Security check.
- There is a free telephone service at major airports to contact any hotel of your choice.

TRAIN

Trains offer a unique experience, and are often an excellent alternative way of getting to and from Goa and Mumbai and South India. The Konkan railway allows you to reach Goa from either Mumbai or Mangalore in under 8 hrs on a comfortable modern train. Equally, the new broad gauge service from Vasco and Margao to Londa allows easy connections to the Indian interior.

Tourists have special quotas on many trains. Thus, when tickets are not available over the general sales counter, it may still be possible to travel on a tourist quota ticket. Indian Railways also offer discounts and special passes for foreign tourists. These can offer excellent value. Payment must be in foreign exchange or in Rupees, as long as you have your currency exchange certificate.

There are the following classes of travel: *1st Class* is very comfortable (bedding provided); *Sleeper* (also known as *2-Tier and 3 tier Sleeper*) are clean and comfortable (*Rajdhani* trains now offer only 1st Class and Sleepers); *Executive Class*, with comfortable reclining seats, available on many *Shatabdi* trains at double the price of the ordinary *Chair Car*. Very cheap by Western standards, the a/c trains are comfortable and good value. They all have toilets (not always very clean); if there is a choice of Western or Indian style it is nearly always better to use the Indian style as they are better maintained. Meals and drinks are available on all the *Shatabdi* and *Rajdhani* trains to and from Goa.

1st Class (cheaper than 2nd Class a/c) can be hot and dusty during the warm weather, these are now being phased out. *2nd Class 2-Tier and 3-tier* provide exceptionally cheap travel and are preferred by some.

It is usually necessary to book train tickets in advance.

Indrail Passes

Tourists (foreigners and Indians resident abroad) may buy passes which allow travel across the network, without route restrictions, and without incurring reservation fees, sleeper charges and supplementary fees. Reservations however must be made, which can be done well in advance when purchasing your Pass. They may be bought abroad for periods ranging from 7 to 90 days. The UK agent is *SD Enterprises Ltd*, 103, Wembley Park Drive, Wembley, Middx HA9 8HG, England, T 0181 903 3411, F 0181 903 0392. They make all necessary reservations, and offer excellent advice.

Other international agents are: Australia: *Adventure World*, 8th Floor, 37 York St, Sydney NSW 2000; *Penthouse Travel*, 5th Level, 72 Pitt St, Sydney NSW 2000. Canada: *Hari World Travels Inc*, Royal York Hotel, 106 Front St West, Arcade Level, Toronto, Ontario M5J 1E3. **Denmark:** *Danish State Railways*, DSW Travel

Indrail Pass rates

Period	A/c 2 tier US$
½ day	24
1 day	40
7 days	150
15 days	185
21 days	220
30 days	275
60 days	400
90 days	530

Konkan Railway

The new **Konkan Railway** plans to have trains running between Mumbai (Bombay Kurla) through Goa down to Mangalore in Karnataka by October 1997. Fast trains will stop at Margao and Canacona and possibly at Mapusa Road. Other stations on this line at Pernem, Old Goa, Verna, Bali and Barcem will be used by local trains. Stations at Revora, Mayem, Sarzora and Loliem are expected to be added to the line. The Old Goa station will be the nearest to Panaji.

The service from Mumbai Central to the Goa-Maharashtra border (Sawantwadi station) was available in early 1997. From 6 September 1997, the timetable was changed and the journey lengthened to over 11 hours, with stops at Dadar and Thane.

Train	Number	Departs	Arrives	Journey
Mumbai-Sawantwadi Exp	*KR111*	*Mumbai Central* at 2230	*Sawantwadi* at 0940	*11¼ hrs*
Mumbai-Sawantwadi Exp	KR112	Sawantwadi *at* 1855	Mumbai Central at 0635	11½ hrs

Buses connect for transfer to Panaji; from Panaji, departs 1600 from Kadamba Bus Stand; Rs 23 for semi-luxury, or Rs 14.

The section between Margao and Mangalore in Karnataka with a stop at Canacona opened at the beginning of August 1997 with a daily service.

Train	Departs	Arrives	Journey Time	Fare (* at end)
Margao Mangalore	*Margao* at 083'0, 1415	Mangalore at 1410, 2100	6-6½ hrs	*Rs 47**
Mangalore Margao	Mangalore at 0710, 1445	Margao at 1345, 2035,	6-6½ hrs	Rs 47*

Patil Tours & Travels are collaborating with 'Wagon-Lits' to introduce a 'luxury tourist train' daily between Mumbai and Goa (Rs 1,500). The a/c chair car train with business facilities will depart from Mumbai (VT) at 0600, and arrive at Margao at 1300 with a stop at Mapusa Road station; return from Margao 1500, arriving in Mumbai at 2200.

Agency Division, Reventlowsgade – 10, DK 1651 Kobenhaven V. Finland: *Intia-Keskus Ltd*, Yrjonkatu 8-10, 00120 Helsinki, Finland. France: *Le Monde de L'Inde et de L'Asie*, 15 Rue Des Ecoles, Paris 75005. Germany: *Asia-Orient*, Kaiserstrasse 50, D-6000 Frankfurt/MI Malaysia: *City East West Travels*, BhD, No 28-A, Loreng Bunus, 6, Jl Masjid India, Kuala Lumpur. Hong Kong: *Thomas Cook Travel Services (HK) Ltd*, 6/F D'Aguilar Place, 1-13 D'Aguilar St, Central, Hong Kong. Japan: *Japan Travel Bureau Inc*, Overseas Travel Division, 1-6-4 Marunouchi, Chiyoda-ku, Tokyo-100. Thailand: *SS Travel Service*, 10/12-13 Convent Rd, SS Building, Bangkok. USA: *Hari World Travels Inc*, 30 Rockefeller Plaza, Shop No 21, Mezzanine North, New York 10112.

The **A/c 2-Tier Pass** is valid for travel on non-A/c First, A/c 3-Tier and A/c Chair car. **A/c 1st Class** costs approximately double the above rate, and **Non-A/c 2nd Class Pass** approximately half. Children

(5-12) travel at half the adult price shown. Senior citizens (65+) may qualify for a 25% discount on journeys over 500 km.

ROAD

Roads offer the only way of reaching many sites of interest within Goa and the neighbouring states. For the uninitiated, travel by road can be a worrying experience since drivers appear to follow few of the traffic rules which apply in the West.

Bus

Special tourist **'luxury' coaches**, which may be a/c,.are the most comfortable. **NB** Average road speeds are very slow. Express buses rarely average more than 40 kmph, and despite advertized timetables the fastest bus from Mumbai to Goa takes at least 16 hrs.

Local buses are often very crowded and quite slow. They have no head support and are often very bumpy, but on many routes they can be a friendly and easy way of getting about, especially for short distances. Even where signboards are not in English someone will usually give you directions.

Bus travel tips

- Avoid the back half of the bus if possible, as the ride is often very uncomfortable.
- **NB** Some towns have different bus stations for different destinations.
- 'Video coaches' which can be unbearably noisy, are best avoided – take earplugs!
- Booking on major routes, particularly for travelling to other states is now computerized, and it is worth booking in advance for longer journeys where possible.
- If your destination is only served by a local bus you may do better to take the Express bus and 'persuade' the driver/conductor in advance to stop at the place you want to get off with a tip. You have to pay the full fare to the first scheduled stop after your intended destination, but you will get there faster and more comfortably.

Car

A car provides a chance to travel off the beaten track, and give unrivalled opportunities for seeing something of Goa's interior villages and small towns. However, the roads are often in poor condition. Furthermore, the most widely used hire car, the Hindustan Ambassador is often unreliable, and although they are relatively spacious and still have their devotees, many find them quite uncomfortable. For a similar price, Maruti cars and vans (Omni) are much more reliable, though the small Maruti 800 has very limited space for luggage. New cars are now often fitted with airconditioning though this is not always as efficient as in cooler climates.

Car hire, with a driver is comparable to (or cheaper than) self-drive rates in Western holiday destinations, though prices rise dramatically in the high season, especially Christmas/New Year, and in luxury resorts. A car shared by 3 or 4 can be very good value. 2 or 3-day trips out of Goa can give excellent opportunities for sightseeing in reasonable comfort and very economically.

Check beforehand if fuel and interstate taxes (if you are taking the car out of Goa) are included in the hire charge. Occasionally drivers are forced to pay small bribes to police to be allowed to continue their journey.

A car with driver (including fuel) may be hired for varying numbers of hours with a specified km allowance, eg 4 hrs/50 km, 8 hrs/80 km, 12 hrs/120 km.

City sightseeing If you exceed the km allowance shown, there is an 'extra km' charge depending on the type of car hired. If you are late returning the car there is an 'extra hour' charge. A typical rate chart is given as a guide (higher rates apply in Mumbai).

Out-of-town A 'km rate' applies when a car is hired for out-of-town journeys. In addition, there is a driver's 'night halt' charge. For example, an Economy car with driver, taken out for one night and covering 200 km would cost Rs 1,560.

Car Hire Rates

Car with driver	Economy Maruti 800 Ambassador	Regular A/C Maruti 800 Ambassador	Premium A/C Maruti 1000 Contessa	Luxury A/C Esteem Opel etc
8 hrs/80 km	Rs 700	Rs 900	Rs 1,300	Rs 1,800
Extra km	Rs 7	Rs 9	Rs 13	Rs 18
Extra hour	Rs 40	Rs 50	Rs 70	Rs 100
Out of town				
Per km	Rs 7	Rs 9	Rs 13	Rs 18
Night halt	Rs 160	Rs 200	Rs 250	Rs 250

Cars can be hired through private companies such as Sai or Wheels which have representatives in cities outside Goa as well. International companies (eg Hertz) also operate in Goa and offer reliable cars. Their rates are generally slightly higher than those of local firms.

Drivers may be helpful in being able to communicate with local people and also make a journey more interesting by telling you about the places and local customs. It is usual for the driver to sleep in the car overnight if the hotel you stay in doesn't provide special facilities for them. They are responsible for all their expenses, including their meals. A tip at the end of the whole tour of Rs 50/day (if you wish to give one), in addition to their inclusive daily allowance, is perfectly acceptable.

Driving conditions

Vehicles drive on the left – in theory. Routes around the major cities are usually crowded with lorry traffic, and the main roads are often poor and slow in comparison with those in Europe or the United States. National Highways are rarely dual carriageway, and many main roads are single track. Some district roads are quiet, and although they are not fast they can be a good way of seeing the country and village life if you have time.

Asking the way can be very frustrating as you are likely to get widely conflicting advice each time you stop to ask, and map-reading is an alien concept in India. Goa's signposting can be frustrating since along the minor roads they are often absent or are old, rusty and difficult to read. On the main roads, 'mile' posts periodically appear in English and can help. Elsewhere, it is best to ask directions often. Fortunately Goa is very small, so you can't get too lost for long!

Car travel tips

Self-drive car hire is still in its infancy though the rates are attractive when compared to 'with driver' rates, especially for out-of-town travel.

Many foreign visitors find the road conditions difficult and sometimes dangerous. If you drive yourself it is essential to take great care. Pedestrians often walk along or across a narrow road, in the absence of pavements; cattle, dogs and families of pigs roam at will. This can be particularly difficult on unlit roads at night since other vehicles often choose not to switch on their lights at dusk and many cyclists don't even have a lamp. Watch out for deep pot-holes and unmarked speed-breakers especially as you approach (and leave) a bridge, a town or a village.

- When reserving the car emphasise the importance of good tyres, breaks, headlamps and general roadworthiness. Check the car (scratches, dents etc) before driving away.
- Find out what happens in case of a break down. Get telephone contact numbers.
- Drivers must have third party insurance. This may have to be with an Indian insurer, or with a foreign insurer who has a national guarantor.

- On main roads across India, petrol stations are reasonably frequent, but parts of Goa are poorly served. Some service stations only have diesel pumps though they may have small reserves of petrol so always carry a spare can.
- Carry adequate food and drink, correct documentation (especially for interstate travel) and a basic tool set in the car.
- Accidents can produce large and angry crowds very quickly. It is best to leave the scene of the accident and report it to the police as quickly as possible.
- The **Automobile Association** address in **Mumbai** is Lalji Narainji Memorial Building, 76, Veer Nariman Rd.

Taxis

'Yellow-top' taxis in large towns are metered, although tariffs change frequently. Ask to see the fare charts which shows you how to calculate the fare from the meter reading. In many towns you may have to pay a surcharge at night and also a small additional amount for each piece of luggage. In some cities taxis refuse to use the meter – the official advice is to call the police. This may not work, but it is worth trying. Other taxis don't always have a meter so a fare should be negotiated before starting the journey.

Taxi tips

- In Goa tourist taxis are not metered. Apart from taxis from the airport which operate on a fixed rate basis, rates are negotiable. Before travelling in an unmetered taxi, ask at the hotel desk for a guide price.
- Elsewhere in India always try to insist on the taxi meter being 'flagged' in your presence. At stations and at Mumbai and Dabolim airports it is often possible to share taxis to a central point. It is worth looking for fellow passengers who may be travelling in your direction. When travelling from Mumbai airport at night always have a clear idea of where you want to go and insist on being taken there. In Mumbai many taxi drivers will do everything possible to convince you that the hotel you have named was 'closed 3 years ago' or is 'completely full'. It may be necessary to insist that you have an advance reservation.

Cycling

Cycling is an excellent way of seeing the quiet by-ways of Goa and particularly enjoyable if you travel with a companion. Indian bikes are heavy and without gears, but on the flat they offer a good way of exploring comparatively short distances outside towns. All cyclists should take bungy cords (to strap down a backpack) and good lights from home; take care not to leave your machine parked anywhere with your belongings, though. Bike repair shops are universal and charges are nominal.

Bicycle hire: bikes are widely available and cost around Rs 3/hr; Rs 20-40/day, depending on the town/resort, season and age of the cycle.

Exploring the rest of India It is also quite possible to tour more extensively and you may then want to buy a cycle. There are shops in the larger towns and the local Raleighs are considered the best, with Atlas and BSA good alternatives; expect to pay around Rs 1,200-1,500 for a second-hand Indian bike but remember to bargain. At the end of your trip you can usually sell it quite easily at half that price.

Imported bikes have the advantage of lighter weight and gears, but are more difficult to get repaired, and carry the much greater risk of being stolen or damaged. If you wish to take your own, it is quite easy if you dismantle it and pack it in its original shipping carton; be sure to take all essential spares and a pump.

Recent travellers found it was comfortably possible to cover 50 to 80 km a day, – "the National Highways are manic but country roads, especially along the coast, can be idyllic, if rather dusty and bumpy". You can even put your bike on a boat for the backwater trip or on top of a bus. Should you wish to take your bike on the train, allow plenty of time for booking it in on the brake van at the Parcels office, and for filling in forms.

It is best to start a journey early in the morning, stop at mid-day and resume cycling in the late afternoon. Night-riding, though cooler, can be hazardous because of lack of lighting and poor road surfaces. Try to avoid the major highways as far as possible. Fortunately foreign cyclists are usually greeted with cheers, waves and smiles and truck drivers are sometimes happy to give lifts to cyclists (and their bikes). This is a good way of taking some of the hardship out of cycling round India.

Suggested reading: Richard Ballantyne's *Richard's New Bicycle Book*, London, Pan, 1990.

Motorcycling

Motorbikes are ideal for Goa – convenient for visiting different beaches and also for longer distance sightseeing. They are very popular and widely available; you will probably be approached by an 'agent' even before you consider looking around. The most commonly available are the automatic Kinetic Honda, Yamaha or Suzuki 100cc and the highly desirable 350cc Enfield Bullet.

On the Kinetic Honda, the headlight is directly connected to the throttle so that it dims whenever you slow down. But help is at hand in the form of a 'Hi-Beam' attachment which connects the headlight directly to the battery and costs just over Rs 100. If you opt for a KH, ask your dealer to fit the attachment or get one from the local repair shop. Tourist pressure may result in all KHs for hire being fitted with a 'Hi-Beam' before long.

Motorcycle hire Rates (without petrol) in high season are about Rs 150-200 for an automatic Kinetic Honda; Rs 150-250/day for a Yamaha/Suzuki 100cc; up to Rs 500 for a 350cc Enfield Bullets. It is usually possible to negotiate reductions for out-of-season or long-term hire. An Enfield Bullet costs Rs 3000-4000 for a month's hire.

NB It is essential to check all bikes thoroughly for safety. If you have an accident you will usually be expected to pay for the damage. Repairs are generally easy to arrange and quite cheap.

Classic Bike Adventure, Casa Tres Amigos, Socol Vado 425, Assagao, T 0832 273351, F 276124, and near the Old Patto Bridge, Panaji, is recommended for reliable motorcycle hire and tours.

Syndicate Tours & Travels, organizes 15-day bike 'adventure tours' starting with 2 days of familiarization in Goa followed by a tour of Karwar, Jog Falls, Mangalore, Mysore, Ooty, Tiruppur, Salem, Pondicherry and finally Chennai costing US$1,200-1,500 (including good hotel accommodation and support vehicle).

If you are intending to travel around India for an extended period and decide to buy a bike, make sure you get up-to-date and valid documents. *Auto Guides*, Dr Dada Vaidya Rd, Panaji, sells new and used motorcycles. A second-hand Bullet sells for about Rs 20,000.

WARNING Police may harass motorcyclists and demand large 'fines'. For not carrying a road licence and insurance certificate, the usual fine in 1997 was Rs 600 (Rs 100 if you could produce them later). For not having a driving license the fine was Rs 950.

Important Check your insurance and get an International Driving Licence (essential for crossing the state border). You can buy the International Licence in your home country from a recognized automobile organisations (eg AA in UK; take your driving licence and a passport photo to apply). Always wear a helmet, carry all documentation and appropriate tools.

Road safety See under 'Car' and 'Cycling' above for general advice. For small-wheeled bikes, sand or gravel roads can be particularly hazardous. Potholes and speed-breakers add to the problems of a fast rider. Goa seems a fun place to ride a bike in a carefree way but many hundreds of bikers, each season, receive the 'Goan Road Tattoo' by way of numerous scabs and scars, and some are seriously injured.

OTHER LAND TRANSPORT

Auto-rickshaws

Auto-rickshaws – "autos" – are the cheapest convenient way of getting about in many Indian cities. In addition to using them for short journeys it is often possible to hire them by the hour (approx Rs 25), half day or full day (approx Rs 200). In some areas younger drivers are often speak some English and know their local areas well. However, rickshaw drivers often earn commissions from hotels, restaurants and gift shops, so advice is not always impartial.

Hitchhiking

Hitchhiking is rare in India, partly because public transport is so cheap. If you try you are likely to spend a very long time on the roadside, although lorries sometimes give lifts. In general it is not recommended, especially for women. In Goa locals often hitch rides on motorbikes/scooters and generally give lifts over short distances. It is good to reciprocate if you have room on your bike and are confident of your riding.

TRAVELLING WITH CHILDREN

Children of all ages are widely welcomed across India, being greeted with a warmth in their own right which is often then extended to those accompanying them. In the big hotels there is no difficulty with getting safe baby foods, though disposable nappies are not readily available in many areas. It doesn't harm a child to eat an unvaried and limited diet of familiar food carried in packets and jars for a few weeks if the local dishes are not acceptable, but it may be an idea to give vitamin and mineral supplements. To help young children to take anti-malarial tablets, one suggestion is to crush them between spoons and mix with a teaspoon of dessert chocolate (for cake-making) bought in a tube.

Extra care must be taken to protect children from the heat by creams, hats, umbrellas etc and by avoiding being out in the hottest part of the day. Cool showers or baths help if children get too hot. Dehydration may be counteracted with plenty of drinking water – bottled, boiled (furiously for 10 mins) or purified with tablets. Preparations such as 'Dioralyte' may be given if the child suffers from diarrhoea. Moisturizer, zinc and castor oil (for sore bottoms due to change of diet) are worth taking. Mosquito nets or electric insect repellents at night may be provided in hotel rooms which are not a/c, but insect repellent creams are a must. It is best to visit Goa in the cooler months, especially when travelling with young children. The biggest hotels provide babysitting facilities.

COMMUNICATIONS

Language

There are few reminders of the Portuguese which was once spoken by Goa's élite. Konkani and Marathi are the most common languages, while English is widely understood. Hindi is India's official language and is quite commonly understood. The use of English is also enshrined in the Constitution for a wide range of official purposes, notably communication between Hindi and non-Hindi speaking states.

Postal services

In recent years the post has frequently become unreliable, and delays are common. It is advisable to use a post office where it is possible to hand over mail for franking across the counter, or a hotel post box. Valuable items should only be sent by Registered Mail. Government Emporia or shops in the larger hotels will send purchases home if the items are difficult to carry. Airmail service to Europe, Africa and Australia takes at least a week and a little longer for the Americas. Courier services are available from major towns.

Sending **parcels** can take up to 2 hrs. Check that post office holds necessary customs declaration forms (2/3 copies needed). Write 'No commercial value' if returning used clothes, books etc. Air mail is expensive; sea mail slow but reasonable (10 kg, Rs 800). Take your parcel in an open cardboard box so items can be inspected. 'Packers' outside post offices will do all necessary cloth covering, sealing etc for Rs 20-50. You address the parcel, buy the stamps from a separate counter; stick stamps and one customs form to the parcel with glue available (the other form/s must be partially sewn on). Post it at the Parcels Counter and get a Registration slip. It is theoretically possible to insure the parcel but may prove difficult in practice.

Poste restante facilities are available in even quite small towns at the GPO, where mail is held for one month. Ask for mail to be addressed to you with your surname in capitals and underlined. When asking for mail at 'Poste Restante' check under Christian as well as surname name. **NB** Any special issue foreign stamps are likely to be stolen from envelopes in the Indian postal service and letters may be thrown away. Advise people who are sending you mail to India to use only definitive stamps (not commemorative).

Telephone services

International Direct Dialling is now widely available in privately run call boxes, usually labelled on yellow boards with the letters 'PCO-STD-ISN'. You dial the call yourself, and the time and cost are displayed on a computer screen. They are by far the best places from which to telephone abroad. Telephone calls from hotels are usually much more expensive (check price before calling). Fax services are also becoming widely available.

NB One disadvantage of the tremendous pace of the telecommunications revolution is the fact that millions of telephone numbers in India go out of date every year. Current telephone directories themselves are often out of date and some of the numbers given in the Handbook will have been changed even as we go to press. Check Directory for the Directory Enquiries number, which varies from city to city.

The international code for India is 00 91. STD codes for towns are printed after the town name.

MEDIA

Newspapers

India has a large English language press. In Goa itself there are 3 local English language newspapers, the Herald, the Gomantak Times and the Navhind Times. The Herald is probably the best written and the most popular. The best known Indian newspapers are *The Hindu, The Hindustan Times, The Independent, The Indian Express, The Times of India,* and *The Statesman*, and now *The Asian Age*. *The Economic Times* and *Asian Age* are possibly the best for independent reporting and world coverage. However, most of these are difficult to get hold of even in Margao or Panaji, though all the Mumbai and South Indian papers may be easier to buy once the Konkan Railway is fully operational. There is however a wide range of weekly and fortnightly magazines. Some of the most widely read are *Sunday*, *India Today* and *Frontline*, all of which are current affairs journals on the model of *Time* or *Newsweek*. There are bookshops in Margao, Panaji, Mapusa and Colva.

Television and radio

India's national radio and television network, *Doordarshan*, broadcasts in national and regional languages. Many Indians have now switched off 'DD', as it is known, to watch satellite TV, including the BBC World, CNN and others. Some international channels are currently relayed through the Star Network. BBC World Service radio has a large Indian audience in both English and regional languages.

Section 5

Rounding up

FURTHER READING

The literature on Goa is significant and growing. Most of the material listed here is available in English though original sources were in some cases in Portuguese. There are excellent bookshops in all the major Indian cities where you will find books are generally much cheaper than outside. In Goa, Panaji has a few good shops, including the one at the *Mandovi Hotel* and *Varsha* near Azad Maidan. In Margao, *Golden Heart* has a wide (possibly the state's largest) collection. *Mapusa's Other India Bookshop* prides itself in covering contoversial issues.

A few suggestions are listed here.

Art and Architecture

Anand, Mulk Raj *In praise of Christian Art in Goa*. Marg, Volume XXXII No 4, Mumbai.

Nunes, Judilia *Monuments in Old Goa*. Delhi, 1979.

Pereira, José *Baroque Goa, the architecture of Portuguese Goa*. Books & Books, New Delhi, 1955. A very detailed and technical analysis.

Pereira, José *Goa Shrines & Mansions*. Knowledeable account of interesting temples and buildings.

Rajagopalan, S *Old Goa*. 3rd revised edition by KV Rao. Archaeological Survey of India, New Delhi, 1994. A short history and guide to the monuments with a few plans and photos, usually available at the site (Rs 10).

Current affairs and politics

Alvares, Claude (editor) *Fish, Curry and Rice, a citizen's report on the Goan environment*. An Ecoforum publication. 3rd revised edition, 1995. Mapusa, Other India Press. Full of up-to-date environmental information, written from a perspective of continuous moral outrage.

Esteves, S *Politics and political leadership in Goa*. Cultural Patterns. New Delhi, 1981.

History: early & colonial

Basham, AL *The Wonder that was India*. London, Sidgwick & Jackson, 1985. Still one of the most comprehensive and readable accounts of the development of India's culture.

Boyajiyan, James C *Goa Inquisition – A new light on first 100 years (1561-1660)* in Journal of the Directorate of Archives, Archaeology and Museum, Panaji, Goa, Volume IV, No 1 pages 1-40.

Spear, Percival & Thapar, Romila *A history of India*. 2 volumes, Penguin, 1978. Compact and authoritative.

Lopes Mendes, S (Portuguese) *A India Portugeza*. 2 volumes, Imprensa Nacional, Lisbon, 1886. An indespensable source book with numerous illustrations.

Marjay, Frederic P *Portuguese India: a historic study*. Livraria Bertrand, Lisbon, 1959. Arrival of the Portuguese and St Xavier, with copies of old maps, prints and photos.

Penrose, Boies *Goa – Queen of the East*. Lisbon 1960. The story of Old Goa with interesting illustrations.

Saldhana, CF *A short history of Goa*. Panaji.

Xavier, PD *Goa: a social history. (1510-1640)*. Rajhans, Panaji, 1993. Detailed chapters on social structure and institutions (slavery, church, position of women, education) with full bibliographies.

History: modern

Saksena, RN *Goa: into the mainstream*. Abhinav Publications, New Delhi, 1972. An account of Goa's political integration with India after its incorporation in 1961.

D'Souza, BG *Goan Society in transition*. Popular Prakashan, Mumbai, 1975.

Literature

Malgaonkar, Manohar Many novels by the renowned Goan novelist include *A bend in the Ganges*.

Menezes, Armando *Chords and dischords*. Poems by a Goan writing in English.

Naipaul, VS *A million mutinies now*. Penguin, 1992. Naipaul's 'revisionist' account of India where he turns away from the despondency of his earlier two India books (*An area of darkness and India: a wounded civilisation*) to see grounds for optimism at India's capacity for regeneration.

Narayan, RK has written many gentle and humourous novels and short stories of South India. *The Man-eater of Malgudi* and *Under the Banyan tree and other stories*, *Grandmother's stories*, among many. London, Penguin, 1985 (India). Also a 're-telling' of the Mahabharata.

Roy, Arundhati *The God of Small Things*. Indian Ink/Harper Collins 1997. Booker Prize-winning novel about family turmoil in a Syrian Christian household in Kerala.

Rushdie, Salman *Midnight's children*. Picador, London, 1981. A novel of India since Independence. *The Moor's Last Sigh*. Viking, 1996. Is of particular interest to those travelling to Kochi and Mumbai because of the settings there.

Vikram Seth *A Suitable Boy*. Phoenix House London 1993, prize winning novel of modern Indian life.

Music

Raghara R Menon *Penguin Dictionary of Indian Classical Music*. Penguin, New Delhi 1995, comprehensive introduction.

People and places

Angle, Prabhakar S *Goa, Concepts and misconcepts*. Goa Hindu Association, Mumbai, 1994. An account of Goa's place in modern India emphasising the significance of its Hindu traditions.

Albuquerque, Theresa *Anjuna: Profile of a village in Goa Promilla*. New Delhi, 1988. An attractive illustrated account of the history of one of Goa's most famous yet little known villages.

Cabral e Sa, Mario & Da Costa Rodrigues, LB *Great Goans*. NNAP, Piedade, Goa, 1985. Brief but interesting account of some of Goa's major modern figures.

Malgoankar, Manohar *Goa*. Govt of Goa, Panaji.

Mascarenhas, Telo de *When the mango trees blossomed*. Bombay, Longmans, 1976. Reminiscences of a freedom fighter some sections of his homeland with years of forced exiles away from Goa, before being able to return.

Singh, KS (ed) *People of India Goa*. Volume XXI, Bombay, Anthropological Survey of India. Popular Prakashan, Mumbai, 1993. A traditional anthropological description of some of the major groups in Goa. Widely available in Goan bookshops.

Rémy (pseud) *Goa: Rome of the Orient*. By Lancelot C Sheppard, London, Arthur Barker, 1957.

Shastry, BS *Goan Society through the ages*. Ajanta, Delhi, 1987

Religion

Eck, DL *Darshan: seeing the divine image in India*. Chambersburg, Pennsylvania.

History of Christianity in India. Volume 1 by M Mundadan, Volume 2 by J Thekkedath. Theological Publications, Bangalore, 1984.

Gomes Pereira, Rui *Goa*, Volume 1, *Hindu Temples and Deities*. Translated from the original in Portuguese by Antonio Victor Couto. Panaji, Printwell, 1978. Detailed listing with some interesting historical accounts and descriptions of practices.

Robinson, F (ed) *Religions in South Asia (in The Cambridge Encyclopedia of India,*

Pakistan, Bangladesh and Sri Lanka). Cambridge University Press, 1989. An extremely well written account of India's major religions, their philosophies and development.

Travel

Cabral e Sa, Mario *Goa*. Lustre Press, New Delhi, 1993. Informative; attractive souvenir with colour photos by Jean-Louis Nou.

Hall, Maurice *Window on Goa*. Quiller Press London (2nd Edition) 1995. Probably the best, most comprehensively illustrated text on Goa's religious and secular sights.

Hutt, Anthony *Goa: a traveller's historical and architectural guide*. Scorpion, 1988. Well-written though not fully comprehensive account of Goan churches, temples and major houses.

Richards, JM *Goa*. Revised edition. Vikas Publishing House, New Delhi. Rather idiosyncratic and dated guide but still with some valuable observations.

Wildlife and vegetation

Ali, Salim and Ripley S Dillon *Handbook of the birds of India & Pakistan* (compact edition). BNHS, Mumbai.

Bole PV & Vaghini, Y *Field Guide to the common trees of India*. OUP. Good for identifying.

Cowen, DV *Flowering Trees and Shrubs in India*.

Grewal B *Birds of India, Bangladesh, Nepal, Pakistan & Sri Lanka*. Odyssey. A well-illustrated (mostly in colour) and comprehensive guide based on Salim Ali's original.

Nair SM *Endangered animals of India*. National Book Trust, New Delhi, 1992. Attractively illustrated slim volume on the species of India's wildlife most at risk and their conservation.

Prater, SH *Book of Indian Animals*, 3rd edition. OUP/Bombay Natural History Society, Mumbai, 1978.

Goa: the independent birder's guide. Eastern Publications, Lowestoft, England, 1996. Recently researched.

MAPS

For anyone interested in the geography of India, or even simply getting around, trying to buy good maps is a depressing experience. For security reasons it is illegal to sell large scale maps of any areas with 80 km of the coast or national borders.

Goa Tourist Offices hand out a reasonable state map (updated with the Konkan railway) in colour. *Findoll Publications* have brought out an updated Goa Yellow Pages accompanied by 2 sheets of colour maps in 1996 (Rs 60 each) aimed at the tourist market. Goa Map 1: State and towns (Panjim, Old Goa, Mapusa, Margao, Vasco, Dona Paula, Porvorim etc). Goa Map 2: Beaches covering all popular ones from Arambol in the north to Palolem in the south. Fairly detailed, including hotels, restaurants, tourist services (banks, travel agents, tailors, beach parties, etc) but not quite up to date (eg Old Goa still shows Camoes' statue at the roundabout, Aguada Sports Complex not included), and not wholly reliable in detail.

The **Bartholomew** 1:4m map sheet of India is the most authoritative, detailed and easy to use map of India available. It can be bought worldwide. **Nelles'** regional maps of India at the scale of 1:1.5m offer generally clear route maps, though neither the road classifications nor alignments are wholly reliable.

Sources of maps outside India: *Stanford International Map Centre*, 12-14 Long Acre, London WC2E 9LP; *Zumsteins Landkartenhaus*, Leibkerrstrasse 5, 8 Mnchen 22, Germany; *Geo Buch Verlag*, Rosenthal 6, D-6000 Mnchen 2, Germany; *GeoCenter GmbH*, Honigwiessenstrasse 25, Postfach 800830, D-7000 Stuttgart 80, Germany; *Libreria Alpina*, Via C Coroned-Berti, 4 40137 Bologna, Zona 370-5, Italy; *Library of Congress*, 101 Independence Ave, Washington, DC 20540, USA; *Michael Chessler Books*, PO Box 2436, Evergreen, CO 80439, USA T 800 654 8502, 303 670 0093; NOAA Distribution Branch (N/CG33), National Ocean Service, Riverdale MD 20737.

Useful addresses

EMBASSIES AND CONSULATES

Australia
3-5 Moonah Place, Yarralumla, Canberra, T 733999. Consulates: Sydney T 927055, Melbourne T 3503351.

Austria
Kaernterring 2, 1010 Vienna, T 222 5058666.

Belgium
217-Chaussée de Vleurgat, 1050 Brussels, T 640 93 73, F 648 9638. Consulates: Ghent T 091/263423, Antwerp T (03) 234 1122.

Canada
10 Springfield Rd, Ottawa, Ontario K1M 1C9, T (613) 744-3751. Consulates: Toronto T (416) 960-0751, Vancouver T (926-6080; **Denmark**, Vangehusvej 15, 2100 Copenhagen, T (01) 18288.

Finland
Satamakatu 2 A8, 00160 Helsinki-16, T 60 89 27.

France
15 Rue Alfred Dehodencq, Paris, T 4520-3930.

Germany
Baunscheidstr 7, 5300 Bonn-1, T 028 5405131. Consulates: Berlin T 37 2482 5306, Frankfurt T 069-1530050, Hamburg T 338036.

Ireland
6 Lesson Park, Dublin 6, T 0001-970843.

Italy
Via XX Settembre 5 – 00187 Rome, T 464642. Consulates: Milan T 02 869 0314, Genoa T 54891.

Japan
2-11, Kudan Minami 2-Chome, Chiyoda-ku, Tokyo 102, T (03) 262-2391, F (03) 234-4866. Consulate: Kobe T 078-241 8116.

Korea
37-3, Hannam-dong, Yongsan-Ku, Seoul, T 798-4257, F 796-9534.

Malaysia
20th Flr Wisma Selangor Dredging, West Block, 142-C, Jl Apang, 50450 Kuala Lumpur, T 03-261 7000.

Netherlands
(Consul), Buitenrustweg 2, The Hague (2517KD), T 070-46 97 71.

New Zealand
10th Flr, Princess Tower, 180 Molesworth St, (PO Box 4045) Wellington, T 736 390/1.

Norway
30 Niels Jules Gate, 0272 Oslo-2, T 443194.

Singapore
India House, 31 Grange Rd, Singapore 0923, T 7376777.

Spain
Avda Pio XII 30-32, 28016 Madrid, T 457-02-09. Consulate: Barcelona T 93/2120422.

Sweden
Adolf Fredriks Kyrkogata 12, Box 1340, 11183 Stockholm, T 08-10 70 08, F 08-24 85 05.

Switzerland
17 Effingstr 45, 3001 Bern, T 031-263111; 9 rue du Valais, 1202 Geneva, T 022 7320859.

Thailand
46, Soi 23 (Prasarn Mitr) Sukhumvit 23, Bangkok 10110, T 2580300.

UK
India House, Aldwych, London WC2B 4NA, T 0171-836 8484. Consulate: Birmingham, Jewellery Quarter, 19 Augusta St, T 0121 212 2782.

USA
2107 Massachusetts Ave, Washington DC

20008, T (202) 939-7000. Consulates: New Orleans T (504) 582 8105, New York T (212) 879-7800, San Francisco T (415) 668-0662, Chicago T (312) 781680, Cleveland T 216/696.

INDIAN TOURIST OFFICES

Australia
Level 1, 17 Castlevegh St, Sydney, NSW 2000, T (02) 232-1600, F (02) 223-3003.

Austria
Opernring 1, 1010 Vienna, T 1 587 1462.

Canada
60 Bloor St, West Suite No 1003, Toronto, Ontario, T 416-962 3787, F 416-962 6279.

France
8 Blvd de la Madeleine, 75009 Paris, T 42-65-83-86.

Germany
77 (III) Kaiserstrasse, D-6000 Frankfurt 1, T 069 23 54 23, F 23 47 24.

Italy
Via Albricci 9, Milan 20122, T 804952.

Japan
Pearl Building, 9-18 Chome Ginza, Chuo Ku, Tokyo 104, T 03 571-5062, F 5235.

The Netherlands
Rokin 9-15, 1012 Amsterdam, T 020-208891.

Switzerland
1-3 rue de Chantepoulet, 1201 Geneva, T 022 32 18 13.

Thailand
3rd Flr, Singapore Airlines Bldg, 62/5 Thaniya Rd, Bangkok, T 2352585.

UK
7 Cork St, London W1X 2AB, T 0171-437 3677/8, F 0171-494 1048.

USA
30 Rockefeller Plaza, Room 15, Mezzazine, T 212 586 4901/3, F 582 3274, New York, NY 10020.

Health in Goa

WITH THE FOLLOWING ADVICE and precautions, you should keep as healthy as you do at home. In India the health risks are different from those encountered in Europe or the USA but the region's medical practicioners have particular experience in dealing with locally occuring diseases.

Theinformation below has been compiled for us by Dr David Snashall, Senior Lecturer in Occupational Health, United Medical Schools of Guy's and St Thomas' Hospitals and Chief Medical Adviser, Foreign and Commonwealth Office, London.

BEFORE TRAVELLING

Take out Medical Insurance. You should have a dental check up, obtain a spare glasses prescription and, if you suffer from a long-standing condition such as diabetes, high blood pressure, heart/lung disease or a nervous disorder, arrange for a check up with your doctor who can at the same time provide you with a letter explaining details of your disability. Check the current practice for malaria prophylaxis (prevention) for the parts of the country you intend to visit.

Medical care

Good hotels can often provide a list of recommended doctors. There are many well qualified doctors in Goa, a large proportion of whom speak English.

However, the quality and range of medical care are much lower in rural areas. Traditional systems of medicine are common and local Practitioners have a lot of experience with the particular diseases of their region. If you are a long way away from medical help, a certain amount of self medication may be necessary.

Medicines

Many drugs available in the west are available from chemists. However, always check the date stamping and buy from reputable pharmacies because the shelf life of some items, especially vaccines and antibiotics, is markedly reduced in hot conditions. Many locally produced drugs are not subjected to quality control procedures and so can be unreliable.

Vaccination & immunisation

The following vaccinations are recommended:

Typhoid (monovalent) 1 dose followed by a booster in 1 month's time. Immunity from this course lasts 2-3 years. An oral preparation is currently being marketed in some countries and a one dose injectable vaccine is also available but is more expensive than monovalent: Typhim-Vi (Mevieux).

Polio-myelitis: this is a live vaccine generally given orally and a full course consists of 3 doses with a booster in tropical regions every 3-5 years.

Tetanus One dose should be given with a booster at 6 weeks and another at 6 months: 10 yearly boosters thereafter are recommended.

Children should, in addition, be properly protected against **diphtheria, whooping cough**, **mumps**, **measles** and **HIB**. Teenage girls should be given **rubella** (German measles) vaccination if they have not had the disease. Consult your doctor for advice on BCG inoculation against **tuberculosis**; the disease is still common in the region.

Meningococcal Meningitis and Japanese B Encephalitis (JVE): immunisation (Japanese or Korean vaccine: effective in 10 days) gives protection for around 3 years. There is an extremely small risk, though it varies seasonally and from region to region. Consult a Travel Clinic.

Hepatitis A Many travellers contract Hepatitis A. Protection is very strongly recommended. Havrix, Havrix Monodose and Junior Havrix vaccine give protection for 10 years after 2 injections (10 days to be effective). Alternatively, 1 gamma globulin injection to cover up to 6 months' travel is effective immediately and is much cheaper.

Hepatitis B This is a sexually transmitted disease, also passed on from blood transfusions or infected needles. A vaccine is available – 3 shots over 6 months. Regular travellers should have a blood test first to check whether they are already immune to Hepatitis A or B.

Rabies Rabies is endemic in India. Pre-exposure vaccination gives anyone bitten by a suspect animal time to get treatment (so particularly helpful to those visiting remote areas) and also prepares the body to produce antibodies quickly; cost of vaccine can be shared by 3 receiving vaccination together.

If you are bitten by a domestic or wild animal, don't leave things to chance. Scrub the wound with soap and water/or disinfectant, try to have the animal captured (within limits) or at least determine its ownership where possible and seek medical assistance at once. The course of treatment depends on whether you have already been vaccinated against rabies. If you have (and this is worthwhile if you are spending lengths of time in developing countries) then some further doses of vaccine are all that is required. Human diploid cell vaccine is the best, but expensive: other, older kinds of vaccine such as that derived from duck embryos may be the only types available. These are effective, much cheaper and interchangeable generally with the human derived types. If not already vaccinated then anti-rabies serum (immunoglobulin) may be required in addition. It is wise to finish the course of treatment whether the animal survives or not.

Small-pox, cholera and yellow fever Vaccinations are not required. You may be asked for a certificate if you have been in a country affected by yellow fever immediately before travelling to India.

FURTHER INFORMATION

The following organizations give information regarding well trained English speaking Physicians throughout the world: International Association for Medical Assistance to Travellers, 745 5th Ave, New York, 10022; Intermedic 777, Third Ave, New York, 10017.

Further information on medical problems overseas can be obtained from the most recent edition of *Travellers' Health: How to Stay Healthy Abroad*, edited by Richard Dawood (Oxford University Press, 1992). We strongly recommend this revised and updated edition, especially to the travellers who go to the more out-of-the-way places.

STAYING HEALTHY

INTESTINAL UPSETS

Almost everyone suffers upset stomachs. Most of the time, intestinal upsets are due to the insanitary preparation of **food**. Under cooked fish, vegetables or meat (especially pork), fruit with the skin on (always peel your fruit yourself) or food that is exposed to flies (especially salads) are all highly risky.

Drinking water

All unbottled **water** is probably unsafe, as is ice. Do not put ice cubes in drinks. If you have no choice but to drink dirty water, strain it through a filter bag (available from camping shops) and then boil or treat. Bringing the water to a rolling boil at sea level is sufficient but at high altitude you have to boil the water for longer to ensure that all the microbes are killed. Various sterilising methods can be used and there are proprietary preparations containing chlorine or iodine compounds.

Pasteurised or heat treated milk is now widely available, as is ice cream and yoghurt produced by the same methods. Unpasteurized milk products, including cheese, are sources of tuberculosis, brucellosis, listeria and food poisoning germs. You can render fresh milk safe by heating it to 62°C for 30 mins, followed by rapid cooling or by boiling it. Matured or processed cheeses are safer than fresh varieties.

DIARRHOEA

This is usually the result of food poisoning, occasionally from contaminated water. There are various causes – viruses, bacteria, protozoa (like amoeba), salmonella and cholera organisms. It may take one of several forms, coming on suddenly, or rather slowly. It may be accompanied by vomiting or by severe abdominal pain and the passage of blood or mucus when it is called dysentery.

Types of diarrhoea

- If you can time the onset of diarrhoea to the minute, then it is probably **viral** or **bacterial** and/or the onset of **dysentery**.

- If the diarrhoea has come on slowly or intermittently, then it is more likely to be **protozoal**, ie caused by amoeba or giardia and antibiotics will have no effect.

Treatment The lynch pins of treatment for diarrhoea are rest, fluid and salt replacement, antibiotics for the bacterial types and special diagnostic tests and medical treatment for amoeba and giardia infections.

All kinds of diarrhoea, whether or not accompanied by vomiting respond favourably to the replacement of water and salts taken as frequent small sips of some kind of rehydration solution. There are proprietary preparations, consisting of sachets of powder which you dissolve in water, or you can make your own by adding half a teaspoonful of salt (3.5 grams) and 4 tablespoonfuls of sugar (40 grams) to a litre of boiled water.

Viral and bacterial diarrhoea Rehydration plus **Ciprofloxacin**, 500 mgs every 12 hrs. The drug is now widely available and seek medical help.

Protozoal diarrhoea Rehydration The following drugs may help if there are severe stomach cramps: Loperamide (Imodium, Arret) and Diphenoxylate with Atropine (Lomotil). **Any diarrhoea continuing for more than 3 days should be treated by a doctor**.

Salmonella infections and cholera

These can be devastating diseases and it would be wise to get to a hospital as soon as possible if these are suspected.

Fasting, peculiar diets and the consumption of large quantities of yoghurt have not been found useful in calming travellers' diarrhoea or in rehabilitating inflamed bowels. Alcohol and milk may prolong diarrhoea and should be avoided during and immediately after an attack. Antibiotics taken before and during travel may help to prevent diarrhoea for short periods but these are ineffective against viruses and, to some extent, against protozoa, so this technique should only be used in exceptional circumstances. Some preventives such as Entero-vioform can have serious side effects if taken for long periods.

HEAT AND COLD

Full acclimatisation to high temperatures takes about 2 weeks. Drink plenty of water (up to 15 litres a day can be needed if taking vigorous exercise), use salt on food and avoid extreme exertion. Tepid showers are more cooling than hot or cold ones.

INSECTS

Insects can be a great nuisance and some carry serious diseases. To ward off mosquitoes sleep off the ground with a mosquito net and burn Pyrethrum mosquito coils. Sprays and insecticidal tablets, heated on a mat plugged into the wall socket, are effective, as are personal insect repellents. The best contain a high concentration of

Diethyltoluamide. Liquid is best for arms and face (take care around eyes and make sure you do not dissolve the plastic of your spectacles).

Aerosol spray on clothes and ankles deters mites and ticks. Liquid DET suspended in water can be used to impregnate cotton clothes and mosquito nets. New style mosquito nets are wider-meshed and impregnated with permethrin (an insecticide). If you are bitten, itching may be relieved by cool baths and anti-histamine tablets (care with alcohol or driving), corticosteroid creams (great care - never use if any hint of sepsis). Calamine lotion and cream have limited effectiveness and anti-histamine creams have a tendency to cause skin allergies and are, therefore, not generally recommended.

Bites which become infected (common in the tropics) should be treated with a local antiseptic or antibiotic cream such as Cetrimide as should infected scratches. Skin infestations with body lice, crabs and scabies are unfortunately easy to pick up. Use Gamma benzene hexachloride for lice and Benzyl benzoate for scabies. Crotamiton cream alleviates itching and also kills a number of skin parasites. Malathion lotion 5% is good for lice but avoid the highly toxic full strength Malathion used as an agricultural insecticide.

SUNBURN AND HEAT STROKE

The burning power of the tropical sun is phenomenal. Always wear a wide brimmed hat and use some form of sun cream or lotion on untanned skin. Always use high protection factor suntan lotions, designed specifically for the tropics or for mountaineers or skiers. Glare from the sun can cause conjunctivitis so wear sunglasses, especially on tropical beaches.

There are several varieties of 'heat stroke'. The most common cause is severe dehydration. Avoid dehydration by drinking lots of non-alcoholic fluid. Put extra salt on your food.

OTHER RISKS AND MORE SERIOUS DISEASES

AIDS

In India AIDS is increasing faster than in most countries. Heterosexual transmission is now the dominant mode and so the main risk to travellers is from casual sex. The same precautions should be taken as when encountering any sexually transmitted disease. The only way to determine whether you have been infected is by having a blood test for HIV antibodies at a place where there are reliable laboratory facilities. The test does not become positive for many weeks.

Injections Ensure that needles used for injections have been properly sterilised or that disposable needles are used. Hepatitis B is the main risk. Blood for transfusion should be screened for HIV but this cannot be guaranteed and remains a real risk. Be wary of carrying disposable needles yourself; customs officials may find them suspicious.

MALARIA

Malaria is a serious disease and is prevalent in India. Certain areas are badly affected, particularly by the highly dangerous falciparum strain. Malaria prevention is becoming more complex as the malaria parasite becomes immune to some of the older drugs. Some of the preventive drugs can cause side effects, especially if taken for long periods of time, so before you travel you must check with a reputable agency the likelihood and type of malaria in the countries which you intend to visit and take their advice on prophylaxis. Be prepared to receive conflicting advice. You can catch malaria even when taking prophylactic drugs, although it is unlikely. If you do develop symptoms (high fever, shivering, severe headache, sometimes diarrhoea) seek medical advice immediately.

Current advice is:

Protect yourself against mosquito bites - cover up exposed skin at dusk, wear light coloured long-sleeved clothes and mosquito repellent cream or Gel, use a net to sleep under. It is now possible to buy lightweight impregnated nets such as the *Repel Trekker*. Enquire from your local travel shop, or in UK the British Airways Travel Shop or Ikea.

Take prophylactic (preventive) drugs. Start taking the tablets a few days before exposure and continue to take them 6 weeks after leaving the malarial zone ('Paludrine' is difficult to find in India).

Remember to give the drugs to babies and children and pregnant women also.

Seek up-to-date advice from the Malaria Reference Laboratory, T 0891 600 350 (recorded message, premium rate) or the Liverpool School of Tropical Medicine, T 0151 708 9393. In the USA, try Centre for Disease Control, Atlanta, T 404 332 4555.

MASTA (Medical Advisory Service for Travellers Abroad) based at the London School of Hygiene and Tropical Medicine, Keppel St, London WClE 7HT, T 0891 224100, publishes a strongly recommended book entitled: *The Preservation of Personal Health in Warm Climates*. Masta also sells a range of health products for travellers.

SNAKE BITE

Death from snake bite is very rare. If you are unlucky enough to be bitten by a venomous snake, spider, scorpion, centipede or sea creature try (within limits) to catch the animal for identification. The reactions to be expected are fright, swelling, pain and bruising around the bite, soreness of the regional lymph glands, nausea, vomiting and fever. If, in addition, any of the following symptoms occur get the victim to a doctor without delay: numbness, tingling of the face, muscular spasm, convulsions, shortness of breath or haemorrhage.

Commercial snake bite or scorpion sting kits are only useful for the specific type of snake or scorpion for which they are designed. The serum has to be given intravenously. If the bite is on a limb, immobilise the limb and apply a tight bandage between the bite and the body, releasing it for 90 secs every 15 mins. Reassurance of the bitten person is very important because death from snake bite is, in fact, very rare.

Do not slash the bite area and try to suck out the poison; this does more harm than good. Hospitals usually hold stocks of snake bite serum.

Best precautions

- Do not walk in snake territory with bare feet, sandals or shorts. Also good to make noise (eg by tapping a stick). Snakes are scared of humans.

WATCH OUT FOR

Dengue fever is present in India. It is a virus disease, transmitted by mosquito bites, presenting with severe headache and body pains. Complicated types of dengue known as haemorrhagic fevers occur throughout Asia but usually in persons who have caught the disease a second time. Thus, although it is a very serious type, it is rarely caught by visitors. There is no treatment, you must just avoid mosquito bites.

Athlete's foot and other fungal infections are best treated by sunshine and a proprietary preparation such as Tolnaftate.

Influenza and **respiratory diseases** are common, perhaps made worse by polluted cities and rapid temperature and climatic changes.

Intestinal worms are common and the more serious ones, such as hook worm can be contracted by walking barefoot on infested earth or beaches.

Leishmaniasis This can be a serious disease taking several forms and transmitted by sand flies. These should be avoided in the same way as mosquitoes.

Prickly heat A very common itchy rash is avoided by frequent washing and by wearing loose clothing. It is helped by the use of talcum powder and/or Boroline ointment. Allow the skin to dry thoroughly after washing.

WHEN YOU RETURN HOME

If you have had attacks of diarrhoea, it is worth having a stool specimen tested in case you have picked up amoebic dysentery. If you have been living rough, a blood test may be worthwhile to detect worms and other parasites.

Useful Konkani words and phrases

Travellers in the 'tourist' areas of Goa can quite easily get by without any knowledge of Konkani or Hindi. Learning and using a few local words, as needed, when visiting a foreign country is always received warmly.

Pronounce

ā as in **ah** **ī** as in **bee**
ō as in **oh** **u** as oo in **book**
ū as in **hub**
t and **d** are usually **soft (dental)** eg **d**ī as in **th**ee
j is often pronounced like **z**
nasalized vowels are shown as aň, iň, em̆, em̆, etc (Place names often end with a nasal vowel eg Pern**em**)
NB These marks to help with pronunciation in this section do not appear in the main text

Useful words and phrases

Hello
Hullo
How are you?(m)
Tūň kosso assa?
How are you?(f)
Tūň kosheam̆ (girl)/ koshi (woman) assi?
My name is ...
Mhūjem nāoň...
Cheers!
Viva!
Good-bye!
Barem̆!/Adeūs!
Pardon?
Kite-m mhalle-m?
Sorry
Tchūk zāli
Thankyou
Deo barem̆ korūň!/obrigād
May I take a photo?
Photo kadum̆?
Yes/No
Hoi/ Na
I
haoň
you
tūň
we
ami
clean
līmp/sāf
closed
bandh
dirty
sooj
drink
pio-mche-m̆/pioňk
food
khānem̆
fruit
pholl
cashew
kazū
coconut
nāll
green coconut
ādsar
mango
ambō
orange
laranja
pineapple
ananas
good
bare-m
hot (temp)
hūň
hot (spicy)
tikh
meal
jevonn
shop
dūkān
water
ūdak
what?
kitem̆?
when?
kenna?
where?
khaiň
which?
khaiiňchem̆?
who?
konn?
why?
kityāk?

Health

medicine
awkhad
Please get a doctor
Matso dotorac affoi
I have a fever
Mhaka zor āila
I feel unwell
Haoñ baro nā
I have a tummy ache
Marjay pottan charpta
I have diarrhoea
Maka bhairī zalya

Hotel

I want a room please?
Mhaka yek room zai mellat?
... with a toilet?
Rooman mhaka toilet zai?
What is the room rate?
Roomacheṁ bhade-m kitte-m?
I'd like to see it
Mhaka room dekhūñ zai
... larger room
... whodlō room
Please clean the room
Matso room sāf kor
There is no hot water/soap
Rooman gorom udak/sabu nā

(Restaurant) Useful phrases

Menu please
Matso menū dī
Bill please
Matshe-m bill dī
I'll have this
Haoñ heṁ khatañ
A bottle of water
Ūdkachi yek bātli
Not chillies please
Mhaka tikh naka
No ice/sugar please
... burf naka/sākhar naka
Sugar and milk please
Matsi sākhar āni dūdh dī
spoon/fork/knife
tchomchō/kanttō/sourī

Shopping

How much is this?
Yay kitlay poishay?
I'll have this
Haoñ heṁ ghetañ
Too much
Ekdom mharaog
Make it cheaper!
Matsheṁ ūnnay kor
... a bigger one?
Whodleṁ assa?
... a smaller one?
Lhañ assa?
... another one like this?
Asleṁ anik assa?
Receipt please
Receipt dī
I don't want it
Mhaka naka teṁ

Travel

I need a taxi
Mhaka taxi zāi
Can I share a taxi?
Taxi bhāgak koruñya?
How much to Colva?
Colwa kitlay podtollay?
Where is the Bus Station?
Bus Station khaiñ assa?
When does the Bus leave?
Bus kenna sūttally?
Next bus?
Dūsri bus kenna?
How far is Panaji?
Poñnji kithli poiss assa?
How long (will it take)?
Kithlō wogauth?
Have I/we reached Panaji?
Poñnji powlay?
I want to hire a cycle
Mhaka yek cycle bhadyak zai

Time and day

right now *attañts*
morning *sakāl*
afternoon *donpara*
evening *sānz*
night *rāt*
at night *ratīñ*
today *āz*
tomorrow *fālya-m*
yesterday *kāl*

Sunday *Āi-tār*
Monday *Somār*
Tuesday *Munglār*
Wednesday *Būdhwār*
Thursday *Birestār*
Friday *Sūkrār*
Saturday *Shenwār*

Numbers

1 *yek*
2 *dōñ*
3 *tīn*
4 *chār*
5 *pānts*
6 *so*
7 *sāt*
8 *āṭth*
9 *nnov*
10 *dhā*
20 *wīss*
100 *shumber*
1,000 *hazār*

Hindi words and phrases for places outside Goa

Useful words and phrases

Hello, good morning, goodbye
namaste
Thank you/no thank you
dhanyavād, shukriyā/nahīn̠'shukriyā
Excuse me, sorry
māf kījiye
Yes/ no
jī hāñ/jī nahīñ
never mind/that's all right
koi bāt nahīñ
What is your name?
āpkā nām kyā hai?
My name is ....
merā nām .... hai
Do you speak English?
āp kō angrezī āti hai?
a little
thorī -sī
Pardon?
phir batāiye
How are you?
kyā hāl hai?
I am well, thanks, and you?
maiñ thīk hūñ, aur āp?
Not very well
maiñ thīk nahīñ hūñ
Where is the ....?
.........kahāñ hai?
Who is ....?
.... kaun hai?
What is this?
yeh kyā hai?

Shopping

How much is this?
iskā kyā dām hai?
That is very expensive!
bahut mahangā hai!
Make it a bit cheaper!
thorā kam kījiye!

The hotel

What is the room charge?
kirāyā kitnā hai?
Please show me the room
mujhe kamrā dikhāiye
Is there an air-conditioned room?
kyā a/c kamrā hai?
Is there hot water?
kyā kamre meñ garam pānī hai?
... a bathroom/fan/mosquito net
....bathroom/pankhā/machhar dānī
Is there a large room?
barā kamrā hai?
Are there 2 beds?
do palang haiñ?
The room is not clean
yah kamrā sāf nahīñ nhai
Please clean the room
yah kamrā sāf karwā dījiye
Are there clean sheets/blanket?
sāf chādareñ/kambal haiñ?
This is OK
yah thīk hai
The bill please
bill dījiye

Travel

Where's the railway station?
railway station kahāñ nhai?
How much is the ticket to Agra?
Agra kā ticket kitne ka hai?
When does the Agra bus leave?
Agra bus kab jāegī?
How much is it to the fort?
killa jāne ke liye, kitnā?
Will you go for 5 rupees?
pānch rupiye leñge?
Is it far?
bahut door hai?
left/right
bāieñ / dāhinā
go straight on
sīdhā / āge chaliye
nearby
nazdīk
Is it near the station?
station ke pās hai?
Please wait here
yahāñ thahariye

Please come at 8
āth bajai ānā
Quickly
jaldi
Slowly
dhire
stop
rukiye

(Restaurants) Useful phrases

Please show the menu
menu dikhāiye
No chillis please
mirch nahīñ dālnā
....sugar/milk/ice
chīnī/doodh/baraf....
A bottle of water please
ek botal pāni dījiye
...do not open it
......kholnā nahīñ
sweet/ savoury
mīthā/namkīn
spoon, fork, knife
chamach, kāñtā, chhurī/chakoo

Time and days

right now *abhī*
morning *suba*
afternoon *dopahar*
evening *shām*
night *rāt*
today *āj*
tomorrow/ yesterday *kal/ kal*
day *din*
week *haftā*
month *mahīnā*
year *sāl*

Sunday *ravivār*
Monday *somvār*
Tuesday *mangalvār*
Wednesday *budhvār*
Thursday *vīrvār*
Friday *shukravār*
Saturday *shanivār*

Numbers

1 *ek*
2 *dō*
3 *tīn*
4 *chār*
5 *pānch*
6 *chhai*
7 *sāt*
8 *āth*
9 *nau*
10 *das*
11 *gyāra*
12 *bārāh*
13 *terāh*
14 *chaudāh*
15 *pandrāh*
16 *solāh*
17 *satrāh*
18 *athārāh*
19 *unnīs*
20 *bīs*
100/200 *sau/ do sau*
1000/2000 *hazār/do hazār*
100,000 *lākh* **10,000,000** *crore*

Basic vocabulary

airport, bank, bathroom, bus, doctor, embassy, ferry, hotel, hospital, juice, police, restaurant, station, stamp, taxi, ticket, train (these are used locally though often pronounced differently eg *daktar, haspatāl*)
and *aur*
big *barā*
café/food stall *dhābā/hotel*
chemist *dawāi kī dukān*
clean *sāf*
closed *bandh*
cold *thandā*
day *din*
dirty *gandā*
English *añgrezi*
excellent *bahut achhā/buriya*
food/to eat *khānā*
hot (spicy) *jhāl, masāledār*
hot (temp) *garam*
medicine *dawāi*
newspaper *akhbār*
of course, sure *zaroor*
open *khulā*
post (office) *dāk khānā*
police station *thānā*
road *rāstā*
room *kamrā*
shop *dukan*
sick (ill) *bīmār*
silk *reshmī/silk*
small *chhotā*
that *woh*
this *yeh*
town *shahar*
water *pānī*
what *kyā*
when *kab*
where *kahāñ/kidhar*
which/who *kaun*
why *kiuñ*
with *sāthh*

Fruit (phal)

apple *seb*
banana *kelā*
coconut *nāriyal*
green coconut *dāb*
lemon *nimbu*
lychee *lichi*
mango *āmb*
orange *santrā*
pineapple *anānās*

Eating out

Eating out in Goa and India is normally cheap and safe but menus can be dauntingly long and full of unfamiliar names. N Indian dishes are nearly universal and offer plenty of opportunity for experiment.

Useful words in Konkani

Popular Goan Dishes

Ambot tik *a hot, sour curry made with shark, squid or ray and eaten with rice*
Apa de camarão *a spicy prawn-pie with flour crust*
Balchão *a preparation of red masala and onions used as a sauce for prawns or king-fish (also meat). A less common dish, not least because it is made without coconut and served with bread*
Caldo/Caldinha *delicately spiced light fish curry*
Cafrial *meat marinated in pepper and garlic and braised over a slow fire*
Chouriço *Goan sausage made of pork pieces stuffed in tripe, boiled or fried with onions and chillies; often eaten stuffed into bread*
Feijoada *Haricot bean (feijão) stew; sometimes served with chouriço*
Guisado *tomato based soup*
Kishmaur *ground, dried shrimp mixed with shredded coconut and chopped onion - an accompaniment*
Recheiado *usually a whole fish, cut in half, served with a hot masala sauce*
Seet corri *fish curry with coconut rice*
Soupa de carne *spicy soup made with meat and rice stock*
Sorpotel *a highly spiced dish of pickled pig's liver and heart, seasoned with vinegar and tamarind; perhaps the most famous of Goan meat dishes!*
Vindaloo *spicy pork or beef, marinated in garlic, wine vinegar and chillies (elsewhere in India 'vindaloo' often refers to a hot, spicy curry)*
Xacutti *('shakooti') hot chicken or meat dish prepared with coconut, pepper and star anise (fr chacontine)*

Goan Bread

Goan bread is good and there are pleasant European style biscuits
Undo *a hard crust round bread*
Kankonn *hard and crispy and shaped like a bangle; often dunked in tea*
Pão *crusty bread rolls, soft inside*
Pollee *like a chapatti, often stuffed with vegetables*
Sannan *Goan version of idli made with ground rice, coconut and fermented palm sap (toddy)*

Goan Sweets

Sweets are sometimes too sweet for the Western palate
Alebele *a sweet pancake with coconut filling*
Bebinca *a layered coconut pancake and jaggery delicacy made with egg yolks, coconut milk, sugar, nutmeg and ghee*
Bolinhas *small semolina cakes*
Doce *fudge-like sweet made with nuts and milk*
Dodol *a mix of jaggery and coconut with rice flour/semolina and nuts*
Neuro *semi-circular pastry*

Useful words in Hindi

dāl lentils, beans
ghī clarified butter
gosht, mās meat, usually mutton (sheep)
jhinga prawns (Bengali *chingri*)
macchli fish
makkhan butter
murgh chicken
panīr drained curds (cubes or pieces)
sabzī vegetables

Vegetables

āloo potato
baiñgan aubergine
band gōbi cabbage
bhindi okra, ladies' fingers
gājar carrots
khumbhi mushroom
lauki green gourd

matar peas
piāz onion
phool gōbi cauliflower
sāg spinach
saym green beans

Methods of preparation

Many items on restaurant menus are named according to well-known methods of preparation, roughly equivalent to terms such as 'Provençal' or 'sauté'.

bhoona in a thick, fairly spicy sauce
do piaza with onions (added twice during cooking)
jhāl frāzi spicy, hot sauce with tomatoes and chillies
Kashmiri cooked with mild spices, ground almonds and yoghurt, often with fruit
kebab skewered (or minced and shaped) meat or fish; a dry spicy dish cooked on a fire
kīma minced meat (usually 'mutton')
kofta minced meat or vegetable balls
korma in fairly mild rich sauce using cream/yoghurt
masālā marinated in spices (fairly hot)
Madras hot
makhani in butter rich sauce
Mughlai rich N Indian style
Nargisi dish using boiled eggs
Peshwari rich with dried fruit and nuts (NW Indian)
tandoori baked in a *tandoor* (special clay oven) or one imitating it
tikka marinated meat pieces, baked quite dry

Ordering from a menu

A ***thāli*** for which you might pay Rs 15 (in small *dhabas*) to Rs 50, is usually the cheapest way of eating; the menu is fixed but refills are normally offered.

When ordering a meal, you might like to try some 'bread' and/or rice, a vegetable and/or meat curry, *bha¯ji, da¯l, raita* and *pa¯pad*. It is perfectly acceptable to order as little as some bread or rice and a vegetable dish or *da¯l*. Sweets are an extra. *Gula¯b ja¯mun, rashmala¯i* and *kulfi* are popular.

Some typical dishes

aloo gobi dry potato and cauliflower with cumin
aloo, matar, kumbhi potato, peas, mushrooms in a dryish mildly spicy sauce
bhindi bhaji lady's fingers fried with onions and mild spices
dāl makhani lentils cooked with butter
dum aloo potato curry with a spicy yoghurt, tomato and onion sauce
kīma mattar mince meat with peas
matar panīr curd cheese cubes with peas and spices (and often tomatoes)
Nargisi kofta boiled eggs covered in minced lamb, cooked in a thick sauce
rogan josh rich, mutton/beef pieces in creamy, red sauce
sāg panīr (*pālak panīr*) Drained curd sautéd with chopped spinach in mild spices

Rice

chāwal plain boiled rice
biriyāni partially cooked rice layered over meat and baked with saffron.
pulao/ pilau fried (and then boiled) rice cooked with spices (cloves, cardamom, cinnamon) with dried fruit, nuts or vegetables. Sometimes served with meat, like a *biriyāni*

Roti – breads

chapāti (*phoolka, roti*) thin, plain, wholemeal unleavened bread cooked on a *tawa* (griddle), usually made from *ātā* (wheat flour). *Makkai-ki-roti* is with maize flour. Soft, thicker version of poori, made with white flour.
nān oven baked (traditionally in a *tandoor*) white flour leavened bread often large and triangular; sometimes stuffed with almonds and dried fruit
parāthā fried bread layered with ghī (sometimes cooked with egg or stuffed with potatoes)
poori thin deep-fried, puffed rounds of flour (Bengali *loochi*, Punjabi *bhaturā*)

Accompaniments

achār pickles (usually spicy and preserved in oil)
chutnī often fruit or tomato, freshly prepared, sweet and mildly spiced
dahī plain yoghurt
papad, pappadom deep fried, pulse flour wafer rounds
raita yoghurt with shredded cucumber, pinapple or other fruit, or *bundi* (tiny batter balls)

Sweets

These are often made with reduced/ thickened milk, drained curd cheese or powdered lentils and nuts. They are sometimes covered with a flimsy sheet of decorative, edible silver leaf.

barfi fudge-like rectangles/diamonds, often with nuts
khīr, payasam, paesh thickened milk rice/vermicelli pudding

gulāb jāmun dark fried spongy balls, soaked in syrup
halwa rich sweet made from cereal, fruit, vegetable, nuts and sugar
kulfi cone-shaped Indian ice cream with pistachhios/ almonds, uneven in texture
jalebi spirals of fried batter soaked in syrup
laddoo lentil based batter 'grains' shaped into orange rounds
rasgulla (roshgulla) balls of flour and curd in clear syrup
rasmalāi spongy curd rounds, soaked in sweetened cream and garnished with pistachio nuts

Snacks

bhāji, pakora vegetable fritters (onions, potatoes, cauliflower, aubergine etc) deep-fried in batter
chāt - sweet and sour cubed fruit and vegetables flavoured with tamarind paste and chillis
chanā choor, chioora ('Bombay mix') lentil and flattened rice snacks mixed with nuts and dried fruit
dosai a S Indian snack that has swept the country; pancake made of a mixture of rice and lentil flour; may be served with a mild potato and onion filling (*masala dosai*)
idli steamed S Indian rice cakes, a bland breakfast food given flavour by its spiced accompaniments
kachori fried pastry rounds stuffed with spiced lentil/peas/potato filling
samosā (Bengali *shingārā*) cooked vegetable or meat wrapped in pastry circle into 'triangles' and deep fried
vadai deep fried, small savoury lentil 'doughnut' rings. *Dahi vada* - similar rounds in yoghurt.

Drinks

chai tea boiled with milk and sugar
doodh milk
kāfi ground fresh coffee boiled with milk and sugar
lassi N Indian cool drink made with yoghurt and water, salted or sweetened
nimboo pāni refreshing drink made with fresh lime and water; ask for added salt or sugar syrup but avoid ice. Safe if made with chilled bottled water, in a clean glass; alternatively ask for fresh lime soda
pāni water

Glossary

Words in *italics* are common elements of words, often making up part of a place name

A

aarti (arati) Hindu worship with lamps
acharya religious teacher
Adinatha first of the 24 Tirthankaras, distinguished by his bull mount
agarbathi incense
Agni Vedic fire divinity, intermediary between gods and men; guardian of the SE
agrashala pilgrim resthouse
ahimsa non-harming, non-violence
ambulatory processional path
amrita ambrosia; drink of immortality
Ananta a huge snake on whose coils Vishnu rests
anna (ana) one sixteenth of a rupee (still occasionally referred to)
antaralaya vestibule between the temple hall and the sanctuary
apsara celestial nymph
apse semi-circular plan, as in apse of a church
architrave horizontal beam across posts or gateways
ardha mandapam chamber in front of main hall of temple
Ardhanarisvara Siva represented as half-male and half-female
Arjuna Hero of the Mahabharata, to whom Krishna delivered the Bhagavad Gita
arrack alcoholic spirit fermented from potatoes or grain
Aruna charioteer of Surya, the Sun God; Red
Aryans lit. 'noble' (Sanskrit); prehistoric peoples who settled in Persia and N India
asana a seat or throne
ashram hermitage or retreat
atman philosophical concept of universal soul or spirit
atrium court open to the sky in the centre In modern architecture, enclosed in glass
avatara incarnation of a divinity;Goan n ouse with ve resistance'descent'
ayah nursemaid, especially for children

B

bagh garden
baksheesh tip
balcao shaded wide verandah of a Goan house
bandh a strike
bandhani tie dyeing (W India, Rajasthan)
bania merchant caste
barrel-vault semi-cylindrical shaped roof or ceiling
Baroque (style) 17th century Italian, bold, exuberant, ornate decoration
bas-relief carving of low projection
basement lower part of walls, usually adorned with decorated mouldings
basti Jain temple
bazaar market
begum Muslim princess; Muslim woman's courtesy title
Bhagavad-Gita Song of the Lord; section of the Mahabharata
bhai brother
Bhairava Siva, the Fearful
bhakti adoration of a god or goddess
bhang Indian hemp
Bharata half-brother of Rama
bhavan building or house
bhumi 'earth'; refers to a horizontal moulding of a shikhara
bidi (beedi) tobacco leaf cigarette
Brahma Universal self-existing power; Creator in the Hindu Triad
Brahman (Brahmin) highest Hindu (and Jain) caste of priests
Brahmanism ancient Indian religion, precursor of modern Hinduism
Buddha The Enlightened One; founder of Buddhism
bund an embankment
burqa an over-dress worn by Muslim women observing purdah

C

cantonment planned military or civil area in town
capital upper part of a column
catamaran log raft, logs (*maram*) tied (*kattu*) together (Tamil)
cave temple rock-cut shrine or monastery
chai tea
chakra sacred Buddhist wheel of the law; also

Vishnu's discus

Chamunda terrifying form of the goddess Durga

Chandra Moon; a planetary deity

chapatti unleavened Indian bread cooked on a griddle

charka spinning wheel

charpai 'four legs' – wooden frame string bed

chattra ceremonial umbrella on stupa (Buddhist)

chaudi town square

chaukidar night-watchman; guard

chauth 25% tax raised for revenue by Marathas

chhatri umbrella shaped dome or pavilion

choli blouse

chowk (chauk) a block; open place in a city where the market is held

chowkidar watchman

circumambulation clockwise movement around a shrine

clerestory upper section of the walls of a building which allows light in

cloister passage usually around an open square

Communidade village assembly/committee

corbel horizontal block supporting a vertical structure or covering an opening

cornice horizontal band at the top of a wall

crenellated having battlements

crore 10 million

cruzado Portuguese gold coin

cupola small dome

D

daal lentils, pulses

dabba meals

dado part of a pedestal between its base and cornice

dahi yoghurt

dais raised platform

dak bungalow rest house for officials

dak post

darbar (durbar) a royal gathering

dargah a Muslim tomb complex

darshan (darshana) viewing of a deity

darwaza gateway, door

Dasara (dassara/dussehra/dassehra) 10 day festival (September-October)

deepmal (deepstambha) temple lamp tower

Devi Goddess; later, the Supreme Goddess

dhansak Parsi dish made with lentils

dharamshala (dharamsala) pilgrims' rest-house

dharma moral and religious duty

dhobi washerman

dholi swinging chair on a pole, carried by bearers

dhoti loose loincloth worn by Indian men

digambara lit 'sky-clad' Jain sect in which the monks go naked

dikpala guardian of one of the cardinal directions mostly appearing in a group of eight

Diwali festival of lights (October-November)

diwan-i-am hall of public audience

diwan-i-khas hall of private audience

diwan chief financial minister

dosa thin pancake

double dome composed of an inner and outer shell of masonry

Draupadi wife-in-common of the five Pandava brothers in the Mahabharata

dupatta long scarf worn by Punjabi women

Durga principal goddess of the Shakti cult

durwan watchman

dwarpala guardian deities at temple doorways (on silver doors of sanctuary)

E

ek the number 1, a symbol of unity

F

faience coloured tilework, earthenware or porcelain

festa Christian saint's day

feni spirit distilled from palm sap or juice of the cashew apple

fidalgo Upper class Portuguese noble

filigree ornamental work or delicate tracery

finial emblem at the summit of a stupa, tower, dome, or at the end of a parapet

frieze horizontal band of figures or decorative designs

G

gable end of an angled roof

gaddi throne

gadi/gari car, cart, train

Ganapati see Ganesh

Gandharva semi-divine flying figure; celestial musician

Ganesh (Ganapati) elephant-headed son of Siva and Parvati

Ganga goddess personifying the Ganga river

ganja Indian hemp

garbagriha lit. 'womb-chamber'; a temple sanctuary

garh fort

Garuda Mythical eagle, half-human Vishnu's vehicle

Gaunkar settler in Goan village

ghat hill range, hill road; landing place; steps on the river bank

ghazal Urdu lyric poetry/love songs, often erotic

ghee clarified butter for cooking

giri hill

godown warehouse

Gopala (Govinda) cowherd; a name of Krishna

Gopis cowherd girls; milk maids who played with Krishna

gram chick pea, pulse

Greek cross cross where each are is the same length

gulal red colour (powder) thrown when celebrating Shigmo

gumbaz (gumbad) dome

gur palm sugar

guru teacher; spiritual leader, Sikh religious leader

H

Haj (Hajj) annual Muslim pilgrimage to Mecca

halwa a special sweet meat

Hanuman Monkey devotee of Rama; bringer of success to armies

harem women's quarters (Muslim), from 'haram', Arabic for 'forbidden by law'

Hari Vishnu Harihara, Vishnu- Siva as a single divinity

Hasan the murdered eldest son of Ali, commemorated at Muharram

hat (haat) market

hathi (hati) elephant

havildar army sergeant

hidalgo Portuguese nobleman

Hiranyakashipu Demon king killed by Narasimha

Holi spring festival (February-March)

hookah 'hubble bubble' or smoking vase

hundi temple offering

Hussain the second murdered son of Ali, commemorated at Muharram

I

icon statue or image of worship

Id principal Muslim festivals

Idalcan (Idalcao) Portuguese' name for Ismail Adil Khan

Idgah open space for the Id prayers

idli steamed rice cake (Tamil)

imam Muslim religious leader

imambara tomb of a Shiite Muslim holy man; focus of Muharram procession

Indra King of the gods; God of rain; guardian of the East

Inquisition special courts to test the Faith and punish deviation from Catholic orthodoxy

Ishana Guardian of the North East

Ishvara Lord; Siva

J

jaggery brown sugar, made from palm sap

jali lit. 'net'; any lattice or perforated pattern

jamb vertical side slab of doorway

Jami masjid (Jama, Jumma) Friday mosque, for congregational worship

jarokha balcony

jataka stories accounts of the previous lives of the Buddha

jawab lit. 'answer,' a building which duplicates another to provide symmetry

jaya stambha victory tower

-ji (jee) honorific suffix added to names out of reverence and/or politeness; also abbreviated 'yes' (Hindi/Urdu)

Jina lit. 'victor'; spiritual conqueror or Tirthankara, after whom Jainism is named

johar (jauhar) mass suicide by fire of women, particularly in Rajasthan, to avoid capture

K

Kailasa mountain home of Siva

Kali lit. 'black'; terrifying form of the goddess Durga, wearing a necklace of skulls/heads

Kalki future incarnation of Vishnu on horseback

kalyanmandapa marriage hall

kameez women's shirt

kapok the silk cotton tree

karma impurity resulting from past misdeeds

Kartikkeya/Kartik Son of Siva, God of war

kebab variety of meat dishes

keep tower of a fort, stronghold

keystone central wedge-shaped block in a masonry arch

khadi woven cotton cloth made from home-spun cotton (or silk) yarn.

khana suffix for room/office/place; also food or meal

kharif monsoon season crop

kofta meat balls

kohl antimony, used as eye shadow

korma rich curry using cubes of meat

Krishna 8th incarnation of Vishnu

kshatriya Hindu warrior caste, second after brahmins

Kubera Chief yaksha; keeper of the treasures of the earth, Guardian of the North

kulam tank or pond (Tamil)

kumar a young man

Kumari Virgin; Durga

kumbha a vase-like motif, pot

kumhar (kumar) potter

kund lake, well or pool

kurta Punjabi shirt

kutcha (cutcha) raw; crude; unpaved; built with sun-dried bricks

L

laddu round sweet snack

lakh 100,000

Lakshmana younger brother of Rama

Lakshmi Goddess of wealth and good fortune, consort of Vishnu

lassi iced yoghurt drink

lathi bamboo stick with metal bindings, used by police

lattice screen of cross laths

lingam (linga) Siva as the phallic emblem

Lingaraja Siva worshipped at Bhubaneswar

lintel horizontal beam over doorway

lunette semicircular window opening

lungi wrapped-around loin cloth, normally checked

M

madrassa Islamic theological school or college
mahamandapam large enclosed hall in front of main shrine
maha great
Mahabharata Sanskrit epic about the battle between the Pandavas and Kauravas
Mahadeva lit. 'Great Lord'; Siva
mahal palace, grand building
maharaja great king
maharani great queen
maharishi (Maharshi) lit. 'great teacher'
Mahavira lit. 'Great Hero'; last of the 24 Tirthankaras, founder of Jainism
Mahayana The Greater Vehicle; form of Buddhism practised in East Asia, Tibet and Nepal
Mahisha Buffalo demon killed by Durga
Maitreya the future Buddha
makara crocodile-shaped mythical creature symbolizing the river Ganga
makhan butter
mandala geometric diagram symbolizing the structure of the Universe
mandalam region, tract of country (Tamil)
mandapa columned hall preceding the temple sanctuary
mandir temple
Manualine after King Manual (1495-1521), ornate entrances and twisted piers often seen in Portuguese churches.
marg wide roadway
masjid lit. 'place of prostration'; mosque
mata mother
math Hindu religious seminary
mausoleum large tomb building
maya illusion
memsahib married European woman, term used mainly before Independence
Mestiços of Portuguese-Indian parentage
mihrab niche in the western wall of a mosque
mithai Indian sweets
Mohammad 'the praised'; The Prophet; founder of Islam
moksha salvation, enlightenment; lit 'release'
mridangam barrel-shaped drum
mudra symbolic hand gesture
Muharram period of mourning in remembrance of Hasan and Hussain, two murdered sons of Ali
mullah religious teacher (Muslim)
Mulattos of Portuguese-African parentage
mundkars tenants
mural wall decoration

N

Naga (nagi/nagini) Snake deity; associated with fertility and protection
nagara city, sometimes capital
nagar khana drum house; arched structure or gateway for musicians (also naubat khana)
nallah (nullah) ditch, channel
namaaz Muslim prayers, worship
namaste common Hindu greeting (with joined palms) translated as: 'I salute all divine qualities in you'
Nandi a bull, Siva's vehicle and a symbol of fertility
Narayana Vishnu as the creator of life
nata mandapa (nat-mandir; nritya sala) dancing hall in a temple
Nataraja Siva, Lord of the cosmic dance
natya the art of dance
nautch display by dancing girls
navagraha nine planets, represented usually on the lintel or architrave of the front door of a temple
Navaratri lit. '9 nights'; name of the Dasara festival
nave central section in a church separating aisles from the choir
nawab prince, wealthy Muslim, sometimes used as a title
niche wall recess containing a sculpted image or emblem, mostly framed by a pair of pilasters
nirvana enlightenment; lit. 'extinguished'
niwas small palace
nritya pure dance

O

obelisk tapering and usually monolithic stone shaft
oriel projecting window

P

padma lotus flower, Padmasana, lotus seat; posture of meditating figures
paisa (poisa) one hundredth of a rupee
palanquin (palki) covered litter for one, carried on poles
pan leaf of the betel vine; sliced areca nut, lime and other ingredients wrapped in leaf for chewing
panchayat a 'council of five'; a government system of elected councils
pandal marquee made of bamboo and cloth
pandit teacher or wise man; a Sanskrit scholar
pankah (punkha) fan, formerly pulled by a cord
parapet wall extending above the roof
paratha unleavened bread prepared with flour and fat
Parinirvana the Buddha's state prior to nirvana, shown usually as a reclining figure
parishads political division of group of villages
Parsi (Parsee) Zoroastrians who fled from Iran to W India in the 9th century to avoid persecution
parterre level space in a garden occupied by flower-beds

Parvati daughter of the Mountain; Siva's consort

Pashupati lit. Lord of the Beasts; Siva

pediment mouldings, often in a triangular formation above an opening or niche

pendant hanging, a motif depicted upside down

peon servant, messenger (from Portuguese *peao*)

piazza cross cross in the church square

pice (old form) 1/100th of a rupee

pietra dura inlaid mosaic of hard, semi-precious stones

pilaster ornamental small column, with capital and bracket

pipal Ficus religiosa, the Bodhi tree

pir Muslim holy man

podium stone bench; low pedestal wall

porch covered entrance to a shrine or hall, generally open and with columns

portico space enclosed between columns

praça open square/area in a town

pradakshina patha processional passage

prasadam consecrated temple food

puja ritual offerings to the gods; worship (Hindu)

pujari worshipper; one who performs puja (Hindu)

pukka lit. 'ripe' or 'finished'; reliable; solidly built

Puranas lit. 'the old' Sanskrit sacred poems

purdah seclusion of Muslim women from public view (lit. curtains)

purnima full moon

Q

qibla direction for Muslim prayer

Quran holy Muslim scriptures

R

rabi winter/spring season crop

Radha Krishna's favourite consort

raj rule or government

raja king, ruler (variations include rao, rawal)

Rajput dynasties of western and central India

Rama Seventh incarnation of Vishnu

Ramayana Sanskrit epic – the story of Rama

Ramazan (Ramadan) Muslim month of fasting

rani queen

rath chariot or temple car

Ravana Demon king of Lanka; kidnapper of Sita

reredos screen behind an altar

rickshaw 3-wheeled bicycle-powered (or 2-wheeled hand-powered) vehicle

rishi 'seer'; inspired poet, philosopher

rupee unit of currency in India

S

sabha columned hall (sabha mandapa, assembly hall)

sacristy place in church where vestments and vessels are kept

sadar (sadr/saddar) chief, main

sadhu ascetic; religious mendicant, holy man

sahib title of address, like 'sir'

Saiva (Shaiva) the cult of Siva

sal hardwood tree of the lower slopes of Himalayan foothills

salaam lit. 'peace'; greeting (Muslim)

salwar (shalwar) loose trousers (Punjab)

samadhi lit. concentrated thought, meditation; a funerary memorial

sambar lentil and vegetable soup dish, accompanying main meal (Tamil)

samsara transmigration of the soul

sanyasi wandering ascetic; final stage in the ideal life of a man

saranghi small four-stringed viola shaped from a single piece of wood

Saraswati wife of Brahma and goddess of knowledge

sarod Indian stringed musical instrument

sarvodaya uplift, improvement of all

sati (suttee) a virtuous woman; later applied to the act of self-immolation on a husband's funeral pyre

Sati wife of Siva who destroyed herself by fire

satyagraha 'truth force'; passive resistance

seer (ser) unit of weight equal to about 1 kg

sepoy (sepai) Indian soldier, private

seva voluntary service

Shakti Energy; female divinity often associated with Siva

shamiana cloth canopy

Shankara Siva

sharia corpus of Muslim theological law

shastras ancient texts setting norms of conduct for temple architecture

shastri religious title (Hindu)

shehnai (shahnai) Indian wind instrument similar to an oboe

Shesha (Sesha) serpent who supports Vishnu

shikhara (sikhara) curved temple tower or spire

shloka (sloka) Sanskrit sacred verse

shri (sri) honorific title, often used for 'Mr'; repeated as sign of great respect

sindur vermilion powder often used in temple ritual

singh (sinha) lion; also Rajput caste name adopted by Sikhs

Sita Rama's wife, heroine of the Ramayana epic

sitar classical Indian stringed musical instrument with a gourd for soundbox

Siva The Destroyer among

Hindu gods

Sivaratri lit. 'Siva's night'; festival (February-March) dedicated to Siva

soma sacred drink mentioned in the Vedas

stambha free-standing column or pillar, often with lamps or banners

stucco plasterwork

sudra lowest of the Hindu castes

Sulabh washed clean (toilets with attendants)

sultan Muslim prince (sultana, wife of sultan)

Surya Sun; Sun God

svami (swami) holy man; also used as a suffix for temple deities

svastika (swastika) auspicious Hindu/ Buddhist emblem

swadeshi home made goods

swaraj home rule

swatantra freedom

syce groom, attendant who follows a horseman or carriage

T

tabla a pair of drums

tahsildar revenue collector

takht throne

taluk (a) administrative subdivision of a district

tamasha spectacle, festive celebration

tandava dance of Siva

tank lake created for irrigation; in temple architecture a masonry-lined body of water, often with stepped sides

tapas (tapasya) ascetic meditative self-denial

tempera distemper; method of mural painting by means of a 'body,' such as white pigment

tempo 3 wheeler vehicle

terracotta burnt clay used as building material

thali South and West Indian vegetarian meal

tiffin snack, light meal

tika (tilak) vermilion powder applied by Hindus to the forehead as a symbol of the divine; auspicious mark on the forehead; now often simply decorative

tikka tender pieces of meat, marinated and barbecued

tirtha (teertha) sacred water

topi (topee) pith helmet

torana gateway with two posts linked by architraves

Trimurti Triad of Hindu divinities, Brahma, Vishnu and Siva

trisul the trident chief symbol of the god Siva

tulsi sacred basil plant

tulsi vrindavan basil enclosure

tympanum triangular space within the cornices of a pediment

U

Uma Siva's consort in one of her many forms

untouchable 'outcastes', with whom contact of any kind was believed by high caste Hindus to be defiling

Upanishads ancient Sanskrit philosophical texts, part of the Vedas

ur village (Tamil)

ustad master

uttarayana northwards

V

vaddo (wado) ward, village 'area'

vaisya the 'middle-class' caste of merchants and farmers

Valmiki sage, author of the Ramayana epic

Vamana dwarf incarnation of Vishnu

Varaha boar incarnation of Vishnu

varna 'colour'; social division of Hindus into Brahmin, Kshatriya, Vaishya and Sudra

Varuna Guardian of the West, accompanied by Makara (see above)

Vayu Guardian of the North-West; wind

vault arched roof (wood, stone or brick)

Veda (Vedic) oldest known Hindu religious texts

verandah enlarged porch in front of a hall

vilas house or pleasure palace

vimana towered sanctuary containing the cell in which the deity is enshrined

vina plucked stringed instrument, relative of sitar

Vishnu a principal Hindu deity; creator and preserver of universal order

vyala leogryph, lion-like sculpture

W

-wallah suffix often used with a occupational name, eg rickshaw-wallah

Y

yagasala hall where the sacred fire is maintained and worshipped; place of sacrifice

yagya (yajna) major ceremonial sacrifice

Yaksha (Yakshi) a demi-god, associated with nature in folk religion

yali hippopotamus-like creature in the ornamentation of Chalukyan temples

Yama God of death, judge of the living; guardian of the south

yantra magical diagram used in meditation; machine

yatra (jatra) pilgrimage

yoga school of philosophy concentrating on different mental and physical disciplines (yogi, a practitioner)

yoni a hole in a stone, symbolising the vagina or female sexuality

Z

zenana segregated women's apartments

TEMPERATURE CONVERSION TABLE

°C	°F	°C	°F
1	34	26	79
2	36	27	81
3	38	28	82
4	39	29	84
5	41	30	86
6	43	31	88
7	45	32	90
8	46	33	92
9	48	34	93
10	50	35	95
11	52	36	97
12	54	37	99
13	56	38	100
14	57	39	102
15	59	40	104
16	61	41	106
17	63	42	108
18	64	43	109
19	66	44	111
20	68	45	113
21	70	46	115
22	72	47	117
23	74	48	118
24	75	49	120
25	77	50	122

The formula for converting °C to °F is:

(°C x 9 ÷ 5) + 32 = °F

and for converting °F to °C:

(°F -32) x 5 ÷ 9 = °C

WEIGHTS AND MEASURES

Metric

Weight
1 Kilogram (Kg) = 2.205 pounds
1 metric ton = 1.102 short tons

Length
1 millimetre (mm)= 0.03937 inch
1 metre = 3.281 feet
1 kilometre (km) = 0.621 mile

Area
1 heactare = 2.471 acres
1 square km = 0.386 sq mile

Capacity
1 litre = 0.220 imperial gallon
= 0.264 US gallon

Volume
1 cubic metre (m^3) = 35.31 cubic feet
= 1.31 cubic yards

British and US

Weight
1 pound (lb) = 454 grams
1 short ton (2,000lbs) = 0.907 m ton
1 long ton (2,240lbs) = 1.016 m tons

Length
1 inch = 25.417 millimetres
1 foot (ft) = 0.305 metre
1 mile = 1.609 kilometres

Area
1 acre = 0.405 hectare
1 sq mile = 2.590 sq kilometre

Capacity
1 imperial gallon = 4.546 litres
1 US gallon = 3.785 litres

Volume
1 cubic foot (cu ft) = 0.028 m^3
1 cubic yard (cu yd) = 0.765 m^3

NB 5 imperial gallons are approximately equal to 6 US gallons

Illustrations

Index

E

F

G

H

I

J

K

T

Maps

COLOUR MAPS

Map symbols

Administration

Taluka border

State / Province Border

State Capitals □

Other Towns ○

Roads and travel

Main Roads
(National Highways)

Other Roads

Jeepable Roads, Tracks

Railways (narrow guage) with
station

Railways (broad guage)

Water features

River *Zuari River*

Lakes, Reservoirs, Tanks

Seasonal Marshlands

Sand Banks, Beaches

Ocean

Waterfall

Canals

Ferry

Topographical features

Contours (approx),
Rock Outcrops

Palm trees

Other symbols

Archaeological Sites

Places of Interest ○

Viewing point

Cities and towns

Built Up Areas

Main through routes
Main streets
Minor Streets
Pedestrianized Streets
One Way Street
National Parks, Gardens, Stadiums

Fortified Walls

Airport ⊗

Banks Ⓢ

Bus Stations (named in key)

Hospitals ⊕

Market Ⓜ

Police station Ⓟᵒˡ

Post Office ⊗

Telegraphic Office

Tourist Office ⓘ

Key Numbers **1 2 3 4 5**

Bridges

Stupa

Mosque

Cathedral, church

Guided routes

National parks, trekking areas

National Parks and
Bird Sanctuaries ◆

Hide ⇧

Camp site ▲

Refuge ⌂

Motorable track

Walking track

Footprint Handbooks

All of us at Footprint Handbooks hope you have enjoyed reading and travelling with this Handbook. As our story starts back in the early 1920s we thought it would be interesting to chronicle our development.

It all started 75 years ago in 1921, with the publication of the *Anglo-South American Handbook*. In 1924 the *South American Handbook* was created. This has been published each year for the last 74 years and is the longest running guidebook in the English language, immortalised by Graham Greene as the best travel guide in existence. Celebrations, presumably, next year as we hit the 75th annual edition!

One of the key strengths of the *South American Handbook* over the years, has been the extraordinary contact we have had with our readers through their hundreds of letters to us in Bath. From these letters we learnt that you wanted more Handbooks of the same quality to other parts of the world.

In 1989 my brother Patrick and I set about developing a series modelled on the *South American Handbook*. Our aim was to create the ultimate practical guidebook series for all travellers, providing expert knowledge of far flung places, explaining culture, places and people in a balanced, lively and clear way. The whole idea hinged, of course, on finding writers who were in tune with our thinking. Serendipity stepped in at exactly the right moment: we were able to bring together a talented group of people who know the countries we cover inside out and whose enthusiasm for travelling in them needed to be communicated.

The series started to steadily grow as we brought out new guides to the Indian subcontinent, Southeast Asia and Africa. At this stage we were known as Trade & Travel Publications, or the people who publish the Handbooks! In 1995 we felt that the time was right to look again at the identity that had brought us all this way. So, we commissioned London designers Newell & Sorrell to look at all the issues.

The result was the launch of our new identity, Footprint Handbooks in September 1996 which has, without doubt, lifted our profile across the globe in the travel guide scene.

For us here in Bath, it has been an exciting exercise working through this dramatic change. We have many new guidebooks in the pipeline and many ideas for the future but central to all of this is to maintain contact with all our readers. Do continue to write to us with all your news, comments and suggestions and in return we will keep you up-to-date with developments here in the West Country.

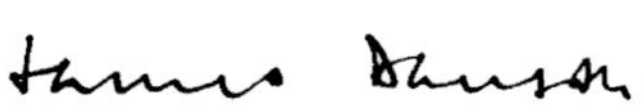

The Footprint list

Andalucía Handbook
Cambodia Handbook
Caribbean Islands Handbook
Chile Handbook
East Africa Handbook
Ecuador Handbook
with the Galápagos
Egypt Handbook
India Handbook
Indonesia Handbook
Laos Handbook
Malaysia & Singapore Handbook
Mexico & Central America
Handbook
Morocco Handbook
with Mauritania
Myanmar (Burma) Handbook
Namibia Handbook
Pakistan Handbook
Peru Handbook
South Africa Handbook
South American Handbook
Thailand Handbook
Tibet Handbook
Tunisia Handbook with Libya
Vietnam Handbook

New in Autumn 1997

Bolivia Handbook
Goa Handbook
Israel Handbook
Nepal Handbook
Zimbabwe & Moçambique
Handbook with Malawi

New in Spring 1998

Argentina Handbook
Brazil Handbook
Colombia Handbook
Cuba Handbook
Jordan, Syria & Lebanon Handbook
Sri Lanka Handbook (new edition)
Venezuela Handbook

Web site

Our website is up and running. Take a look at http://www.footprint-handbooks.co.uk for the latest news, to order a book or to join our mailing list.

Mail Order

Footprint Handbooks are available worldwide in good bookstores. They can also be ordered directly from us in Bath either via the website or via the address below.

Footprint Handbooks
6 Riverside Court
Lower Bristol Road
Bath BA2 3DZ, England
T +44(0)1225 469141
F +44(0)1225 469461
E Mail handbooks@footprint.cix.co.uk